Ari Katorza
Stairway to Paradise

Ari Katorza

Stairway to Paradise

Jews, Blacks, and the American Music Revolution

First published in Israel with the title Madregot Le-Gan Eden: Yehudim, Sheorim, U – Mahapehat Hamuzika Ha-Amerikanit, the Dushkin Foundation of the Hebrew University of Jerusalem and Resling Publishing, Tel Aviv, 2017.

ISBN 978-3-11-126675-6
e-ISBN (PDF) 978-3-11-072316-8
e-ISBN (EPUB) 978-3-11-072320-5

Library of Congress Control Number: 2021935732

Bibliographic information published by the Deutsche Nationalbibliothek
The Deutsche Nationalbibliothek lists this publication in the Deutsche Nationalbibliografie; detailed bibliographic data are available on the Internet at http://dnb.dnb.de.

© 2023 Walter de Gruyter GmbH, Berlin/Boston
This volume is text- and page-identical with the hardback published in 2021.
Cover image: Eshma / iStock / Getty Images Plus
Printed and binding: CPI books GmbH, Leck

www.degruyter.com

Special thanks to De Gruyter formidable staff, Prof. Eli Lederhendler, Dr. Arnon Palty, Dr. Nadav Appel, and Dr. Avi Bauman; my father, David, my kids, Jonathan and Rotem, and my wife, Ganit

This book is dedicated to the memory of my mother, Tamar Katorza

Contents

Prologue —— 1

Chapter 1: Jokerman – The Black Mask of Al Jolson —— 21

Chapter 2: Somewhere over the Rainbow – Jewish Immigration to America and the Struggle for Popular Culture —— 33

Chapter 3: I Used to Be Color-Blind – Irving Berlin, the Ragtime Riot and the Jewish Network in Tin Pan Alley —— 62

Chapter 4: Someone to Watch Over Me – Jerome Kern, George Gershwin and the Jazz Journey in the Musical Comedy —— 75

Chapter 5: It Don't Mean a Thing If you Ain't Got That Swing – Duke Ellington and Irving Mills' Fantasy —— 98

Chapter 6: Heaven With You – Jews, The Record Industry and Rock 'n' Roll —— 113

Chapter 7: Stand By Me – The Black-Jewish Political Alliance and the Decline of the WASP —— 128

Chapter 8: That is Rock 'n Roll! Leiber and Stoller, the White Negro and the Enlargement of America —— 147

Chapter 9: Will You Love Me Tomorrow? Carole King, Black Lolitas and the Brill Building's hit factories —— 166

Chapter 10: River Deep – Mountain High: Phil Spector, Burt Bacharach and the Ghost on the Second Floor of the Bus —— 182

Chapter 11: The Sounds of Silence – Folk, the Blues and the Spirit of Capitalism Between Grossman, Bloomfield and Zimmerman —— 201

Chapter 12: Walk On the Wild Side – Jews, Gangsters, and Rock 'n' Roll —— 221

Chapter 13: Hard Rain Is Gonna Fall – Popular Music, Hegemonic Rifts, and New American Culture —— 240

Epilogue —— 253

Bibliography —— 256

Index —— 265

Author information —— 273

Prologue

"There must be a place like this," Dorothy says to Toto in *The Wizard of Oz*, in search of a place where there is no trouble, "there must be. It's not a place you can get to by a boat or train. It's far, far away … behind the moon … beyond the rain." She says those words just before she begins to sing "Over the Rainbow," which instantly became, in Judy Garland's voice, a symbol of America's significance to the world in that dark period. The song, written by Harold Arlen and Yip Harburg, was released as a single in September 1939, when the Blitzkrieg cut through Poland. The Jewish writers caught the human dreams and hopes in a way that left no doubt. And the Jews, certainly the music and entertainment people, never had any doubt about America. They made it into more than a home – a place somewhere over the rainbow.

They fled the hostile old European world and concentrated in New York and the East Coast of the United States, and later in Hollywood as well. From the 1880s, Jewish immigrants and their descendants built and designed the American entertainment and music industry. They opened publishing houses, ran vaudeville halls and entertainment clubs, established dominant music management companies, opened independent record labels, and controlled successful corporations.

As Europe became a tragic and bloody place, Jewish immigrants and their descendants in America wrote, composed, worked, and produced the best of American music. The German composer Richard Wagner may have accused the Jewish composers of being responsible for everything "mediocre" in nineteenth-century music, but in a kind of collective and unconscious revenge, Jews in America reinvented music. They were responsible for ragtime hits, popular Broadway musicals, soundtracks for the film industry, breakthrough jazz operas, and blues and poetic songs about social justice. Through music they were able to build America as they wished to experience it: liberal, multicultural and cosmopolitan; a place where everyone, no matter what color or religion, would have the opportunity, as one of George Gershwin's tunes preached, "to build a stairway to Paradise."

The journey of the Jews to the peak of American musical creativity was, all along, in the form of a dialogue inspired and in cooperation with another minority: the Afro-Americans. The examples are almost endless: Even before World War One, songwriter Israel "Izzy" Beilin, known to the world as Irving Berlin, stunned America with ragtime music. He based them on Afro-American dances, and turned it into post-Victorian madness. The singer Al Jolson, who was born as

Asa Joelson in Lithuania, wore the mask of the blackface minstrelsy, and in the late 1920s presented the ethnic and racial complex in the film *The Jazz Singer*.

In the second half of the 1920s, the composer Jerome Kern and the lyricist Oscar Hammerstein II changed the face of American musical with *Show Boat*, a work about the American past, mixing races and the demon of racism.[1] In the mid-1930s, the composer George Gershwin introduced his masterpiece, *Porgy and Bess*, a folk-jazz opera based on both black musical and cultural wealth, starring a team of African-American singers, granting legitimacy to multiculturalism in a divided federation. The Jazz musician Benny Goodman combined black and white musicians in his triumphant journey into the heart of American pop culture with swing dance music, which became the sound that represented America during the Depression and World War Two.

The tradition continued after World War Two: Jerry Leiber and Mike Stoller wrote and produced a series of humorous and satirical hits during the 1950s, including the best of the black vocal bands as well as some of Elvis Presley's finest hits. They actually concocted the soundtrack that accompanied the end of racial segregation in the southern United States. The music producer Phil Spector combined Wagner and Leonard Bernstein as he introduced the sound, appearance, and charisma of the black girl groups to millions of Americans in the Kennedy era. The Jewish record entrepreneur and music producer Jerry Wexler recorded the best hymns concerning racial and black pride. Bob Dylan and Paul Simon wrote about the American conscience in the early 1960s with a temporary ideological connection to the Civil Rights Movement led by Martin Luther King, Jr. At the end of that decade, Randy Newman wrote about immigration, the south, narrow-mindedness, and everything in between.

Perhaps the most symbolic anecdote is related to the African-American jazz saxophonist John Coltrane, and his version of "My Favorite Things," originally written for the musical *The Sound of Music* by the Jewish writers Richard Rodgers and Oscar Hammerstein II. The spectacular bestseller of the late 1950s on injustice and persecution during the Third Reich was very relevant in the era of the struggle for equal rights in America. Coltrane turned his interpretation of this Viennese waltz flavor into one of jazz's peaks when he deconstructed and reassembled it into spiritual transcendence and energy with a political power capable of conveying a message of justice, appeasement, and compassion to the world.

---

1 Oscar Hammerstein II was born to a father of German-Jewish origin and a Christian mother. He was educated more as a Protestant than as a Jew.

Minorities, music and history

This book is a story about an unaware and self-aware minority alliance of Jews and blacks. Throughout the twentieth century, these minorities fought together for equal rights and political and social recognition. This fragile alliance was also cultural. The music that emerged from this collaboration and the semiotic power that accompanied it, not only changed American music, but also helped challenge the hegemony of the WASPs (White Anglo-Saxon Protestant), which had dominated American politics and culture since its inception.

At the end of the journey, in the late 1960s, the American melting pot seemed to have experienced a cultural earthquake. The success of the struggle for social justice, the liberal activity of Presidents Kennedy and Johnson, the emergence of student politics and the protest movement against the war in Vietnam, and the bohemian subculture of the hippies, created a rift in the idea of social integration.

The end of that decade was characterized by the breakdown of the liberal dream and the transition to a "salad" of minorities. The end of the 1960s was marked by the echoes of an ethnic struggle in which America was divided into different ethnic, racial and gender groups that redefined their needs. Minorities had replaced the emphasis of the liberal vision on integration by highlighting the ethnic identification of each sector.[2] Feminist, racial, and ethnic politics, along with the activities of various interest groups, sharpened the differences between those minority groups and the Anglo-Saxon white elite.

These processes in American politics and culture weakened the cultural dominance of WASPs and opened the discourse to voices from the margins of society. The 1960s were a time when American liberalism and radical liberalism achieved much, often through court decisions which were the result of the noisy activity and street theater of the counterculture movements. The changes that took place seemed so great that it felt like everything that seemed solid in the past had melted.[3]

---

[2] David R. Colburn and George E. Pozzetta, "Race, Ethnicity, and the Evolution of Political Legitimacy," in *The Sixties*, edited by David Farber, 119–148 (Chapel Hill: University of North Carolina Press, 1995), 137.

[3] Kenneth Cmiel, "The Politics of Civility," ibid., 292. Counterculture is a general term for the liberal and radical liberal activities of a number of political and non-political movements that operated in the 1960s and influenced the public discourse: The New Left (which included several student movements), The Anti-War Movement in the United States, The Civil Rights Movement, Black Power in all its sub-movements, the ecological movement, and the hippies. The aim of the Counterculture was to provide a cultural and sometimes a political alternative to the mainstream American way of life.

The 1960s was also a testimony to many changes in American culture – both high and popular. These were the years in which American culture challenged modernism and adopted diverse aspects of both postmodern and populist sensibilities.[4] The growing popularity of rock music in mass culture in the 1960s was another evolutionary stage – a unique and particularly exciting one – during which popular music took on more importance in everyday life, and at times constituted a social voice and a political soundtrack.[5]

Many American Jews (in a manner inconsistent with their proportion to the American population) took part in the struggle for social justice and the music industry and musical activity from the early twentieth century until the early 1970s (and even later). In both fields, this era witnessed surprising cooperation between the African-American and Jewish minorities. The musical presence of Jewish entrepreneurs and artists in the first half of the twentieth century is well known and accepted in view of the overwhelming representation of Jews in the publishing industry and in popular songwriting, on Broadway and even in jazz. Yet even during the rock era, starting from the mid-1950s, the impact of American Jews was so surprising and unrecognized, that it was even called a "secret history."[6] As in the struggle for social justice, so in the field of music, collaboration began at the end of the nineteenth century, but reached its peak during the 1960s due to the diverse historical events that shaped American society after World War Two.

The struggle for social justice throughout the twentieth century was connected to Jewish activity in music. Many of the songs that were written, produced, and distributed by Jewish musical producers, ranging from classical musicals to blues-gospel performances of African-American operas and high-level poetics from the rock era, were influenced in various ways by the public discourse regarding the struggle for equal rights that was gradually developed throughout the century. The emphasis is on the relationship; this does not mean that the songs influenced the means or activity of the struggle for equal rights.

However, in some cases the hits gave the masses the ideas of equal rights, cultural openness, the image of "another America," racial brotherhood, and the charm and charisma of African-American culture. In so doing, they gradually influenced popular culture. They also took part in the ongoing negotiations over the hegemonic dominance of WASP culture.

---

4 David Steigerwald, *The Sixties and the End of Modern America* (New York: St. Martin's Press, 1995).
5 Ari Katorza, *Come Together: Rock 'n' Roll, Liberalism, Mass Bohemianism and the Sixties* (Tel Aviv: K-Academics Publishing, 2019).
6 Michael Billig, *Rock 'n' Roll Jews* (London: Five Leaves Publications, 2001).

The decline of the WASP

He was supposed to be their man; intrepid in any purpose, real and three-dimensional. The WASP – the mythological model of the White Anglo-Saxon Protestant – was the man who built America and held it together, and was what every immigrant aspired to become, while believing in the endless possibilities that man faces. But the twentieth century was characterized by the ongoing undermining of the hegemonic status of the WASPs. The shattering of the liberal dream of the 1960s, the disintegration of the minority coalition and the crisis of confidence in the WASP's melting pot contributed to this.[7] Contrary to the famous insights on the special way in which American faith was created as a new way of life that, for the first time in human history, provided equality for all races and religions, it may be more reliable to argue that the fathers of the American nation tried to build America in the WASP's image and as the incarnation of the Anglo-Saxon Protestant heritage. They did this by drawing on the Calvinist-Puritan ethic that assumed that the leadership of an exemplary society would be the symbol of them being chosen by God.

While the main source of population that constituted America until 1820 was Anglo-Saxon Protestant, the end of the nineteenth century was characterized by the migration of a mostly non-Protestant population. The WASP hegemony reached its peak in the 1920s with the predominance of the WASP model in the education system, culture, and politics, but it was the cosmopolitan liberalism and the pattern of interests of the new ethnic groups that began to challenge the WASPs.

WASP is not such a solid concept, and in fact it has established itself more through the invention of culture and myths rather than on ethnicity.[8] The texture of the WASPs in the United States was, of course, based on Anglo-Saxon residents, but a considerable percentage of them were also of German and Scottish-Irish origin. Many institutions that were considered throughout American history as "WASPs" were created by a population that is not of English origin only. Some representatives of the mythological heroes of the WASP culture (such as some of the Western conquerors) are not of English descent. In addition, there are Catholic population groups who felt completely WASP.[9]

---

[7] Eric P. Kaufmann, *The Rise and Fall of White-Anglo America* (Cambridge: Harvard University Press, 2002).
[8] Robert C. Christopher, *Crashing the Gates: The DE-WASPing of America's Power Elite* (London and New York: Simon & Schuster, 1986), 23–41.
[9] The WASP concept, which we refer to today, was first published in the press in 1962.

In any case, the fear of immigrants seemed to have troubled the WASP elite since the turn of the century. Between 1921 to 1924, the American authorities managed to make draconian cuts to immigration rates in general, and from Southern and Eastern European and East Asian countries in particular. The Protestant elite, in a sense, managed to control the social balance of power despite their proportional decline, and even if its hegemonic status was no longer taken for granted.

The concepts of WASP and WASP culture are stereotypes created by ethnic minorities, which refer to Caucasians of Anglo-Saxon origin. But WASP culture was not as homogeneous as the ethnic minorities used to presented it. WASP culture was diverse in urban and rural areas, and in various parts of the United States. It is reasonable to assume that the level of conservatism and Puritanism identified with it was not identical everywhere. Thus, the use of the terms "Victorian" and "Puritan" as representing the conservative dimension of the WASP identity is not always accurate, since not all WASPs saw themselves as Puritans. In a sense, this is a stereotype, but in this book we are dealing with the struggle over stereotypes in American culture.

Songs, semiotics, and mass culture

The connection between the popular American music of the Black-Jewish alliance and liberalism is based on historical conditions, which, in fact, allowed popular music to precede several decades of similar processes in parallel cultural sectors, such as television and cinema.[10]

A popular song is a commercial commodity; it is marketed to the masses through the capitalist industry, including record labels, radio, newspapers, and television. Popular songs have a semiotic power stemming from the slogans, the sound, and the image of the performer. Under certain historical conditions, these may influence the fabric of images that constitute the ideology of hegemony.

"Jewish creativity" in this context refers to songs written by artists of Jewish origin. This does not mean that the writers placed their Jewish identity at the center of their work. On the contrary, the overwhelming majority of the writers and musicians have hidden their Jewishness. They were, in many cases, agents

---

[10] Greil Marcus, *Mystery Train: Images of America in Rock 'n' Roll Music* (New York: Plume, 5th ed., 2008); H. B. Schulman, *The Seventies: The Great Shift in American Culture, Society and Politics* (New York: Da Capo Press, 2001), 53–78.

of African-American cultural content in the cultural space of whites and immigrants.

Some scholars point to the influences of Eastern European Jewish music on American pop music at the beginning of the twentieth century, but there are no echoes of these influences in the rock era.[11] The Jewish writers, along with other groups, based their modern vision of American music on Afro-American elements, a vision that was different from the original intention of the WASP composers. The Jewish writers were also pioneers in the composition of folk materials with the elements of European high art in works that were distributed in popular culture.

On the significance of disproportion

The presence of Jews in politics for social justice, in the entertainment industry in general, and in music in particular, is highly remarkable, and does not match their proportion to the general population. Still, this is a small minority group among the general ethnic population.

In the political field, around the struggle for social justice, data shows that in the second decade of the twentieth century, Jewish activists from various fields and institutions – from community institutions, through the Communist Left to the New Left during the 1960s – were working decisively for equal rights. At the height of the process, in the early 1960s, about two-thirds of the young left-wing activists who went south to Mississippi in the summer of 1964 were of Jewish origin; two-thirds of the funding for the struggle for equal rights came from Jewish sources; and about a third of the leaders of the New Left movements were of Jewish origin. Apart from the Afro-American population, the Jews took part in the struggle more than any other American minority.[12]

The Jews were also present in music. The vast majority of the major publishing companies in Tin Pan Alley, which at the end of the nineteenth century became the main production area of the American music industry, were owned and run by Jews. Apparently, about 40 percent of the independent record labels of the post-World War Two era were owned or managed by Jews. In addition,

---

11 Jack Gottlieb, *Funny, It Doesn't Sound Jewish: How Yiddish Songs and Synagogue Melodies Influenced Tin Pan Alley* (New York: University of New York Press, 2004).
12 Arthur Liebman, *Jews and the Left* (New York: Wiley, 1979).

Jews ran and controlled two of the largest and most successful record labels in the late 1960s: CBS Records and Warner Communications.[13]

Jewish songwriters have written the American Songs Book since the beginning of the twentieth century: Irving Berlin, Jerome Kern, George and Ira Gershwin, Oscar Hammerstein II, Richard Rodgers, Lorenz Hart, and Yip Harburg are only some of the writers whose names and works have become an inseparable asset to American music. In addition, Jewish singers, such as Jolson, Eddie Cantor, Sophie Tucker, Fanny Brice, and Molly Picon were prominent in musical activity.

Jewish prominence continued even after World War II. About thirty important artists influenced the popular music in a variety of ways. Few people will dispute that Jerry Leiber and Mike Stoller are among the most important writers of the 1950s, and Phil Spector, Bob Dylan, Paul Simon, Lou Reed, and Leonard Cohen are among the most important figures in rock history.

During the 19th century, Irish and German immigrants were the ones who took part in musical activity, and the twentieth century was characterized by a high presence of singers of Italian origin. Still, compared to other minorities from European countries, Americans Jews were surprisingly dominant in the work, expressing a special connection to black music.

In my opinion, this is not an internal, cultural, and inherent connection between Jews and Judaism and between music and entertainment, but rather a circumstantial-environmental connection. Their encounter at a specific time with the Afro-American minority and its culture was shaped into artistic-commercial-historical chemistry. This chemistry, even if it was not free of conflicts and discourse about exploitation, highly influenced American culture. This encounter of unprivileged minorities in a changing historical period was another chapter in the dialogue between the American culture and its minorities, a dialogue that revolves around the axis of race, liberalism, permissiveness, and cultural openness and against the attempt of the old elite to enforce its historical authority.

---

13 However, the numbers "do not tell the whole story." With the exception of Motown Records, a successful and influential African-American entrepreneur, the two most successful and influential small companies, Atlantic Records and Elektra Records, which merged with the corporations, were wholly or partly owned by Jews and managed by them.

Penny from heaven: Jews in the music industry

From the end of the nineteenth century, Jewish immigrants and their children began to promote their socio-economic status through the mass industry.[14] While most of the Jews in the United States found their livelihood in various branches of trade and professions (although these professions were not always entirely open to Jews), Jews also engaged in mass popular culture.[15] Many of the publishing companies of Tin Pan Alley in New York were founded by Jewish entrepreneurs: Maurice Shapiro, Louis Bernstein, Leo Feist, Isidore Witmark, Joseph Stern, and others. The owners of the publishing houses recruited composers, lyricists, and musical arrangers. As a result of their social background and social connections, many of the recruits were Jews. Cole Porter even admitted during his successful career that "Jewish songs" were a tireless potential for hits.[16]

The writers made their way into the music industry, relying on the Jewish connection between Broadway and the Jewish publishing companies, some of which were owned by Hollywood studios from the late 1920s.[17] Tin Pan Alley dominated the American music industry in the first half of the twentieth century. However, in the mid-1950s, the center of gravity shifted to a new musical genre, which was the fusion of southern Caucasian music and Afro-American culture: rock 'n' roll. This musical style, which would be known from the mid-1960s as rock, was to become the main revenue center of the music industry in the late 1960s.[18] This musical transformation was made possible by changes in the structure of American communications institutions and the emergence

---

14 Stephen J. Whitfield, *In Search of An American Jewish Culture* (London: Brandeis, 2001), 32–59; Leonard Dinnerstein, *Antisemitism in America* (New York: Oxford University Press, 1994); Earl Raab, *What Do We Really Know About Antisemitism and What We Want to Know?* (New York: American Jewish Committee, 1989). In this book, "Jewish immigrants" to America will relate mainly to Jews of Eastern European origin (mainly from Russia, Ukraine, the Baltic countries, and Poland), who began to immigrate to the American continent in large numbers from the 1880s. Yet, German Jews took an active part in the entertainment industry and the establishment of publishing houses.
15 Stephen J. Whitfield, J., *In Search of An American Jewish Culture* (London: Brandeis, 2001), 32–59; Leonard Dinnerstein, *Antisemitism in America* (New York: Oxford University Press, 1994), 32–59.
16 Michael Billig, *Rock 'n' Roll Jews* (London: Five Leaves Publications, 2001).
17 Neal Gabler, *An Empire of Their Own: How the Jews Invented Hollywood* (New York: Crown Publishers, Inc., 1997).
18 Charlie Gillett, *Sound of The City: The Rise of Rock and Roll* (London: Da Capo Press, 1984), 4–6.

of a new consumer audience: the baby boomers and the historic rise of youth culture.[19]

Despite the dramatic change in musical sound and the decline in the power of Tin Pan Alley, Jews became a driving force in the rock industry too, mainly between 1955 to 1970. During this period, Jews took an important part in various fields: management jobs, establishment of publishing companies, radio broadcasters, and the establishment of a professional music press.[20]

American Jews were also responsible for recording and distributing R&B and other styles of African-American artists, such as gospel and doo-wop. Contrary to the popular charm of the "polite" Big Bands of the Swing era, which went through an ongoing process of "whitening," and contrary to the elitist attraction to the avant-garde intellectual modern jazz, R&B was rough, full of extreme jargon and sexual imagery. These songs were perceived by the white mainstream as "obscene," and the major record companies ignored them almost completely even in the post-World War Two era. They concentrated their energies on intensive on promoting the Tin Pan Alley's songs alongside country music, sometimes connecting the esthetics of the two streams together.

On the other hand, many Jewish entrepreneurs, who owned independent labels, were responsible for recording and distributing R&B and rock 'n' roll. In fact, the combination of R&B and gospel and country music, influenced by the concept of white youth culture, was branded as rock 'n' roll during the early 1950s. Syd Nathan, owner of King Records label from Cincinnati, signed, recorded and distributed James Brown; Art Rupe, the owner of Specialty Records located in Los Angeles, introduced Little Richard to the world; the brothers Phil and Leonard Chess turned Chicago into a vibrant blues center; Savoy Records, founded by Herman Lubinsky, recorded black music. The most dominant independent company was Atlantic Records in New York, managed by the Turkish Ahmet Ertegun and Jewish Jerry Wexler, led African-American music into inter-

---

[19] Richard Peterson, "Why 1955? Explaining the advent of Rock Music," *Popular Music* 9 (1990): 97–116.

[20] In spite of the decline in the power of Tin Pan Alley, which enjoyed a prominent Jewish presence, American Jews took part in various fields of the music industry in the rock age: publishing companies (for example, Aldon Music was founded by Al Nevins and Don Kirshner), artists' management (Albert Grossman, Bob Dylan's manager and a music mogul in folk music), broadcasters (Alan Freed, who conceptualized the concept of rhythm and blues as rock 'n' roll), and the contribution of Jews to professional rock journalism (Jann Wenner, the founder of Rolling Stone magazine, and Barry Kramer, the publisher of Creem, an influential subversive rock magazine).

national consciousness while positioning themselves as an economic corporation.[21]

Jewish entrepreneurs not only dealt with Tin Pan Alley, R&B and rock 'n' roll, but also controlled some of the most important independent labels in the field of folk music. Moses Asch recorded the historical recordings of Woody Guthrie in Folkways Records; the Jewish brothers Maynard and Seymour Solomon established their company Vanguard Records in the early 1950s. Elektra Records, for example, founded by Jac Holzman and under the artistic direction of Paul Rothchild, became a very successful folk company, and during the 1960s it also represented some of the more avant-garde and political rock bands identified with the counterculture, including the MC5 and The Doors.

Jews also held senior positions in the major records companies. In 1967, Atlantic and Elektra, with its rich and valuable repertoire, merged with Warner Brothers into the conglomerate Warner Communications. This corporation, which was run by Steve Ross, struggled for the premiere with the CBS Corporation, which was owned by another Jew, William Paley. The corporation's record company was managed by Clive Davis from 1967, and by Walter Yetinnikoff from the mid-1970s – both of Jewish origin. American Jews undoubtedly took part in the historical process in which the major music companies became international corporations.[22] The connection between the independent labels and rock 'n' roll and R&B was not exclusive to Jews, but Jews took part in the promotion of many of the most important artists and worked in some of the most successful record companies.[23]

The Jews of American music

This book will tell the story of the Jewish-Black cooperation, and in certain eras an alliance, in music, from the establishment of the modern music industry in the late nineteenth century to 1965, with Bob Dylan's evolution from civil rights

---

[21] Charlie Gillett, *Sound of the City: The Rise of Rock and Roll* (London: Da Capo Press, 1984), 492.
[22] Fredric Dannen, *Hit Men: Power Brokers and Fast Money Inside the Music Business* (New York: Anchor, 1991).
[23] Charlie Gillett, *Sound of the City: The Rise of Rock and Roll* (London: Da Capo Press, 1984). Sun Records in Memphis, in which Elvis Presley and Jerry Lee Lewis recorded, was a very important field of activity in which black and white culture merged. Vee-Jay Records was one of the most important record labels owned by Afro-Americans, a few years before the Motown Company broke out in Detroit, and there are other examples.

poet to a rock star. This year marked the political peak of the struggle for social justice with L.B. Johnson's 1964 to 1965 civil rights amendments to the American Constitution. The book will focus on some of the most important characters in American music of the twentieth century: the first part of the book will begin with the successful singer and entertainer Al Jolson and blackface minstrelsy, and will continue the process of Jewish immigration to America and the placement of Jews in the entertainment industry. Next we will meet the songwriter Irving Berlin, also known as the King of Ragtime, and the Jewish publishing industry in Tin Pan Alley. This part will be conclude with the world of jazz: from the pioneering journey of composers Jerome Kern and George Gershwin to black music in the world of Broadway musicals, and the relationship between the African-American jazz composer Duke Ellington and his Jewish manager Irving Mills and their influence on American music. A special chapter deals with the social and cultural world of the Jews in the record industry, such as Jerry Wexler, Walter Yetnikoff, and David Geffen.

The second part of this book will be devoted to the formation of the Jewish-Black political alliance in the United States and its growth after the World War Two, as well as to the rock 'n' roll Jews – songwriters and musical producers who created the sound of multicultural America in the era of the struggle for social justice: Leiber and Stoller, Phil Spector, Burt Bacharach, and Carole King. The relationship between folk music and capitalism, e.g., between Bob Dylan, guitarist Mike Bloomfield and their manager Albert Grossman, will receive special coverage. The last two chapters of the book will be devoted to the discourse on exploitation between Jews and blacks, as well as to viewing historical-musical integration through cultural theories.

Jews and the dream of universal America

While the contribution of the Jews to the American canon in the Tin Pan Alley era and Broadway musicals won relatively extensive coverage in the literature, it seems that until the new millennium their contribution to rock was not emphasized enough, at least not as an ethnic diction.[24] The reason for the mystery surrounding the contribution of the Jews, some claims, lies in the history of Jewish identity.

Some scholars have already suggested that in an era were anti-Semitism was still a threatening force, and out of a desire to assimilate into the new world, the

---

24 Michael Billig, *Rock 'n' Roll Jews* (London: Five Leaves Publications, 2001), 10–29.

best Jewish artists – sometimes the first generation, but also second and third generations of immigrants – hid their identity, changed their names, and disengaged from their heritage. The Jews had to invent a new identity so that they could become an integral and important part of the dream industry.

I argue that the creativity of the Jews in American music, even if based on the seclusion of Jewish ethnic identity, shaped a more universal American culture. Based on theories of semiotics, hegemonic negotiations, ideology, and Jungian psychology, it is not difficult to determine that the connection of the Jews to black culture under the cultural climate created by the struggle for social justice contained not only a musical hybrid, but an entire culture of representation, image and language.[25] The Black-Jewish alliance forced America to face its shadow, its primitive and dark side, so that it could begin to heal itself.

There is relatively little evidence that by the end of the 1950s, American popular music (even rock 'n' roll) consciously went against hegemonic culture. Popular music generally avoided taking a stand against the system of discrimination against blacks, racism in general or sexism, or even against class hierarchy. At the same time, the ethnic combinations that characterized it, its black roots over the blunt and spontaneous sexuality that accompanied it, were perceived as a sexual and racial menace. American popular music, ranging from ragtime, jazz, and musicals to rock 'n' roll, sometimes became a political-cultural threat, especially in light of the attack on it, which came from the various institutions that defined it as a moral threat.[26]

Elitist humanism

It is interesting that these Jewish writers and entrepreneurs, who enjoyed promising possibilities of economic mobility in America, took upon themselves the role of identifying with unprivileged minorities. As noted, they were not the only ones in this trend, but they were more dominant than other minorities,

---

[25] Lawrence Grossberg, "Another Boring Day in Paradise: Rock and Roll and the Empowerment of everyday life" *Popular Music* 4 (1984): 225–258; Roland Barthes, *Mythologies* (London: Farrar, Straus and Giroux, 1972); Louis Althusser, *Lenin and Philosophy and Other Essays* (London: Monthly Review Press, 1971); Stuart Hall and Tony Jefferson, eds., *Resistance Through Rituals: Youth Subcultures in Postwar Britain* (Birmingham: Hutchinson, 1976).

[26] African-American musicians took part in the process of sophistication and cultivation of blues and jazz and their connection to high art. The most concrete example is that of Duke Ellington, but also by Bebop artists, such as Charlie Parker, Dizzy Gillespie, Miles Davis, and others.

and they chose to wave the flag of another minority instead of appearing as a minority themselves. Why?

During the last decades, academic scholars were divided in two opposite camps: The first, the *Altruistic* approach, regarding the Black-Jewish alliance in politics and culture describes the ability of the Jews to understand the "other" in general, and African-American culture in particular, better than others ethnic groups. This is the result of the fact that these "unprivileged" minorities share similar mythologies and histories, traditions of suffering, exile, and slavery. This leads to the motivations derived from Jewish humanistic strategies to help the weaker sectors of the population.[27]

The second approach is *Whiteness*, which views Jewish-back relations as a product of the exploitation of African-Americans by the more privileged minority: American Jews. This argument insists that in order to be "white Americans," Jews – who have always been considered the most mixed breed in America – had become "apolitical melting pot agents." They were responsible for turning American culture into a field that served the interests of white hegemony at the expense of African-Americans.[28]

In my view, however, these two approaches do not meet the test of history, and there are too many contradictions that are inconsistent with these assumptions. Regarding the first, "Altruistic" approach, the belief that the Jew "identifies with suffering" simply does not align with the history of the American Jews. Serious historians of Jewish liberalism in America question the "natural" connection many scholars have made between Judaism and universal humanism. They revealed that the struggle of some Jewish organizations in the 1940s and 1950s against anti-Semitism and for equal rights was motivated by political inter-

---

[27] Lawrence H. Fuchs, "Sources of Jewish Internationalism and Liberalism," in *The Jews: Social Patterns of an American Group*, edited by Marshall Sklare (New York: Free Press, 1958), 595–613; Michael Alexander, *Jazz Age Jews* (New Jersey: Princeton University, 2001); Irving Howe, *World of Our Fathers* (New York: Simon & Schuster, 1976); Paul Buhle, *From the Lower East Side to Hollywood: Jews in American Popular Culture* (New York: Verso, 2004); Alfred Kazin, "The Jew as Modern Writer," in *The Ghetto and Beyond; Essays on Jewish Life in America*, edited by Peter Rose (New York: Random House, 1969), 424.

[28] Jeffrey Melnick, *A Right to Sing the Blues: African Americans, Jews and American Popular Song* (Cambridge, Massachusetts: Harvard University Press, 1999); Michael Rogin, *Blackface, White Noise: Jewish Immigrants in the Hollywood Melting Pot* (Berkeley: University of California Press, 1998); Karen Brodkin, *How Jews Became White Folks and What That Says About Race in America* (New Brunswick: Rutgers University Press, 1998). See also: Jon Stratton, *Jews, Race and Popular Music* (Surrey: Ashgate, 2009); Bruce Zuckerman, Josh Kun and Lisa Ansell, ed., *The Song Is Not the Same: Jews and American Popular* (Indiana: Purdue University Press, 2010); Michael Billig, *Rock 'n' Roll Jews* (London: Five Leaves Publications, 2001).

ests, primarily to ensure the security of the Jewish minority. Therefore, the attempt to parallel Judaism and universalism is incompatible with the isolationism inherent in the foundations of Judaism.[29]

History is also inconsistent with the Whiteness tradition and Jews as "melting pot agents" approach. Regarding American film, for example, the number of radical Jewish writers and Hollywood screenwriters with a socialist background, stands in contradiction to this theory. As if against the entertainment stereotype, history shows that Hollywood Jews reacted against the WASP societies and their Victorian values, and Jewish modernist composers fought against the Yankee composers' vision. In the field of music, Jewish entrepreneurs and artists adopted black popular music in a way that the WASPs didn't dare or didn't want to do, as opposition to the elitists Yankees, in both popular and high music. The conception of the Jews as melting pot agents does not fit with the ways that Henry Ford and his team loved to portray Hollywood and entertainment Jews as "a danger to America." These approaches range from the non-existent Jew (the altruist) to the passive-frightened-exploiter Jew (the melting pot agent) – and this book, backing itself with historical facts, rejects these notions.

At this stage, I emphasize that from the end of the nineteenth century and the beginning of the twentieth century, the Jews in Hollywood, Broadway, even the Tin Pan Alley and certainly during the post-World War Two's R&B and rock 'n' roll took part in the struggle against the WASP elites. They created an alternative cultural system to the WASP aspirations, which was less religious, puritanical, and sanctimonious. In my view, they expressed a special kind of "Elitist Humanism" in their version of American culture, and engaged in the cultivation of popular and high culture, since they could express what they saw as their "best." They believed that they knew better than others what the American culture was. The Jews discovered the potential to establish all these advantages in black music, where they felt "at home," since some musical traditions, as well as philosophical overtones, were shared in both cultures.

But the story is not that simple: beyond the success of the Black-Jewish alliance, both in its political achievements concerning the constitutional amendments of 1964 to 1965, and regarding the opening of the monolithic WASP culture to multiculturalism, the discourse relates to exploitation. Jews liked to describe the Black-Jewish cooperation and alliance in heroic terms, while militant blacks

---

29 Stuart Svonkin, *Jews against Prejudice* (New York: Columbia University Press, 1999); Michael Staub, *Torn at the Roots: The Crisis of Jewish Liberalism in Postwar America* (New York: Columbia University Press, 2004); Marc Dollinger, *Quest for Inclusion: Jews and Liberalism in Modern America* (New Jersey: Princeton University Press, 2000).

claimed economic and artistic exploitation. This controversy, which I will address and discuss in this book, still resonates.

This book will describe the Black-Jewish alliance from a psycho-historical perspective. My intention is to examine – through sources, biographies, and autobiographies – the charisma of black culture amongst Jewish writers and businesspersons. Entrepreneurs and artists from these unprivileged minority groups chose to make their way to success, with each side being an asset to the other. This cultural alliance was made possible as long as the African-Americans could maintain their "authentic" culture of promoting the struggle for social justice and enjoying a process of social mobility, while the Jews could define their identity and social cohesion by adopting a charismatic culture with an urban, more cosmopolitan and universal appeal; a culture that would stand aside to the WASP America, which was – at least in terms of image – puritanical and sanctimonious.

This alliance was based on the charisma of each of the sides, but toward the end of the 1960s, due to the separatist political-cultural trend of the blacks, in view of conflicts of interest between the minority groups and a sense of exhaustion, cooperation moderated, and in many ways was even terminated.[30]

About half a century later, we seem to have an immeasurable cultural wealth. An abundance of song books, Broadway musicals, new musical esthetics, historical recordings, exciting collaborations, oppressive labor disputes, many moments of grace, tremendous cultural change and a complete musical revolution. "I'll build a stairway to Paradise," composed Gershwin in one of his early hits, "with a new step ev'ry day," and that is, more or less, the way it happened.

The chapters:
1. Jokerman: The Black Mask of Al Jolson
The first chapter discusses the connection between blackface minstrelsy and the role American Jews took in this field. As opposed to some important works relating to minstrelsy, I propose a different and alternative way to understand this culture, based on cultural studies theories and Jungian psychology. I discuss it through the case study of Al Jolson.

---

30 Murray Freedman, *What Went Wrong?: The Creation and The Collapse of the Black-Jewish Alliance* (New York: Free Press, 1994), 98–201.

2. Over the Rainbow: American Jews and the Struggle for Popular Culture

This chapter discusses Jewish immigration to America and the historical way Jews have entered the entertainment industry, until they finally became a dominant force in this field. This chapter portrays the historical struggle of Jewish entrepreneurs against the WASPs elite in popular culture and the discourse concerning Jewish ethnicity in popular culture. It also deals with the connection between East-European Jewish music and the roots of African-American music.

3. I Used to be Color Blind: Irving Berlin, Ragtime Riot, and the Tin Pan Alley's Jews

This chapter reveals the foundation of Tin Pan Alley (the publishing industry in New York City, that was founded mainly by Jews of German origin) through the story of Irving Berlin. It discusses ragtime music and the way the networking of Jews on Tin Pan Alley helped transform it into the pop tune format that would accompany the twentieth century. This chapter reflects on the way Jewish artists turned these black materials into great successes, while African-American composers such as Scott Joplin usually lacked support of the same powerful networking.

4. Someone to Watch over Me: Jerome Kern, George Gershwin and the Odyssey to Jazz in the Musical Comedy

Kern and Gershwin, two popular songwriters, reached their creative peak by using Broadway's musical comedy as a means through which to combine high art with popular culture. They achieved their masterpieces by exploring African-American cultural materials and American themes concerning racism, exploitation and salvation. Their journey encapsulates the way jazz and black music were evolved into the basis for Broadway musicals and vice versa, and the way their songs had a tremendous influence on jazz music.

5. It Don't Mean a Thing, if it Ain't Got that Swing: The Fantasy of Duke Ellington and Irving Mills

The importance of Duke Ellington to jazz is undisputable and has been widely discussed, but the relationship between Ellington and his Jewish manager Irving Mills has remained in the academic shadows. Their story encapsulates the benefits and problems concerning Black-Jewish relationships. Their fantastic artistic achievements were the consequences of this economic alliance. At the same time, it was a story of anti-Semitism and the limits of culture in shaping racial boundaries.

6. Heaven with You: Jews, the Record Industry and Rock 'n' Roll

This chapter deals with the history of the record industry and the Jewish entrepreneurs in this field. They were mostly from working-class backgrounds, failures in their studies, but cultivated and shrewd. They shared similar psychological traits and were able to turn the record industry into a "Jewish industry."

7. Stand by Me: The Black-Jewish Political Alliance and the Decline of the WASPs.

The post-war era had witnessed the tremendous energy engendered by the political struggle of the Black-Jewish alliance to make America commit itself to its constitution. Jews and blacks under the leadership of Dr. Martin Luther King Jr. created unconsciously an anti-WASP alliance. The political struggle for equal rights was not against the WASP elite, even if it had anti-WASP dimensions. Its results and understanding of the implications of racism following World War Two created the need for a general restructuring of American society. These minority groups were determined to resolve inequality in order to ensure once and for all their security. This chapter discusses the connection between Jews and the American Left during the twentieth century in the context of our story.

8. That's Rock 'n' Roll: Leiber and Stoller and the White Negro

Rock 'n' roll was an expression of post-war liberalism. It was not just its influence on teenagers, but the beginning of an intellectual wave that gradually shaped it and turned it into one of the most important mass cultures in the twentieth century. Rock 'n' roll has been synonymous with democratization processes that cultural discourse had undergone. America may have been divided from the end of the nineteenth century concerning the "color" of American music, but during the 1950s writers and intellectuals came to a decision. They perceived the "black" color as positive and the "white" as "fake." Various discussions dealing with issues of authenticity linked social inferiority and the authentic aura of street culture, which was existential and black. The story of the duo of R&B writers Jerry Leiber and Mike Stoller examines this aspect.

9. Will You Love Me Tomorrow: Carole King and Black Lolita on the Brill Building

The Girl Groups sound was fashionable during the early sixties. Some of the girl groups looked like "neighbors' daughters," domesticated and conservative, but producers also promoted African-American nymphs and Lolitas which merged into a multi-cultural explosion, sometimes full of magic and seduction. This time, for once, women also gave their voices. This chapter discusses Carole King and other feminine voices, feminism and the Brill Building publishing industry.

10. River Deep, Mountain High: Phil Spector, Burt Bacharach and the Ghost on the Second Floor of the Bus

In many ways they were completely different from each other. Bacharach belonged to the jazz generation, Spector to the rock generation. Bacharach was a composer with formal education, while Spector was a talented musician with great intuitions. Bacharach was a man of the existing order, while Spector tried to break every law of the entertainment world. Bacharach looked like an accountant, while Spector was notorious for being one of the mad men of show business. But both continued the trend of integrating popular and high art into works with sweeping influences on American pop music and in general. They both took off in the early 1960s through the New York Brill Building publishing industry. Both came from factories of producing hits with Jewish commercial and artistic dominance and both achieved success by utilizing African-American femininity.

11. The sounds of silence: Folk, blues and the spirit of capitalism between Grossman, Bloomfield and Zimmerman.

Although it was anti-capitalist in its pretense, folk music needed a commercial mechanism to distribute it, and into this void entered several Jewish entrepreneurs who established independent and important record companies in this field.

The instruments were acoustic: accordion, banjo, dulcimer, harmonica violin, mandolin and more. The dynamic was supposed to be anti-commercial and anti-capitalist, rural, communal, leftist and protesting; in short, folk was perceived as a platform for social change. But beneath the surface, the roots of folk were immersed in a kind of transcendence and universal consolation, locked up in images of religious passion. The relationship between Albert Grossman and his clients, Bob Dylan and Mike Bloomfield, tells the problematic story of folk, blues and capitalism through the Jewish discourse.

12. Walk on the Wild Side: Jews, Gangsters and Rock 'n' Roll

American Jews (writers and entrepreneurs) – from blackface minstrelsy, through ragtime and jazz to rock and roll – used African-American musical materials. But these two minority groups moved on different levels in the music field and gained a different power. It was the Jews who controlled African-American cultural products, who were considered good interpreters as creators of these materials and as owners of the means of production: publishers, owners of small and large labels, concert agencies, and others. The success of the Jews in the field of entertainment and music, and their privileged status in this field, were inseparable from the fact that they controlled the sources of music and the careers of artists. The entertainment industry also "enjoyed" the presence of Jewish gangsters, who had their notorious impact concerning exploitation. But was it the exploitation of African Americans, or was it a generally problematic working relationship between those who controlled the means of production and those who did not? This chapter discusses this question.

13. "A hard rain's a-gonna fall": Popular music and Hegemonic Conflict in American Culture

Understanding the influence of the Black-Jewish alliance on American culture is possible through familiarity with the concepts of British cultural studies. These were created during the post-war era at the Center for Contemporary Cultural Studies in Birmingham, England. Their theories will be focused on in this chapter while using post-structuralism as well as postmodern logic to understand conflicts in the American cultural hegemony during the twentieth century.

Chapter 1: Jokerman – The Black Mask of Al Jolson

"Everybody loves me. Those who don't are jealous," wrote singer Al Jolson in an advertisement he published in the *Variety* newspaper in 1919, wishing him a happy New Year and a good year for America.[31] The top figure in the American entertainment industry knew he had a big ego, but there was no one but him who deserved the title of "greatest entertainer in the world." The rising star of the Vaudeville Hall was able to sign a contract with the Shubert brothers on Broadway and starred in the musical comedy *Sinbad* (1918). Hollywood was to be his next prey; it was only a matter of time. In the entertainment industry, as in sports, status or ethnic origin was not important, but what "you are able to do." "He was not a very nice character," said singer George Jessel about two decades after Jolson died. "But he was the best performer I've ever seen."[32]

Jolson was perhaps the most famous artist of his time in the blackface minstrelsy. Wherever he wore a black mask, the audience responded with intensity and excitement. Jolson was also a contradictory character: an immigrant who became an American symbol; a "white" Jew in a black game. He sang with an authentic, heartbreaking drama while playing with his audience through the black minstrel mask. He was a playboy, but he alternately pretended to be an idealist; an ego maniac who played the innocent well. They say he was a mother's child, just as he played in the *Jazz Singer*. The disguise of white-Americans as black entertainers was rooted in a theatrical tradition that became institutionalized during the 1830s and was not too complicated to operate. A make-up mask and a very tightly curled wig were enough to bring about a startling transformation, which turned Asa Yoelson to Al Jolson. One needed to know how to steal and borrow slang, dance steps, and African-American mimicry. But Jolson knew more; he was a trickster, but he had a special ability to give the mask a unique depth. He did it in the minstrel show of Lew Dockstader, and he did it in the film the *Jazz Singer* (1927). Of course, he was not the only Jew to star in this theatrical field, but he was probably the most successful.

At the beginning of the twentieth century, while Jolson entered the field of minstrelsy, it was considered a dying art. The sexual burlesque and polite vaudeville and even the nickelodeon gradually replaced blackface minstrelsy as a popular form of American leisure entertainment. In the following decades, elements

---

31 Michael Alexander, *Jazz Age Jews* (New Jersey: Princeton University, 2001).
32 Ibid.

of the minstrelsy culture became a natural part of the musical comedy of Broadway's musicals and in Hollywood. The blackface minstrelsy was not extinct but changed costumes and form. The black-and-white game was and remains the ground on which American music was built.

African rhythm, European harmony and minority politics

American music is a product of the ethnic, racial and racial history of the United States. American nationalism, class struggles, and European, Latin, and African influences were melted into a boiling pot. But the preoccupation with music was not unique to blacks and Jews. During the nineteenth century, Irish, German, and later Italian immigrants took an active part in shaping the schizophrenic American mix.

For many years, writers, scholars and musicians have insisted that American popular music was created from a "wedding" of Africa and Europe in America. Rock writers liked to describe American music as a fusion of black rhythm and white sentimentality.[33] Jazz scholars also used this dialectic by explaining that jazz was the result of three centuries of mixing European harmony, African rhythms and Euro-African melodies.[34]

But a more sober look at minority relations in the United States reveals that the picture is more complex. The whites were never a monolithic entity, but ethnic groups with diverse traditions. The WASPs defined the new immigrants not as white Americans, but as "half-black mongrels" who had to ensure their place as part of the "white race."[35] Every minority began to identify itself as "American" at a different time and under different historical circumstances. Music, then, was for a long time influenced by groups of immigrants.

Irish, Germans, Italians, and Jews played a central role in shaping American music, but through dialogue with African-American culture. Race relations were always at the center. Movement, dance, rhythms, sound, traditions of vocalization, slang and sexuality that were influenced by black culture gave American music its special style. American music, ranging from the minstrels' songs, ragtime, jazz and blues, to contemporary rock 'n' roll and hip-hop was based on this ethnic-racial soup.

---

[33] Nik Cohn, *WopBopaLooBop LopBamBoom: Pop from the Beginning* (London: Paladin, 1969), 11.
[34] Marshall Stearns, *The Story of Jazz* (London: Oxford University Press, 1970), 282.
[35] David R. Roediger, *Working Towards Whiteness: How America's Immigrants Became White* (New York: Basic Books, 2005).

This combination is now perceived as "natural," but the process through which America adopted schizophrenic cultural features of its "inferior" minority still remains fascinating and raises many questions, especially since this process was so contrary to the Puritan-righteous cultural world upon which the first Americans were based. The story of Al Jolson, the black mask and blackface minstrelsy may reveal to us the nature of the first American mass culture.

Love, theft, racism and everything in between

During the 1920s and 1930s, minstrelsy began to appear in New York City and introduced white artists disguised as blacks.[36] These artists wore black makeup on their faces, sang songs, adopted dance steps and a black body show that contained comedic, parodic and patriotic features, which were mostly available to a white audience. Minstrelsy staged the stereotype of the slave as a source of mockery and ridicule.[37]

One central approach to understanding this phenomenon centered on the conception of American history in the nineteenth century as a process of constructing the ideology of white supremacy.[38] According to this view, blackface minstrelsy was a racist ideology reflected in the conquest by the West and black slavery. This racism contained ancient and varied roots but was radicalized during the first half of the nineteenth century.

The ideology for white supremacy was established during the presidency of Andrew Jackson (1837–1829), which was characterized by attempts by the American bourgeoisie to build institutional cultural institutions and to shape the initial cultural canon. This era was also characterized by the intensification of capitalism and patriotism, and the development of mass media. The Jacksonian era witnessed the intensification of the myth of the conquest of the West (which expresses the supremacy of the white man over the red man) and the development of this first urban mass culture of blackface minstrelsy (which expresses the supremacy of the white man over the black man). The myths about Yankee capitalism and the American dream, the great Westerners and minstrelsy began at the same time, symbolizing the American victory over people of color.

---

36 W.T. Lhamon Jr., *Raising Cain: Blackface Performance from Jim Crow to Hip-Hop* (London: Harvard University Press, 1998), 1–55.
37 Eric Lott, *Love & Theft: Blackface Minstrelsy and the American Working Class* (New York & Oxford: Oxford University Press, 1993), 3.
38 Alexander Saxton, *The Rise and Fall of the White Republic: Class Politics and Mass Culture in Nineteenth Century America* (New York: Verso, 1990).

A far-reaching version of the trend regarding the "aspiration for white supremacy" assumed that this was a historical development of the American working class, convinced that the "white freedom" of the workers depended on black slavery.[39] For working classes, it was argued, racism had become an economic and class benefit, and the black disguise was associated with the pre-modern carnival traditions versus the status of industrialization and the emotional resistance to it. Workers were drawn to the charisma of Afro-American culture as a device that ostensibly restored the pre-industrial era to the myth of the pre-modern village festivities but expressed their attraction by showing hostility to the object of disguise. The minstrel shows introduced the working man to his natural self and the "corrupt nature" of industrialized society. According to this view, the minstrel shows were a racist tool that illustrated the idea of "reward for being white" by appropriating the image of white patriotism and democracy as "white only."

On the other side of the spectrum, there were scholars who saw the minstrelsy as a liberal arrowhead.[40] Blackface minstrelsy, according to this approach, allowed for a safer passage of interracial energies, which were trapped daily in unbridgeable boundaries. The parodist elements of minstrelsy used for blacks and their culture were a self-defense, when in fact they masked a genuine attraction to the charisma of black culture.

The tradition of minstrelsy, according to this view, therefore, is not racist. The attraction of the blackface minstrels to black culture was not based solely on instinct, but on "authoritarian attraction" – the need to receive recognition from "below." Tracking the minstrels reveals that most of them were middle-class Northern Irishmen who were close to the Democratic Party. The attraction to black charisma was the beginning of a bohemian tradition of young people who did not accept Puritan ethics.

Under Freudian influence, it could be concluded that through disguise and mockery the minstrels had in fact shown their love for the seemingly black body, its voice, its movement, and its sexuality; and on the other hand they were stealing black slang, movement, music and passion that often embodied real dimensions of subversion.

Blackface minstrelsy was, according to these approaches, a rebellion against the values of the bourgeois family, Puritan ethics, repressed sexuality, and mid-

---

[39] David R. Roediger, *The Wages of Whiteness: Race and the Making of the American Working Class* (New York: Verso, 1991).
[40] *Eric Lott, Love & Theft: Blackface Minstrelsy and the American Working Class* (New York & Oxford: Oxford University Press, 1993).

dle-class values.⁴¹ It was a collage of sounds, movements and parodies of a black culture that challenged European elitism, creating a deeply rooted American culture.

Minorities and American music

The most successful singers in the years before the civil war were of Irish origin: Stephen Foster, Dan Emmett, Dan Bryant, Joel Walker Sweeney, George Christy and others. The special connection between the Irish and minstrelsy has given rise to various explanations that have not yet been able to provide a complete answer to the phenomenon.

A cynical and penetrating look at this connection might have given the impression that the Irish saw the minstrelsy as an ideological tool for creating a collage and a soundtrack that accompanied the ethnic process in which they moved from a sense of shared fate with the black minority to becoming a racist spearhead. The connection between the Irish and racism, it was claimed, was woven into their American experience and the mediation of the Democratic Party (Jacksonian, anti-federalist and more racist). This gave the "black Irish" – who suffered social and class inferiority – the 'reward for being white' in exchange for their support for the Democratic Party.

This description of the politicization of Irish immigration is inconsistent with liberal, psychological, and class trends that have illuminated other aspects of the phenomenon. The Irish minstrels may have been close to the Democratic Party, but they were also young middle-class bohemians, longing for sexual freedom while defying the culture of parents, who mediated – under the parodic disguise – the charismatic aspects of black culture to a variety of audiences.

In any case, the minstrels parodied Celtic harmonies, Italian and English operettas alongside the Irish fiddle, into entertainment with the African banjo, rhythm, visuals and black dialect.⁴² The minstrels, without awareness or predominant intentions, defined the uniqueness of American music as distinct from that of the Old World: based on European roots but separate from it. They created this uniqueness by means of the parodic and comic dimension and the use of black content. It is also possible that the minstrels created the sense of space, while

---

41 W.T. Lhamon Jr., *Raising Cain: Blackface Performance from Jim Crow to Hip-Hop* (London: Harvard University Press, 1998).
42 William J. Mahar, *Behind the Burnt Cork Mask: Early Blackface Minstrelsy and Antebellum American Popular Culture* (Illinois: University of Illinois Press, 1999).

joining the occupation of the West and were an effective instrument for the promotion of nationalism.[43]

The Irish were prominent in minstrelsy and American music during the middle of the nineteenth century, followed by German immigrants, though to the higher spheres of the entertainment industry. Backed by a magnificent Teutonic music tradition, they began to stand out in the popular and high musical culture. Conductors such as Theodore Thomas and Leopold Damrosch, with Jewish roots, and his son Walter, arranged the German *Kultur* for the American audience. Music critics such as Henri Krehbiel and the musicologist and significant producer Oscar Sonneck, conductor and composer John Philip Sousa and the Steinway family created an aura around the sacredness of German music. The first-generation German immigrants did not succumb easily to minstrelsy, but the story of the second generation of emigration was somewhat different. Paul Dresser and German-Jewish Julius Witmark began their career as minstrels' artists. They continued from there to work as businesspeople at the Tin Pan Alley's publishing houses. The Jewish-Polish minstrel and songwriter Harry Gum (Gambinski) adopted a German aristocratic title, Harry Von Tilzer, to become "a name" in American music. While mediating between the Old World and the New World, immigrant children felt the ideas and sensations that connected different groups. And the Jews, many of whom had German roots, were to set up the publishing industry in the Tin Pan Alley during the last decade and a half of the nineteenth century. It is even possible that this connection between Jews and the entertainment industry was based on their apparent German identity, no less than on their Jewishness.[44] The Jewish immigrants from Eastern Europe who appeared in the music scene after them penetrated this space and continued their trajectory even further. Beginning in the 1880s, Jewish immigrants began to assume the role of the Irish in American music and the minstrelsy, exploiting their connections with the German-Jewish establishment that developed in the Tin Pan Alley. Al Jolson's whistle told the story.

---

43 Alexander Saxton, *The Rise and Fall of the White Republic: Class Politics and Mass Culture in Nineteenth Century America* (New York: Verso, 1990), 172–173; Eric Lott, *Love & Theft: Blackface Minstrelsy and the American Working Class* (New York & Oxford: Oxford University Press, 1993), 169–210.
44 David Suisman, *Selling Sounds: The Commercial Revolution in American Music* (Cambridge, MA: Harvard University Press, 2012).

You ain't heard nothing yet!

No one knows exactly the year of Jolson's birth. The year 1886 is the information he provided, but no records were found at the Shtetl in Sardius, Lithuania. He was born as Asa Yoelson. Like other musical Jews in America, his father Moshe was a cantor. Desperate from the oppression of the Tsar's policies, he left the family in the Shtetl and in 1890 began looking for a rabbinical position in America. Four years later he managed to bring his family to Washington, DC. His mother, Naomi, unfortunately, died a year later. Asa, the youngest son, was particularly heart-broken by this event. He was going to be a big star, but with the eternal soul of a little boy.

Unlike the movie that made him a superstar, The *Jazz Singer*, the process of Jewish assimilation by Asa and his brother Hirsch was the opposite. Frustrated by the crisis of tradition in the Jewish community, his father Moshe was not afraid of integration, but rather hoped that his children would choose to assimilate in various ways. As the old world melted away, the immigrant children saw the light in show business. Asa changed his name to Al, Hirsch became Harry. The last name Yoelson was converted to Joelson and then to Jolson. The streets replaced the "cheder," and warehouses and orphanages the family unit.

From about 1899, when he was about thirteen years old, Jolson entered the real world of entertainment. There was almost no entertainment field that Al Jolson had not experienced: he wandered among traveling circuses, burlesque, and later the vaudeville theaters. During their journey the Jolson brothers landed at the *Kenny Theater* in Brooklyn in a trio performance with a disabled comedian named Joe Palmer. Legend has it that Jolson discovered his comic talent by mistake, out of a need to play a comic role written for him by mistake. It was comedian James Francis Dooley who offered the black mask as a defense and release from stage fright. It changed his life. A blackface mask and lips painted white, a suit and black shoes with socks and white gloves. He searched America and founded his act in the West, but in 1908 joined the Lew Dockstader minstrel show. He also discovered his famous whistle.

Dockstader managed to beat his rivals in several ways: he updated the show to his own era (what is more funny than a parody of President Teddy Roosevelt in blackface?), but he also created something like a complete musical comedy in the blackface costume. In this fantastical world there were no whites; he and Jolson made the audience laugh through the black mask. Every American figure, even the whitest, was supposed to be black.

In between, Jolson successfully passed through the vaudeville auditoriums, one of which was the "Victoria" of the Hammerstein family. This was an achievement and a testimony to his rising power. The legend runs that while the Jewish gangster Arnold Rothstein was busy playing cards in a room next door, Jolson refused to audition for Florenz Ziegfeld, the famous theater promoter and actor. So he joined the Shubert Brothers, one of the biggest Jewish producers on Broadway.

The result was *La Belle Paree* (1911), a musical comedy about a wealthy American widow and her experiences in Paris with music (partly) by the Jewish composer Jerome Kern. Jolson wore a black mask and crossed between minstrelsy and Broadway. He sang "Paris is a Paradise for Coons" which told the truth: Blacks enjoyed more freedom in Paris than in the Yankee homeland. The truth was that the network around him, under Jewish dominance, straitened its position: the Shubert brothers, Hammerstein, and the theater man Lew Fields of Weber and Fields; Fields was originally Moses Schönfeld, who was famous for imitating German immigrants and their dialects in a combination of grotesque and parody; in addition, the "goy" Florenz Ziegfeld, the owner of Ziegfeld Follies, became a close friend and a fan.

Comedy after comedy, night after night, at some point during 1917 the young writer Samson Raphaelson watched the musical comedy *Robinson Crusoe, Jr.*, and was inspired. He watched a frustrated millionaire in the film industry who daydreamed that he was Robinson Crusoe Junior. Jolson played his driver in blackface. Raphaelson was the one who was supposed to publicize the duality and circularity of cantorial music and black music. It began with a short story, "Day of Atonement," a sort of fictional biography of Jolson, which was to become a play on Broadway, the *Jazz Singer* (1925), and then the first important talkie film (1927). Incidentally, the only one who talks and speaks in the film, and more especially sings, is Al Jolson.

The film dealt with the struggle for the identity of Jackie Robin, the son of Cantor Rabinowitz. Jackie loves his parents, but he is drawn to the rhythm of the syncopated ragtime and jazz. When his father discovers this, Jackie must leave home. The Orthodox world of Cantor Rabinowitz is heavy and weighty, while jazz music appears in scenes which express lightness and release (Jackie eats eggs and bacon while listening to jazz). The Jewish ghetto is safe and compact, while the outside world is intriguing, cruel and dangerous. Jackie finds his identity between the hammer and the anvil.

Michael Rogin, one of the representatives of the "whiteness" approach, believed that *The Jazz Singer* was one of a series of films, including the *Birth of a Nation* (1915), directed by the master D.W. Griffith, who dealt with the tearing and splitting of the weakest minority, African-American, in order to unite a nation of immigrants: *The Birth of a Nation* demonizes blacks, it is claimed, while the film

The Jazz Singer exploits their culture with slyness and sophistication.[45] Like the Hollywood tycoons, who have admired their mothers while holding great contempt for their weak fathers, the *The Jazz Singer* has Oedipal aspects. The desire to "kill" the father and the old world is part of the process of building American identity. Blackface minstrelsy, according to Rogin, created a mechanism of racial desire for the material destruction of the other, placing white as superior to black. By trampling the blacks, blackface minstrelsy established an "imagined community" through rituals that turned masses of Americans of a different ethnic origin into one nation.

Affective empowerment, the shadow and blackface minstrelsy

I regard such anti-humanistic approaches with suspicion, since I prefer to diagnose the connection between people and popular culture as a positive act. We need culture to overcome the chronic pessimism tattooed onto everyday life. Based on the theories of Carl Gustav Jung and the American Lawrence Grossberg, I would even add that our mental energies work quite differently than that.

Popular culture moves through different levels of consciousness, sometimes opposing one another.[46] The adoption of the concept of minstrelsy as a racist ideology clashes, for example, with the fact that one of the most recognizable figures in the struggle against slavery, President Abraham Lincoln, has been known as a devout fanatic. The writer Mark Twain, who wrote his masterpieces about the disease of racism, was also a fan.

Jolson's memoirs confirm that the mask was a weapon for saving his performances. Sleepy theaters also reacted strongly to blackface, so it can be concluded that the masking process caused a sensation that was related to the mental structure of the audiences. I would venture to say that the black mask had a therapeutic power. The minstrels placed masses of Americans in front of their personal and collective shadow and the mask enabled them to deal with a variety of things in their encounter with the "other": traces of feelings of inferiority, the primitive sides of the mind, their strange and awkward adjustment difficulties. The mask forced many Americans to deal with the primitive and dark side of

---

45 Michael Rogin, *Blackface, White Noise: Jewish Immigrants in the Hollywood Melting Pot* (Berkeley: University of California Press, 1998), 53.
46 Lawrence Grossberg, *We Gotta Get Out of This Place* (New York: Routledge, 1992).

their unconscious, fantasies of infantilization and resentment, which they concealed within themselves and repressed.[47]

Carl Gustav Jung, one of the fathers of modern psychology, called this archetype the Shadow. He insisted that the Shadow is not only personal but can consist of our cultural complexes. Feelings of racism and group superiority, or even spiritual groups that espouse superiority and self-righteousness, suffer from a lack of awareness of our Shadow. These insights suggest that projection of the inferior sides of the unconscious has enabled many Americans to begin to recognize the sick side of their culture. In other words, the denial of the Shadow within us, along with our dark side, may lead to the projection of the same qualities and feelings we are ashamed of and that we attribute to other groups.

The minstrels, according to this perception, functioned as an affective empowerment field. It was a ceremony that gave the audience a sense of escape from everyday life, the sense of difference and separateness from Europe, and perhaps fragments of "authentic American" identity – also by using the alternative field of black culture. The minstrels turned the black man into a part of American nature and as a result a "natural" part of American heritage and culture, a cultural element that has always existed. The black cultural field was a set of fantasies about sex, alternative possibilities of enjoyment, freedom, escape, language, and an "authentic" American identity. The European man did not consider himself a white American until he confronted himself with the other (black and/or red), and the minstrels appeared to have formed a ceremony that created an affective alliance with their audience, which was an imaginary place. The audience was able to experience – emotionally and materialistically – the vast array of material and cultural possibilities offered by the new American world. The ceremony offered a world rich with territories in the West and endless possibilities of existence separate from European history of class struggles, religious persecution, and more. These were made possible by the blurred presentation of the show. The cultural collage consisted of sounds, slang, visuals and movement, creating a texture of images that signified American uniqueness without any coherent ideological baggage. This collage spoke to masses of Americans, racists from the North, liberals and immigrants alike.

---

[47] Jef Dehing, "Jung's Shadow," (2002), <www.cgjung-vereniging.nl/home/files/jef_dehing.pdf> (last accessed 23.10.2017); C. G. Jung, "Conscious, Unconscious, and Individuation" in *Collected Works of C.G. Jung, Volume 9 (Part 1): Archetypes and the Collective Unconscious*, edited by C. G. Jung, Gerhard Adler and R. F. C. Hull, 2nd ed., 275–289 (London: Routledge & Kegan Paul, 1968).

From minstrels to Broadway and Hollywood

The role of immigrants in minstrelsy has not been the same over the years. While the Irish minstrels operated during the 1930s and 1940s under the protection of the Jacksonians and the Democratic Party, the Jews of the end of the century were not politically identified in the same way. They brought with them different, more liberal ethics. "There's a tear in your voice," says Sarah, Jackie Robin's mother, in the *Jazz Singer*, to explain his uniqueness. Irving Howe believed that the Jews' entry into minstrelsy made it "more rich and humane":

> Perhaps it was no more than shrewd opportunism, an eagerness to give audiences exactly what they seemed to want, which led so many Jewish entertainers to work in blackface; but it is hard to resist the impression that some deeper affinity was also at work [...] when they took over the conventions of ethnic mimicry, the Jewish performers transformed it into something emotionally richer and more humane. Black became a mask for Jewish expressiveness, with one woe speaking through the voice of another.[48]

Michael Alexander believes that Jewish minstrelsy was a show in which the Jews maintained a unique kind of Jewish consciousness, which he says was based on the "tradition of suffering" common to African-Americans and Jews. He writes:

> Jewish minstrelsy in the 1910s and 1920s commonly represented 'the scalawag servant with his surface dullness and hidden cleverness [...] the Jewish minstrel was always one step ahead of the master [...] Jolson's acts were exercises in cultural fluidity and mutual longings for freedom [...] Eastern Jews in America maneuvered to see in African-American life their own story of exile and slavery.[49]

However, the Jews joined minstrelsy while gaining considerable power in the industry. Al Jolson, of course, was not alone. Eddie Cantor, Sophie Tucker, George Jessel, George Burns, the Yiddish actress Molly Picon and Fanny Bryce (in collaboration with Eddie Cantor in 1917) gradually brought new ethics, some of them from their Jewish world and High European art, and connected it to American mass culture. This fusion would become the basis for a unique combination of elitist humanism, which illustrated their cultural advantages in the New World.

The world of the minstrels became the essential reference point for Jewish songwriters about America. Irving Berlin made a fuss with his hit "Alexander's Ragtime Band" (1911), when he recommended that listeners sing the song "Swanee River" by Stephen Foster in ragtime. George Gershwin also relied on the

---

[48] Irving Howe, *World of Our Fathers* (New York: Simon & Schuster, 1976), 563.
[49] Michael Alexander, *Jazz Age Jews* (New Jersey: Princeton University, 2001), 130–131.

phrase "Swanee" in his breakthrough hit, which sold millions thanks to Al Jolson who performed it. Jerome Kern and Oscar Hammerstein II revolutionized Broadway through a musical full of minstrelsy's flavors and Americana on the Mississippi theme boat. Richard Rodgers, for some time, managed the music in the performances of Lew Fields, one of the fathers of Jewish minstrelsy.

American Jews helped to assimilate minstrelsy into the new modern culture industry. The minstrels were recognizable in Tin Pan Alley's songs, Hollywood, Broadway,[50] and later in animation and radio programs, and American Jews were present in all these: Adolf Zukor, Carl Laemmle, Harry Cohn, Lewis B. Mayer, the Warner Brothers and the first producers of all these, built and helped shape Hollywood. The Witmark family, Leo Feist, Shapiro and Stern, Max Dreyfus, and others were prominent in the publishing industry of the Tin Pan Alley; Irving Berlin, George Gershwin, Harold Arlen, Jerome Kern, and other American Jews not only turned minstrelsy and other black music styles into the greatest hits of their time, but connected the black sound to a high culture and formed the foundations of American music.

The Jazz Singer was a great success in the fall of 1927, even among Jewish audiences. Jolson was pleased. The fantasy of this costume juggler about the combination of jazz, Jews and blacks, infuriated America despite the ethnic theme in its foundation. But there was something unresolved in the film, as if it was one side of the coin. African-Americans were removed from the frame as if the KKK were guarding from above. Jazz in the film was also one side of the coin, while in the real-world artists such as Louis Armstrong and Duke Ellington characterized it at the same time as more swinging and African-American, and all the more exciting. Decades would pass before the multicultural ideas in the film really reached completion, but the film was an illustration of Jewish power in the American entertainment industry of the 1920s, while establishing the Jewish-black connection as a central story in the evolution of American music through Jolson's mask and the tear in his voice.

---

50 Gary Giddins, *Riding on the Blue Note* (New York: Da Capo Press, 1980), 32.

Chapter 2: Somewhere over the Rainbow – Jewish Immigration to America and the Struggle for Popular Culture

"We'll turn Manhattan into an isle of joy," wrote Lorenz Hart and Richard Rodgers in their significant breakthrough hit "Manhattan" from the successful musical comedy *The Garrick Gaieties* (1925). The song, which described Manhattan in the light of the small pleasures of a couple, was symbolic of the contribution of Jewish immigrants who helped position the island as the center of American culture.

The history of Jewish immigration to America shaped their fate and American culture itself. Demographics and urbanization, occupational niches, light anti-Semitism, and the crisis of tradition that accompanied Jewish immigration, led talented Jews to entrepreneurship in the field of entertainment and art. The Jews had a particular interest in promoting culture. They came to America and joined the culture industry at a crucial historical moment, during which they could derive economic, cultural, and class benefits from the European canonization of American existence. The Jews realized that in America, their stronghold over European culture gave them many advantages over the WASPs and other minorities. In a world full of possibilities that melded high and popular culture, they could express what they saw as their "best."

First we take Manhattan

Minstrelsy began in New York. The stars of minstrelsy announced their parody of the culture of slavery throughout the northern United States, but New York was undoubtedly the center; the Mecca of Minstrelsy, as described by cultural scholar Eric Lott.[51]

In the first half of the twentieth century, New York was also the largest Jewish city in the world. From 80,000 Jews in 1880, the number increased to 1.5 million by the First World War. During the 1920s, Jews accounted for more than a quarter of the city's population, and therefore constituted the largest group of

---

[51] Eric Lott, *Love & Theft: Blackface Minstrelsy and the American Working Class* (New York & Oxford: Oxford University Press, 1993), 3.

all ethnic groups in the city (though there were more people of Catholic origin in the city).⁵²

New York has always been a multi-ethnic city. The WASPs were never the vast majority there. In 1775, half of the population of the United States was of English origin, but in New York, these percentages were lower given the presence of Dutch and other groups.⁵³ During the 1880s, East European Jews and Italian began arriving in significant numbers. Blacks were already in New York, but their numbers increased significantly after the First World War. The Puerto Ricans came after World War Two.

Minstrelsy did not disappear during the early twentieth century. Vaudeville, Broadway, Tin Pan Alley, and from the 1920s radio programs, the film industry, and many animated films, incorporated aspects of this fading culture. Many New York Jews managed to penetrate the music industry in this time, during the end of the nineteenth century until the beginning of the twentieth century, during which minstrelsy became a modern cultural industry. New York has remained the capital of the entertainment industry and American culture. Isidore Witmark, one of the first successful German-Jewish entrepreneurs in the Tin Pan Alley, and his biographer, Dr. Isaac Goldberg, believe that the Jewish takeover of the musical publishing industry began during the 1880s.⁵⁴

Ain't gonna work in Maggie's farm: Immigration and assimilation

The story of the Jewish immigration to the United States was in every sense a success story.⁵⁵ The Jews proved to themselves and others that the American dream was "more than a myth," claims historian Eli Lederhendler.⁵⁶ Jewish suc-

---

52 Nathan Glazer and Patrick Daniel Moynihan, *Beyond the Melting Pot: The Negroes, Puerto Ricans, Jews, Italians, and Irish of New York City* (New York: The MIT Press, 1970).
53 In the 1940s, the Irish and Germans came to the city in large numbers. In 1855, the Irish accounted for 28 percent of the city's population and 16 percent of the German population. In 1890 these two ethnic groups constituted 52 percent of the city's population.
54 Isidore Witmark and Issac Goldberg, *From Ragtime to Swingtime* (New York: Lee Furman, 1939), 60–65.
55 Nathan Glazer and Patrick Daniel Moynihan, *Beyond the Melting Pot: The Negroes, Puerto Ricans, Jews, Italians, and Irish of New York City* (New York: The MIT Press, 1970), 143.
56 Eli Lederhendler, "American Jews, American Capitalism, and the Politics of History," in *Text and Context: Essays in Modern Jewish History and Historiography in Honor of Ismor Schorsch*, edited by Eli Lederhendler and Jack Wertheimer (New York: Jewish Theological Press, 2005), 504–546.

cess, which was evident even among the Jewish-German emigration during the middle of the nineteenth century, was also part of the second wave of Jewish immigrants who arrived from Eastern Europe in the 1880s. The data reveal an imposing presence in education, in universities, in small businesses (for example, in the garment industry) and white-collar jobs (law, accounting, medicine) in particular niches.[57]

The widespread assumption of immigration history was that, as far as employment was concerned, the Jews had an advantage over other minority groups. While a large percentage of Italian, Polish, Irish, and even German immigrants came as simple laborers, the concentration of skilled and partially skilled workers among the Jews contributed to their impressive success. Until the arrival of the Great Depression, historian Beth Wenger explains, the Jews established their exceptional economic status compared to other immigrants. In less than a generation, they were part of the middle class.[58]

Historians show that the Jews, who arrived, for example, at the time with the Italians, were more connected to white-collar occupations that required skilled occupations and partly-skilled workers in the garment industry, such as furriers, tailors, and sewists. This employment niche undoubtedly played an essential role in the various developments of American capitalism.[59]

Historian Eli Lederhendler maintains that assumption. Jews did not come to America as professionals, he argued.[60] Many of the immigrants adapted to American needs and changed their profession, updated it, or learned a new trade after emigrating. The Jews, he explains, were remarkably adaptable to the American economy because of the way they created an ethnically diverse and sophisticated system of the old world that served as an instrument of integration.

Patterns of consumption also characterized Jewish economic success. The Jews devoted themselves to the myth of abundance, out of a desire to take part in the life of the New World and were engaged in acquiring products that symbolized the American world more prominently than other minorities. They devoted themselves to American capitalism in all aspects of consumerism, transforming consumerism and affluence into an instrument of affirmation of a new

---

57 Andrew Heinze, *Adapting to Abundance* (New York: Columbia University Press, 1992), 109.
58 Beth S. Wenger, *New York Jews and the Great Depression: Uncertain Promise* (New Haven: Yale University Press, 1999), 15–16.
59 Ronald Bayor, *Neighbors in Conflict: The Irish, Germans, Jews, and Italians of New York City, 1929–1941* (Urbana: University of Illinois Press, 1988), 15; Hasia Diner, *In the Almost Promised Land: American Jews and Blacks, 1915–1935* (Westport, Conn: Greenwood Press, 1977), 5.
60 Eli Lederhendler, *Jewish Immigrants and American Capitalism, 1880–1920: From Caste to Class* (Cambridge: Cambridge University Press, 2009).

identity and mental liberation. They emphasized the importance of annual family vacations or purchased a piano for a well-kept parlor, which included the best of the latest consumerist trends.[61]

However, all these aspects do not indicate that the process of assimilation passed with difficulties. Despite the data on their impressive economic success, the Jews suffered from a variety of official and disguised prejudices and showed a presence in specific economic niches.[62] The big firms of Wall Street and public service excluded Jews and denied them access to the oil industry and heavy industries. Despite the success of American Jews of German origin in the area of capital, there were relatively few East European Jews in banking. In response to their exclusion from managerial positions in developing corporations, Jews developed strategies to integrate into the limited spaces that, in fact, also spurred them on. They turned to the economic niches of new and unfamiliar industries, while making use of family and community ties.

There is not a single group of immigrants that reflects the American employment profile in the generation of immigration, and in most cases in future generations, and the Jews are no exception in this respect. Their positioning in specific economic niches, the fact that they settled homogenously in specific urban areas, and especially in New York, and the absorptive capacity of the American labor market, contributed to their integration.[63]

The figures pointing to their success are explicit, but the unresolved issue is related to the psychohistory of Jewish ethnicity. The questions about the reasons that led the Jewish minority to advance beyond other ethnic groups in the process of mobility has remained controversial among historians and social scholars.

Most of the studies explained Jewish economic success in the "inheritance" patterns of European Jewish culture. They pointed to the fact that the Jews had brought these "middle class' cultural characteristics" from the Old World to the New World. Sociologist Nathan Glazer, for example, argued that Jewish immigrants differed from other minorities in their self-perception of the economic possibilities they faced.[64] The Italians and the Irish, he explained, came from

---

61 Andrew Heinze, *Adapting to Abundance* (New York: Columbia University Press, 1992), 3.
62 Henry L. Feingold, *A Time for Searching: Entering the Mainstream 1920–1945* (Baltimore: Johns Hopkins University Press, 1992), 153.
63 Ira Katznelson, "Between Separation and Disappearance: Jews on the Margins of American Liberalism," in *Paths of Emancipation*, edited by Pierre Birenbaum and Ira Katznelson, 157–205 (New Jersey: Princeton University Press, 1995).
64 Nathan Glazer, "The American Jew and the Attainment of Middle-Class Rank: Some trends and Explanations," in *The Jews: Social Patterns of an American Group*, edited by Marshall Sklare (Free Press, New York, 1958), 138–146.

a culture of the working-class with relatively small economic horizons. The Old World, on the other hand, prevented the Jews for centuries from working the land. Therefore, the Jews came to the United States with a more solid background in trade and a broader economic horizon than that of other minorities. In Glazer's view, the Jews came from an unfortunate financial situation, similar to that of the working-classes. Yet, they had a self-awareness of being part of the middle classes. Jewish immigrants, according to this approach, embraced the puritanical ethic of hard work and personal success. In his eyes, Jewish culture had emphasized a kind of ethics of business, morality, hard work, and redemption, some 1,500 years before the birth of Calvinism.

The research displays many similar views: economic historian Simon Kuznets stresses that these characteristics, identified with the middle class, allowed the Jews to achieve an above-average financial success.[65] Various studies by Milton Konvitz, Robert Park and Thomas Sowell, have explained Jewish success in terms of cultural heredity.[66] Their explanations are based on similarities between Jewish and American culture in terms of ambition, entrepreneurship, passion for education, liberalism, social justice, and more. In other words, they argue that the nature of European Jewish culture prepared them for the American experience.

Consumer historians have also explained that Jewish economic success in the United States is rooted in middle-class bourgeois culture patterns that characterized the Jews.[67] Other scholars emphasize the importance of education in Jewish culture, in contrast to the perception of Italian immigrants from southern Italy, who perceived education as an economic burden.

Historian Eli Lederhendler prefers to play down the general concept of "cultural inheritance of middle-class values," explaining Jewish success as a result of the unique motivation given the specific Jewish immigration environment in America. He argues that the encounter of the Jews with America is not at all similar to the somewhat euphoric descriptions that Jewish culture was fitted perfectly to the American economy. On the contrary, the encounter was full of problems regarding assimilation. The "middle-class values" of the Old World – supposedly "inherited" – were completely different from those of the New World. Also, stud-

---

[65] Simon Kuznets, "Economic Structure and Life of the Jews," in *The Jews: Their History, Culture, and Religion*, edited by Louis Finkelstein, 2nd ed. (Philadelphia: Jewish Publication Society of America, 1966).

[66] Robert A. Park, *Race and Culture* (Glencoe: The Free Press, 1950); Milton R. Konvitz, "Judaism and the Pursuit of Happiness," *The Menorah Journal* 49 (1962): 127–128; Thomas Sowell, *Ethnic America: A History* (New York, Basic Books, 1981), 93–94.

[67] Andrew Heinze, *Adapting to Abundance* (New York: Columbia University. Press, 1992), 3.

ies comparing the economic progress of Jews in other countries (e. g., Britain) reveal more modest data on economic mobility, whereby the success of American Jews is not related to cultural inheritance but to the new environment. Besides, the "cultural-hereditary" explanation does not explain the conflict between economic mobility and the loyalty of Jews to American liberalism, and the fact that Jewish voting patterns are opposite to those of influential economic groups.[68]

Therefore, it is appropriate to look very carefully at the experience of Jewish immigration. It was the American environment that shaped the social attitudes of the Jews, much more than any specific heritage they brought with them from Europe. The Jews came not only highly motivated to change their lives but acted against an almost complete lack of conservative restraints in their new American environment. The Jews did not have a religious organization in the neighborhood that would impose its authority on them, as the Catholic Church tried to do with the Irish and the Italians.

The story of the Hollywood Jews, as well as several biographies of musicians and entertainers, reveal that it was the exclusion of Jews from mainstream economic entities that led them to engage in the entertainment industry, which was not considered a promising or entirely legitimate business.[69] Nevertheless, the economic success of the Jewish immigrants explains Jewish progress in entrepreneurship regarding certain capitalist fields, but not why many of them found their place in the entertainment industry. To this end, one must understand why the particular industry of entertainment was open to them. The history of Jewish immigration coincided with a decisive moment in the struggle for American culture.

Hey, white boy, what you doin' uptown? The crisis of tradition and the struggle for American culture

America provided great economic and material opportunities for Jewish immigrants from Eastern Europe, but it also undermined traditional ways of life and values. The Jews in America were safe from looting, capriciousness, royal de-

---

[68] Eli Lederhendler, "American Jews, American Capitalism, and the Politics of History," in *Text and Context: Essays in Modern Jewish History and Historiography in Honor of Ismor Schorsch*, edited by Eli Lederhendler and Jack Wertheimer (New York: Jewish Theological Press, 2005), 504–546.

[69] Neal Gabler, *An Empire of Their Own: How the Jews Invented Hollywood* (New York: Crown Publishers, Inc., 1997), 43.

crees, and pogroms, but one can't ignore the dry statistics of long working hours, meager wages, and severe housing conditions. There were also, as Arthur A. Goren argues, those who suffered terrible distress because of the undermining of the traditional shield of family life and the community.[70] Economic imperatives gnawed at the foundations of Orthodox life, and religious supervision fell into anarchy when the subject of the rabbis' authority collapsed. The biographies of singer Al Jolson and Irving Berlin, sons of the cantors who could not keep their work in America, only illustrate this.[71]

This crisis of tradition occurred as a result of the gap between the modern state and the religious community. The character of the modern Western state, its political structure (sanctity of nationality), and its economy (capitalism), is, in essence, contrary to the separatist ethic that characterizes the Jewish religion. The integration of Jews into the modern state came in many ways at the expense of preserving religious tradition.[72]

The crisis of tradition was a product of the social structure of Jewish immigration to America, composed mostly of young people from Eastern Europe. Without the institutional oversight of the Old World in the form of community, parents, and traditional education, these young people discovered America as a place with liberal opportunities and alternative possibilities for existence from the old European world. Lucy Dawidowicz writes:

> The Jewish immigration was largely a youthful immigration, of young people – teenagers we call them today – and men and woman in their early twenties, many single and without parents [...] They were free, free from parental supervision, from religious obligation, from communal authority. Among some this freedom generated crime and corruption, prostitution and vice, bohemianism and free love.[73]

The data concerning the crisis in Jewish traditions in the United States are tangible: at the end of the Second World War, about 32% of Jews found that they did not participate in religious ceremonies at all, whereas the Catholic and Protestant figures indicated a higher level of religious orientation.[74] The process of sec-

---

70 Arthur Aryeh Goren, "Freedom and its Limitations: The Jewish Immigrant Experience," *Forum* 42/43 (1981): 83–99.
71 Ibid.
72 Mordecai M. Kaplan, *Judaism as a Civilization: Toward the Reconstruction of America – Jewish Life* (New York: Reconstructionist Press, 1956), 16.
73 Lucy Dawidowicz, "From Past to Past: Jewish East Europe to Jewish East Side" *Conservative Judaism* 22, no. 2 (1968): 19–27.
74 Marshall Sklare, *Conservative Judaism: An American Religious Movement* (New York: Schocken Books Inc., 1955), 38–39. About 6 percent of Catholics and 19 percent of Protestants alone

ularization of American Jewish immigrants sanctified American work and created a gap between religious ethics and a changing material society that adapted itself to the new world. The processes of secularization also underwent significant changes. It was not just about breaking previous norms, but about turning existing standards into part of American Jewish ethics.[75]

The discussion of the crisis of tradition was tangible in Jewish popular culture. Yiddish newspapers, for example, highlighted crime stories, the presence of gambling lounges, the description of the street as a "criminal instrument" and the temptations of popular culture.[76] There were Yiddish newspapers that took it upon themselves to encourage young Jews to move away from Harlem, which combined a black cultural renaissance with a growing crime rate. The streets of New York City were the first place where young Jews began to abandon family orthodoxy over their culture and religion.[77] The crisis of tradition is evident in sexual and mental liberation and liberal changes in the culture of working women in the late nineteenth century.[78] The rather active role taken by Jewish gangsters in the United States between the two world wars reveals more than the crisis of tradition. They were the sons of immigrants, or immigrants themselves, who had loosed all the reins to "win" the American way of life.[79]

It seemed that the decentralized structure of the Jewish community was one of the causes of anarchy under religious supervision.[80] Without a robust political and religious mechanism that could strengthen the connection between immigrants and their heritage, "street culture" became the central arena for many immigrants. Opponents to popular music with African-American influences used to point to the "noise" and "sense of street vulgarity," in contrast to the "rural

---

declared that they were not present at religious ceremonies. While 69 percent of Catholics and 36 percent of Protestants admitted that they participated at least once a week in a religious ceremony, only 9 percent of the Jews answered yes to this category; And while 81 percent of the Catholics and 62 percent of the Protestants said that they attended a religious ceremony at least once a month, only 24 percent of Jews fit this category.

75 Eli Lederhendler, *Jewish Immigrants and American Capitalism, 1880–1920: From Caste to Class* (Cambridge: Cambridge University Press, 2009).
76 Hasia Diner, *In the Almost Promised Land: American Jews and Blacks, 1915–1935* (Westport, Conn: Greenwood Press, 1977), 65.
77 Lewis A. Erenberg, *Steppin' Out: New York Nightlife and the Transition of American Culture, 1890–1930* (Chicago: The University of Chicago Press, 1984), 75.
78 Kathy Peiss, *Cheap Amusements: Working Women and Leisure in Turn-of-the-Century New York* (Philadelphia: Temple University Press, 1986).
79 Robert A. Rockaway, *But He Was Good to His Mother: The Lives and Crimes of Jewish Gangsters* (New York: Gefen Publishing House, 1993), 5.
80 Salo W. Baron, *Steeled by Adversity: Essays and Addresses on American Jewish Life* (New York: Jewish Publication Society, 1971), 34.

countryside" of folk music and classical music. But Jewish youngsters in America were urban, rootless cosmopolitans, and the streets were the training ground for Jewish comedians, actors, and singers.[81] Irving Howe wrote:

> The streets are crucial. Forming each day a great fair of Jewish life, they became the training ground for Jewish actors, comics, and singers. You mimicked the hoity-toity Irish teacher who recited Browning in high school, you mocked the snarling rabbi who bored you in Hebrew school, and you made your friends hop with glee. Especially if you were a little fellow and not so good at stick ball, you could gain attention by comic bits, sassy songs, crazy antics, dirty stories; if your father was a cantor [...] you could imitate and parody his chanting [...].[82]

As the old world evaporated, popular culture began to serve as a spiritual substitute in the theaters and vaudeville halls. The Jews jumped on everything new because everything old was associated with a snobbish attitude towards them, anti-Semitism, and hostile conservatism, and thus flooded the cultural life of the city.[83]

The power of detachment from the bonds of the Orthodox past made it easier for the Jews to integrate into American capitalism in general, and especially in the entertainment industry, which was controversial. And the Jews entered precisely at this point and in marvelous synchronization.[84] They challenged the values of conservative Victorian culture by establishing a new, more liberal culture, a trend that was part of a broader struggle over the image of American culture.

At the beginning of the twentieth century, the mass culture industry was a battleground between conservative and liberals. The major Victorian-WASP companies and institutions tended to see this mass industry in all its products from movies to music with African-American influences – as a cultural-moral apocalypse that would corrupt the nation.[85] On the other hand, liberals and other ethnic groups, especially immigrants, viewed the field of entertainment as a barren

---

81 Jeffrey Melnick, *A Right to Sing the Blues: African Americans, Jews and American Popular Song* (Cambridge, Massachusetts: Harvard University Press, 1999), 52.
82 Irving Howe, *World of Our Fathers* (New York: Simon & Schuster, 1976), 558.
83 Nathan Glazer and Patrick Daniel Moynihan, *Beyond the Melting Pot: The Negroes, Puerto Ricans, Jews, Italians, and Irish of New York City* (New York: The MIT Press, 1970), 172.
84 Lary May, *Screening Out the Past: The Birth of Mass Culture and The Motion Picture Industry* (Chicago and New York: The University Of Chicago Press, 1980); Lewis A. Erenborg, *Steppin' Out: New York Nightlife and the Transition of American Culture, 1890 – 1930* (Chicago: The University of Chicago Press, 1984).
85 Ibid. The place of some conservative Jews in the culture offensive of the early twentieth century was not absent, even if they were marginal, reveals May and Erenbeg.

territory that enables their economic and cultural survival. This struggle is evident both in the areas of cinema and music.

The films were an instructive field of struggle between the WASP elite and entrepreneurs of an immigration background. The Victorian political assault on the entertainment industry in general, and the new film industry in particular in the first decade of the twentieth century led to achievements for conservatives: in 1908, New York City ordered the closure of nickelodeons. Neil Gabler discussed the attitude of the WASPs toward morality and the new cinema system:

> Big money, gentile money, viewed the movies suspiciously – economically as a fad; morally, as potential embarrassments. As far as the moral issue was concerned, in February, 1906, when Laemmle opened his first theater, reformers had already begun castigating the movies for their deleterious effects, particularly on children. The content of the movies supposedly undermined moral values [...] and makeshift movie houses themselves – dark, cramped and seductive – supposedly bred iniquity.[86]

In response to these moral attacks, movie companies tried to change their content. Film scholar Lary May showed that the WASP-led companies – in an attempt to imitate the works of the film director D.W. Griffith – began in 1908 to convert the medium to religious, moral and Victorian needs, using the power of photography to shape public opinion.

The year 1908 was characterized by an event of great significance which would dramatically affect the image of the film industry. The WASP companies, led by Thomas Alva Edison, who owned the patents of the films, declared a monopoly over rights. Every film manufacturer, distributor and projectionist was required to pay a license fee and royalties to a monopoly, which his opponents nicknamed the "Trust." The monopoly, led by Edison, also signed an exclusive agreement with Eastman-Kodak, the filmmaker company, thus declaring the end of the free hand era of the film industry. But the independent producers – led by Carl Laemmle (who was on the brink of establishing Universal Studios) – managed to break the monopoly while importing European films and secretly producing new films. Four years later, in 1912, the self-employed managed to take over half of the market.

A combination of several factors contributed to this transformation: the inability of the 'Trust' to enforce its dictates; its arrogance toward its customers, and even the lack of solidarity in its own ranks. However, Gabler writes:

---

[86] Neal Gabler, *An Empire of Their Own: How the Jews Invented Hollywood* (New York: Crown Publishers, Inc., 1997), 53.

> Edison and his cohorts had lost their hegemony [...] they misinterpreted what was at stake. They never seemed to understand that they were engaged in much more than economic battle to determine who would control the profits of the nascent film industry; their battle was also generational, cultural, philosophical, even, in some ways, religious. The Trust members were primarily White Anglo-Saxon Protestants who entered the film industry in its infancy by inventing, bankrolling, or tinkering with movie hardware: Cameras and projectors. For them, the movies themselves would always be novelties. The independents, on the other hand, were largely ethnics, Jews and Catholics, who had entered the industry by opening and operating theaters. For them, outsiders fighting the establishment, the movies would always be much more novelties, they would be the only means available of demanding recognition and exorcising failure.[87]

The beginning of the second decade of the twentieth century was characterized by a mismatch between public demand and the supply of the WASP film companies, which did not adapt to the cultural change that millions of immigrants brought with them.[88] At this point in time one can discern the appearance of Jewish filmmakers. They were free of the moral fear of the new mass industry and filled this economic and moral vacuum. In this historic time and in this occupational niche, when Victorians longed to present the entertainment industry as an anti-American medium, the Jews turned the entertainment industry into a medium based on the connection between European traditions of high culture and the American minstrelsy tradition that had developed throughout the nineteenth century. They shed the virtuous Victorian aspects and combined the root characteristics of the entertainment industry with the needs of the middle class, by creating their own version of the myth of the American dream. Jewish entrepreneurs positioned the entertainment industry as a medium that combined the cornerstones of American culture with Broadway, vaudeville, minstrelsy and comic aspects. The films and music often became a field of parody for Victorian values.

At the beginning of the twentieth century, American music was the scene of a similar struggle. Conflicts around American identity were a struggle between the conservative musical elite and modernist composers, who were an unofficial alliance of Jewish and African-American composers, along with some ethnic figures, and more liberal and progressive WASPs.[89]

---

[87] Ibid., 59.
[88] Lary May, *Screening Out the Past: The Birth of Mass Culture and The Motion Picture Industry* (Chicago and New York: The University of Chicago Press, 1980).
[89] MacDonald Smith Moore, *Yankee Blues: Musical Culture and American Identity* (Bloomington: Indiana University Press, 1985).

On the one side of the divide were educated Yale composers, graduates of Yale and Harvard universities, including Arthur Farwell, Edward Burlingame Hill, John Alden Carpenter, David Stanley Smith, Roy Harris, Charles Ives and Daniel Gregory Mason. The Yankee composers adopted a Puritan-Victorian conception of life and undertook to empower Victorian and rural values and the idyll of nature. They were described as "idealistic" and, in many ways, "humanists and Victorians, connected to culture as a public religion capable of establishing a national conscience."[90] They defined themselves by what they were not: they were not new immigrants, not Catholics or Jews, certainly not black, and certainly not enthusiastic about ethnic urbanization.

The Yankees feared the modernism expressed in the form of ragtime music and especially jazz, which was "frightening" and of course "black." They were afraid that modern music reflected the social problems of the twentieth century, and believed it was mechanical, materialistic, hedonistic, sensual and primitive. They played out the struggle in the popular press but also in academia, dominating the music departments of Yale, Harvard, and Columbia.

The Yankees' rivals were the modernists: George Gershwin, Aaron Copland, the Swiss-born Ernst Bloch, alongside the Czech composer Antonín Dvořák, music critics and opinion-makers such as Carl Van Vechten and the WASPs Gilbert Seldes and John Hammond. Along with them were African-American jazz musicians such as Duke Ellington. The dispute between the two sides was expressed, of course, in the work, but also in its interpretation by the press. One of the focuses of the debate was concerned with Dvořák's article "Music In America" (1895), which dealt, among other things, with the aesthetic future of American music and its components. Dvořák saw black folk materials as an inseparable part of music. He believed that black semantics would separate it from European music. The Yankee composers generally refused or at least were not motivated to accept Dvořák's vision, since they felt that the local color offered a shallow painting of the national portrait.

Beyond the popularity of black songs among the masses, modernist composers saw "color" as an essential commodity of the coincidental nature of American music. The modernist group of composers was headed by urban Jews who stood by the delights of Victorian rural idealism. Without a central religious organization or various political organizations to impose their authority, many Jews more naturally embraced American liberalism, which helped ensure their security, as well as the post-Victorian culture industry.

---

[90] Ibid., 81.

The presence of Jewish composers in high and popular music was due to the power of the Jews in the entertainment industry. American Jews left a social network that positioned themselves as intermediaries of the cultural industry. Many of them were the owners and managers of vaudeville halls. Some of Hollywood's studio owners, for example, began their careers in nickelodeon halls in New York and other cities. The biography of Lew Wasserman and Jules Stein, who turned MCA, a young successful music company in Chicago, into a Hollywood empire, tells the story of this Jewish society as the leading jazz show agency of the vaudeville halls across the United States.[91] Jews were personal agents, publishers, theater owners, and film entrepreneurs. Irving Howe stresses the importance of the Jewish Shubert brothers in financing Broadway and adds that a significant portion of the theater business in New York and beyond had fallen into Jewish hands.[92] At the same time, writers, playwrights, screenwriters, lyricists, composers and musicians found refuge in the endless possibilities in the evolving mass culture.

In the music field, Jews were not afraid to market African-American materials. By virtue of their power in Tin Pan Alley, they became dominant owners of African-American materials and strong interpreters of this culture as American culture. This process was also made possible by the economic weakness of African-Americans, which made it easier for Jewish entrepreneurs to exploit this cultural property.

Stormy weather: The economic weakness of African-Americans

Until 1910, before the massive immigration of an African-American population to New York, there were about 90,000 blacks in the city, less than 2% of the population.[93] With the exception of a thin layer of government officials, most of the black population consisted of unskilled workers, waiters and manual laborers. Their economic position and their inferior status led to their isolation from the rest of the population. During the First World War, their numbers increased impressively – in 1920 the estimate was 150,000 (about 3% of the city's popula-

---

[91] Dennis McDougal, *The Last Mogul: Lew Wasserman, MCA, and the Hidden History of Hollywood* (New York: Da Capo Press, 1998).
[92] Irving Howe, *World of Our Fathers* (New York: Simon & Schuster, 1976), 557.
[93] Nathan Glazer and Patrick Daniel Moynihan, *Beyond the Melting Pot: The Negroes, Puerto Ricans, Jews, Italians, and Irish of New York City* (New York: The MIT Press, 1970), 26.

tion), and by the end of the decade their number had almost doubled to 270,000. In spite of the limited possibilities, New York offered higher wages than African-Americans received in the south. It also offered Harlem.

Black immigration revived Harlem. The quarter became a place where there was a subculture with a prominent presence of music and African-American black artistic creativity. The *Harlem Renaissance*, they called it.[94] The blacks, however, failed to maintain Its appeal, even though they could not escape the fate of poverty. Perhaps because they came from a background of slavery and agricultural labor in the south, without experience and education in commerce and entrepreneurship, Afro-Americans found it challenging to develop businesses in the city. The Jews developed such a robust commercial network that they created confidence in the ethnic employment even during the Depression. The Italians, despite the high percentage of manual workers, were fiercely committed to the ethos of a family structure, and this structure helped them in the process of integration into American life. The Chinese progressed successfully in the food and laundry business. The Irish, who also had difficulty with social mobility, filled police jobs, public service, gas workers, and domestic servants. At the same time, they succeeded in developing a reliable institutional and political system connected with the Democratic Party and the Catholic Church. The Germans managed this faster than the Irish and the Italians and settled in the printing, tobacco, and entertainment business alongside commerce. The African-Americans, on the other hand, failed to create parallel networks. The business development of blacks concentrated on cosmetics. Women who worked in households supported the black community.[95]

As Afro-Americans reached Harlem in the first two decades of the twentieth century, the ethnic puzzle in the district began to change. The Irish-German hegemony gave way to a massive invasion of Eastern European Jews alongside Italians. The Jews began to constitute the majority in this quarter, where they regarded themselves as "a Jewish fortress." They dominated many businesses and community centers, and influential figures from the community took part in urban politics.[96] The dominance of Jewish immigrants in real estate changed the ethnic balance in the city. Harlem was also a bastion of socialist activity,

---

[94] Ann Douglas, *Terrible Honesty: Mongrel Manhattan in the 1920s* (New York: Farrar, Straus & Giroux, 1996).
[95] Nathan Glazer and Patrick Daniel Moynihan, *Beyond the Melting Pot: The Negroes, Puerto Ricans, Jews, Italians, and Irish of New York City* (New York: The MIT Press, 1970), 30.
[96] Ronald Bayor, *Neighbors in Conflict: The Irish, Germans, Jews, and Italians of New York City, 1929–1941* (Urbana: University of Illinois Press, 1988), 14.

and a Jewish working-class population lived in it, but the majority of immigrants from Eastern Europe gradually held white-collar jobs.[97]

Rapid Jewish progress and the perceived backwardness of Afro-Americans inevitably led to social tensions. Norman Podhoretz's famous and controversial essay, "My Negro Problem – And Ours," reveals a tense relationship between the two communities.[98] This essay, dealing with Black-Jewish relations during the 1930s, shows that apart from fixed stereotypes ("the Jews are rich, the blacks are poor"), the gaps in education, economics, and the environment made it difficult for blacks to integrate. While Jews sometimes conspired with other minorities, the blacks – even for a liberal at the time like Podhoretz – looked "threatening," "violent," "physical," and "dangerous." The source of his dual ties to Afro-Americans (jealousy of "athletic superiority" versus fear, for example) is a projection of an American reality, which ostensibly turned whites, liberals, and conservatives in their attitude toward blacks as "sick and distorted."

The tense relationship in the mixed neighborhoods of blacks and Jews was also radicalized by Jewish progress at the expense of blacks. In many places – from housework to public service to private business – Jews became employers of African-Americans.[99] The blacks also failed in developing a robust business mechanism in the field of music, which fell into Jewish hands. Jews were the owners of vaudeville halls, Tin Pan Alley publishing houses, the theaters of Broadway, and the film industry. The power of the Jews in the industry conclusively determined the kind of black image and music that was published.

During the 1920s, a growing presence of Jews (some of them famous gangsters) controlled musical business ventures in Harlem. While the Jews fortified their power in the music industry, the blacks suffered financially from lean years and some unsuccessful attempts on Broadway.[100]

---

97 Jeffrey Gurock, *When Harlem was Jewish, 1870–1930* (New York: Columbia University Press, 1979), 48.
98 Norman Podhoretz, "My Negro Problem – And Ours," in *Black and Jews: Alliances and Arguments*, edited by Paul Berman (New York, Delacorte Press, 1993), 77–96 (Reprinted from *Commentary*, 1963). Podhoretz was the Jewish editor of *Commentary* magazine. He was so pessimistic about the future of the relationship between whites and blacks that he doubted the option of integration. In fact, he believed that the only possible integration would be possible by 'deleting the color.'
99 Nathan Glazer, "Negroes and Jews: The New Challenge to Pluralism," in *Bridges and Boundaries*, edited by Jack Salzman, Adina Back, Gretchen Sullivan Sorin (New York: George Braziller, 1993), 99–107; Irving Howe, "A Fear Beyond Escaping," in Ibid., 70–73.
100 Jeffrey Melnick, *A Right to Sing the Blues: African Americans, Jews and American Popular Song* (Cambridge, Massachusetts: Harvard University Press, 1999), 30.

Even if the Jews didn't display the same racist traditions as the WASPs and Catholics, there was no shortage of exploitation of employer-employee relations. Voices about financial exploitation such as non-payment of royalties and musical exploitation – in other words, the theft of African-American cultural materials – have been regularly discussed in the discourse on black-Jewish relations in the entertainment industry.[101] Entertainment-related legends noted that Jewish gangsters like Arnold Rothstein and Dutch Schultz used the talent of African-American writers to produce successful shows. However, black-Jewish cooperation only increased.

Beyond the physical proximity of Jewish entrepreneurs and musicians to black cultural products, it seems that the Jews' connection to black music was more than accidental. The Jews discovered black music as a fertile ground for activity, and they felt "at home" with it. In other words, there were emotional and musical similarities between black music and Jewish traditions, which strengthened this connection.

Blues dream: Klezmer, cantorial and black music

Throughout history, Europeans didn't consider Jews to be musical pioneers.[102] The nineteenth-century European emancipation allowed the presence of Jewish minstrels for the first time, who presented their version of folk songs combining sentences from the Talmud. These Klezmer bands became entertainers of their time. The cooperation between Jews and gypsies was perhaps an introduction to the Black-Jewish alliance.[103] The Jews' specific use of violin, piano, clarinet, and trombone, with certain forms of improvisation, facilitated their entry into the African-American musical world.

Scholars have noted an aesthetic resemblance between cantorial and gospel and blues.[104] The fathers of some of the best Jewish artists and performers of Afro-American music – Irving Berlin, Harold Arlen, Al Jolson – were cantors. The common claim is that the Jews gave a spiritual feeling to black secular music. The fusion of cantorial and jazz music, Melnick claimed, created the se-

---

[101] Ibid., 36.
[102] Yale Storm, *The Book of Klezmer: The History, the Music, the Folklore* (Chicago: Chicago Review Press, 2002), 23.
[103] Paul Buhle, *From the Lower East Side to Hollywood: Jews in American Popular Culture* (New York: Verso, 2004), 26.
[104] Jeffrey Melnick, *A Right to Sing the Blues: African Americans, Jews and American Popular Song* (Cambridge, Massachusetts: Harvard University Press, 1999), 134–135.

cret heart of the discourse on the musical similarity between African-Americans and Jews. Gershwin himself believed that black music was "natural" for Jews. The "feeling" that a composer must have, he felt, stemmed from Jewish's universalism.[105]

Cantorial music was popular during the 1890s' Vaudeville shows. Despite the decline of the cantor in the Jewish community, he remained a symbol of Jewish culture. For example, the song "Eli, Eli" in Yiddish was popular in the vaudeville and Lower East side shows, where Afro-Americans sang it in Yiddish. The Black singer Ethel Waters said that a PR man persuaded her to add it to her repertoire after another African-American singer, George Dewey Washington, "got great results with it."

Some scholars have focused on musical similarity, including among other things the use of the blue note.[106] These blue notes, which emphasize emotional melancholy, of being bluesy, illustrate the black-Jewish analogy about "the same tradition of suffering." Music critic Gary Giddins has determined that the use of the third minor scale (one of those blue notes), roaring pained vocals and improvisatory poetry, characterizes the similarity between Jewish and black music. "Perhaps our native theorists have over philosophized the blue note of the Negro," claims Issac Goldberg and Gershwin, "for the most popular scale of the khassid has a blue note that is quite as cerulean or indigo as the black man's blues maybe."[107]

Musicologist Jack Gottlieb has tried to explain the way scales and modes from Eastern European Jewish music influenced American pop writing during the first half of the twentieth century.[108] He believes that Jewish modes, including the AM (from the prayer "Adonai Malach"), the MA mode (from the prayer

---

[105] Isaac Goldberg, *George Gershwin: A Study in American Music* (New York: Ungar, 1958), 230.
[106] Blue note. In blues and popular American music of the twentieth century, the blue note characters are the third, fifth and seventh steps of the major scale, which are lowered to a semi-tone. The blue notes create a special sound that results from a combination of chord sounds with sounds up to a semi-tone below them. For example, in the blues style it is customary to play the chord C, which includes the notes C-E-G, with the Eb note, which is bent to a semi-tone under the chord sound (E).
  Blue note is a sound that "decorates" one of the chord sounds (except for the root) by bending the sound down on the instruments where it is possible such as wind instruments, shaking and bending upwards such as a guitar, or by adding additional sound in instruments that can't bend sound like the piano.
[107] Issac Goldberg, *George Gershwin: A Study in American Music* (New York: Frederic Ungar, 1931/1958), 40.
[108] Jack Gottlieb, *Funny, It Doesn't Sound Jewish: How Yiddish Songs and Synagogue Melodies Influenced Tin Pan Alley* (New York: University of New York Press, 2004), 42.

"Magen Avot"), and the AR mode (from the prayer "Ahava Raba") are prominent in American pop music. Jews wrote many of them, but WASP composers such as Cole Porter and Hoagy Carmichael used them as well.

Gottlieb explains that the AM mode is bluesy and is similar to the accessible Mixolydian mode in blues. The AM mode has two octaves. For the first one, the seventh scale degree is bent to a semi-tone to the blue-note, and in the next octave, the bending might happen both on the third and seventh scale degree.

Gottlieb's book is full of examples linking Yiddish music to black music and he displays the influence of the two traditions on American music. For instance, Gershwin's "Summertime," which scholars have perceived since its release as an epitome of Afro-American music, has for years been considered to be influenced by the African-American spirituals "Sometimes I Feel Like a Motherless Child." However, it is more influenced by the Yiddish lullaby "Shlof, Mayn Kind" (Sleep, My child). Gottlieb identifies that Irving Berlin's tune "Blue Skies" is similar to the Yiddish lullaby "Rozhinkes mit Mandlen." The song "Yesterdays" by Jerome Kern and Otto Harbach surprisingly resembles the Yiddish song "Shochen Ad" (Morning Service). Oscar Hammerstein II and Richard Rodgers' classic "My Favorite Things" resembles "Mit A Nodl." The tone of the theme film "Gone with the Wind," by Max Steiner has musical similarities to "My Golden One." Also, the bluesy "When the Sun Comes Out," by Harold Arlen and Ted Koehler, is based on the Jewish AM mode. "Brother, Can You Spare a Dime?" Of Harold Arlen and Jay Gorney relies on the mode MA and reminds him of the melodic structure of "Hatikvah," the Zionist anthem. Frank Loesser's use the AR mode is noted in "Luck Be a Lady." Gottlieb's book contains dozens more examples.

Apart from the musical similarity, I would add that there is a philosophical element in Black blues music that attracted Jewish artists mainly after World War Two. The blues – at least in its primary and raw form within the delta-Mississippi and its associated mythologies – deals with alienation, violence, persecution, and man's inability to control his desires. The blues deals with a person's inner struggles with his dark side, sometimes through dialogue with inner demons, often the "devil" himself. This inner psychological struggle is like a social alienation. All these have been overwhelmingly expressed in mythologies about the blues artist Robert Johnson who was believed to have met the devil at a crossroads and converted his soul in exchange for his unique talent.

Whether the philosophy of the blues was the legacy of mythologies about witchcraft, ghosts and demons from the Black continent, or whether it was a negation of Puritan fears in America, the blues had a mystical appeal to various minorities, including many Jews drawn to the dark, liberating duality of this "Satanic" music.[109]

It is not surprising that Jews, in the shadow of their dark images, were perceived in Christian anti-Semitic terminology as "Satanists" or as those who carry out their work (even their medical abilities were sometimes perceived as "sorcery"). Surveys have revealed the position of blacks and Jews as the most rejected minorities in the United States, even in the post-World War Two era.[110] The essence of life described by the blues – wandering, fear, alienation, and often with a sense of God's neglect – was certainly part of the mythology of that the Wandering Jew. It wasn't just a matter of urban alienation, but also the fact that from childhood, Jews absorbed myths and history about pogroms and persecution. Perhaps the blues also was attractive to all those cantors' sons who were in an internal psychological struggle and conflict between their secular environment and their Orthodox domestic heritage. If so, it is possible – or perhaps unconsciously – that the blues was a musical ground to many Jewish musicians and songwriters who sought alternative identities. The blues, ragtime and jazz actually served as ammunition for Jewish writers to give an artistic expression of their identity. They should have expressed it in the cynical and tough commercial framework of the modern capitalist music industry.

He's a rebel: Elitist humanism and the wages of the American Jews

Some Jewish scholars tended to understand the connection between Jews and popular culture in altruistic terms. The concepts humane ("concern for the feel-

---

[109] In Greil Marcus's *Mystery Train* he describes the blues as the perverse son of Calvinist ethics as shaped by Puritan settlers. The same Puritan ethic, explains Marcus, which in its purpose they built the first American colonies and the notion of the Self-made Man, believed that building a perfect community, hard work and financial success, coupled with contentment and an ascetic lifestyle signified their choice by God on their way to heaven in the afterlife. This belief – which did not come from Africa – was transferred to their black slaves, he explains. But they mainly grasped the gap between fantasy and reality, and the fact that their existential status signified their place not in heaven but at the other end, that is, in hell. The blues singers, Marcus writes, accepted the dread but refused the piety, serving the darker sides of life. In terms of Christian theology, the blues artists expressed the war of man in the devil, that is, the war of man on his dark side. They expressed it within the cynical and tough commercial framework of the modern and capitalist music industry.

[110] Leonard Dinnerstein, *Antisemitism in America* (New York: Oxford University Press, 1994), 157.

ings of the other") and universal ("belonging to and affecting everyone") were associated with Jewish history and mythology about a people who were persecuted and expelled so often during their existence in Europe as a source of understanding their "outsider identification."[111]

Alfred Kazin, for example, emphasized that the Jewish attraction to popular culture was a direct consequence of Jews existing between two cultures: Jewish Orthodoxy on the one hand and the new "Jewish intellectual" who conceived progressive humanism, rationalism, and socialism as values to replace Judaism as a religion and philosophy, on the other.[112]

Paul Buhle subsequently developed this theory, claiming that Jews exhibited a unique talent for popular culture due to the special connection between Jewish culture and tradition and humanistic and universalistic values.[113] The Jews, he argues, possess a particular ability to see themselves in the "other." In consequence, they were able to respond to the mood of the times more promptly than other figures and adopt creative methods appropriate to the needs of the American masses – via the mass consumption culture.

Laurence Bergreen, Irving Berlin's biographer, illustrates this concept by assuming that the success of the Tin Pan Alley stemmed from its ability to meld many styles into a familiar musical language that could be marketed nationally. Regional musical styles, according to this claim, found it difficult to deal with the "Jewish talent for universal products."[114]

Influenced by the philosophy of French continental philosophy (in a combination of postmodern logic, post-structuralism and post-colonialism), new Jewish scholars who were affected by the wave of academic focus on "whiteness," based their theories on the "traditional" role Jews ostensibly played as agents of integration, as cultural products serving as a tool through which the American melting pot could be promoted. The works published in this tradition focus on the ways in which American Jews laid claim to Afro-American cultural traditions as part of their own contribution to the formation of the American melting pot.

---

[111] Michael Alexander, *Jazz Age Jews* (New Jersey: Princeton University, 2001); Lawrence H. Fuchs, "Sources of Jewish Internationalism and Liberalism," in *The Jews: Social Patterns of an American Group*, edited by Marshall Sklare (New York: Free Press, 1958), 595–613.
[112] Alfred Kazin, "The Jew as Modern Writer," in *The Ghetto and Beyond; Essays on Jewish Life in America*, edited by Peter Rose (New York: Random House, 1969), 424.
[113] Paul Buhle, *From the Lower East Side to Hollywood: Jews in American Popular Culture* (New York: Verso, 2004), 21.
[114] Laurence Bergreen, *As Thousands Cheer: The Life of Irving Berlin* (New York: Da Capo Press, 1996), p. 36.

In his book examining the phenomenon of Jewish minstrelsy, Michael Rogin, for example, appeals to the heritage Jews possessed from their European background as agents of national culture. This enabled Jewish immigrants to the New World to naturally adopt the "blackface" mask as an instrument whereby they could assimilate into the American melting pot. At the same time, they also continued the American tradition of devaluing and excluding the weakest ethnic group, Afro-Americans.[115] In Rogin's view, the Jewish use of the black mask was a method Jewish minstrels utilized in order to turn the musical and theatrical medium (in its negative sense of contempt for and parody of Afro-American slavery) into a tool for the construction of white American identity.

In a similar approach to Rogin's, Jeffrey Melnick argues that Jewish American entrepreneurs, performers, and composers employed their interpretation of Afro-American music and theatrical styles to emphasize their white American authenticity as a healthy part of the American identity and its melting pot.[116] Relying on other scholars such as Sander Gilman and Martin Buber, Melnick analyzes the history of the Jewish race as that of a "cross-breed." Diaspora life, outside their religious homeland, together with the emancipation characteristic of the modern era, transformed modern Jewish identity: Jews preferred to see themselves as pan-Europeans. According to this theory, the Jews may be the most hybrid and universal of all races.

Melnick further suggests that the success of the American Jews in the entertainment industry in general, and the music industry in particular, proves that Jewish products could be enjoyed as "American" by everyone. In the music field, he adds, Jewish songwriters constructed their own image as "all-Americans" by integrating African-American rhythm and sounds – i.e., true American folk music – in their own high-quality interpretation of the latter. Fear of what they might lose in the process of assimilation was overcome by the belief that they were performing a vital role in the service of integration.

Jewish cultural products revealed an image of the Jewish race as characterized by its fusion. According to Melnick, the fact that Jews contributed to American cultural capital without demanding political power enabled them to create an American national culture imbued with hidden Jewish elements.

---

115 Michael Rogin, *Blackface, White Noise: Jewish Immigrants in the Hollywood Melting Pot* (Berkeley: University of California Press, 1998), 61.
116 Jeffrey Melnick, *A Right to Sing the Blues: African Americans, Jews and American Popular Song* (Cambridge, Massachusetts: Harvard University Press, 1999), 128–129.

Another scholar, Josh Kun, relates American music to a multi-layered field of voices that created different identities. Yet, his writing is not far from the latter tradition. He perceives the Jewish performance as a masquerade and as the conversion of "lingering notions of Jewish difference and otherness," though he argues for the "continuing pull of assimilation and the desire for invisibility into American whiteness," with the fusion of Afro-American material and Jewish traditions.[117]

I would like to suggest an alternative method for understanding the relationship between American Jews and the entertainment industry than the two approaches outlined above. I believe that these interpretations overlook significant factors relating to the history of American music industry and Jewish immigration alike.

I propose, first of all, that the popular assumption that American Jews consciously took upon themselves the role of agents of the melting pot must be reexamined. This hypothesis fails to take several important factors into account. Regarding films, for example, these include the number of radical Jewish authors, Jewish screenwriters from a socialist background, the history of Hollywood Jews' struggle against WASP companies (e. g., Edison's Trust monopoly), and their rejection of the Victorian values which characterized the latter's motives and strategies in the initial film era. Nor does the "melting pot" thesis take into account music history as the story of opposition on the part of modernists composers (who were, as I mentioned above, mainly Afro-Americans and Jews and "outsiders") to the Yankee elite and to the aesthetics and ideology of the latter composers.

In my opinion, those scholars who argue for the "melting pot" version of historical and cultural development disregard the fundamental fact that the very concept of the melting pot was diversely interpreted by different ethnic groups. From the perspective of the WASP elite, this phenomenon indicated the adoption of WASP values and its image as a way of life. From the Jewish or ethnic standpoint, however, the melting pot was perceived as pluralism – certainly not subordination to WASP hegemony, even when the latter defined cosmopolitan values as all-American. These two perspectives differ greatly from one another. If the Jews acted in such a way as to accelerate their integration, how is their consistent struggle against the WASP monopoly to be explained? In other words: from where did the WASP propaganda portraying Jews in the entertainment in-

---

117 Josh Kun, "'If I Embarrass You, Tell Your Friends': The Musical Comedy of Bell Barth and Pearl Williams," in *The Song is Not the Same: Jews and American Popular Music*, edited by Bruce Zuckerman, Josh Kun and Lisa Ansell (Indiana: Purdue University Press, 2010).

dustry in general, and Hollywood Jews in particular, as a "danger to America" derive?[118] Peter La Chapelle demonstrated this aspect in his writing concerning Ford's racist vision of America and its culture.[119] I'll add that the fear concerning alien immigration greatly disturbed the WASP elite more dramatically from the beginning of the twentieth century.[120]

The assumption made by scholars that American culture should be identified with the melting pot constitutes a facile preconception. Is it necessarily true that every cultural creation reflects a drive to forge a national identity? Is there no place for an alternative identity? And more to the point, were Jewish musicians and entrepreneurs so self-consciously preoccupied with the idea of the melting pot?

With respect to the "altruistic" approach, I suggest that the common assumption of "natural" Jewish identification with the suffering of unprivileged social groups is erroneous. This theory is undermined by several volumes of significant contemporary research – such as those of Stuart Svonkin, Michael Staub, and Marc Dollinger – which reexamine the ostensibly integral association between Jews and liberalism in America.

Svonkin investigates the battle against anti-Semitism and on behalf of civil-rights justice waged by some of the most important Jewish organizations during the 1940s and the 1950s. He reveals that the struggle was motivated primarily by political interests intended to secure Jewish ethnic existence.[121]

Michael Staub resents an even more complex version of the relationship between Jews, humanism, liberalism, and civil rights than that proposed by the "altruistic" version. [122] Staub exposes a conflictual and ambivalent political attitude within the Jewish organizations towards the radical liberalism and civil-

---

[118] Henry Ford, for example, consistently made this claim in the pages of his newspaper during the 1920s: see Henry L. Feingold, *A Time for Searching: Entering the Mainstream 1920–1945* (Baltimore: Johns Hopkins University Press, 1992).
[119] Peter La Chapelle, "Dances Partake of the Racial Characteristics of the People Who Dance Them: Nordicism, Anti-semitism and Henry Ford's Old-Time Music and Dance Revival," in *The Song is Not the Same: Jews and American Popular Music*, edited by Bruce Zuckerman, Josh Kun and Lisa Ansell (Indiana: Purdue University Press, 2010).
[120] Leonard Dinnerstein, *Antisemitism in America* (New York: Oxford University Press, 1994); Earl Raab, *What Do We Really Know About Antisemitism and What We Want to Know?* (New York: American Jewish Committee, 1989).
[121] Stuart Svonkin, *Jews against Prejudice* (New York: Columbia University Press, 1999).
[122] Michael Staub, *Torn at the Roots: The Crisis of Jewish Liberalism in Postwar America* (New York: Columbia University Press, 2004).

rights ethics of the 1960s. He further reveals an ideological ambiguity within the Jewish organizations regarding their attitude toward Afro-Americans.[123]

Marc Dollinger, who researched the history of Jewish liberalism between 1932 and 1975, asserts therein that on those occasions on which the Jewish organizations and leaders were faced with a choice between support for liberal politics and their own ethnic interests, they preferred to support their pursuit of integration.[124] According to Dollinger, Jews were more concerned with ensuring their own ethnic survival and welfare than with national interests.

Returning now to the issue of popular culture and the entertainment field, I wish to argue that the assumptions made by the altruistic approach fail to coincide with the disregard for Afro-American existence displayed in early Hollywood musical films such as *The Jazz Singer* (1927), or with the complicated relationship between Jewish employers and black employees in the music business. Moreover, the equation of Judaism with universalism does not always correspond to the sense of isolation which has characterized Judaism since the fourth century C.E., when Christianity obtained its privileged place in the Western world.

I believe that the attraction of Jewish immigrants to popular culture and the entertainment business was not due to the inheritance of altruistic values but rather to specific historical circumstances that enable the Jewish ability to create a particular brand of elitist humanism whose synthesis of high and low cultures constituted a source of economic and class-status standing. In other words, Jews were able to raise their personal status by promoting the development of American culture. In so doing, they merged images of humanistic and universal values with a cultural elitist and high aesthetic which exhibited their unique advantage in the new world. Jews flourished in American culture because they arrived in America during the mass immigration era – i.e., in a period during which neither low nor high culture was fully established. They both sensed and recognized this fact – and filled the void with their own ideas concerning popular entertainment, combining their European heritage with the American-rooted culture of blackface minstrelsy in films, music, and the theater.

In order to emphasize this point,' I'd like again to refer to the film world. As Gabler has demonstrated, this fusion of elitist humanism is prominently reflect-

---

123 Staub explain that on the one side stood the liberal pro-civil rights political camp, countered on the other side by reactionary and conservative organizations, as well as such influential public figures as (the sociologist) Nathan Glazer, (the journalist) Norman Podhoretz, and others, all of whom questioned the effectiveness of the black-Jewish alliance.

124 Marc Dollinger, *Quest for Inclusion: Jews and Liberalism in Modern America* (New Jersey: Princeton University Press, 2000).

ed, for example, in the life of Adolf Zukor, the founder of Paramount Pictures, who obsessively sought to amalgamate high and low culture:

> Whenever or not there was a specifically Jewish component in Zukor's sudden preoccupation, it was true that many if not most of the producers who would take up the banner of feature films were Jewish, and the idea was certainly compatible with the deepest strains in Jewish life where culture had always been held in special esteem. In America, where ambitious Jews could conceivably ride culture into higher social strata, this esteem carried a greater force. It was the Jews, like Zukor, who were most sensitive to the movies low esteem, and the Jews who had most to gain by raising it.[125]

Irving Thalberg, Louis B. Mayer's right hand man, may also be adduced as a further example of a person who believed that he knew "better than everyone" what the American people desired and needed:

> One reason even highly talented individuals suffered Thalberg's interference – and often suffered it gladly – was that in the legend his instincts were regarded as close to infallible [...] another MGM writer remembered Thalberg leaning over the desk and declaring imperiously, "I more than any single person in Hollywood have my finger on the pulse of America. I know what people will do and what they won't do.[126]

This tendency of American Jewish writers in popular culture to portray a picture of "Enlarging America" is well suited with their sense of elitist humanism, meaning that they know better than "others" what kind of culture America needed and deserved. We can observe that in the journey of Kern, Gershwin and other composers from the Tin Pan Alley district to the heights of Broadway musicals and in Gershwin's jazz-opera. Civil rights, justice, anti-racism is very distinct and noticeable in the best of Broadway musicals. Gershwin is a good case-study in this matter. He was probably the most proud and outspoken Jew in arguing for the fusion of African-American materials in American music. His lingo was full of superlatives for African-American vocal abilities and jazz sensibilities. But he didn't compose *Porgy and Bess* from pure altruistic motivations, nor from solely exploitative interests, but rather from his drive to accomplish American high art at its best via the power of multiculturalism. His journey toward this jazz opera was similar to the anthropological voyage to Charleston, North Carolina, to learn about black folk material, as the rich literature regarding Gershwin

---

125 Neal Gabler, *An Empire of Their Own: How the Jews Invented Hollywood* (New York: Crown Publishers, Inc., 1997), 25–26.
126 Ibid., 224.

reveals. It was more a "game" of challenging the American mainstream of the 1930s than assimilating to it.

Actually Jeffrey Melnick was trapped in his Whiteness tendency when he wrote:

> Gershwin's biography has stuck to this line [...] the composer's affinity for African-American forms derived from his belief that blacks and Jews [were] the same in relation to the rest of society. The British critic Wilfrid Mellers has articulated a similar position, suggesting that although Gershwin, unlike Porgy, was not a physical cripple, he was a psychological cripple: an archetypical white Negro, a poor boy who made good, a Jew who knew about spiritual isolation. Of course, this misses the key point that even if the White Negro is responding to some perceived lack in his home culture or some personal disability, he also always operates from a position of power.[127]

Indeed, Gershwin operated from the position of power – the power of Jews in the music industry – but was it the real power to exploit African-American or rather exactly the contrary, the power to present songs with a semiotic force that uplifted the status of African-American culture in American society? I believe in the second option.

Such an elitist game and the challenging of WASP norms may also be found among the younger generations of songwriters. Jerry Leiber and Mike Stoller, the most famous rhythm and blues writers of the 1950s, constitute an example of figures who adapted Afro-American music not out of altruistic ideas or the desire to forge a "new melting pot vision" but as an elevated cultural instrument whereby they could turn life into art. Michael Billig describes the post-war generation of Jews as those who maneuvered between the tales of old anti-Semitism and a hostile dangerous world for Jews, but Leiber and Stoller's memoires fail to share such feelings.[128] Rather, it was a world dominated by the provocation of WASP norms and adopting African-American's music as an elitist and humanist weapon at the same time. Stoller himself acknowledged:

> Even though we were white, we didn't play off a white sensibility. We identified with youth and rebellion and making mischief. We thumbed our nose at the adult world. We crawled inside the skins of our characters, we related to the guys in the singing groups, and that was a cross-cultural phenomenon: A white kid's take on a black kid's take of white society.

---

[127] Jeffrey Melnick, *A Right to Sing the Blues: African Americans, Jews and American Popular Song* (Cambridge: Harvard University Press, 1999), 128–129.
[128] Michael Billig, *Rock 'n' Roll Jews* (London: Five Leaves Publications, 2001), 7–13; Jerry Leiber and Mike Stoller with David Ritz, *Hound Dog: The Leiber and Stoller Autobiography* (New York: Simon & Schuster, 2009).

Color lines were blurred, but the motif was always absurdity. We were putting a twist in Caucasian traditions, turning folk heroes on their heads.[129]

Music Producer Phil Spector might be seen as another example of this elitist humanist tendency for multiculturalism and American Jewish artists to reveal America as more cosmopolitan, multicultural and sometimes even anti-WASP. Like Burt Bacharach and Hal David's work with Dionne Warwick, and their reflections regarding black femininity, Spector was famous in his work with African-American girl groups (the Crystals and the Ronettes) and for his Wall of Sound production technique – a combination of melting high European music with R&B and rock 'n' roll through recording manipulations. He became highly successful during the early 1960s, portraying himself as a real tycoon of the teens. However, as his biographies reveal, he never acted from altruistic motivations, nor from his desire to assimilate as a melting pot agent. It was closer to cultural resistance, or an attempt to gain alternative power in the music industry field. The writer Nik Cohn describes Spector's elitism and his obsession with mass media success, as well as his vision of America:

> Anyhow, Phil Spector was the first man to see pop as the new natural refuge of the outsider. The place you could make money and cut yourself off from filth and also express whatever you wanted without having to waste half your lifetime looking for breaks. The way he saw things, America was sick and pop was healthy. It was uncharted territory and its potential was endless [...] His most persistent image of himself was paranoid – creative Phil Spector hemmed in by cigar-chewing fatties, beautiful Phil among the uglies, groovy Phil versus hair-tugging America. His records were his best revenge.[130]

The Jews were able to achieve significant triumphs by fusing low and high culture. While the European cultural elite, with its combination of nationalism and romantic myths, was closed to them, the new world was a very different story. The American ethos was based on enlightenment and rationalism, and despite its attitude towards slavery, was a more welcoming territory.[131]

---

129 Jerry Wexler and David Ritz, *Rhythm and the Blues: A Life in American Music* (New York: Alfred Knopf, 1993), 134.
130 Nik Cohn, *WopBopaLooBop LopBamBoom: Pop from the Beginning* (London: Paladin, 1969), 95.
131 Ira Katznelson, "Between Separation and Disappearance: Jews on the Margins of American Liberalism," in *Paths of Emancipation*, edited by Pierre Birenbaum and Ira Katznelson (New Jersey: Princeton University Press 1995), 157–205. Although European nationalism was born in France, out of the values of the enlightenment, following the revolutionary and Napoleonic wars mid-European nationalism adopted a more romantic vision.

While the American "national tradition" was not fully developed or "invented," to borrow a concept from Eric Hobsbawm, the Jews came armed with the best of European culture – a culture which ironically had been denied them for more than two thousand years.[132] They combined this heritage with the American experience and its rooted culture of blackface minstrelsy in films, music, books, and theater.

Jews also succeeded on the basis of their elitist humanistic vision because the mass media was governed by middle class desires. Such scholars as Simon Frith, William Webber, and Paul DiMaggio have revealed the process in which, with the rise of the bourgeoisie to power during the nineteenth century, high culture became a kind of a new "secular religion." The latter was characterized by a combination of the genius rite, the sanctity of performance, and transcendentalism.[133] In contrast to its stereotypical image, Frith explains, mass culture was not only a working class phenomenon but was governed by middle class ethics.[134]

In this new secular religion – which combined a constant negotiation between high and low culture – the Jews were not relegated to an inferior position. On the contrary, it afforded them an arena in which they could gain power inaccessible to them in other fields. Not only did they stand here on more equal terms but they also possessed a European cultural heritage frequently unavailable to other American minorities, including WASPs.

The Jews recognized that immigrants had changed the face of America and its culture, and were the first to respond to these changes when they created their version. In the fields of music, Jewish humanistic elitism consciously and unconsciously led to the creation of a new, more liberal and universal representation of America. The Jewish musicians were the ones who helped turn the melting pot into a salad. The negotiations in the musical field were several decades ahead of the results that would be evident on the surface towards the end of the 1960s.

---

132 Eric J. Hobsbawm, *Nations and Nationalism since 1780: Programme, Myth, Reality* (Cambridge: Cambridge University Press, 1992); Eric J. Hobsbawm and Terence Ranger, *The Invention of Tradition* (Cambridge: Cambridge University Press, 1992); Benedict Anderson, *Imagined Communities* (New York: Verso, 1983).
133 Simon Frith, *Performing Rites: On the Value of Popular Music* (New York: Oxford University Press, 1996), 28; William Weber, *Music and the Middle Class: The Social Structure of Concert Life in London, Paris and Vienna* (London: Routledge, 1975), 19–21; Lawrence M. Levine, *Highbrow/Lowbrow* (Cambridge: Harvard University Press, 1988), 107; Paul DiMaggio, "Cultural Entrepreneurship in Nineteenth-Century Boston. Part 2: The Classification and Framing of American Art," *Media Culture and Society* 4 (1982): 317.
134 Simon Frith, *Performing Rites: On the Value of Popular Music* (New York: Oxford University Press, 1996), 36.

WASP culture established its supremacy in the first half of the twentieth century in the education system, higher culture, and bureaucratic institutions, but it also saw itself as facing "danger" in view of the enormous scale of immigration of Catholics and Jews. It faced ever greater conflicts between the progress of secular science and culture, along with the need to preserve Protestant supremacy.[135] This desire for supremacy was achieved, among other things, by a growing demand to strengthen the dominant culture and to stop the progress of foreign immigrants, including American Jews.

But while the WASP elite was late in understanding the power of modern mass culture and its cultural possibilities, the Jews took key positions in various fields of this industry: cinema, music, theater, satire, radical literature, comics, animation and more. They combined elitist humanism with moral and religious freedom, and established their power in different cultural fields. In music, this process was conducted in a fascinating, charged and revolutionary dialogue with African-American culture. The story of Irving Berlin, ragtime music and the Tin Pan Alley will open the hatch on it.

---

135 David A. Hollinger, *Science, Jews, and Secular Culture* (New Jersey: Princeton University Press, 1996), 1–10.

Chapter 3: I Used to Be Color-Blind – Irving Berlin, the Ragtime Riot and the Jewish Network in Tin Pan Alley

> A wave of vulgar, filthy, and suggestive music has inundated the land [...] Nothing but ragtime prevails and the cakewalk with its obscene posturing, its lewd gestures. It is artistically and morally depressing should be suppressed by press and pulpit. (The Musical Courier, 1899)[136]

"Syncopation is the soul of every real American [...] someday I'm going to write a syncopated grand opera," said Irving Berlin about ragtime, the new craze that gripped America.[137] Only good musicians could play it, too few managed to sing it, but "everyone" danced to it. Representatives of the Victorian world were perplexed by it, but ragtime music ruled from the end of the nineteenth century until America joined World War One in 1917. In fact, the ragtime never disappeared, but was absorbed into the new madness, jazz, which was about to sweep the swinging 1920s. The people of the era did not really know the differences between the two styles, which brought the taste of "African-American brothels" to the realm of many conservatives. The Victorian world of the late nineteenth century experienced a real cultural shock, but America could only surrender to the syncopated rhythm that defined it.

Jews were not the first to write ragtime hits, but they were probably among the biggest earners from this musical style, not only as entrepreneurs in the Tin Pan Alley, the publishing industry in New York, but as songwriters. Irving Berlin was really the king of ragtime. He was a lyricist and composer, a businessman who became a legend in the history of American music. He was thin, small and gray in appearance, yet sharp, witty, quick-paced, and had the special ability to distill a social and personal feeling for a two-and-a-half-minute song. "The Franz Schubert of America," George Gershwin called him.[138] And of course Berlin was not alone, but part of a group of highly-talented songwriters who changed the face of American music.

---

136 Ian T. Whitcomb, *After the Ball – Pop Music from Rag to Rock* (New York: Allen Lane/Penguin, 1972), 16

137 Ibid.; Andre Millard, *America on Record: A History of Recorded Sound*, 2nd ed. (Cambridge: Cambridge University Press, 2005), 108.

138 Stephen Birmingham, *"The Rest of Us": The Rise of America's Eastern European Jews* (New York: Syracuse University Press, 1999), 188.

There's no business like show business

Irving Berlin was born as Israel Beilin in 1888. He was five years old when he arrived with his family on their journey from Antwerp to New York, during which it was reported that not all the passengers had survived the journey and there was a great fear of cholera. The Beilin family, who were a part of thousands of immigrants who landed in New York every day, docked at Ellis Island. Cantor Moshe Beilin, his wife Leah and their six children spoke Yiddish, which made it difficult to communicate with American institutions. Moshe introduced himself as a "kosher butcher" in order to appear "respected" by the authorities.

Like other immigrant families from Eastern Europe, the Beilin family came from an Orthodox background. They were characterized by wearing typical Jewish outfits and were constantly concerned and insecure about their adaptation to the noisy, dirty, immigrant-rich new world. Like new Jews in the city, they acclimated to dormitories in cramped apartment buildings stinking of gas, smoke, and shocking sanitary conditions. From one ghetto in the old world they moved to another ghetto in the New World, the Lower East Side; Cherry Street to be more precise, once a fairly well-known place, but waves of immigration from Ireland, Italy, and Eastern Europe made it reckless and dangerous.

But Izzy looked at the glass as half full. "Everyone has to have a Lower East Side in his life," he said years later. Like Gershwin later, perhaps because he was the youngest in the family, Izzy felt more at home in New York than any member of his family.[139] "I did not feel poverty because I did not know anything else," he explained. And perhaps one should not be surprised at his positive spirit, given the past of the Beilin family in their hometown of Mogilev in Belarus. Berlin claimed that he had no memories of the old world except for one – where he lay beside the road while watching his house go up in flames. It is not clear whether this was a pogrom or an accompanying result, but the family had no choice but to leave.

Father Moses never returned to being a cantor in America, where Jews, even compared to other minorities, were conspicuous in breaking the chains of Old World tradition. He became a Kosher supervisor, and later had no choice but to paint houses for his living when he was middle-aged. The other members of the family helped to make money, as did young Izzy, who began selling newspapers by broadcasting the news in a loud voice. Sometimes he was forced to sell

---

[139] Jeffrey Magee, *Irving Berlin's American Musical Theater* (New York & Oxford: University Press, 2012), 9; Laurence Bergreen, *As Thousands Cheer: The Life of Irving Berlin* (New York: Da Capo Press, 1996), chap. 1, Kindle.

family valuables for single cents. The rest of the time, he visited the school and the "room" for bar mitzvah studies, without enthusiasm in both cases. "He just dreams and sings to himself," said one of the teachers. And he did sing with his father. "I suppose it was singing in shul that gave me my musical background," he recalls. "It was in my blood."[140]

Izzy was thirteen years old when his father died. After eight years in America, the family returned almost to their starting point. It was not long before Izzy left school and the family's house, moving between one living room and another. What remains is his voice. He began to sing popular ballads from the time in the Bowery salons in the vicinity of gambling houses, brothels, and a crowd of sailors of various nationalities. His success and livelihood depended on the popularity and euphoria of the songs he chose to sing. In 1902, he received his first role as a choir member. He worked in the theater and became a "boomer" or a "plugger." In short, he marketed songs – at this stage, he used to dress up as one of the audience, pretending to be enthusiastic for specific hits over and over. Under these circumstances, he met Harry Von Tilzer and the publishing industry of the Tin Pan Alley.

Song publishing was not new at the beginning of the twentieth century. As we have seen, various musical performances existed throughout the nineteenth century: from operettas, minstrelsy, later vaudeville, burlesque, English, and Irish ballads in the Appalachians, prisoner songs, slave songs, religious songs in white and African-American churches. In the bourgeoisie's homes, they used to keep a piano, and classical German music enjoyed a status of "sanctity" in contrast to popular music that they perceived as everyday, forgettable, and trivial songs with "little or no value."[141]

Since the 1880s, the popular song had became a real product. The industry formed in New York was modern, making songwriting a profession in every respect. Like Hollywood, the Tin Pan Alley was diverse but created homogenized products. The source of the nickname is controversial, but it is customary to cite the Jewish journalist and songwriter Monroe Rosenfeld on 28 West Street as the one who gave the name to the area between Broadway and Fifth and Sixth Avenue in Manhattan, where many of the publishers located their offices. Rosenfeld gave it a nickname with connotations of the cacophony that arose from a visit to offices and listening to music that was heard from different pianos and singers in various positions without synchronization. Over the years, this nickname has be-

---

140 Laurence Bergreen, *As Thousands Cheer: The Life of Irving Berlin* (New York: Da Capo Press, 1996), chap. 1, Kindle.
141 David Suisman, *Selling Sounds: The Commercial Revolution in American Music* (Cambridge: Harvard University Press, 2012), chap. 1, Kindle.

come the generic name of the music publishing industry. Finally, it became the description for American pop songs of the first half of the twentieth century.

Entrepreneurs hired composers and lyricists regularly to create popular songs, written to guidelines and restrictions. Charles K. Harris, a Jew who wrote one of the greatest hits of the 1890s, the Victorian waltz "After the Ball" and founded a publishing company that bears his name, recommended his authors to work on songs that were not hard to sing in order not to make it difficult to sell them. Another Jew, Harry Von Tilzer, who added a German aristocratic prefix to his mother's family, believed that songwriters must bend their desires to the tastes of the audience. Von Tilzer, who was born as Harry Gumm, which was even short for Gambinsky, was the prototype of the new industry.

Before the foundation of the Tin Pan Alley, the publishing industry was decentralized in various places and was part of a music business that included a variety of activities, such as selling musical instruments, marketing musicians. A highly successful composer's average royalties, like those of Stephen Foster's, were ridiculous compared to what was accepted after the Tin Pan Alley's foundation. Composers who sold a few hundred copies of a song considered it a success, and there were very few options for earning profits. So, as Von Tilzer explained, there were not many people interested in writing songs.[142]

The Copyright Act of 1891 changed the industry. The law promised to protect the copyrights of imported works, and therefore also guarantee the rights of American companies, thus opening the way to the 1890s boom. However, the commercial revolution in the publishing houses began a little earlier, in the 1880s, because of the need to provide songs for the vaudeville halls, which replaced minstrelsy. Vaudeville required a combination of comic sketches, dance, acrobatics, and live music adapted to the tastes of the middle-classes. Restrictions related to smoking, alcohol, prostitution, and sexual censorship, but the need for songs was inevitable, and the publishers began aggressive marketing with attractive covers and active public relations.

Tin Pan Alley marketed its products to middle-class audiences, without regard to age differences. A song had to be circumvented by age, class and ethnic group, and be acceptable for a bourgeois family with their home piano, and represented by a white artist. Black artists were discriminated against in industry and the mass media reflecting the general prejudice regarding blacks. The consumption possibilities of the white population attracted the publishing companies. But the song industry was also a complex and problematic place where

---

[142] Ibid., chap. 1, Kindle.

Afro-Americans could move forward and integrate, even in smaller doses than some of the other ethnic groups. The music was marketed using music sheets for the piano. Later on, Tin Pan Alley designed its products for the home audio system.[143]

American Jews, many of them of German origin, began to set up publishing houses in the last decade and a half of the nineteenth century. The Witmark brothers launched M. Witmark & Sons. The amateur pianist Joseph W. Stern started Joseph W. Stern & Co. Leopold Feist founded Leo Feist, Inc.; Patrick Howley and Frederick Benjamin Havilland, two publishing salesmen, founded Howley, Haviland & Co., but the company's executive manager was Max Dreyfus, a Chicago Jew who would later become an essential figure of Tin Pan Alley.

In the late 1990s, Max Dreyfus abandoned Howley, Haviland & Co. and joined the brothers Thomas and Alex Harms in what would be TB Harms & Francis, Day & Hunter, Inc. Dreyfus bought the Harms brothers a few years later and was the one who cultivated the songwriters Jerome Kern, George Gershwin, Vincent Youmans, Richard Rodgers and Cole Porter.

The Jews Maurice Shapiro and his brother-in-law Louis Bernstein formed a company with Von Tilzer under the name Shapiro, Bernstein & Von Tilzer. Irving Berlin, who began his musical career as a song plugger, a friend of another Jew, Ted Snyder, to eventually become Waterson, Berlin & Snyder, Inc. Charles K. Harris opened a publishing company bearing his name.

In the first decade of the twentieth century, Tin Pan Alley continued to be in full swing. Of course, not all the publishing houses operated in New York, and some of them were not owned by Jews, such as Jerome H. Remick and Company. This businessman from Detroit based his power by taking control of the company of Shapiro and Bernstein. In this publishing house, young Gershwin began his career as a song plugger.

In the first decade of the twentieth century, the African-American publishing company Gotham-Attucks Music Company appeared, even if there were no more than a handful of companies owned by Afro-Americans for many years. This fact further strengthens the discourse regarding the exploitation of Afro-Americans, both by Tin Pan Alley and in the relations between Jews and Blacks.

The Jews of Tin Pan Alley did not emphasize their Jewishness. Even in the autobiographies they published, they barely, if ever, reveal their ethnic identity. Still, the impressive representation of Jews among the top publishers was a

---

143 Simon Frith, *Sound Effects: Youth, Leisure and the Politics of Rock'n'Roll* (New York: Pantheon Books, 1981), 32–33; Reebee Garofalo, *Rockin' Out: Popular Music in the USA* (Boston: Prentice Hall, 1997).

source of criticism with an anti-Semitic tone. Journalist Dr. Arnoth, for example, found the Jewish publishing houses "cheap, inane, vulgar."[144]

He did not believe that "sounds so vulgar and horrible can come out of cultural throats." But the publishers, who mostly were in their twenties, were in full swing and had previous business experience: Isidore Witmark sold water filters, Joseph Stern – ties; Dreyfus – picture frames, etc. Music was a product for sale, and they sold it imaginatively and aggressively.

Some of the publishers came to the field after an experience in the American pop culture of the period. Von Tilzer said that he had joined the circus as a teenager, and later joined a burlesque crew as a minstrel singer. Charles Harris defined himself as a banjoist, a songwriter and a man who grew up on minstrelsy and the racial parody of these performances; Julius Witmark began his career in minstrelsy. The family publishing house not only held a department of minstrelsy but also published the guide and encyclopedia for fans of blackface minstrels, *The Witmark Amateur Minstrel Guide and Burnt Cork Encyclopedia*.

But let's return to Von Tilzer. Like many Jews in the entertainment industry, he seemed to have created himself out of an illusion. His roots were Polish, but he preferred to present himself as a German. He could not read music but claimed he had written more than 8,000 songs, of which he published about 2,000, and at least a dozen of them had sold more than a million copies. Even if we regard these figures very carefully, Von Titzer was a famous name in the industry. He wrote ballads and "coon" songs with an African-American dialect. One of them, "Alexander Do not You Love Your Baby No More?", would be an inspiration for Izzy, as well as Von Tilzer's success, clothes, and German name. Izzy used "everything" around Von Tilzer in his dazzling transformation from Beilin to Irving Berlin.

Izzy became a well-known name in the Jewish network; he worked for a time in Von Tilzer's service as a promoter of songs for the artists who appeared in vaudevilles. From there, he moved to opium-ridden Chinatown, and joined Blind Soul, promoting blind Afro-American songs while learning a little piano. He was almost sixteen, and the next target was as a singing waiter at Cafe Pelham in Chinatown, which was known as "Nigger Mike's." 'Nigger Mike' Salter was a Russian Jew who opened a musical bar, which became a meeting place for gangsters and Italian, Irish and Jewish gangs. Alongside Izzy was a pharmacist student named Joe Shenk, who later became one of Hollywood's most prominent Jews.

---

144 David Suisman, *Selling Sounds: The Commercial Revolution in American Music* (Cambridge: Harvard University Press, 2012), chap. 1, Kindle.

From singing, Izzy switched to lyrics. "Marie from Sunny Italy" was his first song, signed in the company of Joseph Stern for pennies, and did not succeed commercially. But the credit for the cover sheet, I. Berlin, was the first step in the creation of his persona in the world of entertainment. Berlin abandoned Von Tilzer and joined an almost deaf diamond merchant named Henry Waterson, who founded a publishing company with a 25-year-old Jewish songwriter, Ted Snyder. Berlin was appointed a full-time lyricist for $25 a week with the addition of royalties. Finally, he was to be an essential partner in this publishing house.

There were unofficial rules in the Alley, which some writers outlined and had to adapt to. For example, a songwriter was supposed to understand the head and ear of the audience, examine competitors, and make use of recognized materials that were public property. The songwriter should avoid vulgarity and slang, and words with many syllables; and Berlin believed that it was essential to reach the refrain and idea quickly and strengthen them as much as possible. Songs often began with a repetitive line between the speech and the melody of the verse. The songwriters had to engrave the refrain in the audience's mind and transformed the songs to 32 bars with a bridge of eight bars. It became the standard.

The songwriters had to fill the bars with substance. "The best songs came from the gutter," explained publisher Edward Marks, and Berlin knew the streets.[145] He also knew the vaudeville singers and songs also came under their inspiration. One of them, George Whiting, did not hesitate to join him for the show on the pretext that he was free because his wife "left for the village." In a short evolutionary process, Berlin turned the slogan into one of his first hits, "My Wife's Gone to The Country (Hurrah! Hurrah!)."

It was one of the amusing examples of the new post-Victorian mood in the Alley. This work by Berlin and Snyder dealt with the momentary euphoria of men's release from the bonds of marriage. It became a hit that had sold hundreds of thousands of copies by the end of the decade. Berlin's inability to play and compose at this stage encouraged him to use the repertoire from "public property." "The Spring Song" by the German composer Felix Mendelssohn was saddened by "That Mesmerizing Mendelssohn Tune," which was a bigger hit than his predecessor.

Yet by this time, at the end of the first decade of the twentieth century, he realized that to leave his mark, according to Stephen Foster's model, one must

---

145 Laurence Bergreen, *As Thousands Cheer: The Life of Irving Berlin* (New York: Da Capo Press, 1996), chap. 1, Kindle.

grasp the "essence" that "shocks" America so that the song can enter the museum. Black music caught his imagination, and especially ragtime. The nickname referred to the noisy rhythm and was another way of describing syncopation. This piano style contrasted one hand that plays a "straight" rhythm while the other hand emphasizes the "weak beats." You needed to be an excellent pianist to play it properly. Berlin was not, but the black composer Scott Joplin was the real thing.

Joplin, who won a musical education from the German Jew Julius Weiss, arrived in New York in the second half of the decade with a series of instrumental hits that defined ragtime as a unique aesthetic. He even issued an opera under his hand, A *Guest of Honor* (1903), but now he offered another opera: *Treemonisha*. Difficulties in finding a publisher obliged him to produce a self-financed and modest version of the opera for investors. It ended in a ferocious fiasco that led to bankruptcy and depression, even if what came to him a few years later was far worse: syphilis from which he had suffered attacked his mind and killed him in the spring of 1917.

Joplin lacked the social and professional network of Berlin and its financial power in the world of entertainment and publishing, but he also lacked Berlin's more penetrating view of pop culture. Berlin believed that the meaning of ragtime was much more than style, but a way of life – something that would be identified a decade and a half later with swingtime, and then rock 'n' roll, that is, a freedom that was a release from the modern Sisyphean experience. This understanding turned him from an instant hit producer with a somewhat ridiculous German name to Irving Berlin, the King of Ragtime.

At first, with his partner, Snyder, he wrote pseudo-rag songs, including one in Yiddish-Jewish-Russian flavor: "Yiddle On Your Fiddle Play Some Ragtime." The publishers Waterson and Snyder made a good profit from their new talent, but Berlin also made an impressive income for himself until the *New York World* newspaper decided to publish an article about him. The newspaper piece emphasized that the young tyro had earned $15,000 in the last year (1910).

Berlin did not slow down; although the few piano lessons fatigued him, according to the myth he had created for himself at least he began to write songs on the black keys. He called them the "Negro Keyboards." He probably did not know but playing on them sets up pentatonic scales: the major and the minor. The first is popular with the minstrels' songs while the second appears in blues, which may have helped him find motifs of Afro-American music. "The Key of C," claimed Berlin, "is for people who studied music," but in practice, he wrote in a variety of scales and harmonies. Although he found it hard to accompany himself, mechanical development allowed him to switch between musical scales.[146]

Now he felt he could cope, in his way, with the devil's music. To him, Joplin's rags were obsolete as a potential source for religious anthems, but the syncopation seemed attractive. He started composing a new piece, "Alexander's Ragtime Band," still without words. He tried to promote it at the Ziegfeld Follies, a place that had already included some of his songs, but his new work did not stand out. So he decided to add lyrics. "Three-fourths of that quality which brings success to popular songs is the phrasing." he explained. "I make a study of it – ease, naturalness, every-day-ness – and it is my first consideration when I start on lyrics. 'Easy to sing, easy to say, easy to remember and applicable to everyday events' is a good rule for a phrase."[147]

The lyrics seemed to combine the primitive elements of "Alexander's Ragtime Band" and made it a hit. The success of the song was due to effective New York marketing under the management of his business partner Max Winslow, while running 75 publicists in every important place. The singer Emma Carus of Chicago often performed it, as did Al Jolson wherever he appeared. By summer, the song had sold more than half a million copies of sheet music, and by the end of the year – more than a million. A million copies were sold the following year, at least according to a Berlin biographer. Even if one had to be wary of the sales figures in the era, the song was a sensation, elevating ragtime music into a mass frenzy.

Dvořák hoped for and had predicted this development in the world of concert music, but Berlin created the image of popular American music all over the world. The song included a mix of march, coon songs, and minstrelsy performances, using approach notes that would later be part of blues and jazz, as well as the proto-swing rhythm, thus creating a model for the twentieth century's music. In an interview from 1915, Berlin accused American composers of imitating meaningless European music. "I'm doing something they all refuse to do: I'm writing American music!"[148]

In Britain, the media introduced Berlin as the inventor of ragtime. Scott Joplin, who until Izzy's breakthrough believed himself to be the king of that style, claimed that Berlin was an impostor. But it did not help him. The song "Alexander's Ragtime Band" – one of the greatest bestsellers of the period – was crowned the sensation of the decade. "The melody [...] started the heels and shoulders of

---

146 Ibid., chap. 4, Kindle.
147 Ibid., chap. 4, Kindle.
148 Ibid., chap. 4, Kindle.

all America and a good section of Europe to rocking," Berlin explained, adding, "[t]he lyric, silly though it was, was fundamentally right."[149] The demand to listen to Alexander's band saw it conquer the world.

The question was, who is Alexander? On the cover of the notes were white musicians, even if it was felt that Berlin had written about the conductor of an Afro-American orchestra. Berlin borrowed the name from Von Tilzer's Afro-American dialect. Alexander was a fancy name, perhaps too elegant, attributed to one of the greatest military generals in the history of civilization. It was customary to attach it to Afro-Americans as a form of mockery. It seemed like an impossible gap between their status and the halo attached to the name. This gap created an impulse to respond to it as if it were paradoxically a friendly way to deal with the terrible and disturbing shadow of American life. The song seemed to turn to the primitive side, to feelings of inferiority and darkness hidden in the collective unconscious of the listeners, as if awakening a monster until you had to go with it. It defined an era just as "Rock Around the Clock" did during the mid-1950s. So, was Berlin a liberal and colorless, or a cynical and exploitative songwriter of African-American culture? I believe that he was an "ordinary" Jewish immigrant with progressive, cosmopolitan aims, who thought that Americans could and should accept the "other," even if he did so from a position of strength and also if he merely acted in the spirit of the times. Joining the orchestra was an allegory of America as a whole.

Although actually moving between two tonal centers, the song was perceived as "primitive" and dripped with a black dialect and an American past drawn from the multi-dimensional imagination of Berlin. He finally composed the song in relation to "Swanee River," Stephen Foster's heritage ("If you care to hear the Swa-nee Riv-er played in rag-time"), like minstrelsy still remained alive through Berlin's liberal vision.

In 1920, in a retrospective view of his victory, Berlin explained the method: a song must be within the range of the average amateur singer. He believed that the name of the song should be simple and be planted in the song, with the possibility to repeat it over and over; he explained that the idea should fit both men and women, and that songs – even if comical – should have pathos. With the exception of originality, he argued that lyrics should deal with emotions and objects familiar to everyone, be easy to memorize and sing, and that the songwriter should look at his work as a business.

But the cynical commercial strategy and the "Negro keyboard" issue are highly misleading. Berlin's songs are colorful and rich in music. It is unlikely

---

149 Ibid., chap. 4, Kindle.

that he only used black keys, because his songs, despite his musical ignorance, are rich, like those of Gershwin, Cole Porter, Burt Bacharach, Lennon and McCartney, and the best of the twentieth century melodists: chromaticism, modal interchange, pentatonic motifs and blue notes, multi-sonic textures, modulations and changes between tonal centers, alongside layers of harmony from the end of the Romantic era.[150] It is interesting that despite the myth he created for himself about the "Negro Keyboards," his songs are not based on the pentatonic scales that are typical of blues but only as nuances and segments at best. These sounds, which were popular in blues and rock, were certainly not typical of the Tin Pan Alley composers. Years of experience with various musicians had sharpened his ears about the harmony of his songs, which even if he was not solely responsible for it, he was the one who approved it.

Berlin could have been among the first singer-songwriters and certainly wanted to move forward as a singer, but only by "bad luck" was he ahead of his time by half a century. "When I Lost You" (1912) was dedicated to the death of his wife a few months after their marriage. The song "I Love a Piano" used the piano as an allegory for an elegant woman. With the exception of some patriotic songs from World War One, he devoted a whole series to the South (e.g. "When It's Night Time in Dixie Land") and a whole series of songs about love, such as "A Pretty Girl Is Like A Melody" (1919), a hit at the Ziegfield Follies, which used athletic metaphors to synchronize themes of infatuation and "flare" about the beauty of music.

Philip Fouria explained that the charm of Berlin's songs stems from the contrast between words and music, a kind of lyrical-musical counterpoint.[151] Romantic songs such as "Always" (1925), written as a gift to his then-fiancé Ellin Mackay, were based on slight syncopated accents that lent counterweight to romance. The song "All by Myself" (1921), a "depressing" statement about loneliness, turned Berlin into a writer of a sweet-bitter humanistic anthem with a touch of optimism. The song "Blue Skies" (1926) uses the ambiguous meaning of the word "blue" as sad versus happiness, and the contrast of the sadness of the house against the B part that smiles at it.

Berlin's was a story of victory. His publisher, Waterson, Berlin & Snyder, Inc., became the new "star" in the industry because he was one of the most prolific and successful songwriters. In 1927, with the birth of "Talkies" he also penetrated

---

[150] David Carson Berry, "Gambling with Chromaticism? Extra-Diatonic Melodic Expression in the Songs of Irving Berlin," *Theory and Practice* 26 (2001): 21–85.
[151] Philip Furia, *The Poets of Tin Pan Alley: A History of America's Great Lyricists* (New York: Oxford University Press, 1992), 47–62.

the heart of the Hollywood action. One of the memorable scenes from the movie *Jazz Singer* was the performance of Al Jolson to Berlin's "Blue Skies."

Towards the end of the 1920s, with the jazz takeover of the popular song, lyrics also changed to adopt greater sophistication, parody and satire. Ira Gershwin, Oscar Hammerstein, Lorenz Hart, and Cole Porter became the new pop poets of Tin Pan Alley. Berlin was like the old man of the tribe, but he had enough energy and credibility to go all the way to Hollywood, where the studios were still in sync with him. Motivated by the demands of cinema, Berlin, as well as his colleagues who would jump at the chance of going to Hollywood, including the Gershwin brothers, Hart and Rodgers, and others, had to transcend themselves. "Puttin' On the Ritz" (1929), which was later immortalized by Fred Astaire, was a masterpiece of the opposite: a pioneering syncopated phrasing of the verses in one part, versus a relatively straight cut in the second. But it was more than that – it defined the aesthetics and sound that dominated American songs during the era. The biographer of Berlin identifies it with the Coon tradition as a parody of the Harlem Renaissance, but in Hollywood it was performed by an ensemble of multi-racial performers, and was synchronized with the swing rhythm. It sounded like Europe and America distilled together in Duke Ellington's vision. The song was written back in the fat 1920s, so that the sense of splendor that now emanated from it offered the perfect fantasy for millions of Americans who had to experience the Great Depression. And regarding Ellington – his Jewish manager and lyricist Irving Mills bought the company of Watson, Snyder and Berlin while implementing Berlin's future slogan: "There's no business like show business."

Against the background of the economic abundance of the 1920s, Tin Pan Alley experienced an impressive flowering. Along with the popularity of jazz was born a new dance style, the Charleston, which also penetrated Broadway. Jazz and blues sold better in record format, thanks to the launch of radio in the early 1920s.

A real musical development took place with the arrival of the "talkies." Hollywood realized that ownership of the songs themselves made them a valuable property. Warner Brothers, who introduced *The Jazz Singer* in 1927, acquired the companies of the Witmark brothers and Harms, which was owned and operated by Max Dreyfus, and took control of Jerome Remick's company. MGM bought the repertoire of Leo Feist and smaller companies, and the film companies created new methods for publishing the songs using their own cinematic medium: the 1920s were peak years for publishing songs until the Depression. Tin Pan Alley was now stronger than ever and in Hollywood's hands.

Looking back, the scale of the Jewish presence in the publishing houses of the late nineteenth and early twentieth centuries is still astonishing. Later estimates changed, but at least until the late 1960s, Jews were prominent activists in the publishing industry, and consequently in the music industry as a whole. But the top songwriters had never been satisfied with the success of Tin Pan Alley's cynical and limited production line. They wanted more than that; they dreamed of infiltrating the world of musical comedy and Broadway musicals, where they could realize particularly challenging artistic ambitions. Irving Berlin was one among them who earned the prestige, honor and achievements, but the Jewish composers who led the movement were Jerome Kern, George Gershwin and Richard Rodgers, and they paid Berlin respect: "Irving Berlin has no place in American music," Kern explained, "he is American music," even if the man who made ragtime to the sound of America claimed sometime, "I never did find out what ragtime was."[152]

---

[152] Laurence Bergreen, *As Thousands Cheer: The Life of Irving Berlin* (New York: Da Capo Press, 1996), Ch. 4, Kindle.

Chapter 4: Someone to Watch Over Me – Jerome Kern, George Gershwin and the Jazz Journey in the Musical Comedy

The origin of all music lies in the theater, claimed Leonard Bernstein, emphasizing folklore, songs, and dances of prayer, or love, words and ideas. Where did the music really develop from he wondered, if not in the church? The most fabulous theater of all, he insisted. And the Jews in the world of music loved the theater.[153]

They were the counts, the princes, the dukes, and the kings of the musicals. Many of the most prominent and significant figures in American musical comedy, mainly from the 1920s, were American Jews: Oscar Hammerstein II and Jerome Kern, George and Ira Gershwin, Lorenz Hart and Richard Rodgers, Vincent Youmans, Yip Harburg, Harold Arlen, Gus Kahn, and of course Irving Berlin, to mention only a few. The pairs changed over the years: Hammerstein joined Rodgers for a series of bestsellers; Stephen Sondheim, a trainee of Hammerstein, joined Leonard Bernstein to write unforgettable musical hits. Jews always stood out on Broadway.

They wrote songs, comedies and dramas about America. At first, they called it musical comedy, and later – musicals. The principal scholarly tendency has been to think that these were shows concerning the melting pot, but in fact, it was the picture of America as they experienced it. Indeed it was not the righteous and religious-Protestant America of the Victorians, but rather a more multicultural, liberal, and more justice place that merged with the echoing combination of popular culture and high art.

The musicals adopted a variety of elements from the stage of theater and music. The music and sporadic skits of the revues and the porous sexuality and dimensions of the burlesque were influential. The musical circus, minstrelsy, and elements of the vaudeville and even operettas were the roots of this art form. Jewish artists did not initially create this American culture, but they certainly helped in its design, especially in the combination of the American musical elements in the shows. It was the field where the songwriters of Tin Pan Alley were able to embroider their musical "concept albums" half a century before The Beatles did it in practice. The best musicals were like lighter operas in which American Jews could express their cosmopolitan vision, as in the works of Ham-

---

153 Leonard Bernstein, *The Unanswered Question: Six Talks at Harvard* (Cambridge: Harvard University Press, 1976), 43–44.

merstein and Kern and the Gershwin Brothers, whom I will concentrate on in this chapter.

There were many pioneers of the American musical theater, but the most significant were Gilbert and Sullivan, the British duo of the Victorian era, whose comic operas permeated works of American composers in their combinations of drama, satire, parody, and music. Leonard Bernstein, who wrote his master's thesis on the uniqueness and identity of American music, was convinced that the American musical comedy was the first stage of development in creating a genuine American sound. From its European influences, it was supposed to evolve into an American soup, since jazz was in American hands. He believed that it would be the beginning of another direct line, which would develop from folk music, and be naive, intellectual, and exciting. The musical comedy was the realm of this development, and it would have its impact on concert composition.[154]

However, this process was shaped somewhat differently than expected. At the end of the journey, jazz music – of which essential parts influenced the field of musical comedy – would achieve the aesthetics of high art and constitute a format representative of America. The musical comedy itself was shaped into a uniquely American genre and became a junction where pop music and high composition were melded together as products for the masses, and through this format, America influenced the world. Bernstein may have idealized the famous Jewish composer Aaron Copland as the American model, and perhaps he was right. But it seems that the real event in the battle for the pulse of American music as a combination of popular culture and high art took place in the work of two other composers: Jerome Kern and George Gershwin.

Kern and Gershwin represented different generations. Kern, who was older, succeeded Victor Herbert at the turn of the century in a time when British productions dominated Broadway shows, and he set up Broadway's first original American aesthetic with a subtle, continuous, and conservative blend of black music. Gershwin, who showed enormous pride in his Jewish identity, was the person who led the second renaissance on Broadway, which was marked by Jewish dominance, with a host of hits by Hart and Rodgers, Hammerstein, and Berlin. The myth claims that even a WASPish composer such as Cole Porter claimed that he discovered the secret to writing hits in Jewish music.[155] But this Jewish music was a long journey to the soul of black music, and Gershwin was one

---

[154] Ibid., 57.
[155] Jack Gottlieb, *Funny, It Doesn't Sound Jewish: How Yiddish Songs and Synagogue Melodies Influenced Tin Pan Alley* (New York: University of New York Press, 2004), 88.

of the great missionaries in integrating African-American music in his performances.

Both Kern and Gershwin were self-taught and had only partial high musical educations. Both were enormously inspired by Europe, but they balanced it with an American vision. The differences between the two composers tell the story of American music in the musical comedy in the first half of the twentieth century.

Jerome Kern: All the things you are

Jerome Kern is a famous name in the history of American music, but his image as a composer remains mysterious. Richard Rodgers, Cole Porter, George Gershwin, and the New York musical elite adored him. Some described him as "the most gifted composer in American music." He was a model and an icon. His biographer David Ewen called him "a genius," while others saw him as part of the folklore of the nation.[156]

But there seem to be relatively few Americans who can hum his songs on the street today. Sometimes they know his famous bestsellers, but do not associate them with him. But one great musical about the south, a series of Hollywood hits and one memorable jazz standard established his iconic status.

Kern was born in 1885 in New York City and moved during his youth to New Jersey. He was the sixth son of Jews of German-Czech origin and grew up in a middle-class family. His father was a businessman; His mother was born in America and played the piano. She gave him love and a foundation of musical education. At the age of ten, his father took him to Broadway for the first time, and this visit left a mark. While still at school, he wrote music for two minstrels' performances, one of them based on *Uncle Tom's Cabin* for the Newark Yacht Club. His school friends described him as a sensitive child.

During his youth, Kern admired the Irish-American composer Victor Herbert, and probably also the British duo Gilbert and Sullivan. Still, he had a particular fascination with German culture, which even intensified after his parents' death, sometime after he turned 20. Until his teens, musical education was autodidactic and partial (he learned some college music courses later), but he won his first job in the music business through the Jewish connection; in his case, the musical entrepreneur William Hammerstein, the father of Oscar, his future partner.

---

[156] Stephen Banfield, *Jerome Kern*, 1st ed. (New Haven: Yale University Press, 2006), chap. 1, Kindle.

As in many other cases, at first, it was difficult to identify his qualities, perhaps because of his conventional, heterosexual, and conforming world. He was not a street boy like Gershwin, and he had no partner like Lorenz Hart, who gave a psychological dimension, as the self-destructing gay victim in Richard Rodgers' melodies. Like other aspiring composers, he had not yet found the right environment.

Shortly before the age of 20, he joined the publishing company "Harms" under the direction of Max Dreyfus, the Maharaja of the New York publishing industry, and was quickly appointed to be their representative in London in 1905. From that point on, Kern began to take off, moving from New York and Broadway to London, where he had connections with the who's who of British theater.

Between these worlds and his additions to the British shows, he found the right partners on the way to becoming the undisputed icon of the American musical comedy, especially towards the end of the 1910s, when the British influence on Broadway weakened. Kern devoted years to additions to translations of German operas and participated in a series of original productions with the Shubert brothers on Broadway. The interpretations of the European shows were responsible for the cultivation of the American transcripts.

Paradoxically, despite his German influences, the patriotic and anti-German spirit of the First World War strengthened Kern's status as an original American composer and a figure of Broadway's independent identity as rooted in American culture. He celebrated a significant achievement with the ballad "They Didn't Believe Me," which premiered at the theater in 1914 and included some of Kern's hallmarks, including rich vertical melodies. The British statesman David Lloyd George, who was later appointed prime minister, declared the song "the most haunting and inspiring melody I have ever heard."[157]

A year earlier, Kern was one of the founders of ASCAP, which was responsible for collecting royalties and served on the Board of Directors at various times. But no less important to him personally, he established what resembled the aristocratic group of Broadway with the British-American Guy Bolton and the British writer P.G. Wodehouse. The musical Oh, Boy! was not only a bestseller but the "moment" when the American musical comedy moved from the Victorian to the modern era.

The year in which America joined the World War, 1917, was particularly busy for Kern with a list of musical comedies in the Princess Theater and other halls. At this point, Rodgers, Porter, and Gershwin discovered him while seeking to understand the commercial and artistic potential of musical comedy. During the

---

157 Ibid., chap. 1, Kindle.

first half of the 1920s, Kern experienced a series of lukewarm and relatively forgotten musicals with the playwright Anne Caldwell, but these did not prevent him acquiring fame, popularity, money, and status among the elite of musical comedy. He was finally at home at 40 years old.

It is not clear how good Kern was as a pianist. At the beginning of his career, he worked as a plugger in the publishing houses, but he certainly was not a virtuoso like Gershwin. Yet, his abilities as a pianist gave him enough ammunition to determine not only the harmonic dimensions, such as attraction to modulations, voice leading, and the circle of fifths, but the central ideas of arrangement he scribbled on notepaper. Various orchestrators, including Frank Saddler and Robert Russell Bennett, developed these ideas in writing for the orchestras.

Like other composers, he clung to the familiar 32 bars used by Tin Pan Alley and its standard lyric structures but managed to pour fresh content into these limited structures with the help of chromatic and multidimensional harmonies, combining march, polka, waltz, and ballads. Kern matured in a generation that had not yet discovered the blues, and even syncopation was relatively "foreign" to him as a composer. His compositions could have come out of Arthur Sullivan's work, but gradually he seemed to have established a language of his own in catchy melodic patterns alongside space for musical transitions and in the form of writing more reminiscent of German chorales than the sound of a burlesque. Kern combined the best of the British comic opera with solid harmonics from Germany along with French rhythms, combined with American elements: the blue notes, blues harmony, seventh chords, and syncopated rhythms.

Paradoxically, as the designer of American musical comedy, Kern was a conservative. The composer who gave jazz one of its most popular standards was slow to assimilate it. In his Hollywood biography, *Till The Clouds Roll By* (1946), which is a romantic and unreliable version of the composer's real character, Kern is portrayed as having suffered a writing crisis due to the death of his mentor and orchestrator Frank Saddler. In fact, in the first half of the 1920s, he experienced some commercial disappointments, and more conspicuously, his admirers – Gershwin, Porter, and Rodgers – who were more in sync with the spirit of the times, threatened to transcend him. He had to adapt to the colorful jazz era, even if he composed a work that was more reminiscent of an opera of minstrelsy. He did it with *Show Boat*, which he created with Oscar Hammerstein II in 1927. This work was not only a breakthrough in the field of musicals but was popular because it was like a hot iron on the great wound of issues of American identity, the entanglement of race, and the meaning of America.

The novel *Show Boat* by Edna Ferber came out a year earlier and dealt with the phenomenon of boats sailing in the rivers to the south between the years

1880 to 1920 to provide entertainment for residents of remote towns. Ferber based the work on primal and tragic fears of racism and the danger of mixing races. According to the novel, Julie La Verne, one of the women on the ship's entertainment team, is a white-black mongrel who is white visually, but of course hides the fact that "black blood" flows in her blood. Her marriage to Steve Baker, a white performer on the boat, is illegal in the south. A conflict between them and the ship's technician who desires Julie reveals this secret after he tells the sheriff. The law authorities force her to leave the area and the boat, and this drama drives the convoluted and penetrating plot in combination with the story of Magnolia Hawks, the daughter of the ship's owners.

Critics and the audience recognized the breakthrough of the musical in real-time marketing as "setting new standards." This musical was exceptional since Kern and his partner based it on an entire novel and the cultural history it reflected. There was something in the format of the musical that softened the southern horror. Still, it eventually managed to express the madness of segregation, hopelessness, social diseases, and all the dark secrets that lay along the dangerous long river, even if the mixing of races here was just a backdrop for a dramatic American family story.

Hammerstein (who defined himself more as a Protestant than a Jew) and Kern (who rarely emphasized his ethnic identity) were possibly attracted to the story in the racist south because of their own origins. Perhaps they felt that the amusement ship was unintentionally an illustration of the circumstance of Jews of German descent who succeeded in the entertainment industry with all its inherent dangers. Maybe the fear of mixing black and white races could have been interpreted as a fear of a Jewish-Christian mix, which both of them had experienced. Perhaps Magnolia, one of the main characters in the plot, who is married to the charming and incompetent gambler Gaylord Ravenal, reminded them in part of the danger of integration that pervaded ethnic mythology. The amphitheater was a restricted and confined world in contact with the surrounding environment, not unlike the Jewish ghetto. After all, in parallel to the ghetto, only the on the "boat" Magnolia felt safe. Or maybe it was just a good story.

However, *Show Boat* came a long way from the musical comedies produced a decade earlier by the Bolton-Wodehouse foundation that catered for Anglo-American tastes, saturated with farce and burlesque with the grotesque imitations of the American and British upper classes.

The book itself was in line with the realism of Charles Dickens and Emile Zola. The opera heritage was no stranger to interpretations of the novels, and there were precedents. In fact, Kern and Hammerstein's handling resembled an operatic treatment, even if it was still a very serious and pioneering musical with a combination of melodrama, music, blues, dance, burlesque, and minstrelsy.

It is doubtful whether Kern knew the roots of the blues that had formed in the Delta-Mississippi plantations, so his approach to different aspects of black music was based on second-hand materials and mainly on the legacy of minstrelsy, which is present with the use of the banjo and the major pentatonic scale. It was undoubtedly a re-creation of the sound of antebellum America. Kern himself said that the inspiration for "Ol' Man River," one of the essential songs in the musical, came after he was thrilled by the appearance of the African-American singer Paul Robeson. Perhaps this was in advance of Gershwin's anthropological journey in search of the black music of South Carolina as he worked on the composition of the jazz opera Porgy and Bess.

Musicologist Stephen Banfield believed that the instrumental overture, beginning with a minor triad chord, was composed by a Faustian pact of orchestration that combined a southern flavored banjo with trumpets, that sound like Morse code, which joins elements reminiscent of the British composer Edward Elgar.[158] The major pentatonic scale is evident both at the overture and throughout the musical. Kern used it as a motif that moves between a variety of scenes and characters, back and forth. Banfield also finds a similarity between Bach's "May Safely Graze" and the dynamics of "Ol' Man River" and a similarity between the harmonious moves of this song and Dvořák's compositions. The opera Carmen, with its motif of fate, as well as the burlesque noise, was reminiscent of the sacrament motif in the opera Tosca by Giacomo Puccini. Kern uses various musical instruments and musical motifs for different characters and scenes, such as secondary dominants to suspensions of tension, old musical styles (e. g., waltz) to counterpoint themes as a leitmotif that emphasizes locations and time in history.

However, an essential theme is the black heritage that passes from generation to generation. The blues song "Can't Help Lovin' Dat Man" stands at the center of the musical and is performed by several characters at different times, linking the past, present, and future as a song that exists in the collective American unconscious. And this is not a well-known religious anthem, but a "secret legacy" – it is like a more in-depth, unique acquaintance, the idea of a liberal America on the cruise ship at its best. The song, with its apparent blues style, symbolized the American direction music would go in the 1930s.

In the novel itself Edna Ferber mentioned "river songs," but Kern, with the encouragement of Hammerstein, based the idea of the river and fate on his an-

---

[158] Ibid., chap. 3, Kindle.

them, "Ol' Man River," blending the apparent influences of minstrelsy, various religious hymns alongside Dvořák into one of his greatest songs. The African-American singer Paul Robeson (who admitted he felt an affinity to the Jewish race) gave the song a religious and universal feeling.[159] It is reasonable to assume that Kern developed the song in continuous harmonious negotiation with his orchestrator Robert Bennett, and there are gaps between Kern's sketch and the final version.[160] In any case, it is customary to see the song's performance as a Greek choir that responds to dramatic events, even if this choir belongs to one singer.

In 1994, the singer Aretha Franklin appeared before President Bill Clinton and his wife, Hillary, and performed this song in the style of a beautiful gospel after dedicating it to all those fathers and mothers who had to work courageously in cotton fields, from sunrise to sunset, including her grandmother's family. She did not mention the writers, as if it were an original African-American song.

The end of *Show Boat* is less impressive, but the reviews were fantastic and defined this musical as a milestone in the history of musical comedy. *Show Boat* was what *Sgt. Pepper's Lonely Hearts Club Band* was to rock music, a model. Like other masterpieces at different times, the whole was more significant than the pieces. The musical contained features that Kern developed and charmed with in "All the Things You Are" from his later musical *Very Warm for May* (1939), which symbolized the return of the composer from Hollywood to Broadway. Kern's song, paradoxically, was a masterpiece of movement between tonal centers, seventh chords, modulations, and a melody that is efficient enough to become one of the most pervasive standards in the history of jazz.

George Gershwin: It ain't necessarily so

Few composers in the history of music, not just the American tradition, have made phenomenal tracks like those of George Gershwin. His journey was so spectacular and tragic that he remained controversial. Not many have won so much popularity in both popular music and concert music. In many respects, we ought to understand Gershwin's work while realizing that these two sides were, in fact, one integral whole of the history of American music.

---

159 Jeffrey Melnick, *A Right to Sing the Blues: African Americans, Jews and American Popular Song* (Cambridge: Massachusetts: Harvard University Press, 1999), 181.
160 Stephen Banfield, *Jerome Kern*, 1st ed. (New Haven: Yale University Press, 2006), chap. 3, Kindle.

Gershwin had a unique talent, but he was also lucky. He grew up in an age when popular American song became a mass consumer product. A new understanding of the potential of popular songs required an efficient and thriving music industry into which this young phenomenon entered. Of all the Jewish composers, he was among those who were the most proud of their ethnic identity and ability to grasp multiculturalism as a source of power. It can be seen as a success story of an unusually gifted and determined Jewish immigrant son in a highly developed Jewish network.

Gershwin's parents came from St. Petersburg, Russia. His grandfather, Jacob Gershowitz, was the son of a rabbi, but he served in the army and won a privilege within the Czar's realm: He was permitted to live where he wished. His son, Morris, was apparently influenced by his father's integration skills. He later fell in love with Rosa Bruskin, the daughter of an affluent furrier from St. Petersburg, and before they both married, they immigrated to New York at different times.[161]

Lost, without knowledge of English and in search of his relatives, Morris changed his name to Gershwin (initially with the spelling Gershvin) and settled in the Bowery. The vibrant Jewish community in New York was able to soften his hard landing. Like many Jewish immigrants, Maurice became a shoemaker in a women's shoe factory, quickly becoming a junior manager. In 1895 he found Rosa and they married. A year later Ira was born, followed in 1898 by Jacob Gershwin. The family name was distorted to Gershwine, and Jacob was changed to George. The couple had two more children.

At home, they did not speak Yiddish or Russian, so the children grew up with English as their mother tongue, as if preparing them for the New World. During the Gershwin brothers' childhood the economic situation became more challenging. Morris moved from one business to another and found it hard to persevere. Luckily, he and his wife Rosa were friendly, communal, saturated with visits from neighbors and friends from the Yiddish theater community. They were on the verge of a permanent crisis of livelihood, but they lived with a sense of bourgeois class, in contrast to the way Gershwin was presented in the Hollywood biography. Morris was full of humor and was a free spirit in everyday life, while Rosa was incredibly tough and realistic. Ira, on the other hand, lived in a world of imagination. He liked to read, from Sherlock Holmes to Oscar Wilde. He was a collector of newspaper articles and information, an amateur painter and graphic artist, a vaudeville fan, a theater, and a filmmaker.

---

161 Ean Wood, *George Gershwin: His Life and Music* (New York: Sanctuary Publishing, 1999); Howard Pollack, *George Gershwin: His Life and Work* (Los Angeles: University of California Press, 2007).

George was different; a street kid. Restless, aggressive, competitive, and athletic, he grew up in a sometimes violent environment of ethnic street gangs. The music was going to refine him.

The Gershwin brothers grew up during a musical renaissance of songs and a new world of popular music, which got a boost in the press (writing competitions) and of course through Tin Pan Alley and the publishing industry that was established between 28th Street and Broadway and Sixth Street. The Gershwin family was not particularly musical, but despite the economic shortage, they adopted bourgeois aspects: they were among the first in their neighborhood to have a Victrola – then an audio device with social prestige. And despite the gap between the machismo that characterized street life and music, Gershwin was quickly conquered by the new magic of music.

George's first encounter with music took place at age six on 125th Street in Harlem, while listening to "Melody in F" by the pianist and Russian-Jewish composer Anton Rubinstein. His attraction to music prompted him to establish musical friendships and his first acquaintance with the piano until, finally, the family purchased one.

Although Ira Gershwin was the natural candidate for music studies, 12-year-old George was the one who took the opportunity. The biographies describe Gershwin as a natural, innate talent, who once he touched the piano managed to play the hits of the era. Gershwin admitted that the piano transformed him from a bad boy to a good child, that it made him feel more serious. Within six months, he was a different person.[162]

His mother had set him out to be an accountant and sent him to the School of Commerce, but Gershwin had progressed beautifully as a pianist in his lessons with Miss Green. To the fervor created by classical music he added the style of ragtime. Irving Berlin's poems were undoubtedly the model. "The Franz Schubert of America," Gershwin later called him. After a summer break in Catskill, he decided to become a composer.

He began studying with Charles Hambitzer, a composer and theoretician who passed Gershwin through a rigorous training regime. Hambitzer revealed to him the great composers, from Bach to Ravel. Three years before the breakthrough of jazz, when the concept was still quite esoteric, in a letter to his sister from 1914, Hambitzer said that he was teaching a "genius" that want to pursue jazz, even if, he says, he prefers to teach him classic modernist elements.

---

[162] David Schiff, *Gershwin: Rhapsody in Blue* (Cambridge: Cambridge University Press, 1997), 194.

Jerome Keren's music was George's next discovery. He made a gesture by writing songs that were in imitation.[163] Gershwin loved the changing of the tonal centers and the triplet sequences of the rising star in the field of musical comedy.

At this stage, Ben Bloom, a Jewish friend, and singer directed Gershwin to serve as a pianist demonstrating songs in the company of Jerome Remick, one of the publishing houses in Tin Pan Alley, while his mother – despite insisting on his lack of suitability for commerce – pushed him towards the fur business. However, Gershwin left his studies to go straight into the world of entertainment, and the ragtime hits of Scott Joplin and Eubie Blake. These African-American pianists and composers wrote music influenced by African-American dance. While one hand often played a "straight" rhythm on the strong pulse, the other hand emphasized the syncopation and weaker pulses. The music was connected to dances that took their names from the animal world, and they were like a painful scratch to the restrained, righteous Victorian world.

Nevertheless, Jewish music tradition had its impact. Although at this stage Gershwin didn't exhibit his Jewishness, he carried with him memories and a conscious and hidden love of the Yiddish music he had heard during his childhood. Jewish traditional melodies had an impact on modern music, Gershwin explained in 1925, adding that Jewish music has the quality of a cry that gives it universal appeal.[164] In another interview, he linked Jewish oppression throughout the generations to the talent of writing music, admitted that his music had Jewish and American feelings, and although Gershwin's home was not a Jewish religious folklore, George assimilated at least some of the Eastern European sounds from his frequent visits to the Lower East Side and his visits to the Yiddish theater.[165]

In the Yiddish theater, many of the elements that appeared in the musicals could be found, such as satire, humor, unique metaphors, and heartbreaking tragedies. The Yiddish theater developed in America throughout the second half of the nineteenth century and began with the work of Abraham Goldfaden, who was a kind of Stephen Foster of the theater, through Joseph Rumshinsky and ending with Sholom Secunda. Some claimed that the spirit of Yiddish lullabies influenced almost everything Gershwin wrote. Scholars and biographers liked to find Jewish sources for his songs, even if the characteristics most identified with

---

163 Ibid., 293.
164 Howard Pollack, *George Gershwin: His Life and Work* (Los Angeles: University of California Press, 2007), 42.
165 Ibid.

East European Jewish music – church modes with a minor affinity, and Jewish modes – did not characterize his works and were not identified with them.

Parallel to the Yiddish theater, Gershwin moved in the social circles of publishing companies. These included playing in cafes in the evenings and recording piano pieces for audio systems of the era while visiting classical music concerts. His teacher, Hambitzer, introduced a new teacher of composition, the Hungarian immigrant Edward Kilenyi. He also sought out musicians and other influential sources: he became acquainted with the original ragtime pianist Les Copeland, and in early 1915 witnessed the first creative sparks from Afro-Americans such as Willie "The Lyon" Smith, Luckey Roberts and James P. Johnson, who would capture the "freedom" of the 1920s with the Charleston. The Stride piano style was a continuation of ragtime, only freer, harder to play, and more complex. Even before the Original Dixieland Jass Band broke out with the first jazz recording in 1917, Gershwin listened to the music of James Reese Europe – an African-American pianist from Alabama, a classicist by training who found his vocation in the fashionable world of proto-jazz. At the beginning of the second decade of the twentieth century, he was already working with his black band at the Manhattan Casino, combining classical, ragtime, mixed with the sounds of the blue note, but with less emphasis on New Orleans improvisation.

Gershwin loved W.C. Handy, the African-American composer of "Saint Louis Blues." He even dedicated his breakthrough in the classical world, "Rhapsody in Blue," to him as a career gesture. At the time he also knew the Jewish lyricist Irving Caesar, who would write his first big hit, "Swanee," as well as Fred and Adele Astaire, the dancers in the vaudeville halls, who began their careers as child protégés and were about to have their breakout in Broadway.

Although he worked as a pianist demonstrating songs for the Remick publishing house, the company did not hasten to sign him as a composer. So he released his first song with the help of Jewish singer Sophie Tucker along with Harry Von Tilzer. George's track was already clear: influenced by the musical comedies of Kern and the ambition of Berlin – who has just devoted a complete musical comedy – "Watch Your Step" (1914) – to ragtime music, he decided to position himself as a composer in the field of the comic theater. He strengthened his connections with his brother Ira, won the role of a pianist in the Ziegfeld Follies, and joined up with the African-American musical director Will Wodery. The latter was to give him his first serious concert music opportunity.

That he used his social network has been consistently established: the singer Al Jolson had heard of the music Gershwin wrote for *La La-Lucille!* (1919) and became the sponsor who led him to the masses with "Swanee." It was the product of three American Jews: Gershwin, Irving Caesar, and Jolson. This huge hit, according to Howard Pollack, based on a modal aroma untypical of George, was written in the Gershwin home, while parents and family members were busy playing poker. Despite a harmony that might sound Eastern European, as in the case of Irving Berlin, this success required the most American of codes: the excellent minstrel star, Al Jolson, who would sing a fresh adaptive adaptation using the expression "Swanee" from the song "Swanee River" by Stephen Foster. Gershwin's father, Maurice, remembered that when he had finished writing, he accompanied them with a comb and paper. Above all, the piano – powerful and flamboyant – stood out as the instrument that outlined the path of the young phenomenon. It did not take long for Jolson to conquer the song. The recording became a big hit, as were the sheet notes. Gershwin scored an important achievement.

He did not slow down with the success of "Swanee." He enrolled in Columbia University's Summer Semester for two courses in harmony and orchestration, even though Gershwin would always stand out as a composer and a songwriter rather than as an orchestrator and "painter" of sounds like Ravel or Debussy.[166] At the same time, the attraction to the world of African-American rhythms only increased and became a kind of obsession. His new song, "I'll Build a Stairway to Paradise," drew attention, and not only jazz musicians discovered it, but also classical musicians such as Oscar Levant, who became a close friend.[167]

Gershwin's career had three phases: the early period, culminating with the success of "Rhapsody in Blue" in 1924. The second, middle period, in which he based his romantic, post-romantic, and jazz influences, includes his most famous songs, such as the beautiful "Someone to Watch Over Me" from the musical comedy *Oh, Kay!* (1926) and his classical compositions such as "Concerto in F" (1925) and "An American in Paris" (1928). The third period started at the beginning of the 1930s and continued until his death in 1937, during which he achieved his greatest artistic achievements. The period begins with "I Got Rhythm," which became one of the most influential songs in the history of jazz, culminating in challenging theatrical compositions in the epic jazz opera *Porgy and Bess* (1935), which dealt with the African-American world with a brave attempt to present another vital aspect of the soul of America.

The composition "Rhapsody in Blue" was not a total surprise. Gershwin had already experimented with classical composition, and even tried to write an

---

166 Robert Wyatt and John Andrew Johnson, eds., *The George Gershwin Reader (Readers on American Musicians)*, 1st ed. (Oxford: Oxford University Press, 2007), 10.
167 Ibid., 8.

opera with the African-American Will Wodery, which music scholar David Schiff describes as a "disaster."[168]

The piece "Rhapsody in Blue" was written at a time when classical music was at a crossroads. After decades of tonal development and the positioning of hierarchical rules, composers had begun to go more and more in directions that blurred the tonal center, while giving an ambiguous approach to harmony and multidimensionality: from Chopin's tonal elucidation through Debussy's 12-tone and impressionism, Wagner's multi-layered chromaticism and of course Gustav Mahler' work. But in the first decade of the twentieth century, the break was even deeper: on the one hand there were composers such as Igor Stravinsky, who turned composition into an eclectic performance to the point of a circus. Stravinsky used the entire arsenal, including polytonality and superimposed polychords, yet these were still ultimately subject to a particular tonal center. On the other hand, there was Schoenberg and his students from the second Viennese school, who strove for atonality. The American Charles Ives also presented in "The Unanswered Question" one of the most impressive works of the early twentieth century, with a disharmonic trumpet that seems to be questioning the future of music with its polytonality spectrum.[169]

Against these dramatic changes, "Rhapsody in Blue" was modest in its demands, but in some respects no less revolutionary – if not to the classical world, then to popular American music. After all, it was a controversial classical piece that had established African-American ingredients in American pop music.

"Rhapsody in Blue" was commissioned by Paul Whiteman, a successful conductor and head of one of the most famous orchestras in the United States. Whiteman sought it from Gershwin for a special concert that would concentrate on jazz as original American music. "Rhapsody in Blue" has one of Gershwin's great introductions, and not only because of the clarinet that demands the attention of the listener in an unforgettable glissando, but in its chromatic harmonies, as well as in the dazzling blue note, which embodies Gershwin's entire vision of American modernity as exemplified by this work.

There is something unresolved about "Rhapsody in Blue." On the one hand it is an exciting drama with beautiful melodies in all its sections; on the other hand, Ferde Grofé, one of Whiteman's employees, wrote a somewhat vulgar orchestration. Gershwin was still inexperienced in this work and needed an orchestrator. David Schiff points to the contrast between the orchestra's unchang-

---

[168] David Schiff, *Gershwin: Rhapsody in Blue* (Cambridge: Cambridge University Press, 1997), 144.

[169] Leonard Bernstein, *The Unanswered Question: Six Talks at Harvard* (Cambridge: Harvard University Press, 1976).

ing atmospheres versus the dynamic richness of the piano. He also points out the difference between the foxtrot and the romantic dynamics of the concert world. Schiff further emphasizes that the unconventional movement between the tonal centers was a reflection of Gershwin's abilities with modulations from his days as a song plugger. Gershwin used harmony influences from Franz Liszt and the Romantic era but ignored the form. Musical modulations were evident in Romantic classical music as well as in Tin Pan Alley music.[170]

"Rhapsody in Blue" was written in 1924, even before New York got to know Louis Armstrong's swing. The most celebrated jazz artists had not yet left their mark on New York, which was not the center of jazz, and far from New Orleans, Chicago, and Kansas. But "Rhapsody in Blue" is saturated with jazz. Composer and critic Virgil Thomson defined jazz as a combination of foxtrot-four-on-four rhythms and syncopated melodies along with this rhythm, while composer Aaron Copland emphasized the contribution of polyrhythms. Gershwin's Rhapsody glows with the use of blue notes, modulations, glissando, and combinations of 4/2 and 4/4 rhythms.[171]

This is not surprising given the influence of Handy, who was the recipient of a warm dedication on score of "Rhapsody." After all, Gershwin's youth was accompanied by coon songs written by Afro-Americans. But the influence of the delta-Mississippi blues seems to have been gentler, perhaps only indirectly through Handy's works.

Gershwin fully expressed his liberal manifesto in the *New York World Sunday Magazine*, on May 4, 1930:

> The idea for Rhapsody of Blue, for example, came to me quite suddenly. The vivid panorama of America life swept through my mind – its feverishness, its vulgarity, its welter of love, marriage, and divorce, and its basic solidarity in the character of the people. All the emotional reactions excited by contemplating the American scene, with all its mixture of races.[172]

Despite Gershwin's modern American vision, Leonard Bernstein was also ambiguous in relation to the achievement. He believed it "breathed" Tchaikovsky's tricks, some of Debussy's influences, with flashes of Liszt's piano. He also believed that it was American music, yet had some problems with its development,

---

170 David Schiff, *Gershwin: Rhapsody in Blue* (Cambridge: Cambridge University Press, 1997), 27.
171 Ibid., 28.
172 George Gershwin, "Making Music," in *The George Gershwin Reader (Readers on American Musicians)*, edited by Robert Wyatt and John Andrew Johnson, 1st ed. (Oxford: Oxford University Press, 2007), 134.

even though the melodies were fantastic. But melodies are not the same as compositions and Bernstein was not totally satisfied.[173]

The Rhapsody had a dizzying pace, and it became a crucial part of Gershwin's compositions. Decades after his work became famous, the world listens to Gershwin in a very different way than he intended. Years of swing and big band adaptations of many of his proto-swinging jazz songs stunned the greatness of playing his phenomenal piano. His piano-playing influenced the composition and the relationship between melody and harmony in his repertoire. The song "Fascinating Rhythm," for example, not only has uneven bars but a horizontal and minimal theme, which is completed by the rhythmic dynamics. In this sense, Gershwin challenged Berlin and Kern, and perhaps preceded Burt Bacharach, or what songwriters like John Lennon would do in the later Beatles' songs, even if Gershwin's other songs resembled Paul McCartney's future vertical melodies.

In the second half of the 1920s, Gershwin continued to expand the creative spectrum: "Concerto in F" (1925) and "An American in Paris" (1928) established his abilities as a composer combining European music and jazz. In a series of children's concerts in the late 1950s, Bernstein began with a demonstration of American music with a reconstruction of Gershwin's work in Paris and his expression of longing for home in America through the blues, even if he still had reservations about his compositional abilities and the mechanism that he felt borrowed too much from Strauss and Ravel.

Biographers described Gershwin's meetings with Ravel, Stravinsky, Schoenberg, and other prominent composers as Gershwin's desire to learn from the masters. Although these mythic meetings have witnesses, the European masters never confirmed them. They say that Gershwin's financial success convinced the Europeans that he really had something to teach them. But even if we assume this gentle curiosity is a rumor, the effect was mutual. Maurice Ravel was probably impressed by the American composer.

While Gershwin was perhaps controversial in the world of classical music, his influence on songwriting and the development of jazz and theatrical composition is indisputable. Jazz itself has come a long way since its breakthrough in 1917. In the mid-1920s, Louis Armstrong introduced the world to the sense of swing and a bit later, to scat singing. Fletcher Henderson began by designing the jazz orchestration that would be the basis for swing during the 1930s, and Duke Ellington found a fresh and elegant harmony in his jungle music, obses-

---

[173] Leonard Bernstein, *The Unanswered Question: Six Talks at Harvard* (Cambridge: Harvard University Press, 1976), 55–56.

sively using rhythm, seventh chords, polytonality, and a more closed voicing and dissonances that reflected the American way of life. Gershwin listened to everyone and found great beauty in Ellington's music.

"I Got Rhythm," including the improvisational variations that were published, were Gershwin's hallmark. This simple song was released in 1930, and became the basis from which jazz would develop in the next two decades. Ira Gershwin conducted several experiments until he found a direction for the words – and this is not the first time he used the phrase "rhythm." The Gershwin brothers had already included the term in their "fascinating rhythm" from the mid-1920s, which included irregular four- to three-five-bars as part of its aggressive use of extinct syncopation. But their next achievement caused an unexpected musical explosion.

The song "I Got Rhythm" was a success as part of the musical comedy *Girl Crazy*, but not necessarily as sheet music, since it requires skill both as a performer and as a singer. The popularity began with recordings of the song by jazz artists: Fred Rich and Paul Small recorded their version six days after the premiere of the musical comedy. Soon "I Got Rhythm" became a standard in structure, style, rhythm and atmosphere, while the melody was the basis, relatively marginal, for improvisation and interpretation. The harmonic structure was to be named Rhythm Changes. Jazz artists continued to reuse the harmonic degrees (I-VI7-ii7-V7) with the second-minor-fifth-seventh (ii7-V7) being a movement and a cadence that was the basis for jazz harmony. The jazz artists also liked the bridge, which is based on secondary and extended dominance. These, along with his built-in syncopation, make "I Got Rhythm" a base from which others will build the modern jazz world.

The singer Ethel Merman, in the original musical comedy, found a way to excite the audience, and others did what Gershwin himself did in the variations he recorded for the song. This paved the way for many interpretations of African-American jazz artists. Pianist Art Tatum, an eclectic virtuoso, added the circle of fifths to this work, while only hinting at the original melody. Sidney Bechet transferred it to "Shag" (1932). Fletcher Henderson used it in "Yeah Man" (1933) and Chick Webb in "Stomp it Off" (1934), Benny Goodman in "Do Not Be That Way" (1938) and Duke Ellington in "Cotton Tail." Almost every one of the popular swing bands of the time performed a version of Gershwin's song, as did the African-American bebop artists who challenged the swing era. Drummer Max

Roach recalls that publishers never sued the bebop players since there were no copyrights on harmony and chord progression.[174]

The most prominent artist in these rewritings was Charlie Parker. He went back and forth to Gershwin's Rhythm Changes and recorded many pieces based on these chords while sometimes using a strong riff that becomes the base of the song while the other part becomes free to improvise, as in the "Steeplechase" and "Moose the Mooche" sections. The chord progression became significant in the design of bebop. Thelonious Monk, Sonny Rollins, Bud Powell, and Miles Davis continued to develop jazz pieces based on Gershwin's Rhythm Changes. Hundreds of recordings of the song came out after the end of World War Two until the end of the 1960s.

Gershwin's massive influence on jazz and black music in particular, and on American culture in general, was reflected in his most significant achievement: the jazz opera, which Gershwin insisted on calling the folk opera, *Porgy and Bess* (1935). It was more than a gesture to the black cultural world, it was an artistic breakthrough in every sense: a combination of present and past, America, Africa and Europe; and above all in a psychological discovery, it constituted Gershwin's crushing encounter with the racist demon that was shaping America's confrontation with its shadow: the racial disease, and a prelude to the possibility of healing this society.

The unique power of black music should speak for itself, Gershwin observed in 1925:

> I think it [jazz opera] should be a Negro opera [...]. Negro, because it is not incongruous for a Negro to live jazz. It would not be absurd on the stage. The mood could change from ecstasy to lyricism plausibly, because the Negro has so much of both in his nature.[175]

The satirist and playwright John Howard Lawson influenced popular music with *Processional: A Jazz Symphony of American Life* (1925), but Gershwin's ambition was much greater. He sought the appropriate libretto influenced by the leaders of modernist ideology, such as critics like Carl Van Vechten. Looking for a suitable libretto, he wrote:

---

[174] Robert Wyatt and John Andrew Johnson, eds. *The George Gershwin Reader (Readers on American Musicians)*, 1st ed. (Oxford: Oxford University Press, 2007), 167.
[175] Howard Pollack, *George Gershwin: His Life and Work* (Los Angeles: University of California Press, 2007), 567.

I shall write it for niggers[!]. Blacks sing beautifully. They are always singing, they have it in their blood. They have jazz in their blood too, and I have no doubt that they will be able to do full justice to a jazz opera.[176]

The idea for this opera appeared in the mid-1920s, at the same time that Jerome Kern and Oscar Hammerstein embarked on a journey with *Show Boat*, the pioneering musical that preceded his preoccupation with southern racism. After one rehearsal for the musical *Oh, Kay!* (1926) Gershwin sank into a reading of the promising Southern writer, DuBose Heyward, author of *Porgy* published a year earlier. He loved the tension and humor and the world he had before him, and by morning he had written to Heyward about his desire to turn the book into an opera.

Heyward, who was of WASP and French-Huguenot origin, was known as one of the most promising voices in the Southern literary renaissance of Charleston, South Carolina. The book describes the life of the African-American community, centered on the beggar Porgy. Heyward based it on a real figure from the city (named Goat Sammy), who was prominent in Heyward's use of folk songs and hymns and the Gullah language. It was too good a source for Gershwin to pass.

In the early 1920s, Gershwin composed the failed black culture project "Blue Monday," regarding Harlem, so that despite Gershwin and Heyward's enthusiasm for the project, it took them nine years to get their premiere in Boston in September 1935. Before Gershwin began his composition, Dorothy, Dubose's wife, turned the book into a successful play on Broadway, but Gershwin declared his desire for free time to compose – probably in order not to repeat his previous failure in serious theatrical composition. He wrote to Heyward about his desire to collect thematic material before the composition began.

Gershwin's desire to turn S. Ansky's *The Dybbuk* into an opera caused another delay. Since he did not obtain the rights, he returned to his original plan. Another barrier on the way was Gershwin's successful career in the field of musical comedy that took up most of his time. In the early 1930s, he entered, with the help of various writers, into a new phase that contained a musical comedy of satirical proportions. From *Strike Up the Band* (1930), via *Of Thee I Sing* (1931) and *Let 'Em Eat Cake* (1933), satires that were popular at the time and whose current value is not clear, but for our purposes they consumed Gershwin's time from writing the opera until 1933. However, the delay became an advantage due to the impressive knowledge he accumulated during this period. Gershwin combined his experience of writing a concert in the world of musicals and composing hits into a rare moment. He was ready to set out on his way from his perform-

---

176 Ibid, 568.

ances to musical comedies, satirical comedies, and opera. Gershwin devoted almost a year to composition and about nine months to its orchestration.

The exchange of letters between Gershwin and Heyward follows their desire to avoid the blackface minstrelsy syndrome and employ only African-American singers, a standard already laid out in the play, which also shifted the plot from the end of the nineteenth century to the twentieth. They gave up nominating the Jewish star Al Jolson, who in the past had stimulated Gershwin's career, but was now perceived as not authentic or artistic enough for the opera, even though Jolson's recruitment would have guaranteed its funding. It was an essential step in giving authenticity to the opera, with excellent coordination between Heyward and Ira Gershwin, who joined to reinforce the team responsible for songwriting.

Gershwin also spent several days with Heyward in Charleston in late 1933 and early 1934, and Heyward stayed in New York for several weeks in the spring of 1934. The *Charleston News and Courier* documented Gershwin's first visit on November 25, 1933, and wrote: "Mr. Gershwin is also anxious to listen in on some of the fish and vegetable hucksters," while perhaps unconsciously emphasizing the anthropologist overtones of Gershwin's trip. At the same time, the newspaper quoted Gershwin on his devotion to Jazz: "There can be no question but that jazz is the first real American music. When you look into any other kind you find the influence of some other country, but not so in jazz [...] I have tried, myself, to do more than a song [...] I've tried to grasp the real spirit of our people."[177]

There were disagreements about the libretto, which Heyward felt ought to be the center of attention, and that Gershwin, who was probably influenced by the work of Schoenberg and Berg, preferred to give musicality to the characters of all races.

In preparation for his anthropological visit to Charleston, Gershwin wrote to Heyward that he would like to see the city and listen to the local music. During his visit, he was particularly impressed by the markets that may have reminded him of New York City's Jewish Lower East Side and the religious anthems in the churches. After sensing that he had not absorbed enough inspiration, he returned with his close friends to Polly Island, a few miles from Charleston, where he even found a Jewish delicatessen shop.

---

[177] The Charleston News and Courier, "George Gershwin Arrives to Plan Opera on Porgy," in *The George Gershwin Reader (Readers on American Musicians)*, edited by Robert Wyatt and John Andrew Johnson, 1st ed. (Oxford: Oxford University Press, 2007), 210.

Gershwin, who brought a piano to the spacious house he rented near the sea, deepened his familiarity with local folk culture while spontaneously joining the vocal groups and musical street bands. On his way back to New York, in Hendersonville, he and Heyward listened to a black vocal ensemble performing some contrapuntal melodies of perhaps 12 voices, which would inspire a variety of opera tracks, especially in the "Gone Gone Gone" requiem.

Gershwin finished composing in the winter of 1935 and began to work on the orchestration while claiming that there were many more notes to write. The result was profound. He charged the encounter between the soul of the composer and the fabric of the characters and the scenes. It has various leitmotifs, while scene after scene, sometimes interwoven with layers of polyphonic and polyrhythmic textures, bring the characters to completion. This begins with the fugue that opens the opera, through the Yiddish-black combination of the lullaby "Summertime" with its tonal and multidimensional harmony, and near quotations from his previous concert compositions ("Cuban Overture," which was a successful promotion for the opera). The opera contained echoes from Debussy, Puccini, Kern, Stravinsky, and Berg, along with African-American folk-jazz (from W.C. Handy to Cab Calloway and Duke Ellington), and often religious anthems. Even unskilled listeners might swear that "It Take a Long Pull to Get There" is reminiscent of the melody of Jewish liturgical music.

Porgy and Bess is full of hits. These focus the episodes in a community saturated with fraternity, violence, grief, prejudice, faith – but without racism, in an entirely original musical texture. The composer defended his popularity by suggesting that almost all of Verdi's operas include hits and that "Carmen" is practically a collection of singles.[178]

The opera projects Jungian archetypes: the Trickster character of Sportin' Life, played with the help of blue note, the blues scale and biblical images in "It Aint Necessarily So," through the dark shadow of the assassin Crown, and above all, Porgy, who suffers for the entire community with an uncompromising love for Bess, which represents the archetype of the unattainable Anima. These are tantamount to releasing involuntary dynamic forces, which turn the listener into a victim. The opera in Jungian terms is numinous as if it were communicating with the listener through transcendent forces in our collective unconscious. It was a musical prayer founded by a Jewish composer in a black dream.[179]

---

178 Robert Wyatt and John Andrew Johnson, eds. *The George Gershwin Reader (Readers on American Musicians)*, 1st ed. (Oxford: Oxford University Press, 2007), 219–220.

179 Carl Gustav Jung, *The Archetypes and The Collective Unconscious (Collected Works of C.G. Jung)*, Vol. 9, Part 1, 2nd ed. (New Jersey: Princeton University Press, 1968).

Gershwin was clear about his popular intentions regarding the operas, as he wrote to the *New York Times* in October 20, 1935:

> The reason I did not submit this work to the unusual sponsors of opera in America was that I hoped to have developed something in American music that would appeal to the many rather to the allured few.[180]

In his *New York Times'* essay, Gershwin continued and explained his artistic driving force regarding the fusion of humor and tragedy, as well as the urge to create not just a "regular" opera but a folk-opera (since "its people would sing folk songs"). He insisted that "the Negroes, as a race, have all these qualities inherent in them," and that "they are Ideal for my purpose."[181] And finally, he balanced his tendencies toward the popular by claiming: "I chose the form I have used for *Porgy and Bess* because I believe that music lives only when it is in serious form."[182] Again, this elitist-humanist approach is very evident in many if his writing and interviews.

The achievement was both impressive and controversial, but Leonard Bernstein could not remain indifferent while claiming that with the appearance of Porgy, you suddenly realize that Gershwin was a great stage composer rather than just a symphonic writer.

The pianist Oscar Levant, who was a close friend of Gershwin, said that the composer listened a lot during the writing process to Wagner's "Die Meistersinger von Nürnberg." Others pointed to the battle fugue as relying on the German composer, and the Tristan chord as the basis for "Summertime." Even if we think we know what Wagner would have thought about the Jewish opera, the unpleasant surprise came from African-American voices. The opera moved the black singers to tears, but there were other, very critical voices. It is not surprising that during the 1960s, black radicals like Harold Cruse disliked the stereotypes dripping from the opera, but even in real-time, composer Duke Ellington declared that this was not authentic black music. It's time to remove the black soot over Gershwin, the famous composer suggested.

---

[180] Gershwin, George, "Rhapsody in a Catfish Row: Mr. Gershwin Tells the Origin and Scheme for His Music in That New Folk Opera Called Porgy and Bess," in *The George Gershwin Reader (Readers on American Musicians)*, edited by Robert Wyatt and John Andrew Johnson, 1st ed. (Oxford: Oxford University Press, 2007), 218.
[181] Ibid.
[182] Ibid., 219.

In 1959 Bernstein believed that America was musically located where Germany was in the seventeenth century. It was immersed in the musical comedy like Germany was fifty years before Mozart. Bernstein believed that this was a period that America must pass through before it can reach a true American style in concert music. But Bernstein's prophecy seems to have materialized only partially. In my opinion, the most important musical event took place in the field of composition for Hollywood films. Jazz became the elitist high culture music that represented America. While the musicals, like rock music afterward, became symbols of capitalism, cultural imperialism, and the American dream. Kern and Gershwin played a decisive role in this development. Kern had a decisive influence not only on Richard Rodgers and the generations of musical composers, but on excellent pop composers like Burt Bacharach and almost all the aesthetics employed by Walt Disney, Pixar, and the like.

Gershwin defined the direction in which American popular music and classical music would both go. His black and European combinations influenced not only high composition but the routes taken by great songwriters like Harold Arlen. His works have regularly been reinterpreted by the best jazz artists, ranging from Louis Armstrong and Ella Fitzgerald to Miles Davis, who dedicated an album to Porgy and Bass in the late 1950s. Jewish jazz musicians such as Benny Goodman and Artie Shaw continued his legacy and openness to blacks. Furthermore, and no less critical, Gershwin's achievements were the point at which the Jewish composers of rock and the British duo of Lennon and McCartney continued their rewarding ride on the Blue Note.

Chapter 5: It Don't Mean a Thing If you Ain't Got That Swing – Duke Ellington and Irving Mills' Fantasy

"She knew how to live with passion and style. She knew Duke Ellington," says Irving Rosenfeld (Christian Bale) about Sydney Prosser (Amy Adams) in the movie *American Hustle* (2013). In one of the most beautiful scenes in his film, Irving and Sydney, the con-couple, listen to "Jeep's Blues," a recording by Duke Ellington from the 1950s; and Irving enthusiastically, proudly, and exultingly, declares: "Who opens a song like that?" While magnetized to the mesmerizing sound. "It's magic," Sydney agrees as she looks at the cover of the record. The spirit of reinvention of themselves as crooks with a supreme grace is reinforced by their shared love for the spirit of Duke Ellington's reinvention during his slump in the first half of the 1950s.

The story of Ellington as one of the twentieth-century's jazz giants is overall well known, but the Jewish angle in his success has been less often emphasized. It is not new that behind every musical genius stood a highly talented businessman, and behind Ellington, until the late 1930s, stood the Jew Irving Mills, his partner in songwriting and business. But Mills was more than that; he was a branding wizard before we even used that idea. He not only made Ellington a celebrity and a bandleader, but a musical giant, one of the most influential American musicians ever. It is doubtful whether a black artist, however charismatic, could have achieved so much without a character from the "White" world, or rather, without a character from the Jewish world of the music industry. Mills managed to brand Ellington in a racist society, and luckily the music industry was more liberal than the society they lived in, thanks to its ethnic fabric. Mills managed a black artist in a world of overt southern apartheid and latent northern discrimination, but also in a music industry that had a Jewish privilege. He made his client one of the undisputed American jazz and music icons, while at the same time his own name remains almost unknown, not only to the general public but also to jazz fans.

The Duke of American music

There is a photo from 1932 that tells the story. Ellington is photographed sitting at the piano, alongside the classical composer Percy Grainger, as he gazes in amazement at the "great musician who makes a huge contribution to American music." Mills stands next to them, proud and happy in his work: Duke Ellington, the Duke, the king of American music. But what is America's music?

American music is a variety of styles, colors, and genres, which have also evolved at different times. And the truth is, there is far more resemblance than differences between ragtime, swing jazz, and rock, which are all variations of musical aesthetics created from the fusion of African and European traditions.[183]

African characteristics came through the slave trade mainly from West Africa: from Senegal in the north to Angola in the south. Africans brought with them to America forms of percussion-based musical communication. The tribal music, especially from northwestern Africa, entailed a variety of stringed instrumental traditions – banjo and various types of harps and guitars – played by "riffs," and on top of which they built melodies into a multi-sonic textured of call-and-response.

Compared to the highly educated European tradition, Africans brought with them rough vocals based on groans, sobs, and screams, which were influenced by African witchcraft mythology and voodoo rituals. Compared to absolute European standards, African vocalization may have slide down in pitch to a semitone during the act of emotional and musical ecstasy.

The tradition of the pitch-tone-language, meaning changing the vocal pitch and the stretching and trembling options of different instruments such as banjo and guitar, have created different ways of expressing music. The African slaves exhibited melodic patterns of pentatonic scales into unique versions, created because they were in a "collision" with European harmonies. So while the blues musicians based their songs on 12 bars of major chords or seventh chords, the melody might have been decorated with notes that were bent down a semitone into what is known as the blue note. These gave a pungent, bluesy feeling that created one of the unique and vital features of the African-European encounter in America. It also changed the blues harmony to become unique in its own right.

All of these elements – indeed based on the imitation of African-American dances – began to emerge in the second half of the nineteenth century into syncopated rhythmic musical patterns that were the basis of ragtime, jazz, blues, and rock 'n' roll. The swinging rhythm (characterized by the second and fourth beats of the bar and the dotted eights), was a continuation of a dialogue with

---

183 Gunther Schuller, *Early Jazz: Its Roots and Musical Development* (New York: Oxford University Press, 1986); Robert Palmer, *Deep Blues: A Musical and Cultural History, From the Mississippi Delta to Chicago South Side to The World* (New York: Penguin Books, 1982).

syncopation. While musical traditions across the globe may contain different types of blue notes, call-and-response, and polyrhythm, the swing rhythm belonged to America. And it permeated a variety of styles, including the blues and rock 'n' roll of the 1950s, which was an abstraction of music that America knew from the Big Bands era. Jerry Leiber and Mike Stoller, the famous Jewish songwriters of the 1950s, were right when for Elvis Presley they wrote the phrase "The band was jumping and the joint began to swing" in the single "Jailhouse Rock" (1957).

Not all of these traditions became noticeable in all American genres. However, the musical negotiations between Europe and Africa had established most of them in an American evolution. Jazz artists took these elements and gradually combined and developed more elaborate chords, brash dissonances, and denser harmonic movements. Above all, however, as Duke Ellington and Irving Mills tried to explain: it didn't mean a thing if it ain't got that swing.

Ellington was born in Washington, DC, in 1899 to a middle-class black family. Compared to many places in America, Washington was more friendly to African-Americans. Many came from the south to survive, and some even achieved much more than that. There was a good college for African-Americans, which gradually created the black middle class. There was no official segregation in Washington, but in fact, blacks lived in separated districts until the post-war era. The blacks lived in their areas where only they could spend or purchase a home. The separation was even present in the cemeteries. While in the South racial lines were cruel and explicit, in Washington they were more complex, both between whites and blacks and between blacks and themselves.

Around 1900, only about 87,000 blacks lived in Washington, DC. Although Ellington claimed that the capital was good for him, he left as soon as he could. His parents belonged to the black bourgeoisie. His father came from North Carolina to Washington around 1890 and was a senior butler and confidant of the physician with whom he worked. He shaped the family according to the manners he acquired in his work. Ellington's mother, on the other hand, came from a slightly more privileged family, and she had black, white, and Native American (Cherokee) roots, which were evident in the color of her skin. She was a regular visitor to the church, a reasonable pianist, and elitist in taste.

Ellington's parents had marital problems, but it was doubtful whether they affected him. Ellington admired his mother. He was a spoiled and proud kid and grew up with a sense of security. Discourse about racism at home was minimal. His parents protected him from the cruel world outside, just as his manager Irving Mills did years after. Ellington read Sherlock Holmes, visited the church on Sundays, and began taking piano lessons with one of his neighbors. He was an average student and had not yet shown much attentiveness to music. He was even more interested in painting.

His internal revolution occurred when, at the age of 14, he listened to the ragtime composition "Junk Man Rag" by Luckey Roberts while on a trip to Philadelphia. That's how he wanted to play the piano.[184]

He returned to Washington, learned from friends, and soon succeeded in playing. He also joined bands for events and parties. Fortunately, a boiling musical steam fed Washington. Before 1920, Washington, DC had more clubs than Harlem. The presence of popular music was so dominant that churchgoers, both white and black, feared ragtime.

Ellington discovered the ragtime in the late days of the genre. In some circles, they started calling the new style jazz music. Meanwhile, Willie "The Lyon" Smith, Luckey Roberts, James P. Johnson, and Eubie Blake merged ragtime into something more virtuous and complicated: stride. Some were loyal to classical music, but none of them was familiar with New Orleans jazz. The great paradox, as mentioned above, was that the black bourgeois used to react with horror to their children's attraction to ragtime, but not Ellington's parents. However, they did not consider music a profession and sent him to a technical school, but he received a scholarship from the National Association for the Advancement of Colored People, and the frequency of performances dictated its direction.

In 1917, the age of jazz began. Two years later, Ellington was already married and led a band in Washington. People who knew him used to tell about his unique charisma, a passion for people, and his ability to harness them in his favor. It's hard to say how much he listened to jazz records and how much the giants of the era influenced him, but he learned harmony privately with a local teacher, Henry Grant. "I discovered that F-sharp is not a G-flat," Ellington said, "That was the end of my lessons [...] because I found out what I wanted to know."[185] With relatively little theoretical ammunition, he set off. Unlike Gershwin, for example, he was not interested in classical music. He copied the stride wizards until he sounded just like them. In 1923, he encountered jazz from New Orleans and did not forget the "power and imagination" experienced by Sidney Bechet.

Racial riots in Washington, which lasted four nights (amid suspicions that an African-American had raped a navy officer's wife), convinced Ellington to move to New York. His progress was rapid. He settled in Harlem and became

---

[184] Terry Teachout, *Duke: A Life of Duke Ellington* (New York: Gotham Books, 2013), chap. 1, Kindle.
[185] Ibid., chap. 2, Kindle.

part of the Renaissance, the unofficial capital of Black America at the time. Black and white intellectuals were looking for the "new Negro," the one who could take part in American civilization, a jazz hero who can connect the entertainment world with the African-American spirit world. Ellington was in the right place and at the right time and was perfect for that goal.

His band, The Washingtonians, associated with the Hollywood Club near Broadway and became a kind of a collaborative group. The jazz world slowly began to internalize the gospel brought by King Oliver and his Creole Jazz Band. King Oliver and Louis Armstrong of New Orleans stunned those who watched them at their new location in Chicago. The wah-wah effect with mute horns in the solos sounded like something coming out from space. The players in Ellington's lineup began to adopt the style. At the end of the journey, Ellington took over the band and became its leader. Because he did not read notes well, they did not use ready-made arrangements but instead played by oral coordination resembling the rock bands of the following decades. Ellington recalls that he was looking for "colors." Fletcher Henderson's arrangements, who was the first to design the New York jazz sound, fascinated Ellington as did white orchestras such as Paul Whiteman's. He began meeting Will Marion Cook, an African-American musician, and conductor who became his mentor. Cook studied violin in Berlin and some composition with Antonín Dvořák. Being African-American, he was unable to play in the segregated classical orchestras. Cook began to work as a composer and arranger of popular music. He collaborated with the black poet Paul Laurence Dunbar on *Clorindy, or The Origin of the Cake Walk*, one of the first African-American shows on Broadway. Ellington says he used to travel with Cook in a taxi around Central Park, and his mentor would give him lectures in music, with suggestions for improving compositions, transforming other forms and ideas, some of which he still applied after many years. Ellington got from Cook the inspiration for the concept of "developed Negro music." Cook suggested that he find the logical way, then avoid it, and let his "self" become manifest.

From Russia with love

The National Prohibition Act, which inaugurated the dry period in the United States, was one of the most unnecessary constitutional amendments in American history. Throughout the 1920s, it may have precipitated the official closure of entertainment venues, but on the other hand, it spurred crime organizations (in which Jews took a particularly active part). Unexpectedly, it fit into the seemingly dangerous spirit of jazz. In forbidding alcohol the new law created a result opposite from its original intention – now not only did men drink, but women, too. What was supposed to save the Victorian legacy became the accelerator of its decline. The turbulent 1920s released the bridle: "In the twenties [people] could love," recalls one of the documentaries of the era, "[t]hey could travel, they could stay up late at night as extravagantly as they pleased."[186] The mythology of these hedonistic years revolved around cabaret and dancing, drinking, and the beauty of capitalism, all because enforcement was tenuous. Against the background of this era, jazz soon rose to be part of the world of the American high-bourgeoisie. Someone needed to mediate the music from the Harlem clubs to the new audience, and that is where Irving Mills came in.

He was born Isadore Minsky in 1894 on the Lower East Side, Manhattan, to a Jewish family of Russian origin. People have described him as a "hard-nosed businessman," who accomplished his aims with innocent and humorless enthusiasm. Like many Jews in the entertainment industry, he and his brother Jack started as pluggers – songs salesmen. Intrigues, bribes, violence and flattery were needed to promote songs, and Mills had that, as well as a barefoot baritone voice that resembled a megaphone.

Not surprisingly, the Minsky brothers, who became the Mills, began their journey at the Jewish network in Tin Pan Alley. In 1919, the Mills Brothers launched a publishing company. They teamed up with the tenor star Enrico Caruso in their first significant song release, but after Mamie Smith ignited the passion for the blues of the 1920s, the Mills brothers followed suit. Other publishing houses, including those who were owned by Jews, had been selling black music-based songs for years but were still somewhat distant from working with black artists. The Mills brothers penetrated this space with gusto. "[...] [A] dollar don't care where it's from," Irving Mills said, "whether it's black [or] green."[187]

Mills, on the whole, treated his African-American writers fairly. Before embarking on his professional affair with Ellington, he promoted works by Fats Waller, James P. Johnson, and Fletcher Henderson, among others, and of course published works by white songwriters such as Hoagy Carmichael. However, Ellington learned that Mills "corrected" new writers' songs and shared their royalties. Ellington admitted that Mills "feels the song." Even if he was not the writer, he would direct the lyricist and refine the form of expression. Irving Mills claimed that he gave all the song names to his artists and that he was talented at it. Either way, many of his writers discovered after the release that they shared credits with another writer, Irving Mills.

---

186 Ibid., chap. 3, Kindle.
187 Ibid., chap. 3, Kindle.

He was a wonderful host and was notorious for the excellent cigars he offered. People who knew him said he was a hustler, a street boy with a Lower East Side jargon and limited vocabulary. Industry people liked to patronize him. John Hammond, one of the most enthusiastic WASP missioners of black music, was duly in touch with him. On the one hand, he disliked the exploitation of the songwriters, and on the other, he appreciated the work that he was doing as the only one who cared about promoting black artists during a time when nobody cared. At the beginning of the Depression, the Mills Brothers company acquired several small publishing companies, including Waterson, Berlin & Snyder, Inc. They bought the Berlin company cheaply ($5,000; Berlin was only really associated with the company at the time by name) and got their hands on a rich repertoire. They also moved to the Brill Building on Broadway.

Ellington has visited Tin Pan Alley several times since arriving in New York, but the encounter with Mills changed his fate. It is unclear when Ellington first met Mills, because the memories of both are different. Ellington once said it happened in his early months in New York, when he sold the Mills Brothers a handful of blues songs for "fifteen to twenty dollars."[188] In another memory, they met sometime in 1926 when Ellington's band played "Saint Louis Blues." Mills remembers another date and that he had Ellington sign up on the back of a menu after Duke's band played "Black and Tan Fantasy." Anyway, in November 1926, after signing a management contract with Mills, Ellington and his band completed recordings at Brunswick Studios.

Mills was a pioneer entrepreneur during the 1920s, just as the Turkish Ertegun brothers, and the Jewish Jerry Wexler, who founded Atlantic Records (with the aim of legitimizing black music), would be after World War Two. He wasn't an idealist like them, and probably lacked their charisma, but he knew that successful marketing of songs lay in their connection to a successful artist. Because blacks wrote many songs in his company for black performers, Mills needed an African-American band. He tried Fletcher Henderson and his band for a while, but there were always chaotic problems: singers and players came and went, and he was late in delivering arrangements on time. Mills fell in love not only with Ellington but also with his excellent musicians and memorable solo pieces. And he understood something more profound – the broad potential of this composition, the way to brand Ellington as a true musical duke.

Ellington occasionally recorded music from Mills' publishing repertoire, but for the most part, they concentrated on his compositions, and Ellington recognized this contribution to his career development. From the beginning, Mills

---

188 Ibid., chap. 3, Kindle.

positioned him as a great American musician and the first to capture "the true spirit of jazz." Mills also understood the contribution of the soloists in the band and allowed them to write.[189]

Musicians joined, others went, but the direction was of a buildup as the band expanded and slowly grew. The recordings became more frequent, and the colors were more vibrant, the tones more interesting, the harmonic changes more frequent. The band even mimicked a train noise like something from Musique concrète. Ellington's piano playing was sometimes sloppy, some of the musicians still evolved, but all quickly improved under one vision. The recording of the work "East St. Louis Toodle-Oo" featured low-pitched saxophones, a mysterious tuba playing the bass, a steady swing banjo, and a wah-wah trumpet sound by Bubber Miley. Over the years, Miley got credit as a composer. Gunther Schuller has unequivocally argued that the players supported Ellington's greatness and that they were at their best with him.[190] He had that trait of making the musicians around him transcend themselves. The arrangements during this period (and afterward) were, for the most part, unwritten. Yet, "East St. Louis Toodle-Oo" serves as one of the perfect examples of mid-twenties jazz.

Early on, musicians and critics noted the colors regarding the recordings of The Washingtonians. The band distinguished themselves from the rest of the dance bands. There were critics who drifted into Mills' branding attempts and crowned Ellington as the Ravel and Strauss of the jazz orchestra. These reviews identified Ellington as a composer in comparison to a medium primarily produced by instrumentalists. Mills had a significant hand in consulting in the studio. "He was respectful of what I did in the recording room" Mills said. "I created the balances. I cut out the arrangements. Whatever they did, I thinned it out. His music was always too heavy. He over arranged."[191]

Some musicians in the band remembered it quite differently. Mills, so to speak, would "change things" just for the sake of his ego. "Man, we had some arrangements, and then this monkey comes in, and that's when everybody began to get down on Duke. They'd say, 'How can you let this man louse up your band?,'" remembered musician Louis Metcalf. The band would complain to Ellington about his manager; However, Duke enjoyed Mills' treatment, which included publishing sheet notes of his songs.

---

[189] Ibid., chap. 3, Kindle.
[190] Gunther Schuller, *Early Jazz: Its Roots and Musical Development* (New York: Oxford University Press, 1986); Robert Palmer, *Deep Blues: A Musical and Cultural History, From the Mississippi Delta to Chicago South Side to The World* (New York: Penguin Books, 1982), 327.
[191] Terry Teachout, *Duke: A Life of Duke Ellington* (New York: Gotham Books, 2013), chap. 3, Kindle.

Mills opened Duke Ellington Ltd., which he and his composer jointly owned, as well as the lawyer who handled the company. He made a large profit, but Ellington knew he couldn't function at the high levels of the entertainment industry without a "white" manager. Mills gave him preferential treatment and excused him from all the day-to-day duties on the way to becoming a jazz artist in every sense of the word, but it had a cost. Not only did he bite into Ellington's profits, but he undermined the relationship within the band.[192]

Another contribution by Mills was to connect all the components of the entertainment industry in Duke's favor, like the Cotton Club. In 1927, Harlem was a place where everyone searched for alcohol and sex. The Cotton Club, which advertised itself in the press as an elitist venue, was the place where the mobs, jazz artists, and New York's rich people could mingle. The club was one big, grotesque fantasy. While prestigious New York clubs were owned and run by Jews, the owner of the Cotton Club was the Irish-American gangster Owney Madden (who acquired it from a Jewish businessman). It made it a place reminiscent of a southern estate, with African-American waiters in tuxedos looking like they were brought in from the pre-Civil War era as if to give the rich the slave's sense of entertainment for one evening. However, Ellington, Mills, and the gangster had excellent relationships. Some have remembered the place as horribly expensive, luxurious, and often with poor food. Ellington, for his part, related in his autobiography that it was a place with class.[193] Payments to artists were high, and he was confined to a club that consisted of about 20 dancers and beautiful show girls and celebrities. The club ran a selection policy, but allowed very famous black artists to enter, though the great African-American composer W.C. Handy was not even allowed to enter a show featuring his own works.

The club was the epitome of the bountiful 1920s era illustrated by a cultural blooming. Ellington's band performed twice a night, based on Mills' workspace: the songs were written by composer Jimmy McHugh, a plugger who worked for the Mills brothers' company, and Jewish lyricist Dorothy Fields, one of the industry's first female songwriters. Ellington said he loved the materials. "They wrote some wonderful material, but this was show music and mostly popular songs."[194] The Cotton Club was a social world (at least two of Ellington's musicians married dancers and show girls from the club), and in this work Ellington learned to submit almost complete arrangements to the band.

---

192 Ibid., chap. 3, Kindle.
193 Duke Ellington, *Music is My Mistress* (New York: Da Capo Press, 1976).
194 Terry Teachout, *Duke: A Life of Duke Ellington* (New York: Gotham Books, 2013), chap. 4, Kindle.

In 1929, CBS Radio broadcast Ellington's show from the club. The broadcast was pioneering and exposed millions of Americans throughout the federation to black music at a time when the radiophonic medium was growing tremendously (from 16 million radios in 1925 to 60 million in 1930). Ellington acknowledged that the Cotton Club had a decisive influence on his success and exposure. It turns out it was Gershwin, a regular visitor to the club, who gave Ellington's music the name "jungle music," and it stuck.

In the late 1920s and early 1930s, African-Americans tried harder to penetrate Broadway and produce their own shows. Louis Armstrong appeared in *Hot Chocolates*, an African-American show composed by Fats Waller. Ellington and his band performed in *Show Girl* (1929) with Gershwin's music and Florenz Ziegfeld's production. Will Wodrey, the African-American musician who once gave Gershwin a chance with *Blue Monday* (1922), took care of that. Ellington received informal lectures from him through which he learned about chromatics, structures, and alterations on extended compositional options, and then Ellington embarked on breaking Hollywood. Gradually, non-black musicians began joining the band, such as Puerto Rican trombone player Juan Tizol.

Mills connected Ellington not only to the white world but to Europeanism, as well as to a concert with Frenchman Maurice Chevalier. Ellington posted an ad in the *Variety* newspaper in which he mentioned Chevalier, *Show Girl*, The Cotton Club, the record label Victor, and thanked Irving Mills for his confidence and judgment. A few months later Mills made sure the *New York Age* newspaper praised it:

> Mills signed Ellington, and after years of work and study he developed this organization into one of the most talked of musical combinations in the world [...] Mills personally supervises every orchestration and arrangement the band plays. He arranges the bookings and directs the exploitation in general. He selects the records made for the various phonograph companies and is master of the destinies of Duke Ellington.[195]

The next step was the integration of Ellington's Cotton Club with the Hollywood movie *Check and Double Check* (1930) at RKO Studios, which was a reincarnation of the minstrelsy world with Amos 'n' Andy, a radio show in which two white actors played several characters from the black community in Harlem. The brighter musicians in Ellington's band, including the talented Puerto Rican trombonist, had to make their skin black to enter the role-playing game.

Watching the film reveals the role of African-American jazz bands in the pre-bebop era. Jazz and entertainment were linked through roles and stereotypes,

---

[195] Ibid.

whether dull, grumbling, brilliant, and stereotypical a-la Uncle Tom, while Duke stood over the piano, revealing his charismatic smile and humbly bowing in gratitude to the audience. Decades later, black artists would dare to be more militant, but Mills knew that the only way to sell Ellington to the American mainstream would be by making a compromise on Africanism. Ellington had to balance America and Europe, ideally, to successfully open the door for more black artists to penetrate Hollywood. Louis Armstrong's genius was thus linked to the image of the clown entertainer, but Ellington at least never compromised his "dignity." It was hard to explain, but Ellington was not only handsome, but he also carried something special, a smile of uncommon confidence.

The jazz borrowing

Cultural scholars have dealt with Jewish and black relations and the way Jewish composers have exploited African-American's cultural wealth.[196] However, the effects were also the opposite, and blacks sometimes exploited each other more blatantly. Ellington was one of them. The famous track, "Old Man Blues," mentioned elements and segments by Jewish composer Jerome Kern from *Show Boat* (1927). "Ol' Man River" was also a purposeful display of the band's excellent colors. Yet, the sound was original. "Mood Indigo," recorded weeks later, was another overwhelming example of Ellington's talent as a master of big bands orchestra.

Ellington loved to cast a mythology around his works. He used to say that he composed "Mood Indigo" while waiting for a dinner his mother made. He also said that after the band played it on the radio from The Cotton Club and received rave reviews, Mills added lyrics to the music, so Ellington earned royalties from his lazy wait for dinner. But the story was more complicated. Clarinet player Barney Biggard claimed to have added the second part. Mills was credited as the lyricist, but apparently the Jewish songwriter, Mitchell Parish, wrote it (he worked at Mills' company and was a successful Tin Pan Alley lyricist in his own right). Later, singer Gene Austin, who was the first to record a vocal version

---

[196] Jeffrey Melnick, *A Right to Sing the Blues: African Americans, Jews and American Popular Song* (Cambridge, Massachusetts: Harvard University Press, 1999); Michael Rogin, *Blackface, White Noise: Jewish Immigrants in the Hollywood Melting Pot* (Berkeley: University of California Press, 1998); Karen B. Sacks, *How Jews Became White Folks and What That Says About Race in America* (New York: Rutgers University Press, 1999).

of this work, stated that Mills was responsible for the lyrics. Either way, it was a hit and a critical success that gave birth to many offspring.

Gunther Schuller explained that Ellington's lack of knowledge of tonal harmony (his voicing was due to his finger on the piano) and counterpoint gave rise to a new language of close harmonic blocks with a unique tone.[197] Schuller also noted that his bandmates wrote some of his most famous works. He used to listen to some melodic lines and made them work. Saxophonist Otto Hardwick and trombonist Lawrence Brown experienced how Ellington took a chromatic melodic line they improvised that became "Sophisticated Lady" (1933). He weaved polychords orchestral (with two different chords playing at the same time) and a polytonality move.[198] Mills added lyrics, and the credit was given to "Mills and Ellington," without the original contributors (later Parish's name was added to the credits).

Ellington was a talented lick robber, and Mills took over where he could. The trombonist Juan Tizol, who composed the masterpiece "Caravan," claimed that Ellington was a "crazy thief."[199] The musicians sold him some of their artwork for $25, and later some claimed it. Others felt very bad about using their materials. His musicians accused him of musical kleptomania and the band as being a joint material production plant. Lawrence Brown defined his boss as a "compiler" of works rather than a composer. But the truth is that without Ellington, these ideas would have remained in the improvisation closet.

Schuller described Ellington's art at its best as a balance between composition and improvisation. Initially, Ellington longed to be Fletcher Henderson, but apparently Jelly Roll Morton's work was a more significant challenge. Ellington certainly also tried to cope with Gershwin's accomplishments. Ellington had mixed feelings, embedded in envy, admiration, and resentment towards the composer. He described his work in *Porgy and Bess* as good but negligible in its uniqueness and character. Mostly, like many African-Americans, Ellington despised the stereotypes of the ghetto. After all, style and modernity were the essences of his life.

Nevertheless, in a press interview held after Gershwin's death, he crowned him the most celebrated American composer of all time. Under his influence,

---

197 Gunther Schuller, *Early Jazz: Its Roots and Musical Development* (New York: Oxford University Press, 1986); Robert Palmer, *Deep Blues: A Musical and Cultural History, From the Mississippi Delta to Chicago South Side to The World* (New York: Penguin Books, 1982), 336–343.
198 Arnon Palty, *Connecting Points in Jazz Dialects: The Metamorphic Process* (Kiryat Ono Academic College, 2017), 65–66.
199 Terry Teachout, *Duke: A Life of Duke Ellington* (New York: Gotham Books, 2013), chap. 6, Kindle.

he began to expand his compositions into longer works. He decided to dedicate them to the depiction of African history through slavery until the liberation in Harlem, as reflected in "Creole Rhapsody" (1931).

Ellington made statements about his composing plans as early as the 1930s, but it was Mills who steered the program to take his treasure trove of American art forward and achieve American recognition. He spurred Ellington and nearly burned his ties with two major record companies to record the pieces. It is quite possible that Ellington, who was always busy with performances, composed sections he already had for "a long work." Mills worked vigorously on the branding. He published a complete advertisement entitled "Duke Ellington: America's Newest Hot Fashion (Different Music Type)." Various images of Ellington and Whiteman focused on the conductor's desire to play the piece and emphasized that this was a new stage in jazz's development.

Even Schuller, who was an avid fan of Ellington's compositions, was skeptical of the contexts that critics and composers such as Constant Lambert made between French and English impressionism and Ellington. For him, the terminology was more condescending than correct. To him, the random tendency towards extended chords (9, 11) did not justify an impressionist categorizing but was the basis for seeing Ellington's work as a more original complex.[200] Mills managed to conquer the media in America and the United Kingdom. Critics and classical musicians recognized his works. Composer Percy Grainger invited Ellington to meet his students at the University of New York. He then began teaching a course on Ellington and placed it alongside Bach and Frederick Delius on the list of great composers of all time. Paul Whiteman played Ellington's music at Carnegie Hall as genuine American music. Ellington had nothing left but to pass on his role at the Cotton Club to his African-American colleague Cab Caloway and travel across America to establish his status as a star.

The Duke is still a king

The Great Depression that began in 1929 shrunk the music industry, which suffered a drastic decline in record sales. Mills' way of dealing with the crisis was to increase advertising and navigate towards a broad and stable bourgeois audience. Personally, Ellington barely felt the slump and always appeared in

---

200 Gunther Schuller, *Early Jazz: Its Roots and Musical Development* (New York: Oxford University Press, 1986); Robert Palmer, *Deep Blues: A Musical and Cultural History, From the Mississippi Delta to Chicago South Side to The World* (New York: Penguin Books, 1982), 347–348.

fancy attire with a plethora of closet suits. It was said that if he knew he needed four suits, he would carry four crates with forty outfits. Collaborating with the pop star of the 1930s, Bing Crosby, in "Saint Louis Blues," was another step in building mainstream reception. But something about the natural flow of his career stopped for a moment.

At the start the Cotton Club brought prestige, money, women, and status, but a few years of the Depression saw the emergence in society of unpleasant and racist feelings. Mills suggested they go on a tour in England. Although aristocrats honored Ellington, his players and staff were forced to stay in cheaper hotels.

Mills, for his part, began having difficulties in the second half of the 1930s. The Cotton Club lost its appeal after a riot in Harlem and was temporarily shut down. His business had expanded dramatically, and perhaps too much. He had less time for Ellington, and more trouble with the record companies he opened. He failed to secure proper overseas distribution contracts, which made it challenging to invest further in Duke's expensive project. But he still supported the Duke. He initiated a documentary in 1937, *Record Making with Duke Ellington and His Orchestra*, which dealt with Ellington's recordings with an emphasis on their technological quality. He published a newspaper ad on a page explaining that "the Duke is still a king."

Jewish clarinet player Benny Goodman broke the bank starting in the mid-1930s with his effective swing (using the arrangements of African-American Fletcher Henderson) that magnetized young people on the dance floors. While Goodman occupied Carnegie Hall, Mills did not dare bring Ellington there for fear it would not pay off. The composer, for his part, defined the music of the younger generation as "monotonous," "reproduced," and "commercialized." However, the press charged Mills with exploitation, which may have been more refined had he not been a Jew. Ellington began to internalize, among other things, the writings of John Hammond, who accused Mills of the excessive exploitation of Duke. Other newspaper articles accused Mills of exploitation through slavery and using such terminology and painting Ellington as a cotton picker at Mills' factory.

After returning from a tour in Europe in 1938 with it on the verge of war, *Music Magazine* reported that he and Mills had terminated their contract. Ellington moved to another Jewish company originally, the William Morris Agency. They closed Duke Ellington Inc. But Mills tried to hold on to his power, among other things, with the Cab Calloway band and said he thought Ellington had chosen a different and wrong direction. Ellington's biographers report that he asked to "open the books." One day he even went to the office to browse them, and it's unclear what he found, but he put on his hat, put on his jacket, walked out the door, and never came back.

Even if Ellington had a slight feeling of exploitation, inside he knew Mills had protected him for years from a harrowing racist environment. And maybe he thought everything was relative in life, probably given the difficulties that plagued him down the road. He eventually remembered Mills for the better. His parents and manager tried to protect him, but the walls fortified with his personal charm, eternal smile, incredible charisma, and inner belief were never hermetically sealed. After all, he might not have forgotten that during a meal with music scholar Marshall Stearns and his students at Yale University, one student raged out of the dining room saying, "I don't eat with niggers." If it had happened to Ellington, it could have happened to anyone.

It is doubtful whether an apolitical man like Ellington thought about it at all, but assimilation and charisma alone were not enough; liberalism needed a broader move. The ethnic collaborations that shaped the musical world would connect after World War Two to political partnerships aimed at forcing America to commit to its principles and promises. Music and politics were about to intersect at the crossroads.

Chapter 6: Heaven With You – Jews, The Record Industry and Rock 'n' Roll

Singer Michael Jackson in conversation with Walter Yetnikoff, president of CBS Records, after completing his best seller *Thriller* in 1982:

> Jackson: "I told you I'd do it, I told you I'd outdo *Off the Wall*."
> Yetnikoff: "You delivered [...] you delivered like a mother-fucker."
> Jackson: "Please don't use that word, Walter."
> Yetnikoff: "You delivered it like an angel. Archangel Michael."
> Jackson: "That's better. Now will you promote it?"
> Yetnikoff: "Like a mother-fucker." (Walter Yetnikoff, *Howling at the Moon*, 2003)[201]

That's how Michael Jackson's rise to his position in the global music industry began. A combination of great talent, strength, and finances created all the possibilities he could only dream of as he began his musical career with his brothers. A well-known saying in the music industry has it that behind every musical genius stands a marketing genius. Still, one can settle on the assumption that various factors attributed to artistic success – musical abilities, image, and archetypes, marketing, and timing – that come together in a dynamic and multi-revolutionary industry.

Jewish-blacks-WASP relationships characterized the record industry. Tremendous victories and resounding frustrations, timeless recordings, and hard struggles – between Jews and themselves, blacks, WASPs, Italians, and in any order – were the background music of the soundtrack that accompanied America (and the world) during the twentieth century.

The relationship between Walter Yetnikoff, director of the CBS Records Corporation, and Michael Jackson, the world's biggest star in the 1980s, was another link in a long line of employer-employee relations between Jews and blacks in the record industry. Yetnikoff, a savvy lawyer devoid of any musical learning, became known as Jackson's "rabbi." His confidante, advisor, and full-fledged father figure of the genius black phenomenon. Yetnikoff's resume as a lawyer who advanced through the corporate ranks was a familiar and typical side of the Jewish story in the American record industry.

Jews functioned as promoters and distributors of records, managers, and executives, and most importantly, entrepreneurs and owners of small labels and

---

[201] Walter Yetnikoff and David Ritz, *Howling at the Moon: The Odyssey of a Monstrous Music Mogul in an Age of Excess* (New York: Abacus, 2003), 153–154.

major corporations. While the Tin Pan Alley of the late nineteenth century was mostly a German-Jewish story, the record industry gradually absorbed the second generation of Jewish immigrants from Eastern Europe. Many of these helped shape the industry through their relationship with African-American music and culture.

From Tin Pan Alley to the record industry

The publishing industry in New York was the center of the American Music Center from the late nineteenth century, but in the early twentieth century, entrepreneurs began to realize the potential of selling music on a record and audio device (a phonograph, gramophone, etc.). Three manufacturers controlled the industry: Victor Talking Machine Company, Columbia Records, and Edison Records. These companies took advantage of the patent laws set by the US legislature to prevent the entry of competitors into the industry for years, but in 1915 other companies entered the race.

Victor was the first to discover the potential of content. Its earnings from record sales, through its label *Red Seal*, surpassed the sales of gramophones, and it positioned its record label as a high-end art marketplace in the middle-class consumer goods industry. Victor's first recordings, by Italian tenor Enrico Caruso, were popular opera pieces. Naturally, the first singers on Victor Company came from a background of classical music. However, from the beginning, Victor also based its repertoire on comedy pieces, instrumental music, and famous singers of the era.

In 1917, the year when American soldiers began marching into the European inferno, Victor made the first jazz recording with the Original Dixieland Jass Band, a New Orleans jazz band based on its white color purity and inaugurating a new era. Jazz intersected with media and technological revolutions and historical events: the advent of radio, the talking movie, black immigration to the north, and the Great Depression of the late 1920s that threatened American sanity. In between, the Prohibition law fed the subversive dimension of jazz. The efforts to control alcohol and jazz, were probably one of the reasons for the attraction of millions to this "forbidden fruit" and its popularity over the decade.

The 1920s were tumultuous and intoxicating. The radio, stationed as a capitalist medium, radiated modernity and progress.[202] The radio networks broadcast programs designed for the American family. The Hollywood studios had ac-

---

[202] David Kellner, *Television and the Crisis of Democracy* (Oxford: Westview Press, 1990), 32.

quired a significant portion of the essential companies in Tin Pan Alley following the success of *The Jazz Singer* film and understood the potential of owning the song rights. Not only did the physical vaudeville halls become cinemas, but the movies now contained the spirit of the vaudeville show.

At the same time, the radio giants began to take over the record companies. In 1929, RCA, under the leadership of the American Jew David Sarnoff, acquired Victor, and renamed it RCA-Victor. Its rival, Columbia, which went bankrupt for a variety of reasons, was sold to a receiver and came into the hands of William Paley, the Jewish owner of the CBS broadcast network.

The corporations' takeover of the music industry intensified with the onset of the economic depression of 1929. The Great Depression had shrunk record sales and shattered small record companies. The depression created Oligopoly, a limited number of major record companies – RCA, Columbia, EMI, Decca, and Brunswick – which owned radio, film, and electronic products. Fewer people could buy records, but the radio companies were able to broadcast music to broader audiences. Influenced by the interests of the major media companies (which included the radio giants and record companies), radio re-energized their interest in short, fast, and light music; the Tin Pan Alley songs swept across America.

Faced with the slump, the companies tried to lower record prices, but this strategy alone failed to secure the industry. The big British company, Decca, opened a US branch in 1932 and was responsible for transcribing the Hollywood model into the marketing branch of the music industry; building up a singer's image embodied fantasies of success. Music scholar Simon Frith mentions that the significance of the aggressive selling methods and the star system of the 1930s was a new recording method. The companies were less interested in utilizing big names, but in building stars from the ground up as recording artists.[203]

President Roosevelt's *New Deal* revived American music with the swing bands. The band's singers began to gain more power on behalf of the orchestra's directors. Perry Como, Bing Crosby, Frank Sinatra, and many others became American pop idols. The singers began to forge their ties with the publishing houses of Tin Pan Alley, now owned by the Hollywood studios and extend their power that until then was mainly in the realm of the movie stars.

The lean 1930s signaled a power shift from Tin Pan Alley to the Hollywood broadcast networks, from publishers to the entertainment star-making system.

---

203 Simon Frith, *Music for Pleasure: Essays in the Sociology of Pop* (London: Routledge, 1988), 8.

Pop song production began to adapt to the limited framework of the 78 rpm records.[204]

By the 1950s, American popular music was under the control of the major record companies, but the aggressive sound of the South was about to cause a stir. Youth, mass culture, communications, and technological innovations had created a new consumer market. The rock 'n' roll artists stood at the gate.

From Tin Pan Alley to rock 'n' roll

American music historians have highlighted the connection between the emergence of American youth culture and rock 'n' roll, but the rock revolution was also technological and institutional.[205] The media revolution began to change the power relations between the copyright organizations. The ASCAP, which was responsible for enforcing royalties from the best Tin Pan Alley writers, was challenged by BMI, an alternative set up by the National Association of Broadcasters, and representing a repertoire of blues, gospel, and country music. ASCAP purported to seek compensation for its losses during the Depression, demanding higher royalties from the radio networks, which refused and relayed the catalog of the competing organization.

The changes in the structure of radio, the rise of BMI, and the appearance of the 45 rpm record format led to the break-up of the monopoly held by the major record companies. In the late 1950s, music by small record companies was felt more strongly in the top-ten published by Billboard.[206]

---

[204] The 12 inch 78-rpm record was used for most industrial models starting in the mid-1920s.
[205] George Douglas, *Postwar America: 1948 and the Incubation of Our Times* (New York: Krieger Publishing Company, 1995); Richard Peterson, "Why 1955? Explaining the advent of Rock Music," *Popular Music* 9 (1990): 97–116.
[206] Columbia launched the LP after World War Two with 33.3 rpm. RCA, working on an alternative system, developed the 45-rpm record format, which challenged the 33.3 record. This dispute between the record companies, called the Battle for Speed, has been resolved by the government's intervention. The rival companies reached an agreement that directed the 33.3 records to classical music, and the 45 records to pop songs.

Small labels, big sounds

The rise of jazz during the 1920s was in sync with the founding of small independent labels aimed at urban and rural audiences, partly black.[207] Harry Gennett, the owner of Indiana's Piano Store, led this wave after winning a lawsuit against Victor for his right to produce records. His company, Gennett Records, which specialized in African-American jazz, is remembered for its wealth of recordings, including King Oliver's Creole Jazz Band, a famous Chicago orchestra led by a black trumpeter from New Orleans, King Oliver, and his 'deputy' Louis Armstrong.

Gennett Records' legal victory led to the tide of new small independent labels. They recorded all the new jazz sensations from New Orleans: The creole pianist Jelly Roll Morton, Louis Armstrong, King Oliver, Freddie Keppard, and others. The small labels also released recordings of hillbilly music, which became country and western.[208] While the independent labels were distributing fringe music, the major companies, including Victor and Columbia, continued in the mainstream line: opera singers, vaudeville stars and big orchestras. However, at the height of the jazz era, Victor and Columbia followed the little labels and began recording the big jazz stars alongside some country and western singers.

The launch of the radio in the early 1920s changed the structure of the music industry. Although the first half of the decade was successful for Victor, the demand for radios gradually increased over phonographs and gramophones. The beginning of this crisis and the impact of the Great Depression led to the takeover of radio networks by the major record companies.

The independent labels had trouble surviving the Depression. Gennet was among those who declared bankruptcy. However, the New Deal managed to secure the record industry and resurrected other independent labels.[209] A modern

---

[207] Rick Kennedy and Randy McNutt, *Little Labels – Big Sound: Small Record Companies and the Rise of American Music* (Indiana: Indiana University Press, 1999).

[208] Black Swan Records is noteworthy, a record company owned by the African-American Harry H. Pace, to whom other black investors joined. The company, supported by African-American intellectuals, was a product of the 1920s' Harlem Renaissance. This entrepreneurial effort had been trying to influence the politics of music production, questioning what music would be recorded, under what circumstances and who would benefit. The company went bankrupt in late 1923 and was sold to Paramount Records, but during its brief time of operations it exposed larger companies to an African-American target audience.

[209] Charlie Gillett, *Sound of The City: The Rise of Rock and Roll* (London: Da Capo Press, 1984), 4. From 1938 to 1936, the American Record Corporation label recorded the blues singer from Delta-Mississippi, Robert Johnson, who became known as one of the greatest influencers of rock in the 1960s. The label Commodore Records, which came out of a small record store in Man-

jazz avant-garde movement, the bebop, had been shaping Harlem for some years now, promoting itself with new labels. Nevertheless, the most popular genre on the margin of the music industry was rhythm and blues (then still categorized as race music), which was blues in its urban version. Contrary to the European traditions embedded in Tin Pan Alley and bebop pieces, rhythm and blues seemed too primitive to its racial opponents, who found it saturated with sexual slang. However, its relatively inexpensive production, the birth of regional radio, and the age of post-war affluence that boosted teenage consumption increased its popularity. In light of these changes, dozens of Jewish entrepreneurs left their mark.

The Jewish network in the music industry

In the early 1950s, a handful of major record companies dominated the music industry.[210] The British firm Decca, founded in 1934, was the first to respond to the popularity of rhythm and blues among young audiences with the "Rock Around the Clock" recording (1954–1955) performed by Bill Haley & His Comets. A year later, the song became a sensation as the theme song in the famous teenage movie *Blackboard Jungle* (1955), but Decca did not outline a rock 'n' roll recording policy.

Particularly notable in this paradox was the veteran RCA-Victor, who signed Elvis Presley in late 1955 after acquiring his contract from the Sun Records label. Nevertheless, they avoided continuing down this line. Their catalog offered Tin Pan Alley crooners alongside some country singers and esteemed black pop performers. Its big rival, Columbia, didn't even show any signs of jealousy at RCA's success with Elvis Presley, continuing down the line of Tin Pan Alley and Broadway.[211] At the same time, the power of small independent labels increased. Like ragtime and jazz before it, rhythm and blues evoked antagonism among the mainstream industrial establishment; however, many Jewish entrepreneurs

---

hattan, recorded Billie Holiday and a variety of jazz and swing records. Blue Note Records was launched in 1939 in New York.

210 David Pichaske, *A Generation in Motion: Popular Music and Culture in the Sixties* (Granite Falls, MN: Ellis Press, 1979), 156.

211 Other major companies – Mercury Records (founded in the mid-1940s), Capitol Records (founded in 1942 and purchased by EMI in the mid-1950s), MGM (record company founded in 1946) and ABC-Paramount Records (founded in 1955) – were no exception in their approach to rock 'n' roll music.

were responsible for recording and distributing race music, which would be rebranded in the late 1940s as rhythm and blues and later as a rock 'n' roll.

Brothers Phil and Leonard Chess, owners of Chicago based Chess Records; Art Rupe, owner of Specialty Records located in Los Angeles; Syd Nathan, label owner King Records of Cincinnati; Savoy Records Founded by Herman Lubinsky – every one of them and hundreds of others recorded and distributed black artists. The most dominant small record company of all was Atlantic Records, led by the Turk Ahmet Ertegun and his Jewish partner Jerry Wexler, which contributed a significant breakthrough in the popularity of African-American artists.

A close study of independent labels by rock historian Charlie Gillett (1970) reveals that slightly more than 40 percent of the independent labels were owned or run by American Jews. However, the influence of Jews was more considerable, since a decade later the repertoire of independent companies became the mainstream sound. During the second half of the 1950s, the small independent labels began to release more songs that made the top 10 of the *Billboard* chart.[212] The success of the independent labels forced the major record companies to adapt themselves to the new age, and the most successful ones were those that were able to build an accessible rock catalog.

Two of the most successful independent companies, Atlantic Records and Electra Records, were owned and managed by Jews. These two companies, which held a valuable repertoire, merged in 1967 with the Warner Brothers' record label. This merger was made possible by the auspices of Kinney National Services, managed by Steve Ross, a New York Jew who acquired Warner Brothers. Kinney turned into Warner Communications from 1971, and over the years would become the Time Warner conglomerate. From the early 1970s, it also bought the repertoire of Asylum Records, the successful Californian singer-songwriters catalog owned by David Geffen. Beginning in the second half of the 1960s, Warner based its output on a rock repertoire, and for the next three decades, competed with CBS.[213]

The old Jewish music company MCA, founded in the 1920s by Jules Stein, later became a Hollywood empire under the leadership of Lou Wasserman and took over Decca. The German giant BMG swallowed RCA-Victor that lost the lead in the industry. Columbia, which was Victor's competition for years, was owned by William Paley, son of a Jewish businessman who understood the po-

---

[212] Charlie Gillett, *Sound of The City: The Rise of Rock and Roll* (London: Da Capo Press, 1984), 492.
[213] Connie Bruck, *Master of the Game: Steve Ross and the Creation of Time Warner* (New York: Penguin Books, 1995).

tential of radio networks in the late 1920s. Paley became a real tycoon and entrusted Columbia's artistic management to Goddard Lieberson. Until the mid-1960s, the latter maintained a repertoire of Tin Pan Alley songs, basing most of its power on Broadway musicals, from *My Fair Lady* to *West Side Story*. The company signed Bob Dylan and the folk-rock band The Byrds during the first half of the 1960s, but its activity in the rock industry remained limited. It was the new Jewish director, Clive Davis, who changed the trend after attending the Monterey Festival in June 1967. Davis understood the commercial potential of the baby boomers and opened the company to a new line of rock that made CBS Records one of the two leading corporations.

Waiting for my man: The Jewish entrepreneur

They were independent, courageous and unrestrained, risk-averse, street-loving cats. The record companies played a key role in American music in both majors and independent companies. Among them were Jerry Wexler (Atlantic Records), Jac Holzman (Electra Records), Albert Grossman (Bob Dylan's manager), Walter Yetnikoff (CBS-Records' lawyer and CEO), Neil Bogart (King of the Bubblegum music), and David Geffen ("the Golden Boy" of the industry). These Jews were, for the most part, second-generation Jewish immigrants from Central and Eastern Europe, who made their way through the Jewish social networks. Others had free professions (especially lawyers) who, in the face of the barriers they faced in WASP companies developed prosperous careers in the music field. It's not as if the Jews also lived in harmony among themselves. Sometimes the competition was harsh and bitter. However, their dominant presence made the music field a "natural" place for Jews to advance in.

To the credit of the Jewish mother

Some Jewish entrepreneurs who were second and third-generation Americans owed their success to the maternal push. The parents, who were first and second-generation immigrants, hoped and looked forward to a better future for their children. The pressure for higher education as a recipe for social mobility appears in their recollections, as well as the way immigration difficulties affected their parents in creating their urge for success.

Jerry Wexler was vice-president of Atlantic Records and a partner in the company from 1953. Alongside the charismatic Turkish Ahmet Ertegun, he co-founded one of the most important musical institutions of the era of authentic black music for America. Wexler previously worked as a publisher in Tin Pan Alley and a journalist (he was the one who recommended branding race music as rhythm and blues) but discovered his vocation as a successful record man and music producer. Wexler lacked any musical knowledge nor did he have any technological know-how. Like Hollywood's Jewish founders, he was endowed with a failed father and a strong mother whom he admired. While his father, a member of a Jewish Hasidic Polish family, worked as a window cleaner in New York, his mother Elsa, who was of German-Jewish descent, hoped for a "better life" for her son. Although he was irresponsible (wasting the precious $50 meant for his education in a city pool game), his mother did not give up. "She would not, she insisted, give up my own education," he recalls.[214]

Walter Yetnikoff served as CBS Records' president from 1975 for a decade and a half.[215] He began his career as a lawyer in the early 1960s and progressed rapidly through the corporate ranks. CBS belonged to William Paley, who, despite his origins, tried to introduce to the public an all-American company by only appointing Protestant board members. Yetnikoff admitted that Paley revealed his Jewish background only in the way he passionately ate his meals. But while WASPs ran CBS radio and television, the record company was attractive ground for young Jews. Many of them started as young lawyers, such as Walter Yetnikoff and Clive Davis, who would run the record company.

Yetnikoff, like Wexler, was born in Brooklyn to a working-class family. His father was a maintenance worker at a New York hospital, supporting his family frantically. His mother was very dominant and had higher aspirations for herself and her son. She believed, he said, that her son would be the "savior" of the family. Yetnikoff recalls that his mother said: "'Our Walter is a genius [...] He has the IQ of a genius. He'll get rich [...] He has to."[216]

David Geffen became known as the pioneer of the music business from the early 1970s.[217] Born in Brooklyn, he started in the mailroom and emerged as a

---

[214] Jerry Wexler and David Ritz, *Rhythm and the Blues: A Life in American Music* (New York: Alfred Knopf, 1993), 25.
[215] Columbia was founded in the mid-1980s and was one of the two major music companies, alongside Victor (from 1929 it was renamed RCA-Victor). In the 1920s, also due to the death of its dynamic manager Edward Easton, the company suffered from financial difficulties and was sold to a receiver. In the late 1930s, a young Jewish entrepreneur, William Paley, took over and bought it.
[216] Walter Yetnikoff and David Ritz, *Howling at the Moon: The Odyssey of a Monstrous Music Mogul in an Age of Excess* (New York: Abacus, 2003), 44.
[217] By the end of 2005, David Geffen became known as one of the three owners of the studio Skg – Dreamworks, alongside two other Jews, Steven Spielberg and Jeffrey Katzenberg (the studio was sold to Universal in October 2005). Geffen began his career in the mail room at William

businessman with rare instincts. In his mid-20s, he launched a successful record label, Asylum, under the auspices of Warner Communications. Like Wexler, Geffen was a mediocre school student and perceived his father as "weak and unsuccessful," while his mother was a very dominant woman who unreservedly believed in her son's talent. "King David," she used to call him. Still, Geffen had dropped out of college in Texas. He started his career from "below" in the mailroom at a successful booking agency. His biographer, Tom King, describes him as a student with a hard-work ethic he learned from his mother. "Geffen simply worked harder than anyone else," King explained. "He came early and stayed late. Each weekend, four trainees were sent down the street to help out with small jobs on *The Ed Sullivan Show*, which the agency had 'packaged.' Geffen frequently volunteered for the task."[218]

A street without God

The music industry's Jews grew up in the seam between the old European world and the new American world. They could not and did not want to maintain their religious tradition (even if some, like Yetnikoff, became known as enthusiastic Zionists), but American street culture provided them with their desires. "I can't remember a time I wasn't a doubter. Never," Jerry Wexler recalled of the atheism he had embraced, "not for a hot minute – have I believed in God […] Yet I see myself as deeply spiritual. My feelings for literature, art, movies, food and wine are all invested. All that meant going to Harlem, he adds," I loved the Harlem of the thirties, loved its look and feel, its dance halls and night clubs and especially its sound."[219]

Growing up in Brooklyn's grandparents and extended family, Walter Yetnikoff was unmoved by his mother's embarrassment because of their economic and social status and their location in a working-class neighborhood. Yetnikoff gravi-

---

Morris Artists Agency and emerged as a businessman with rare instincts. In his mid-twenties, he launched a successful record label, Asylum, under the auspices of Atlantic at Warner Communications. After a series of successes, he sold it to Warner for $7 million. He became one of the board members and concentrated on film making. In the early 1980s, he started a new record label, which he sold to Universal for an estimated half a billion dollars toward the end of the decade.

218 Tom King, *The Operator: David Geffen Builds, Buys, and Sells the New Hollywood* (New York: Broadway Books, 2000), 48–49.
219 Jerry Wexler and David Ritz, *Rhythm and the Blues: A Life in American Music* (New York: Alfred Knopf, 1993), 15.

tated to urban Brooklyn. "I liked the clock, I liked the streets, I liked bustling neighborhood of pushcarts on Blake Avenue," he reiterated, "where old-world Jews peddled everything from pickles to piece goods [...] and the shouts of hungry merchants and excited shopper collided with the radios on windowsills playing swing time Benny Goodman and Artie Shaw."[220]

Jac Holzman was the owner and president of Electra Records from the early 1950s to the first half of the 1970s. Electra became known as a successful folk company, but in the mid-1960s, Holzman crossed the line toward rock that was identified with counterculture. Holzman revealed that he grew up in a liberal family under a father who was a successful doctor and who had no faith in his son. His maternal grandmother, he explained, wrote a speech for F.D. Roosevelt in the past, and his grandfather was a rabbi who married Jews and gentiles, as well as Jews and blacks, and "for which he was forever banished to an obscure synagogue in Hoboken, New Jersey."[221]

Albert Grossman became known as one of the most influential artistic directors of his time. The man behind Bob Dylan, Peter Paul and Mary, The Band and Janis Joplin, made his artists very successful with his reliance on his "street guts." Peter Yarrow from Peter Paul and Mary testifies to him being "very intuitive. Very gutsy, very street. He was also brilliant. A genius in my opinion." He added, "[b]ut he immediately established his dominance in our relationship, which was always there."[222]

You've got a friend

One of the characteristics of the Jewish network was how American Jews recruited other Jews into the industry and facilitated their penetration into this economic sphere. In contrast to the heavy industries, banking, Wall Street and the like, the music industry was one of the only areas of activity in which Jews were not discriminated against, and they benefited in diverse ways from the ethnic context. Jerry Wexler recalls how Shap (Meyer Shapiro), "one of those wonderfully mellow, hip Broadway press agents, an old-time publicist who was working for BMI," arranged for him to work for Joe Carlton, Billboard's music editor. Wex-

---

[220] Walter Yetnikoff and David Ritz, *Howling at the Moon: The Odyssey of a Monstrous Music Mogul in an Age of Excess* (New York: Abacus, 2003), 28.
[221] Jac Holzman and Gavan Daws, *Follow the Music: The Life and High Times of Elektra Records in the Great Years of American Pop Culture* (Santa Monica, CA: FirstMedia Books, 2000), 263.
[222] Fred Goodman, *The Mansion on the Hill: Dylan, Young, Geffen, Springsteen, and the Head-On Collision of Rock and Commerce* (New York: Vintage, 1997), 87.

ler talks about a sense of outsider fraternity among his industry peers who opposed both WASPs and the Jewish 'establishment.' They identified with the pioneers of independent labels and BMI leaders because they "broke the stranglehold of the pop record labels." His boss, Paul Ackerman, recalled Wexler, "admired Russ Sanjek and BMI for similar reasons [...] Paul was my guru."[223]

In the early 1960s, Jac Holzman, owner of Electra Records, recruited Paul Rothchild, a young Jewish music producer who was responsible for discovering new talents. The collaboration between the two led to immediate results with the Paul Butterfield Blues Band, a Chicago blues band he joined soon after with the excellent guitarist Mike Bloomfield. Rothchild recalls how their common Jewish origins and a "half hour of intense intellectual Jew at each other" were part of the band's attraction to sign with the phenomenal Jewish guitarist Bloomfield.[224] "He [Bloomfield] found a kindred soul, I found a kindred soul, it was wonderful," recalls Rothchild.

Albert Grossman built a Jewish web of connections. His management company was primarily a Jewish initiative. He – apparently unnoticed – shaped Bob Dylan's business environment as such: The song publisher was the Jew Artie Mogull, who in the 1960s led a later incarnation of the Witmark brothers' company; also, his tour agent was the Jewish folk entrepreneur Harold Leventhal.[225]

Walter Yetnikoff recalls how his Jewish friend Clive Davis, then a young lawyer who worked with him in a small Jewish law firm, turned his attention to the limited travel opportunities in the small Jewish firms in the business world compared to the full open music world, and how the Jewish connection brought them both together: "Remember Harvey Schein?", Davis said, "[h]e used to work at Roseman, now he is at CBS [...] You don't have to know music, you have to know contracts. Harvey's practically alone in the legal department. He wants to bring me along," Clive Davis explained to Yetnikoff. Shortly after that, they both landed one after the other in Columbia's law department.[226]

---

[223] Jerry Wexler and David Ritz, *Rhythm and the Blues: A Life in American Music* (New York: Alfred Knopf, 1993), 59–60.
[224] Jac Holzman and Gavan Daws, *Follow the Music: The Life and High Times of Elektra Records in the Great Years of American Pop Culture* (Santa Monica, CA: FirstMedia Books, 2000), 114.
[225] The first publisher of Dylan's poems was the Jew Joe Levy, whom Dylan reached through John Hammond. Dylan was released from his contract with him because Grossman preferred for business reasons to move him to Artie Mogul. In the 1970s, David Geffen (for a period of time), and most notably his Jewish partner, Elliot Roberts, became Bob Dylan's tour managers.
[226] Clive Davis became known as one of the most successful figures in the American music industry in the second half of the twentieth century. He began his career in the early 1960s as a Columbia Company lawyer and served as director of the CBS record label from 1973 to 1967. After

Booking agencies, PR offices, law firms, as well as personal relationships between records companies execuitives and service providers comprised the Jewish network. Walter Yetnikoff recalls that his appointment as director of the record company became possible thanks to the fact that he and CBS General Manager, his boss, the WASP Arthur Taylor, shared the same lawyer, Stanley Schlesinger.[227]

Neil Bogart (Bogatz originally) became known in the late 1960s as the king of bubblegum music, which mainly appealed to a young audience and was the opposite of the hippie underground rock music scene. The bubblegum music industry was, in fact, a Jewish sub-industry. Two Jewish music producers and entrepreneurs, Jerry Kasenetz and Jeffry Katz, and Joey Levine, who was the lead singer in all of their bands (most often acting in parallel), led this endeavor. Many employees of Bogart's record company, Casablanca Records, were his relatives. "Promotion maniac," journalist Fredric Dunnan called him, while "nepotism was another Bogart trait."[228]

After 15 years in the music business, Bogart reaped the fruits of his activity through the release of dozens of successful disco records, including hits by Donna Summer and Village People. European giant PolyGram bought shares in Bogart's record company and made him a millionaire. Buying a series of roofless Mercedes cars illustrated the success of his dream.

Elitism and popularity

The most significant independent Jewish labels placed themselves in an artistic line that combined elitism and popularity. This sensibility also seems to have stemmed from their personality and desire for charismatic authenticity. Jerry Wexler was primarily looking for new and authentic black singers and sounds from the South; Jac Holzman located his label in the line of protesting white folk music; Albert Grossman believed he possessed a better artistic judgment than those around him and sanctified the "artistic freedom" of his clients. David Geffen built his career by promoting the singer-songwriters from the Los Angeles bohemian scene with an emphasis on artistic uniqueness.

---

being ousted for improper use of the company's money (to fund his son's Bar Mitzvah party), he founded Arista in the mid-1970s and with it achieved outstanding commercial success that included bestsellers by Barry Manilow, Whitney Houston and many other artists.
227 Walter Yetnikoff and David Ritz, *Howling at the Moon: The Odyssey of a Monstrous Music Mogul in an Age of Excess* (New York: Abacus, 2003), 53.
228 Fredric Dannen, *Hit Men: Power Brokers and Fast Money Inside the Music Business* (New York: Anchor, 1991), 166.

These entrepreneurs might have come from working-class backgrounds but were influenced by a home-grown bourgeois ethic for education that emphasized the importance of art and culture. They went to the music industry armed with semi-intellectual tastes, or at least the accompanying jargon (or adopted something similar), but with a finger on the pulse of consumer culture.

When Jerry Wexler first met David Geffen, he didn't think the young agent was going to be one of the most influential people in the music industry. Geffen, then another agent at the outset, sought to release musician Stephen Stills to form a new trio he managed, Crosby Stills and Nash (CSN). Wexler threw the young agent out of the office in shame. It was Ertegun who identified Geffen's business talent and signed the trio in the company. This mistake was to cost Wexler dearly, who in any way was not suitable to the corporate environment.

Success and comfort were Wexler's wishes as Atlantic merged with Warner's corporation, but also tainted the very identity of those who loved to experiment on the wild side of musical activity. Wexler was impatient with extended board meetings and felt adrift. He went down south to record artists he loved but found himself pushed aside. He did sign Led Zeppelin, which was a massive success during the 1970s, but even that didn't stop him from becoming a relatively marginal force. After a tumultuous meeting and a devastating confrontation with Geffen, Wexler was forced to retire.

In 1975, Yetnikoff became CEO of the CBS record company. Although he was devoid of musical learning, he led CBS into the 1980s as he leaned on his charisma and human relationships with some of the world's greatest stage artists, including Bruce Springsteen, Billy Joel, Barbara Streisand, James Taylor, The Rolling Stones, and Paul McCartney. While addicted to sex, alcohol, and cocaine, he had a special relationship with the world's greatest singer-dancer, Michael Jackson, whose albums sales helped Yetnikoff make CBS stay a leading company.

David Geffen made his fortune during the 1970s grooming the Los Angeles-based post-hippie scene of figures like Joni Mitchell, Neil Young, Crosby-Stills-Nash, and The Eagles, who produced a post-psychedelic soundtrack for millions of Americans. After a series of dizzying musical successes and while still a millionaire in his twenties, he tried his hand at cinema, but did not initially demonstrate the same brilliant ability he had in the musical world. In the 1980s, he managed a label bearing his name and slowly and steadily won a series of successes: from the heavy rock of Guns N' Roses to the grunge of Nirvana, which established a new era in the 1990s. Along with Irving Azoff (head of MCA for most of the 1980s), Yetnikoff and Geffen managed a triumvirate in the music industry characterized by friendship, tension, animosity, and suspicion.

In late 1987, Yetnikoff arranged the sale of CBS to the Japanese Sony company. As the mediator between Tokyo's head of capital and American talent, he saw himself as the king of the record industry since he was in control of the 'king of pop' himself. In his recollections, he recalls his conversation with Michael Jackson:

> Jackson: "I'm in a helicopter flying over Long Island."
> Yetnikoff: "You with the monkey?"
> Jackson: "Bubbles is back in California. It's important, Walter. David Geffen just called. He's producing the soundtrack for Tom Cruise's new movie [...] He wants to use one of my songs. I don't want him to. But I told him yes."
> Yetnikoff: "Why did you say yes when you wanted to say no?"
> Jackson: "Well, you know Geffen [...] I am saying yes, you're saying no [...] When are you coming back to Wonderland?"
> Yetnikoff: "When you get rid of the zoo. Your peacocks hate me. They're jealous."[229]

So, finally, Yetnikoff refused to lend Jackson's music to Geffen. Months later, Yetnikoff was ousted, presumably due to a host of instances of inappropriate behavior and a dispute with one of his big stars: Bruce Springsteen and his (Jewish) manager Jon Landau. Yetnikoff's charisma, which saved him many times, wasn't sufficient for such a crisis with such an influential artist. Jackson never called to express his empathy, and in fact, none of the other artists tried to stay in touch either. The press reported that Geffen, once a friend and now an enemy, pulled strings, and the fall was painful. Despite running one of the most significant musical operations in the world he remained powerless, even if Yeitnikoff now had enough time, he says, to "count my money. And believe me, that's going to take some time."[230]

It is difficult to know how popular music would have evolved without the dominant presence of Jews in the industry, but the music world would have advanced in ethnic diversity compared to other industries and to society itself. The ethnic fabric is responsible for the music we listen to throughout the world, and thus the structure of the industry, for the plethora of hungry Jews to fulfill the American dream, has had an overwhelming impact on pop culture across the globe.

---

[229] Walter Yetnikoff and David Ritz, *Howling at the Moon: The Odyssey of a Monstrous Music Mogul in an Age of Excess* (New York: Abacus, 2003), 4–5.
[230] Ibid., 263.

Chapter 7: Stand By Me – The Black-Jewish Political Alliance and the Decline of the WASP

> Because it was the last moment when nearly all Americans (all white Americans) shared, at least rhetorically, a common vision, it became frozen, a kind monument to the old WASP ideal [...] The year 1945 was the last time we were together, the last time we had genuine confidence in the integrative, Americanizing qualities of the old WASP ideal.
> (Peter Schrag, *The Decline of The Wasp*)[231]

> [...] [T]he idea for the March on Washington was conceived by King some ten days before the president announced his support for an omnibus civil right law...following Birmingham king took over the idea transformed it into one of the most memorable events in American civil rights history [...] (Stanley) Levinson argued that at least 100,000 people had to be brought to Washington for it to be a success. Mass demonstrations were rare in Washington in those days [...] Ordinary citizens of various colors and religious persuasions poured into Washington by the tens of thousands, along with constant stream of teachers, trade unionists, priests, pastors and rabbis. Countless groups were represented, but Jewish representation was particularly strong. (Freedman Murray, *What Went Wrong?*)[232]

In the early 1960s, Jewish duo Jerry Leiber and Mike Stoller produced and co-wrote with African-American singer Ben E. King the hit "Stand by Me" – a track with a gospel feel, Latin flavors, European orchestration, and altruistic lyrics. King's voice stitched together religious and lyrical imagery, both personal and public, through the airwaves across the liberal America of the early Kennedy era. The message "Stand by Me" was not cynical at all. In politics, as in music, Jews and blacks collaborated. For one crucial moment in American history, they crossed the bridge over troubled water to force America to commit to its constitutional ideals.

There was no direct link between music and politics, but a conceptual connection. These were parallel phenomena that were not dependent on the other but influenced by each other. In most cases, Jewish musicians did not actively enlist in the struggle for equal civil rights, and most did not write about "politics," but the public discourse fed many of the songs regarding the fight for equal rights. As mass consumer goods, the songs circulated and promoted diverse ideas and images across America about equality of civil rights, cultural pluralism, and racial fraternity. In doing so, they gradually influenced the fabric of images that shaped the American popular culture of those years.

---

231 Peter Schrag, *The Decline of the WASP* (New York: Simon and Schuster, Inc., 1973), 50.
232 Murray Freedman, *What Went Wrong?: The Creation and The Collapse of the Black-Jewish Alliance* (New York: Free Press, 1994), 98–201.

https://doi.org/10.1515/9783110723168-008

As noted earlier, Jews and blacks under the leadership of Dr. Martin Luther King, Jr. formed an unconscious anti-WASP alliance. These minority groups were determined to solve inequality to ensure once and for all their own security.[233]

"When the moon is the only light you see"

The idea of the black-Jewish alliance began to develop in Atlanta in the second decade of the twentieth century, in a case that resembled an American Dreyfus trial. The Jew Leo Frank, a Texan engineer formerly and director of the National Pencil, was arrested on suspicion of murdering a white Protestant young woman. He was killed in 1915 by an angry mob in a vicious lynch (later on Frank was proven innocent).[234]

Frank's trial, imprisonment, and lynching caused concerns among the Jewish community about Old World's insecurities. Although in comparison to Eastern Europe America was a dream come true, discrimination in education, em-

---

[233] Jewish-American research on Jewish and black relations is multifaceted. This study suggests a link based on the experience of suffering, which I will divide into three major research approaches to the Jewish-Black alliance concept. The first, an approach that derives from the same tradition and methodology of suffering, namely the belief that these two minorities were united in the face of a past with similarities and of trying to secure their existence and security. This approach is reflected in Lawrence H. Fuch's classic article, "Sources of Jewish Internationalism and Liberalism" in *The Jews: Social Patterns of an American Group*, edited by Marshall Sklare (New York: Free Press, 1958), 595–613.

A second approach holds that American Jewish bodies are behind black struggles to safeguard the interests of the Jewish community itself. This approach is reflected, in part, by Hasia Diner's important book *In The Almost Promised Land* (1977), and David Levering Lewis's article, "Parallels and Divergences: Assimilationist Strategies of African-American and Jewish Elites from 1910 to the early 1930s," in *Bridges and Boundaries*, edited by Jack Salzman, Adina Back and Gretchen Sullivan Sorin (New York: George Braziller, 1993), 17–31.

A third approach, which I would call revisionist, purports to place Judeo-black relations within the study of whiteness, namely the perception of Jewish-black relations as the way in which Jews secured their position as part of the white color and defined themselves as "white Americans." See Stephen Steinberg, *The Ethnic Myth: Race, Ethnicity, and Class in America* (New York: Beacon Press, 2001); Karen Brodkin, *How Jews Became White Folks and What That Says About Race in America* (New Brunswick: Rutgers University Press, 1998); Taylor Branch, "The Uncivil War," in *Bridges and Boundaries*, edited by Jack Salzman, Adina Back and Gretchen Sullivan Sorin (New York: George Braziller, 1993), 50–69.

[234] Paradoxically, it was the African-American Jim Conley, who worked as in the factory, who killed the victim.

ployment, and acceptance into prestigious universities and faculties was maintained until the mid-1960s.[235]

Despite their constant prominence, the Jewish minority joined the struggle for social justice in impressive numbers, even if it was not a popular Jewish mobilization, but an alliance of political bodies. The polls show that the vast majority of those in the Jewish community supported the struggle for social justice.[236]

Jewish activists were involved in the black struggle of the early twentieth century, but after World War Two, they began a more obsessive, committed, and competent offensive. The mobilization was varied and came from different circles: the central bodies of the Jewish community, alongside the Old Left, and later the New Left. All of these had conflicting interests.[237]

Fear, lust, abundance and consensus

The roots of the civil rights revolution and the alternative culture that grew with it lay in the unique conditions of post-war America. The consciousness of the possible consequences of racism and the new liberal consensus between the left and the American right marked the beginning of a euphoric era full of fear of Communism.

The New Liberal Alliance paralleled a time of unprecedented economic abundance in United States history. This post-war affluence was symbolized by American domination as the leader of the "free world." It was also manifested in its commitment (Marshall Plan) to rebuild the economy of European countries,

---

[235] Leonard Dinnerstein, *Antisemitism in America* (New York: Oxford University Press, 1994), 155.
[236] Marshall Sklare, *Jewish Identity on the Suburban Frontier: A Study of Group Survival in the Open Society* (Chicago: University of Chicago Press, 1979), 322. Sklare found that 93 percent of Jews who participated in his sample survey believed that the term "good Jew" meant "a man who leads an ethical and moral life." And 67 percent said it was "necessary" to support humanitarian causes while 29 percent said it was "desirable" to support those goals. Forty-four percent of respondents thought it was "necessary" to fight, but for blacks this did not change their definition of Jews, while only one percent thought it "necessary" not to work for equality for blacks.
[237] On the one hand, Jewish bodies could be against anti-Semitism and for universal ethnicity, and at the same time support the Cold War and banish members suspected of Communism. On the other hand, some of the Jewish activists closest to Martin Luther King were leftist members of the Communist Party. Some of them, who became King's soul mates, helped their various connections across the northern United States, especially in the media, transform the Civil Rights Movement from a marginal southern movement into an organized national movement. However, King himself was an anti-Communist. The Jewish activists in the Communist Party were sometimes outraged over his political contacts with the Kennedy brothers.

not only of its allies but also of its former enemies. Economic affluence varied in many ways in the different population groups, but the primary beneficiaries of the affluence were the white working class, and especially the white middle class.

The white working class had to struggle – with the help of President Truman on pensions, federal backing for loans and raising minimum wages – to enjoy the affluence.[238] The white middle class, on the other hand, reaped the abundance of fruit faster and more meaningfully with the development of bureaucracy, the intensification of capitalism and the expansion of corporations.[239] At the individual level, more people than ever bought homes, sent their children to colleges, and could afford to purchase a car and various electronic domestic appliances.[240]

It was an unstable economic abundance, built on a continuing war economy (World War Two, Korea, and Vietnam), and which continued to produce a high price of high inflation and low investment. It was also unequal economic affluence.

The economic boom, some of which was real and some artificial and misleading, rested on a new economic strategy, which combined Fordism and Keynesianism. The goal of the US government was to expand the consumer market by increasing the number of people who were part of it. It was a logical continuity of Henry Ford's recognition that he could make more significant profits if his employees were his consumers. The goal required that the competing interests of labor and capital (employers and workers) be put aside for the benefit of a joint effort. The capital, labor, and government compromise was needed between capital and workers. The compromise insisted on was that by increasing

---

238 The end the war and dismantling the military industry led to widespread layoffs, a wave of strikes, inflation and a temporary crisis, but cooperation between President Truman and labor unions created an opportunity for a rise in living standards, a rise in minimum wages, federal backing for bank loans, pensions and more. See George Douglas, *Postwar America: 1948 and the Incubation of Our Times* (New York: Krieger Publishing Company, 1995), 9.

239 Between 1945 and 1957 the number of clerical staff increased by 23 percent. The most important trend was the transition of small business workers (36% in 1900, 28% in 1940 and 16% in 1960) to work in large corporations and government organizations, a change that created a new order of work within a neo-capitalist technocratic system. See Ibid.

240 Between 1940 and 1955, the income per individual grew by 293 percent, but that did not help to moderate the "consumer appetite," so consumer overdrafts grew by 55 percent between 1952 and 1956. In 1950, there were one and a half million TVs in households, while in 1954 there were more than 30 million TVs. The United States, with 6 percent of the world's population, had 60 percent of the worl"s cars, 58 percent of the phones, and 45 percent of its radios. See Lawrence Grossberg, *We Gotta Get Out of This Place* (New York: Routledge, 1992), 138.

productive salaries, the production cycle would widen, and profits would increase. Business and labor were united in a joint economic effort as the state mediated between them.

This policy required another political, social, and democratic compromise: the expansion of the consumer market allowed those who were outside the mainstream labor force, especially blacks and migrants, to join the working class. Integration into economic affluence required the expansion of the social and political rights of these lower classes. The connection between capital, workforce, and the mobility of the subclasses formed into an ideology known as "New American Liberalism."

At the level of political politics, the two major parties agreed not to disagree, at least on the new concepts of economics. It was a temporary era of "the end of ideology." This new liberalism lasted as long as the ideological differences between the parties did not entail specific meanings for the states' activities. It also attracted leftist intellectuals into this optimism.

At the level of social politics, the new liberalism had, as it were, complex solutions to the question of existence and social differences. It seemed to offer the end of ideological divisions in class as well. As mentioned, this form of liberalism directed social dissent at an external enemy, Communism, which became a real threat to America. Liberalism illustrated that status had an important cultural significance related to taste, aesthetics, difference, and style. Social motives were made possible by creating economic characteristics and not necessarily by cultural capital. The working class and the middle-classes based their tastes on the expanding consumer culture, and not necessarily the desire to be "upper class."

It was as if social movement was available for anyone who wanted to work hard in the manner of the old Puritan ethic, and this liberalism believed that the world was entering a new era primarily based on the possibilities for the individual in everyday life.

Conformity versus subversion

The liberal consensus created a conformist image for the 1950s. Economic abundance influenced the individual and family life. Middle-class white citizens moved to the suburbs and filled their homes with electronics and forms of mass media. However, the investment in the family went hand in hand with public investment in the military-industrial complex and corporate profits. Americans saw the family as a broader commitment to contributing to the strength of the United States, fulfilling the dream of peace and prosperity, and protecting against "godless" communism. As it stood, conservatism, which created a traditional isolation at the family level, was grounded in the political consensus.

The post-war levels of economic abundance, as well as the legacy of the war, led to an unprecedented wave of births in American history, termed the "baby boom." A low marriage age (average age 21) and high marriage percentage (92 percent) characterized the 1950s. Various scholars and writers liked to point out the impact on women's status, especially in popular culture, through representation on television and in books, supposedly based on patriarchal imagery.

But it was not so clear that reality was so conservative. Although women made room for soldiers who returned home, and labor unions worried that employers would push aside minorities and women, the number of employed women increased from year to year.[241] Even the Kinsey reports, which were best-sellers and explored the sexual behavior of the human male, proved that attitudes to sexuality was more liberated than before.[242]

Intellectuals also criticized notions of conformity and the new lifestyle of the "corporate person" who became a "small screw" within a "soulless" hyper-technocratic system. William Whyte wrote:

> They are not workers, nor are they the white-collar people in the usual, clerk sense of the word. These people only work for the Organization [...] they are the ones of our middle class who left home, spiritually as well physically, to take the vows of organization life [...] they are the dominant members of our society nonetheless [...] it is their values which will set the American temper.[243]

In spite of the criticism regarding conformism, there were also voices of balance. Even in the late 1950s, intellectual Daniel Bell argued that the new political-social structure in the United States allowed more subversive and critical voices from the margins than previously; not necessarily a classic ideological leftist criticism, but a new form of criticism grounded in popular culture.[244]

---

[241] George Douglas claims that in 1960 the number of women employed was double that of 1940. The large percentage of working women was among married women over the age of 35, although only about 20 percent still held senior positions in their jobs and many jobs were part-time. See George Douglas, *Postwar America: 1948 and the Incubation of Our Times* (New York: Krieger Publishing Company, 1995), 96.
[242] Beth Bailey, "Sexual Revolution," in *The Sixties: From Memory to History*, edited by David Farber (Chapel Hill: The University of North Carolina Press, 1994), 237.
[243] William H. Whyte, *The Organization Man* (New York: Simon & Schuster, 1956), 298.
[244] Daniel Bell, *The End of Ideology* (Illinois: Free Press, 1959).

Bell explained that even at a time when Communism became such a tangible threat to democracies through a host of achievements in Eastern Europe and East Asia, it hardly threatened America. Although the United States was an industrial, urban, and democratic state that decomposed traditional community ties, Communism could never rise politically, since the constitution and the establishment of immigrant society's formation left minimal space for Communist solidarity.[245]

It seemed that Americans were naturally critical of "everything that is wrong with their society," due to the American balance in the form of pressure groups – from farmers, blacks, to Jewish and ethnic groups. Bell also paid attention to the impressive presence of the American media and press, the massive investment in both higher education and popular culture, and the formation of the leisure company, which created the world's largest consumer society. He believed in the liberal American social structure, which gave American society more opportunities for self-criticism and repair.

Bell doubted the social psychologists' assumptions about the era who believed that Americans had turned conformity into a religion He noted the subversiveness of various bohemian groups and even of Hollywood itself. As far back as the 1920s, he said, the film industry was an American attempt to provide an alternative to the European monarchy, and in the 1950s not just the producers and moguls, but the stars were of ethnic origin (Sinatra, Dean Martin, Sammy Davis Jr.) who were an alternative to the old Hollywood order. On the cultural fringe, it was the Beat poets who suggested an alternative way of life to that of the mainstream. In the past, bohemians had criticized the Puritans and the Victorians. In the 1950s they confronted the shallowness of mass society.

And still, minority groups began to criticize the ills of the liberal consensus. Despite the rhetoric, blacks partially benefited from the general economic affluence and suffered from institutional discrimination in the South and non-institutional discrimination that was prevalent throughout the states. Continued lynching in the South and disappointing homecomings for veteran African-American soldiers only illustrated the dissonance between World War Two objectives (war on racism) and the promise of the new age (the new liberal consensus) in the face of existential reality.[246]

---

245 Ibid., 31.
246 Although the wages of blacks rose, it did not compare to the wages of whites. In the 1940s, the average salary of a white citizen was $2,982 a year while that of an African-American citizen was $1,828 a year. In the 1950s, however, the average salary of a white citizen was $5,137 a year, while a black citizen earned an average of $3,075 a year. In fact, the gap between the standard of living of whites and blacks only increased. The economic power of blacks was worth $15 million

Compared to the black minority, American Jews experienced impressive mobility. Jews entered the mainstream starting in the 1920s and after the war established their hold as a middle class.[247] Still, employment and educational discrimination continued even after the war, and public fears of the imaginary and imaginative power of the Jews was still prevalent.[248] Polls showed that nearly 60% of the population still claimed that Jews had too much power in the United States.[249] This sense of insecurity drove Jewish organizations to fight alongside blacks for equal rights and to unequivocally demand that the United States commit itself to its constitution.

The involvement of Jews in the black "business of politics" after the war was not self-evident, and was a matter of controversy within the Jewish community; some feared that standing by the blacks would 'drag the Jews down.' However, the vast majority, led by Rabbi Stephen Weiss, the head of the American Jewish Congress, decided in favor of the need to fight for shared Jewish and black interests.

Jewish leadership also underwent significant changes during these years. The veteran leaders, mostly of German-Jewish origin, were conservative and produced a conservative politics. They supported the Republican Party and dealt with the problem of equality with elitism. In contrast, the new leaders came from a background of social work and public law, and the origins of many were from families with socialist experience. These activists believed that a humanitarian utopia might solve black poverty.[250]

The new Jewish leaders believed that one of the most effective anti-discrimination weapons was the use of state-of-the-art social science research on racism. They were assisted by a group of European social scientists, especially Jews who were refugees from Nazi Germany, who set up a new field of research that sought to test racism as a psychological distortion of mankind. These scholars (including Theodor W. Adorno and Max Horkheimer, Hannah Arendt, Erich Fromm, Erik Erikson, and Kurt Lewin) tried to understand the motives for the totalitarian takeover of World War Two in general, and the Nazi extermination ma-

---

a year, but these hardly benefited from the fruits of plenty. See Douglas T. Miller and Marion Nowak, *The Fifties: The Way We Really Were* (Garden City, N.Y.: Doubleday & Co., Inc., 1977), 184.
247 Henry L. Feingold, *A Time for Searching: Entering the Mainstream 1920–1945* (Baltimore: Johns Hopkins University Press, 1992).
248 Leonard Dinnerstein, *Antisemitism in America* (New York: Oxford University Press, 1994), 155–157.
249 Murray Freedman, *What Went Wrong?: The Creation and The Collapse of the Black-Jewish Alliance* (New York: Free Press, 1994), 131–132.
250 Ibid., 134–136.

chine in particular. To this end, they used, among other things, Sigmund Freud's theory about the pessimistic and irrational element of the human soul, along with anthropology and sociology.

Erich Fromm based his theoretical work on the authoritarian type facing the humanitarian type.[251] Adorno also went on to deal with this issue of the authoritarian figure, and Lewin based his research on society and racism at the Research Center for Group Dynamics at Massachusetts Institute. Later on, Jewish civil rights activists used social studies in the struggle for social justice. Supreme Court Justice Earl Warren was persuaded to make the decision to abolish segregation in the education system, too, due to sociological studies brought to his attention by Jewish activists who dealt with the damage done by southern racism among children of black communities.[252]

After the war educational integration was interpreted as the positive side of every minority. The power of the United States, according to this new rhetoric, stemmed from the power of all and varied groups. Instead of becoming stigmatized, cultural differences and pluralism became acceptable.

The last hope of the American left

The revolution for equal rights was encouraged by the mobilization of the American Left in favor of the struggle. The fact that Jews, more than any other minority group, formed part of the American Left, was in retrospect vital. The Jewish political network on the Left, due to its ties to American media in general and New York in particular, helped bring Martin Luther King, Jr.'s activities on to the American agenda.

The explanations for the tangible presence of Jews on the left-wing political spectrum were varied. Some scholars believed that socialism was a secular religion and a substitute for Judaism.[253] Other studies have explained that Jews favored an anti-religious leftist world, where religion was not an obstacle.[254] Some

---

[251] Erich Fromm, *Escape from Freedom* (New York: Open Road Media, 2013 [1941]); Erich Fromm, *Man for Himself: An Inquiry into the Psychology of Ethics* (New York: Open Road Media, 2013 [1947]).
[252] Murray Freedman, *What Went Wrong?: The Creation and The Collapse of the Black-Jewish Alliance* (New York: Free Press, 1994), 139.
[253] Moses Rischin, *The Promised City: New York Jews, 1870–1914* (Cambridge: Harvard University Press, 1970), 166; Nicolas Berdyaev, *The Russian Revolution* (Michigan: Ann Arbor Paperbacks, 1961), 69–70.
[254] Arthur Liebman, *Jews and the Left* (New York: Wiley, 1979), 12, 620.

also recognized that the Jews' tendency to turn "left" was the product of a distortion of national culture, leaving Jews outside the circle of nationalism and in the arms of socialism.[255] Other left-wing scholars believed that Jewish socialism was a form of Jewish subculture created by the encounter with Eastern European capitalism.[256] Studies combining history and psychology, for their part, believed that the connection between Jews and socialism was inherent in the familial and psychological structure of the Jewish family.[257]

Counter voices argued that Jewish socialism in America was a unique American historical experience, made possible by the specific encounter of Jewish immigrants with American capitalism.[258] Although American Jewish socialism became a mass movement in the second decade of the twentieth century, it seems to have been a product of the experience of immigration, rather than an established ideological movement. Socialism, in other words, was the way for immigrants to ensure their survival. It improved the conditions of their employment and served as a social home, but was never ideologically rooted and did not rise politically.[259] Socialism was fed by the politics of labor unions and the rhetoric of Jewish intellectuals, more than from calculated and successful movement activities. And so, when the first and second generation of immigrants began to enter the mainstream, socialism lost its meaning and influence.

In the early 1950s, trade unions, which until then were characterized by the massive presence of Jews, lost their status. After all, the sons of union members rose to their standard of living and entered middle-class work circles. Jewish labor union leaders emphasized integration and "social commitment," in the sense of modern living, across ethnic-religious interests, and, in many ways, the role of labor organizations was an integration agent for American life.

Surprisingly, the post-war anti-Communist atmosphere reinforced the alliance of blacks and Jews from the left. The McCarthyite witch hunt could not allow the left to organize any more politically. Leftists leaders and activists had to face investigative conferences by the House of Representatives. Many

---

[255] Bernard K. Johnpoll, *Pacifist's Progress: Norman Thomas and the Decline of Socialism* (Chicago: Quadrangle Books 1970), 27, 54, 55.
[256] Arthur Liebman, *Jews and the Left* (New York: Wiley, 1979).
[257] Stanley Rothman and Simon Lichter, *Roots of Radicalism: Jews, Christians, and the Left* (New York: Transaction Publishers, 1985).
[258] Eli Lederhendler, *Jewish Immigrants and American Capitalism, 1880–1920: From Caste to Class* (Cambridge: Cambridge University Press, 2009).
[259] Irving Howe, *World of Our Fathers* (New York: Simon & Schuster, 1976), 355.

have lost their reputations and livelihoods while facing accusations regarding subversive activity.

The Communist Party lost its grip in tandem with the rise of King and his supporters. Soviet leader Nikita Khrushchev's publications about Stalin's crimes and Khrushchev's invasion of Hungary in 1956 markedly weakened the Communist Party, which remained without recruits. Jewish leaders of the left considered moving the party through a process of "Americanization." Other socialists declared support for the "black mass search" and created the grounds for the left's alliance with Martin Luther King.[260] At the same time, the American left sought ways to approach the center, while broadening ideological rhetoric and moderating criticism of capitalism as an economical method.[261] The left-wing intellectuals withdrew from their old beliefs and for the most part, joined Truman's crusade against the Communists.

Against the backdrop of the Cold War, intellectuals and left-wing public opinion shapers realized that irrational forces had taken over Europe's eastern half. Recognizing the failure of their previous vision drew them to Sigmund Freud's pessimistic theory of man and neo-orthodox theologies. The new liberalism rejected all forms of totalitarianism and supported only minor reforms in capitalist society. This liberalism recognized the complexity of reality, the rooted sense of sin in human nature, and the corruption that resulted from the ability to control the power of the masses. In short, this liberalism recognized capitalism as the least terrible of all economic systems.

Social and spiritual scholars have thus marked the 1950s as the era of "the end of ideologies." They insisted on how ideology, ideas that turn into power that would lead to social change, lost its meaning. The 1950s left no room for it: the results of World War Two, the emergence of 'fair capitalism,' the formation of the welfare state, and the influence of Freud's ideas, questioned the ability of any ideology to create a utopia and social harmony. "The old ideologies have lost their 'truth' and their power to persuade," Daniel Bell explained, and "[f]ew serious minds believe any longer that one can set down 'blue prints' and through 'social engineering' bring about a new utopia of social harmony."[262]

The new liberal manifesto of the left relied on the publications of Arthur Schlesinger and John Kenneth Galbraith, who lessened antagonism towards the big corporations. These believed that the government had learned the lessons of the past and would not allow a 1929 economic collapse, while presenting an

---

[260] Murray Freedman, *What Went Wrong?: The Creation and The Collapse of the Black-Jewish Alliance* (New York: Free Press, 1994), 160.
[261] J. A. Matuso, *The Unraveling of America* (New York: Harper and Row, 1984), 4.
[262] Daniel Bell, *The End of Ideology* (Illinois: Free Press, 1959), 371.

optimistic vision of economic relations.²⁶³ Intellectuals also explained that the liberal consensus was an extreme response to Communism stemming from the anti-radical roots of the American nation.²⁶⁴ Richard Hofstadter's writing was influential, as he argued that America was not the only nation suffering from "paranoia" about foreign bodies, yet it was a relatively small right-wing front that adopted the "paranoid style."²⁶⁵

However, towards the end of the 1950s, left-wing intellectuals changed their tone slightly and suggested some minor changes "within the system," while correcting consumer concerns and balancing investment in the public sectors.²⁶⁶ Critics had been engaging in social sectors that the liberal consensus had left behind, explaining that, despite affluence, a quarter of the United States population lived below the poverty line.²⁶⁷

The rise of alternative protests grew parallel to the great wave of immigration of blacks to the north.²⁶⁸ There they found new difficulties: high rents, poor municipal services, disadvantaged schools, crime, and increased violence. But these were dwarfed by the situation in the South, where constitutional improvement was more rhetorical than tangible. The federal government had difficulty enforcing the 1954 constitutional amendments to the education system (following Brown v. Board of Education of Topeka). Although the media praised the legal victory as an example of American altruism, the social reaction in the southern states and the enforcement difficulties created a situation where blacks were forced to explicitly exercise their right to equality.

Because of the left's inability to harness the masses in support of its old Marxist ideology, mobilization for the struggle for social justice served as a

---

263 Arthur M. Schlesinger, *The Vital Center: The Politics of Freedom* (New York: Transaction Publishers, 1947); J.K. Galbraith, *American Capitalism: The Concept of Countervailing Power* (New York: Martino Fine Books, 1952).
264 Douglas T. Miller and Marion Nowak, *The Fifties: The Way We Really Were* (Garden City, N.Y.: Doubleday & Co., Inc., 1977), 23.
265 Richard Hofstadter, *The Paranoid style in American Politics and other Essays* (Cambridge: Harvard University Press, 1962), 9–11.
266 J. K. Galbraith, *The Affluent Society* (New York: Library of America, 1958).
267 Michael Harrington, *The Other America: Poverty in the United State* (New York: Penguin Books, 1962), 1–2.
268 The Black Odyssey to the north has transformed the subject of social justice from a moral failure that characterizes social margins into a topic that is at the top of the national consciousness. From 1940 to 1910, the African-American population of New York grew from 60,000 to 250,000. In Philadelphia the number of blacks increased from 84,000 to 250,000. Chicago, too, became an African-American center: from 30,000 blacks in 1910, the number after the war increased to about 277,000.

lever for renewed relevance. The fight from the courts to the streets began with the appearance of Martin Luther King, Jr. King became the movement leader as early as 1955, after Rosa Parks' famous refusal to move to the back seats of the bus she was traveling on. King's boycott was not the first African-American attempt to combat southern discrimination in public transportation, but it was the first time that African-Americans had joined in large numbers in the fight and stood behind a dominant leader.

King himself was an unknown pastor until the 1955 Montgomery bus boycott, and he lacked any real experience as a leader of a political-social protest movement. King's rise to leadership occurred as he aligned with members of the leftist Jewish radical community, which leveraged the black struggle for national public consciousness.[269] The Jews brought with them organizational capabilities, media relations, funding, and legal knowledge. But most of all, they were the catalyst for blacks to start taking their political destiny into their own hands. They were the ones through which King understood how far they could reach. While the administration widely accepted the veteran Jewish leaders of the National Association for the Advancement of Colored People, the new activists, such as Stanley Levinson and Ella Baker, were left-wing radical Jews.

Radicalism as an experience

While the leveraging of the black struggle into public consciousness helped the momentary success of the Old Left, it was the younger radicals of the New Left who expressed the cultural transformations of post-war alternative culture. Throughout universities and campuses, young student movements (SDS, SNCC, and others) began to fight for civil rights and combat racism and poverty, but they turned their activities into cultural protests. They replaced the 'class war' with insights into the experience of alienation. The New Left enjoyed an ethnic presence. Its leadership, with a high radical Jewish presence, anchored their activity in exhibitionistic protest that radiated anti-WASP overtones.[270]

Historians are unanimous in the perception that student politics received a boost of energy with John Kennedy's election in 1960. Kennedy's charisma and pragmatic liberalism, and hope for a better future for minorities and liberals, fair

---

[269] Murray Freedman, *What Went Wrong?: The Creation and The Collapse of the Black-Jewish Alliance* (New York: Free Press, 1994), 164–167.
[270] Arthur Liebman, *Jews and the Left* (New York: Wiley, 1979), 160.

capitalism, the promise of scientific progress all made him a positive force in young American and liberals' lives.[271]

Kennedy's great influence did not stem from his actions, but his rhetoric and image. The image of a white house in a flurry, the resolution of international crises (e. g., the Cuban Missile Crisis), his considerable charm, his appearance as an intelligent and witty man, his effective control of the media, and the speed of his response to the world.

Kennedy's rhetoric moved the wheels on the path to more democratization. He felt that more Americans could and should enjoy the fruits of participation in public life – a process that was supposed to eliminate poverty and racism. Despite his sweeping rhetoric, Kennedy's actions were careful and conventional. He conducted a pragmatic and cautious policy but released hidden energies. He was the first Irish Catholic president of the United States, and his election symbolized the extent to which the United States stretched the political options of the ethnic minorities. The activities of the Civil Rights Movement reinforced the recognition that America suffers from social diseases, and Kennedy's liberalism created the belief that this social malady could be solved. This new wave of liberalism led to an awareness of injustice, and this awareness was the primary basis for those movements of the 1960s.

The New Left defined itself as free from a strict dogma, committed to the present elements in an attempt to practice radicalism through 'experience.' Young students volunteered in the summer of 1964 to combat racism in the South, but it was a fashion of protest rather than strict Old Left ideology. They were attracted mainly to new radical intellectuals, such as Herbert Marcuse, Charles Wright Mills and Paul Goodman, who were close in their agenda to the Beat poets.[272] Goodman and Miles criticized capitalism not only in the economic sense, but also in a cultural one. They believed that capitalism shattered the beauty of traditional community life and created a 'meaningless' culture. In their opinion, economic prosperity destroyed the values of good society and created a soulless technocratic civilization. In addition, members of the New Left were drawn to the writings of Jean-Paul Sartre and Albert Camus that preached

---

271 Edward Morgan, *The Sixties Experience: Hard Lessons about Modern America* (Philadelphia: Temple University Press, 1991), 1–20; J. A. Matuso, *The Unraveling of America* (New York: Harper and Row, 1984), 3–5.
272 See Morris Dickstein, *Gates of Eden: American Culture in the Sixties* (New York: Basic Books, 1977); Todd Gitlin, *The Sixties: Years of Hope, Days of Rage* (New York: Bantam, 2013); Charles Kaiser, *1968 in America: Music, Politics, Chaos, Counterculture, and the Shaping of a Generation* (New York: Grove Press, 2018); David Farber, *The Age of Great Dreams: America in the 1960s* (New York: Hill and Wang, 1994).

Existentialism and the responsibility of the individual. The New Left founders wrote in the Port Huron statement:

> We are people of this generation, bred in at least modest comfort, housed now in universities, looking uncomfortably to the world we inherit [...] We regard men as infinitely precious and possessed of unfulfilled capacities for reason, freedom, and love [...] We oppose the depersonalization that reduces human beings to the status of things.[273]

Despite the moral liberal intentions of the New Left – which included pacifism, eradication of poverty, equality, democratization and personal fulfillment – the detachment from the old Marxist ideology created a situation where emphasis was placed on alienation rather than class war. It was a tool of utopian and humanistic socialism, which had devoted very little space to the proletariat as a subject, and therefore, as a political body, they endowed it with less ideology than the Old Left, and perhaps it was not an ideology at all.

Psychology scholars such as Kenneth Keniston believed that young people's commitment to radicalization was made possible by a new postmodern maturation experience that resulted from the new historical conditions created by mechanization and affluence. Psychologically, the radical young people felt mature. Sociologically, however, they were defined as adolescents, with no connection to the institutional structure of society, and thus found their purpose in the liberal political activities of the movements.[274]

The psychological theorist Erik Erikson argued that the basis for the formation of the youth political movements stemmed from the young people's recognition of the dangers to mankind by the technological revolution and the arbitrariness of the supernatural mechanisms that might replace human morals and conscience.[275]

Nevertheless, the new young generation's extroverted conduct and the use of "radicalism as an experience," kept them away from the labor unions and the old socialist bodies. The leaders of the movements (Abbie Hoffman and Tom Hayden, for example) led an overt approach to exhibitionism, a kind of "street theater."[276]

From the mid-1960s, especially after the civil rights amendments to the constitution, the altruism of the early decade seemed to have given way to a more

---

[273] Arthur Liebman, *Jews and the Left* (New York: Wiley, 1979), 239.
[274] Kenneth Keniston, *Young Radicals: Notes on Committed Youth* (New York: Harvest, trade paperback edition, 1968).
[275] Erik H. Erikson, *Identity: Youth and Crisis* (New York: W. W. Norton, 1968), 19–36.
[276] Christopher Lasch, *Culture of Narcissism* (New York: W. W. Norton & Company, 1979), 165.

prominent narcissism of the leaders. At this point, the student movements didn't run neat campaigns, were not well connected with the Old Left, and were unable to produce effective politics. In this way, as a political movement, their contribution to the war on poverty was not much greater than the bohemian alienation statements of the Beat poets, but they did acknowledge the restlessness of young culture, the generation gap and the importance of cultural openness.

The Jews were an impressive part of the New Left, though, despite their large numbers, they did not constitute the majority in the movement. The research displays that only 30% of Jewish students were members of the New Left, and only a minority of Jewish students were radicals. However, the leadership had a strong Jewish presence, and Jews constituted the senior group among minorities. Many students at SDS (Students for Democratic Society) were Jewish; Jews composed half of the movement's delegation to the 1966 convention, and many of the campus leaders were of Jewish origin, as were 30% to 50% of the left-wing editorial staff.[277]

Two-thirds of radicals headed south during the fight for equal rights, and of the one-third to half of the activists who volunteered in Mississippi in the summer of 1964, 45% of activists in Chicago, one-third of activists at Columbia University, and 90% of University of Wisconsin radicals came from Jewish backgrounds. Forty percent of participants in the March of Washington in 1963, and three of the four who were killed by police in a rally in Kent State in 1970 were Jews. Jews – who constituted less than three percent of the population and about 10 percent of students in the United States – constituted the majority among the leadership.

Despite the rhetorical differences between the Old Left and the New, there was more continuity between these political movements than differences. The university background that was also the ground for the rise of the Old Left during the Depression; the family background, the institutional structure of the Jewish community – all formed bridges between the Old Left and the New Left.

Other explanations linked the place of Jews in radical circles with the structure of the Jewish family, which is less patriarchal compared to other ethnic groups. The mother in the Jewish home is more dominant, they argued, while fathers were weaker. Against this family structure, adolescents adopted aggressive impulses and defenses in the form of identification with masculine, charismatic, and influential radical leaders, alongside the adoption of weak minority groups.

Either way, the Jewish radicals did not feel "Jewish" and their attitude toward the Jewish establishment was characterized by ideological controversies.

---

[277] Arthur Liebman, *Jews and the Left* (New York: Wiley, 1979), 540.

Disagreement over Marxism, race relations, and the State of Israel strained relations over time and more specifically since 1967.

Many of the Jewish radicals came from families with a socialist background with anti-WASP resentment. Nevertheless, the anti-WASP protest seemed to have been more a product of the movements' activities than a clear and structured agenda. The New Left's challenge to ruling culture inevitably led to its positioning of politics as a "cultural guerrilla war."

The protest of the New Left, in particular, and of the counterculture in general, was influenced by new voices mostly influenced by the larger bohemian circles that were more tangible than ever in the 1960s with the presence of hippies. *The Psychedelic Experience* (1964), Timothy Leary's book (and other writers), established – while relying on Zen Buddhism – a pseudo-religious framework for the drug LSD. The book had a significant impact mainly on bohemian circles, but also as a fashionable pastime for students.[278]

Another underground book considered the forerunner of the sexual revolution was Norman O. Brown's *Life Against Death* (1959).[279] Brown was a Freudian who called for free and group sexuality to unleash the same inner and creative impulse of man, the Eros, which seemed to be repressed by society. In radical circles, students liked to blatantly demonstrate the adoption of the lifestyle that was influenced by the relationship between rock and bohemians. Still, many of the cultural issues developed by the new radicals were characteristic of ancient European movements and traditions. Among other things: bohemianism, the free expression of sexuality, and even the desire to break down the idea of the nuclear family.

The anti-bourgeois protest of the New Left was no different from many other revolutionary agendas of the modern era, and yet the dissent of the radical students was intensified by the power of cultural resistance. The New Left's anti-establishment temperament, as scholars Lichter and Rothman explained, encompassed a rejection of the 'usual politics' of political and economic institutions, of social traditions and sexual codes, and even of Western culture itself.[280]

The New Left became an eclectic movement that carried the flag of the unsatisfied, a political-cultural expression of middle-class psychological alienation. The political-cultural fusion of the New Left contained elements of anar-

---

[278] Timothy Leary, *The Psychedelic Experience: A Manual Based on the Tibetan Book of the Dead* (Boston: Progressive Press, 1964).
[279] Norman O. Brown, *Life Against Death: The Psychoanalytical Meaning of History* (New York: Vintage, 1959).
[280] Stanley Rothman and Simon Lichter, *Roots of Radicalism: Jews, Christians, and the Left* (New York: Transaction Publishers, 1985), 387.

chism, socialism, pacifism, existentialism, humanism, bohemianism, populism, the effects of mysticism, and echoes of black nationalism. And above all, it was a pluralistic radicalism. This pluralism was the key to the cultural alternative it presented.

The decline of the WASP

The struggle for civil rights, radical liberalism, and the rise of pluralism and difference continued to undermine the dominance of the old elites. The WASP, who was a "bigger man than life," "the one who built the state," "the one who held the nation all together," the one who "worked hard and feared God," and the one who presented the possibilities of modernity, was in the process of decline.

Historians and sociologists dealt with the decline of the WASP hegemony. They pointed to the way that cosmopolitan liberalism and the fabric of interest of the new ethnic groups began to present an alternative to WASP dominance. The weakening of the WASP center was gradual. Throughout history, the American elite was more receptive to outsiders than was usually represented, but the 1960s constituted the culmination of a change in the hegemonic pattern, especially since liberals, at least, perceived the Vietnam War as a WASP failure.[281] Peter Schrag described the 1960s as an era in which the decline of the WASP, as a representative of Puritan-Calvinist ethics and the inexhaustible possibilities of American modernism, was evident. That mythological figure, the conqueror of the West, who built America with rare optimism, worked hard and feared God, was in the late 1960s just another voice among the various Americans voices. Schrag wrote:

> It happens gradually, but you notice suddenly: A new crowd, new faces, new styles, a new sound: un-WASP, Non-WASP, anti-WASP. The center has begun to disappear, and the action originates at the periphery, Jews and Negroes, Catholics and immigrants.[282]

The black life of the ghetto, the long hair, the hashish, the Indian gurus, the Zen philosophy, the warriors, the black radicals, Cuban guerrillas, Jewish anarchists, and rock music, were all part of the new cultural landscape. The changes were

---

[281] Robert C. Christopher, *Crashing the Gates: The DE-WASPing of America's Power Elite* (London & New York: Simon & Schuster 1986), 23–41; Eric P. Kaufmann, *The Rise & Fall of White-Anglo America* (Cambridge: Harvard University Press, 2002).

[282] Peter Schrag, *The Decline of the WASP* (New York: Simon and Schuster, Inc., 1973), 13.

indeed evident everywhere: in American academia, that opened itself to new voices from a press managed by the children of immigrants.

Protestant Christianity, which marched toward the modern age as the most influential and most institutionalized culture of the Western world, and dominated the doctrines that accompanied it in all spheres of life, found itself under attack in the 1960s. As the twentieth century progressed, this empire of knowledge and power, as described by historian David Hollinger, experienced difficulties in establishing itself as the primary source of the cultural capital of the Western world.[283]

American culture witnessed far-reaching transformations in the adoption of extreme liberalism: the liberation of language in popular culture, the rise of pornographic culture, a revolution in standards of dress and hair length. These were many achievements of liberals, sometimes through court decisions that expanded the insight and interpretation of the concept of legitimate liberalism, most of which reflected non-WASP styles and ideas.

Against the background of these processes, the Black-Jewish musical alliance brought with it ideas, styles, and passions that saturated popular culture. The Jewish-Black musical collaboration exuded non-WASP connotations, which – in many cases, unintentionally – created a new awareness of "another America." Gershwin's liberal world was about to intensify in the universal and black vision of the rock 'n' roll Jews.

---

[283] David A. Hollinger, *Science, Jews, and Secular Culture* (New Jersey: Princeton University Press, 1996), 1–10.

Chapter 8: That is Rock 'n Roll! Leiber and Stoller, the White Negro and the Enlargement of America

> Elvis Presley: "Hey, Mike [...] how do you guys write all these great songs?"
> Mike Stoller: "Well, Elvis [....] we just kinda sit down and jam."
> Elvis Presley: "It's amazing to me. I guess I just ain't much of a writer."
> Mike Stoller: "You don't have to write songs. You're Elvis."[284]

More than blackface minstrelsy, ragtime, swing, and Jazz, rock 'n' roll of the 1950s was the most antithetical to stereotypes of diaspora Jew throughout the ages. Wild, blunt, sexual, and saturated with gibberish that resembled a code language for teenagers, rock 'n' roll seemed to have shed the European influences of previous American musical styles. Conservatives marked it as a danger to American children. Even if America had experienced similar cultural riots in the past with ragtime and early jazz, rock historians have loved to describe in particular color the noise associated with the new genre. Rock 'n' roll resembled an unbearable incompatibility that disturbed the rest of the nation. The preachers, the church, the House of Representatives, and governments of the states, tried to censor and block the new music coming from the South. The criticism of the previous generation of artists, such as Ira Gershwin and Frank Sinatra, regarding rock 'n' roll's alleged poor quality, added more oil to the fire. Everyday life in the burgeoning, lush, pervasive, consensual America of the post-war era came with unexpected cultural noise as if the same old national, racial shadow had emerged again to confront America with itself.

The rock 'n' roll of the 1950s fused blues and country music. It adopted the blues' 12-bar structure, electric guitars, pentatonic melodies, blue notes, and roaring vocals. However, it also embraced elements of swing music that a vast audience was familiar with from the Big Bands era. And yet, compared to Broadway's musical richness, rock 'n' roll sounded primitive. Some felt it was not music at all, but others believed it was the most exciting thing ever.

Rock 'n' roll was an expression of post-war liberalism.[285] It was not just its influence on teenagers full of adolescent hormones but the beginning of a gradually growing wave of intellectuals that made rock music one of the most cele-

---

284 Jerry Leiber and Mike Stoller with David Ritz, *Hound Dog: The Leiber and Stoller Autobiography* (New York: Simon & Schuster, 2009), Ch. 11, Kindle.
285 Simon Frith, *Sound Effects: Youth, Leisure and the Politics of Rock'n'Roll* (New York: Pantheon Books, 1981).

brated examples of mass culture of the twentieth century. Rock 'n' roll was in sync with the democratization processes that cultural discourse had undergone. America may have been divisive from the late nineteenth century in discussing the "color" of American music, but in the 1950s, writers and intellectuals came to a decision. They perceived "black" music as positive and "superior" to "white," which in this discourse was perceived inauthentic and "fake." Diverse discussions regarding authenticity linked social inferiority to an authentic aura of street culture that was existentialist and black. It was, as it were, against the high bourgeois culture that expressed "hypocrisy."

In the heyday of post-counterculture rock, influential critics and editors, such as Jon Landau of *Rolling Stone* magazine, purported to present this mass culture of rock as folk music. Landau believed that the artists connected behaviors, styles, and emotions of original and real experiences and that the social situations helped produce these experiences.[286] Other critics, such as Nik Cohn, have presented a different position and sought to see the power of rock music in the concepts of mass culture mythology. "It should be, fast, funny, sexual and obsessive," Cohn wrote, insisting that rock 'n' roll needs a mass media's images and aura rather than high-culture influences. The gibberish of black singer Little Richard remains the ultimate symbol of the medium.[287]

The democratization of culture influenced these attitudes, which permeated both academia and popular culture. The White Negro, which already had precedents in the Harlem Renaissance during the 1920s, achieved its full glory. The book *The White Negro: Superficial Reflections on the Hipster* (1957) by Norman Mailer saw how the Beat Poets in their various writings praised existential African-American "savagery" against the forgery that characterized the middle-class world and its corporate subordinates.[288] The critical romanticism of rock music was a natural sequel.

Paint it black

African-American's rhythm and blues songs were popular on the margins of American music even before World War Two, but rock 'n' roll broke into Amer-

---

[286] Simon Frith, *The Sociology of Rock* (London: Constable, 1978), 182.
[287] Nik Cohn, *WopBopaLooBop LopBamBoom: Pop from the Beginning* (London: Paladin, 1969), 243.
[288] Norman Mailer, *The White Negro: Superficial Reflections on the Hipster* (San Francisco: City Lights Books, 1970 [1957]).

ican public consciousness in 1955. Except for the youth revolution that created a vast audience, explanations of its appeal are explained by American media history, starting with the struggles between radio and the ASCAP organization (which was responsible for enforcing royalty payments by Tin Pan Alley writers) and the strengthening of a competing BMI organization with its catalog of southern and racial music, through the development of the transistor, and to the appearance of regional radio and the 45 rpm record format.[289]

Rock 'n' roll reached public consciousness in Hollywood with "Rock Around the Clock," performed by Bill Haley & His Comets. Jewish singer-songwriter Carole King remembers that this song divided her life into the pre era of rock n 'roll and after.[290] The song served as the soundtrack to the successful movie *Blackboard Jungle* (1955), and became the icon of the era. The news and images of rioting teenagers in movie theaters at the end of the film had already become a myth in the 1950s. Carole King remembers that boys feared that the image of delinquent youths in the movie might happen in reality in their neighborhood.[291] So if its black roots weren't enough, rock 'n' roll music was identified from the outset with vandalism, violence, juvenile delinquency and disorder. All of this is quite surprising given the naïve lyrics of the song, which appealed innocently to the joys of dancing incessantly.

Contrary to its great myth, during the 1950s, rock 'n' roll was hardly against the dominant culture. While almost entirely silent about the system of discrimination against blacks, racism, or sexism and class hierarchy, rock 'n' roll matched the post-World War Two liberal consensus. The emergence of rock 'n' roll at the time of the "end of ideologies" made it difficult for it to enter into 1950s political struggles.

But rock 'n' roll came out of Southern racial and religious tensions. The music expressed blatant sexuality and defiance. It resembled a puppet theater that was out of control and was nothing more than cartoon-like subversion. Its black and white artists came from poor and religious families. They expressed tensions that resulted from the gap between the religious community's restrictions which country music and sacred gospel music projected. At the same time, they desired to escape those boundaries and limitations with a secular blues.

Most notably, the black roots, blatant sexuality, and "wild" spontaneity that accompanied rock 'n' roll made it a sexual and racial threat. The "behind the

---

289 Richard Peterson, "Why 1955? Explaining the advent of Rock Music," *Popular Music* 9 (1990): 97–116.
290 Carole King, *A Natural Woman: A Memoir* (New York: Grand Central Publishing, 2012), 28.
291 Ibid.

back" attack on it came from various institutions: the church, the music industry, the legal system, and the law, which defined the music as a moral hazard. The attack on rock 'n' roll, historians explain, not only reflected a Southern paranoia but that of an entire nation. The reaction against the music created a historical link to reactions to African-American sounds we already knew from ragtime and jazz's association with "Devil's Music."

The songs did not attack the political-economic consensus, but unintentionally rock 'n' roll managed to rock the cultural boat.[292] It presented a new image of the possibilities of everyday life; it affirmed identities of diversity and differentiation and offered diverse voices that were inherently authentic. It weaved images that not only did not conform to the institutional norms of the dominant culture but gradually became semiotic weapons that showcased the charisma of black culture.

Black rebellion, Jewish script

Rock 'n' roll may have landed in the mainstream culture like a complete surprise but it was marginalized for at least two decades under the name "race music," even if musically it was an abstraction of many elements that America recognized in the swing era. In the late 1940s, Jerry Wexler, a Jewish writer for *Billboard* magazine at the time, recommended replacing the term "race music" with "rhythm and blues," since it was more suitable for more "enlightened times."[293] In the early 1950s, Cleveland-American Jewish broadcaster Alan Freed converted the nickname rhythm and blues to rock 'n' roll, which was African-American slang for a craving for sexual intercourse, branding it as the new-upcoming style, and the name has remained ever since.

The major record companies tried to ignore rhythm and blues, sometimes forcing artists to replace the original lyrics. They preferred to concentrate on the more subtle songs of Tin Pan Alley. Contrary to the mass magic of the swing Big Bands or the bebop avant-garde elitism, rhythms and blues was perceived, as Nik Cohn called it, "downright filthy."[294]

---

[292] Lawrence Grossberg, *We Gotta Get Out of This Place* (New York: Routledge, 1992), 178.
[293] Jerry Wexler and David Ritz, *Rhythm and the Blues: A Life in American Music* (New York: Alfred Knopf, 1993), 62–63.
[294] Nik Cohn, *WopBopaLooBop LopBamBoom: Pop from the Beginning* (London: Paladin, 1969), 15; Glenn G. Altschuler, *All Shook Up: How Rock 'n' Roll Changed America* (Oxford: Oxford University Press, 2003), 35–66.

Rhythm and blues songs contained sexual codes that left no doubt about their meanings but did not frighten everyone, probably not a stingy Jewish merchant with a big mouth and street guts like Syd Nathan, the owner of King Records in Cincinnati. The latter recorded and circulated Billy Ward's "Sixty Minute Man" and Hank Ballard's "Work with Me, Annie," both littered with sexual cues; "Baby Let Me Bang Your Box" by The Toppers, sounded childish but was about lust; it was distributed by Herb Abramson, who co-founded Atlantic Records, the heroine of this chapter.

Atlantic Records was founded in 1947 by Ahmet Ertegun, the son of the Turkish ambassador in Washington, together with a Jewish student for dental studies, Herb Abramson. In 1953, while Abramson was forced to participate in the war effort in Korea, Jerry Wexler, an American Jew who formerly wrote for *Billboard* music magazine and worked for publishing companies in Tin Pan Alley, joined the label. Wexler and Ertegun, two American outsiders, established one of the greatest revolutions of American popular music.

Ahmet Ertegun was obsessed with the blacks' jazz and R&B. People who knew him defined him as a champion with personal charm, an unrivaled promoter, and a charismatic man. He justified every rumor about him, as he used to wear three-piece suits and led a flamboyant nightlife.

Wexler was the son of a Jewish immigrant from Poland and a Jewish mother of German descent who devoted her life to nurturing him. Wexler, who was a failure in his studies and saw his father waste his life as a window cleaner in New York, fled to music, to the freedom of Louis Armstrong's sound and other jazz heroes. He was a compulsive collector of music and had a brilliant taste and encyclopedic knowledge of the topic. All this helped him become one of the most essential musical producers of all time, even though Wexler lacked musical education. He was different from Ertegun, more neurotic, obsessive, and frantic, but like his partner, he had sharp senses.

Together, the pair complemented one another and stormed into a musical world mixed with racial prejudices. Because of their ethnic origins, they were free from American racial traditions and made the African-American markets into a vital source of profit. Their first goal was to brand Atlantic as a sound for the older black audience, one that trusted the tradition of blues and jazz. The first artists who joined the label were purely African-Americans: Ruth Brown, The Drifters, "Big Joe" Turner, and Clyde McPhatter. Ray Charles, a young blind singer with phenomenal musical abilities, turned out to be their savior and forged a fusion between blues and gospel into early soul music. However, a mix of multi-ethnic talents helped their breakthrough: a series of Jewish songwriters from New York City alongside African-American performers, who led rock 'n' roll to some excellent artistic achievements. These ran an ethnic network throughout New York with various Jewish forces, particularly in the Brill Building area, the place housing several publishing companies. These focus areas included songwriters, producers, musicians, publicists and promoters, artist managers, and live show agents. Nobody had time to breathe. There was a lot of money that they could and should have made.

Atlantic was a small company full of Jews. Not only in the management and the bureau (Miriam Beinstock, Abramson's divorcee, controlled the office) but also in the creative department. With the exception of partner and producer Jerry Wexler, Jerry Leiber and Mike Stoller, who wrote to Elvis Presley and the best of rhythm and blues artists, worked there; Bert Berns and Jerry Ragovoy, two music producers of Latin and black music; and Phil Spector, who began as Leiber and Stoller's assistant and finally designed the sound of the girl groups.

The great rise of Atlantic happened with the help of Leiber and Stoller.[295] They "blew in like a fresh breeze from the coast, "Wexler said. "The comic spin of their musical vignettes, their reflections on black American life [...] made an inestimable contribution to Atlantic's success."[296] The multiethnic scene thrived in New York but echoed to Los Angeles. A few years before the cultural earthquake that occurred during the British invasion, American music came out of an ethnic space formed of a reunion of Europe and Africa and a particularly pungent Latin flavor.

Leiber and Stoller were born in Baltimore and New York, respectively, and in their youth both moved to minority neighborhoods in Los Angeles. In many ways, Leiber and Stoller continued the traditions of Jewish songwriters from previous generations: Leiber was reminiscent of Irving Berlin in his lyrical talent, only more pointed and focused in his writing on the young black world. Stoller – though he did not consider himself a great jazz pianist – played in the stride style a la George Gershwin, but his music would sound more like firsthand boogie-woogie and with less post-Romantic influences. Like Gershwin, he, too, was confined to Latin music. Their musical productions combined the European approach that characterized Jerome Kern's music, as well as giving them a taste of Americana, even if they had less of a sense of empathy with black culture from "below." Like Harold Arlen, they excelled in an authentic interpretation of African-American musical traditions. However, they felt more distance from white

---

[295] Jerry Leiber and Mike Stoller with David Ritz, *Hound Dog: The Leiber and Stoller Autobiography* (New York: Simon & Schuster, 2009).

[296] Jerry Wexler and David Ritz, *Rhythm and the Blues: A Life in American Music* (New York: Alfred Knopf, 1993), 133–134.

mainstream culture than their predecessors. If we adapt Norman Mailer's jargon, we might refer to them as cool 'white negroes.'

In many ways, there are significant differences between African-American culture and Jewish culture: Anthony Rotundo believes oral culture and human physicality (vocalization and dance) defined black culture, while the written word defined American Jewish culture.[297] Still, it seems that even if the Jewish artists did not exhibit any real sense of Jewish identity, the emphasis placed on writing in their parents' Jewish culture linked them to their role behind the scenes as songwriters and music producers. The fact that they came mostly from middle-class environments and at least had aspirations to display the image of middle-class culture, which emphasized high culture, affected their contribution to rock 'n' roll.

In my view, how these songwriters cultivated the popular song did not express Jewish altruism for the lower classes or their role as melting pot agents, as many scholars have argued, but rather their importance was in fusing high and popular music and culture, and cementing its value. They expressed a special kind of elitist humanism with an attraction to the alternative sides of the WASP cultural tradition, through which they emphasized their need for American culture and society.[298] They established themselves as the forerunners of the European canon, which historically and paradoxically avoided them for generations. With the help of this elitist humanism, they contributed not only cultural wealth, but a new picture of everyday life expressed in a different, more universal and cosmopolitan American world, through the use of the African-American cultural world. As Greil Marcus wrote in praise of The Coasters' recording collection: "Stepin Fetchit [a black comedian] as advance man for black revolt, with script by two Jews, Jerry Leiber & Mike Stoller [...] this was rock 'n' roll."[299]

---

297 E. Anthony Rotundo, "Jews and Rock and Roll: A Study in Cultural Contrast," *American Jewish History* 72.1 (1982): 82–107.
298 See chapter 2. See Ari Katorza, "Walls of Sound: Leiber and Stoller, Phil Spector, the Black-Jewish Alliance, and the 'Enlarging' of America," in *Mazal Tov, Amigos: Jews and Popular Music in the Americas*, edited by Amalia Ran and Moshe Morad, 78–95 (Leiden: Brill Academic Press, 2016).
299 Greil Marcus, *Stranded: Rock 'n' roll for a Desert Island* (New York: Random House Inc., 1978), 263.

The Gilbert and Sullivan of rock 'n' roll

Leiber was born in Baltimore, and the first language he spoke was Yiddish. His father, a Jewish immigrant from Poland and a milkman, passed away when Jerry was five. His mother became known as a tough woman (there were stories that she once threw someone from her grocery store with her own hands). Jerry used to deliver coal to the homes of African-American clients in Baltimore, where he discovered the blues. He said he was the only white boy in the neighborhood to do errands for African-Americans. "They liked me because I brought the light. I became part of their families," he recalls, "Inside those households, radios were always playing [...] My heart was flooded with boogie-woogie."[300]

He was a street boy and not a bad boxer. By the age of nine, he was smoking like his father. His mother was forced to educate him toughly so that "he would not finish in the electric chair." Jerry and his mother moved to Los Angeles when he was 12, right at the end of the war. On his travels around Hollywood, he met Irving Berlin pondering new words to write, and director Cecil B. DeMille, who gave him some bits of advice on body care, and he left school, to work in the theater every day. Leiber went through something similar to a revelation as he listened to the radio show *Harlem Hit Parade*. Whatever it was, this Jewish dandy from Los Angeles did not return to being the same person.

Mike Stoller was born in Queens to a slightly more established family. His mother participated as a chorus girl in the musical comedy *Funny Face* (1927) by Gershwin and even dated the composer. She was artistic, cosmopolitan, and sad, and his father struggled to support the family with two day-jobs. In 1941, his parents sent him to a racially mixed camp where, alongside studying Hebrew folk songs, black singer Paul Robeson performed. "I was eight years old, at a sleepaway camp in New Jersey," Stoller recalls, "and hearing boogie-woogie for the first time. The piano player was a black teenager [...] Boogie-woogie was a new and magical world for me [...] I can't explain why, but the music was changing me."[301]

On neighborly advice, his parents sent him to piano studies with James P. Johnson, a phenomenal African-American pianist who had previously been an inspiration for Gershwin. "Understanding a structure," explained the stride wizard "is the key to confidence."[302] In New York, Stoller was still able to witness

---

[300] Jerry Leiber and Mike Stoller with David Ritz, *Hound Dog: The Leiber and Stoller Autobiography* (New York: Simon & Schuster, 2009), chap. 1, Kindle.
[301] Ibid., chap. 1, Kindle.
[302] Ibid., chap. 2, Kindle.

the bebop shamans revolutionize jazz, but he still remained true to the blues, and his ears would reveal the symphonic and Latin world as well.

At the age of 16, he also came to the City of Angels, where, in his words, the "white" world caused him "alienation and boredom." He preferred an environment of Mexicans, Asians, and blacks. Above the piano in his house, was a picture of Gershwin with a dedication to Stoller's mother. So, it is not surprising that he chose to study composition with Hollywood composer Arthur Lange. He soon met Leiber. Although Stoller tried to impress and introduce himself as a bebop and classical music lover (Monk and Bartok), they set about on what would bring them world fame: rhythm and blues.

From the beginning of their careers, Leiber and Stoller approached African-American street culture, in addition to presenting a robust agenda for their musical tastes and perceptions of American culture: "We were two guys looking to write songs for black artists with black feelings rendered in black vernacular."[303] They had started writing songs when they were teenagers, recorded by a host of artists in the early 1950s. Los Angeles was overflowing with black music with lots of rhythm and blues, and jazz. Quite a few independent Jewish labels settled there or opened branches.

Their development as writers occurred gradually but rapidly. The first songs communicated with relatively standard blues messages. They turned biblical anecdotes to temporary relevance, wrote about the difficulties of life, and when the black singer Charles Brown recorded their song "Hard Times," they believed it was high art.[304] Their immense love for black music was perfectly expressed in "K.C. Lovin'" (known as "Kansas City") which was a tribute to the Kansas City music scene, the town of Count Basie and Charlie Parker.

In 1953 they wrote the song "Hound Dog" for the black singer, Big "Mama" Thornton, and it finally became their breakthrough hit. "When Jerry and I arrived and heard her start to sing, we looked at each other in amazement," Stoller recalls. "Her voice was a force of nature […] There was something monstrous about Big Mama," Leiber states, "but I saw her as the perfect instrument for the blues that we and Mike loved."[305]

They knew that in the south, the phrase "this dog would hunt" was used, so the phrase "hound dog" had the correct rural-funk-feel, and Big Mama brought out a massive tongue toward them to illustrate what she was going to do with it.

---

303 Ibid., chap. 9, Kindle.
304 Ibid., chap. 2, Kindle.
305 Ibid., chap. 6, Kindle.

When Leiber suggested for a moment that she should attack the song from a different angle, she pointed toward her crotch: "Attack this," she hissed.[306]

Based on the blues, the single preceded Aretha Franklin by more than a decade demanding respect while declaring both female and African-American power. Full of complaints over her partner's disloyalty, Thornton seems to be barking it, while using the slang phrase "hound dog." Yet, it was Elvis Presley who turned it into an international hit (he became more familiar with a cover version of this song by Freddie Bell and the Bellboys).

Today "Hound Dog" is considered a true classic and was even chosen by *Rolling Stone* magazine as one of the greatest American songs of the rock era. "Hound Dog" was slang for infidelity, filled with rage and contradictions, and the magic was in the space between the language, its meaning, and Presley's vocal performance.[307]

They joined the industry with the help of Lester Sill, an American Jew who was an active and successful publisher of songs from Los Angeles. They started working with a black vocal band, The Robins, and established the label Spark Records, where they recorded the band, but still most of the songs were, at best, local hits. "We couldn't get through the Rockies," Stoller said. But Nesuhi Ertegun, a professor of jazz history and Ahmet's brother, became their "savior."

Jerry Wexler described Leiber as extravagant and rebellious, magical, messy and unruly. Stoller, whose appearance reminded him of Robert Oppenheimer, was a piano wizard, "who looked like he came from Venus or Jupiter."[308] Leiber and Stoller mentioned the Jewish jazz musician Mezz Mezzrow; Like him, they were a recent version of the White Negro, which Norman Mailer described in his famous book. They even used to date young black and Asian women (Stoller's first girlfriend was Filipino). "[...] [I]n another life," composer Burt Bacharach said about Leiber," he had definitely been African-American."[309] They identified with the fringes, one might even claim to be an imaginary fringe, but really played humorously with identities and turned them on their heads.

The rhythm and blues and the first rock 'n' roll songs centered on sexual codes and defined everything that was taboo or boring. Little Richard's "Tutti Frutti" (1955), which combined fruit and sex associations, was the prototype for many hits of the era. Chuck Berry was one of the only people who managed

---

306 Ibid., chap. 3, Kindle.
307 "The 500 Greatest Songs of All Time," *Rolling Stone* (February, 2004).
308 Jerry Wexler and David Ritz, *Rhythm and the Blues: A Life in American Music* (New York: Alfred Knopf, 1993), 134.
309 Burt Bacharach, *Anyone Who Had a Heart: My Life and Music* (New York: Atlantic Books, 2014), 99.

to create a lyrical world concerning 1950s youth culture that resembled Pop Art. Lyrically, Leiber and Stoller were closer to Berry, but they also drew influences from musical comedy through the ages and poured realistic and in-depth content into the blues frames. One by one, recording masters of satirical mini-operas began coming from California.

At the height of his success, Elvis Presley recorded "Hound Dog" (1956), changed the lyrics a bit, performed it on television, rocked his thighs, and made it an international hit. At first, Leiber and Stoller felt a distance from Presley's performance, which was more fast-paced than the original, and the change of lyrics was unsettling, but with the coming of royalties, the feeling was much more comfortable. In meeting the king of rock 'n' roll they were impressed by his varied abilities and impressive knowledge of the blues. His physical beauty captivated them, and despite his status as the biggest star in America at the time, something was charming about his manners and modesty, even though his southern parochial environment was foreign to them.

The Jewish network in the form of Hill & Range, a publishing company that oversaw Presley's songs, established the relationship of the duo with Presley. The Aberbach brothers and Freddie Beinstock (his wife was Miriam, one of Atlantic's founders) owned and managed the company, and Leiber and Stoller showed off their excellent abilities. They wrote some of the best of Presley's repertoire, including "Jailhouse Rock" (1957), a rock 'n' roll song with a musical flavor that reached the top of the *Billboard* chart, but they preferred to work outside the paranoid management environment outlined by Colonel Tom Parker. Although Elvis called them the Gilbert and Sullivan of rock 'n' roll, a bright future awaited them outside of Hollywood's mainstream.

Hyperrealism, outsider eyes

Leiber and Stoller marked their own multicultural vision with two Afro-American vocal groups: The Coasters and The Drifters. Critic Robert Christgau thought highly of the way they portrayed realistic scenes from the urban black world: "Leiber takes off from Louis Jordan no less than Chuck Berry does; though his hyperrealism is more calculated, he brings the same bemused, admiring outsider's eye to the details and universals of black urban life that Berry brought to bobbysoxers."[310]

---

[310] Robert Christgau, Experience Music Project, Seattle, Washington (April 16, 2005).

One of their images from black urban youth can be found in "Young Blood" (1957), written for The Coasters with another Jewish writer, Doc Pomus. This romantic narrative of a youth's sexual attraction gained deeper sensual layers with the repetition of black slang and masculinity. The recurrence of "Look a-there" four times; the paradoxes and contradictions ("I tried to walk but I was lame / I tried to talk but I just stuttered") portrayed the tension and sexual energy that pass between a very attractive female, this "young blood," and the group of black male singers. Critics highly valued the humor, wit, and ingenuity of Leiber and Stoller's satires.[311] They are somewhat reminiscent of the multicultural gang reflected in the video of the global hit "Uptown Funk" (2014), the work of British Jewish producer Mark Ronson and singer Bruno Mars, recorded almost six decades later.

Critics praised the wit with which Leiber and Stoller documented adolescents' lives in the 1950s, as well as their independence and creative originality, and even emphasized the humor of their writing. Leiber and Stoller liked to admit that they relied on the musical comedy tradition and vaudeville acts, but there was a unique and mature multicultural feel to their songs, even if they were aimed at teenagers. "The material was strong, the metaphors sometimes hidden, but the hook was always dramatic," Leiber explained. "We used humor to blunt the edges."[312] Unintentionally, they continued the work of the Gershwin brothers, Hart and Hammerstein and all the great writers of musical comedy. The single "Yakety Yak," for example, was a hybrid of rock 'n' roll and a musical, describing a scuffle between a neighborhood thug and his parents, in a song about freedom and youth. Sometimes they played with black humor: the song "Poison Ivy" (1959) brought the preoccupation of a black band with sexually transmitted diseases to the top 10 in the pop and rhythm and blues chart. "In the back of our minds, we wanted to write musicals, "said Stoller. "We liked the idea of writing a collection of songs illustrating a dramatic story. But no one was asking us to do that."[313] Everyday African-American life merged into mainstream America through Leiber and Stoller's vision.

Perhaps the duo's contribution to multicultural rock poetry and America can be summed up with "Searchin'" (1957), another hit filled with black gospel imagery, yet focusing on obsessive secular love with a black preacher texture

---

[311] Nik Cohn, *WopBopaLooBop LopBamBoom: Pop from the Beginning* (London: Paladin, 1969), 38–39.

[312] Jerry Wexler and David Ritz, *Rhythm and the Blues: A Life in American Music* (New York: Alfred Knopf, 1993), 135.

[313] Jerry Leiber and Mike Stoller with David Ritz, *Hound Dog: The Leiber and Stoller Autobiography* (New York: Simon & Schuster, 2009), chap. 14, Kindle.

("Well, now, if I have to swim a river / You know I will"). Again, the strategy of repetitiveness with "Gonna find her" and the sanctification and obsession with youthful love portrayed a respectable black America that culturally welcomed the 1960s' Civil Rights amendments and the end of Southern segregation.

Nevertheless, despite the use of black language, it is not the expression of an African-American world, but as one critic described it, a semiotic universal world that happened to be black.[314] Leiber and Stoller contributed to the breaking of racial stereotypes with the humor, wit, and poetry of everyday life that turned ugly racial issues into caricatures, and therefore opened possibilities of acceptance.

A magic moment in Spanish Harlem

Rock 'n' roll was a sound. The development of recording studios, multi-track tapes, echo chambers, including reducing the dynamic range of the recorded signal and controlling it with compressors and limiters have shaped the musical production work. In the beginning, the tasks of directing and organizing recordings belonged to the head of the repertoire of a record label. It was now in the hands of a music producer (or record producer), and he became a critical link in the production line.[315]

From Memphis, Tennessee came recordings of Elvis Presley and Jerry Lee Lewis by the label Sun Records. Slapback-delay, glittering country guitars licks or thunderous boogie-woogie piano and sexual staccato vocals blended into such beautiful records that it became a stereotype of 1950s sound. From Chicago came Chess Records' blues-rock 'n' roll, full of "natural" slightly distorted guitars, encrypted Delta-Mississippi riffs and roaring vocals. The multicultural movement was sometimes in the opposite direction: African-American Chuck Berry drew from country and western and combined those with fine writing on youth in the 1950s.

Leiber and Stoller were among the first to "write records." They continued their work with another black vocal band, The Drifters. They chose a different line of sweeter entertainment, incorporating European orchestration of strings, Latin rhythms, and more universal songs. They focused on musical production while recruiting a host of songwriters – most of them from the Brill Building Jew-

---

314 Robert Christgau, Experience Music Project, Seattle, Washington (April 16, 2005).
315 Ari Katorza, *Come Together: Rock 'n' Roll, liberalism, Mass Bohemianism and the Sixties* (Tel Aviv: K Academics Publishing, 2019).

ish network: Phil Spector, Carole King and Gerry Goffin, Doc Pomus and Mort Shuman, Hal David and Burt Bacharach. They were probably one of the first to have a fully autonomous production deal. This privilege allowed them to be independent but protected, daring yet commercial, and their recordings showcased a multicultural display combining high European art with Latin-black soup.

Composer Burt Bacharach, who learned about the art of production from them, recalled that they had "four guitars, three percussion players, drums, a string section, background singers, [...] Whenever I watched him work, all I could say was 'Wow!' Jerry would get in that room with the musicians and the singers and set the groove and the feel."[316]

Stoller recalled that the work with The Coasters was fun, and he shared Leiber's work with the vocals and interpreting singers and his work with the musicians. At its best moments, the production and songs blend into one essence. "Parent Lecture with a Saxophone," critic Dave Marsh wrote about "Yakety Yak" which dealt with the neighborhood bully's freedom and his parents.[317]

The big breakthrough was in The Drifters single "There Goes My Baby" (1959). The song featured a unique strings arrangement by Stanley Applebaum, along with untuned tympani drums and a Brazilian baion rhythm. "'There Goes My Baby' deserves to be enshrined, for the moment when those strings entered," explained critic Dave Marsh. "[...] Rhythm and blues took an irrevocable step toward soul music. This next step in the evolution of record-making made it even more decisively a producer's music, concocted in the studio without much reference to what happened on stage or in doo-wop hallways with perfect echoes."[318]

Jerry Leiber recalled that arranger Stanley Applebaum had written something that sounded like a "Caucasian" take-off. "We had this Latin beat going on this out-of-tune tympani and the Drifters were singing something in another key," he explained, " but the total effect-there was something magnificent about it."[319] Jerry Wexler thought otherwise. It sounded to him like two radio stations playing simultaneously and an exercise in cacophony. Ahmet Ertegun didn't express great enthusiasm either, but the song was a great hit and a real symbol of the era.

---

[316] Burt Bacharach, *Anyone Who Had a Heart: My Life and Music* (New York: Atlantic Books, 2014), 100.
[317] Dave Marsh, *The Heart of Rock & Soul: The 1001 Greatest Singles Ever Made* (New York: Da Capo Press, 1989), 62.
[318] Ibid, 27.
[319] Ibid.

Due to their many commitments, Leiber and Stoller began to use additional writers. "Save the Last Dance for Me" (1960) – written by two Jewish writers, Doc Pomus (N. Jerome Felder) and Mort Schumann, and produced by Leiber and Stoller – reached the top of the charts. It was not just a model for writing and production, but popular art.

Pomus and Shuman wrote songs for Elvis Presley, and Italian-American stars and groups (Fabian and Dion and the Belmontes, for example) that were momentarily popular in the pre-British invasion era. They also wrote African-American rhythm and blues. The single "Save the Last Dance for Me" was a remarkable achievement that managed to combine the personal and the public. The lyricist Pomus was disabled and wheelchair-bound due to a polio illness that had paralyzed him in his youth. He connected his physical limitations to a profound emotional statement. Due to his actual inability to dance, the writer asks his partner to keep "the last dance" for him, as the dance is symbolic of life itself.

While the vast majority of African-American songwriters came from a working-class background, Pomus was from the middle-class and romanticized the creation myth of the lower classes. He, too, was a White Negro. Pomus had experienced journalistic writing, music criticism, and fiction, and in fact, began his career as a writer for African-American singers (and even tried his hand as a performer). However, even if he was engaged in high art, he confessed that a successful writer possessed versatility and universal and accessible aspects.[320]

The most memorable hit was "Stand by Me" (1961), which started from an improvisation by Ben E. King, who was The Drifters' lead singer, on a gospel song from the early twentieth century ("Stand by Me Father") and designed by Leiber and Stoller into a pop song with a religious gospel flavor. Stoller used the same harmonic degree of "There Goes My Baby" (I-vi-IV-V7) for an up-to-date doo-wop harmony.

Latin rhythm and European string arrangement (also by Stanley Applebaum) enveloped Ben E. King, who sang in "Stand by Me" as if "the fate of the world lies on the lyrics." What makes the performance memorable is King's vocal intonation, which negates his defiance ritual: "'I won't cry, I won't cry,' he cries," Dave Marsh explains; this contrast illustrates a combination of panic and regeneration, terror and security.

The song is familiar to younger audiences as a soundtrack from Rob Reiner's film bearing the song's title (1986). It sounds unusual in the 1980s, but the subject remains eternal. In the 1960s, the gospel spirit served as a moral conscience

---

320 Bruce Pollock, *In Their Own Words* (New York: Collier, 1975).

for this request to a friend in times of trouble, and it was a perfect soundtrack to the days of struggle for equality.

The bass role, which British singer Duffy sampled years later for her hit "Mercy," laid the foundation for the song. The percussion was borrowed from Latin music, the gospel vocals combined with the cello and string processing, which develops seductively throughout the song. These were also down to Motown Company's production line.

Tom Dowd, who served as Atlantic Record's chief recording engineer (and later became a successful producer in his own right), was the one who accompanied Leiber and Stoller in their productions. He claimed that technology influenced their writing. They not only looked for new sounds, Dowd said, but were interested in the double-tracking. The multi-track recording device not only allowed them to produce better records but to think about songwriting from a production perspective.[321]

The connection between the black world and the use of classical strings instruments was not always enthusiastically received by the critics, and some criticized The Drifters' soft line, but most critics appreciated the professionalism, sophistication, and depth of the songs. Leiber and Stoller succeeded with songs that had both sophisticated and "tough" string orchestras, careful to avoid kitsch, thus "orchestrating" post-war youthful life.[322]

Cuba in three chords

The Jewish network around Leiber and Stoller was able to present some of the best popular music before The Beatles and the British invasion of America began in February 1964. However, even before the shock of the new American Anglophile, there was trouble at home. As early as the beginning of the decade, Atlantic and Leiber and Stoller were in financial disputes over royalty payments, which led to their departure (in favor of United Artists Records). Later on, they set up a new label, Red Bird Records, with George Goldner, a talented, devious New York Jew, who had already been with a few records label for rock music, and was a compulsive gambler. They managed to fit in the wave of girl groups and released hits but seemed to lose interest. They lacked the hunger they had at

---

[321] Stuart Grundy and John Tobler, *The Record Producers* (London: St. Martins Pr., 1982), 1–10.
[322] Greil Marcus, *Stranded: Rock 'n' roll for a Desert Island* (New York: Random House Inc., 1978), 266–267.

the beginning. Goldner's gambling habits didn't help, nor did his ethics and relationship with the mobs, so they gave him the label as a gift.

Atlantic tried to revive Ben E. King's and The Drifters 'career, but America was already concentrated elsewhere: with Motown's hits, Bob Dylan's folk messages, and The Beatles' fantastic musical abilities that overpowered Leiber and Stoller with their melodic and harmonious accomplishments. The leaders at Atlantic tried to fight back with soul music talents, but later on they also moved towards new groups from the UK.

In the early 1960s, Wexler and Ertegun turned in different directions. Ertegun, betrayed by Ray Charles' departure, sought white rock that generated a lot of revenue over the decade. Wexler stayed with his firm love of black music. The euphoric days of the beginning, during which they moved back and forth in the racially segregated South, turned into a heavily atmosphere of suspicion. Ertegun feared that a pure Jewish alliance of Wexler, Leiber and Stoller was going to take over Atlantic Records. It wasn't supposed to happen, nor did it happen.

In the meantime, Wexler recruited Bert Berns, a Jewish rhythm and blues producer, whom he called a "doctor groove." Like Leiber and Stoller, he too was a street cat, making things happen, connected to everyday people. Wexler remembered that his father used to clean the windows in Berns's parents' clothing store. He hadn't had a good childhood either, as his parents had focused on their business so much that they sent him to an orphanage. His parents left him with mental scars that stood out until his early death.

Berns had an obsession with power. Hypnotized by gangsters, he said he used to trade weapons in Cuba before Castro. He loved Latin music and made the three basic chords of "Guantanamera," a well-known Cuban folk-patriotic song, ammunition for his many hits; among others, "Twist and Shout" – one of the most famous songs of the twentieth century in a variety of performances, including The Beatles. The three chords were the basis for dozens of hits in rock history.

Berns worked with solo singers like Salomon Burke with partial success, but his masters started making noise around a young Jewish singer and songwriter by the name of Neil Diamond who was thrown out of Leiber and Stoller's Red Bird label and came to Wexler, who decided to sign for a new label he created under the name BANG, jointly with Bert (B), Ahmet (A), Nesuhi (N) and Jerry Wexler (G).

Speaking to journalist Nik Cohn in London in the mid-1960s, Berns told the curious young lad that The Beatles' genius and sophistication would further lead to "the ruin of us all."[323] The three chords were the model for a successful series of productions, especially when connected to symphonic depth. Berns produced Neil Diamond, as well as the excellent Irish singer Van Morrison, and brought him with his band Them to America. In these sessions he discovered the brilliant guitarist, Jimmy Page, who would later turn his band, Led Zeppelin, into Atlantic pot of gold. He even co-wrote Jerry Ragovoy's "Piece of My Heart" for singer Erma Franklin, which features a chorus that leans on the same three basic harmonic degrees (I, IV, V7) – the same chords that would give Janis Joplin worldwide fame.

Rock writer Barney Hoskyns describes Berns as the "master of symphonic soul," an "uptown New York sound" which combined a multilayered orchestra with attractive gospel singing.[324] Berns, Hoskyns wrote, created the sound like the "kind of records Bacharach and David might have cut had they ventured down to Stax, or Pomus and Shuman down to Muscle Shoals."[325] According to him, Berns created exemplary and rugged soul ballads with a powerful emotional impact.

Ragovoy was his partner and in a sense, even Berns's student. His character was documented in the feature film *Not Fade Away* (2012) by David Chase, the *Sopranos* TV series creator, as one of New York's most notable musical characters in the 1960s. Ragovoy and Berns presented productions that combined secular gospel with European strings orchestration, such as the symphonic production for the solo song "Stay With Me" (1966), written for African-American singer Lorraine Ellison. Ragovoy pushed the orchestra intended initially to record with Frank Sinatra to "volcanic highs" that released and returned as they pushed the singer's soul into despair with a three-chorus chorus.

However, the production did not rely on sound, but it is the vocal performance that is at the center of interest. Ragovoy, for example, became known as a vocalist producer. He explained that Singers usually achieve fame for their singing style, and the producers remain in the background, "but the style [...] is my style," he emphasized in an interview, since he "gave it" to the singer, as if the singing games concerning the vocals were utterly his inventions, explained Ragovoy.[326]

The collaboration between Ragovoy and Berns is another example of what I termed elitist humanism. "Bert was a meat-and-potatoes four-chord basic kinda

---

323 Dave Marsh, *The Heart of Rock & Soul: The 1001 Greatest Singles Ever Made* (New York: Da Capo Press, 1989), 51.
324 Barney Hoskyns, "Bert Berns," *Mojo* (March 1998).
325 Ibid.
326 Cleothus Hardcastle, "The Unearthing of Howard Tate," *Rock's Backpages* (April 2001).

guy with a street feel that other people would have killed for," said Ragovoy, who believed Berns' talent was greater than his own. However, he couldn't hear beyond four chords while, compared to him, he was musically sophisticated. Berns, he said, ruled out over-sophistication such as "bebop," meaning avant-garde.[327]

Under the Atlantic Records umbrella, Berns, sometimes alongside Ragovoy, produced many crucial black soul music artists. The Texan singer Janis Joplin, who broke through into public consciousness in 1967, made Ragovoy's songs internationally famous even though her versions were not to his taste.

Unfortunately, with that success, the balance in BANG deteriorated. Demands for excessive royalties, battles over control, and the filing of lawsuits destroyed the initiative of the Ertegun brothers, Wexler and Berns in BANG. The informal alliance of Jewish writers and black performers in the Atlantic trickled into other places, labels, and other people. Enraged by his demons, in 1967 Berns died of heart problems. Wexler admitted he didn't attend the funeral.

The black-Jewish cooperation secured fantastic artistic achievements under Atlantic Records' umbrella. The primitive sound of rhythm and blues became high-quality and legitimate mainstream music with a host of hits, TV shows, and singles in the Top 20. Blacks gave the Jews the sense of authenticity that they sought so much, and the Jews presented a broader and more liberal America.

However, when Jews chose their business partners, they preferred to do so from their own ethnic group. They did not form business partnerships with African-Americans. Jerry Wexler had chosen Bert Berns to set up BANG Records, a publishing company, and a sideline label for Atlantic. Jerry Leiber and Mike Stoller established Red Bird Records with George Goldner. There are dozens more examples, and this trend culminated with the people of the Brill Building. Soon the issue would become more lurid. Radical black voices would argue against continued exploitation.

Leiber and Stoller continued their journey. In the mid-1960s, they felt tired and too old for rock 'n' roll labels and turned to musical writing and publishing. They no longer led a movement, but mostly rested on their glory. In the mid-1990s, a successful Broadway show, *Smokey Joe's Cafe*, celebrated their songs. Without huge names, the stars were the songs themselves, which four decades before had turned America on its head. Baby, that was rock 'n' roll!

---

327 Barney Hoskyns, "Bert Berns," *Mojo* (March 1998).

Chapter 9: Will You Love Me Tomorrow? Carole King, Black Lolitas and the Brill Building's hit factories

They came to work every morning at the Brill Building on 1619 Broadway. They went into the hit factories and wrote songs that helped the masses skip their daily troubles. The talented and the lucky ones managed to spread their wings and fly between the skyscrapers and airwaves. The others remained in the same small cubicles, waiting for their life's chance with piano and chair, lyric stand, ashtray, coffee mug, and the cacophony that came from music in nearby rooms. A multitude of songs performed simultaneously hoped to find the song that would continue the previous hit. They all sounded alike, but not all of them would be hits. Singers, bands, secretaries, marketers, and audiences sometimes stayed up to the small hours of the night dumbfounded about recording demos for songs. In America, music doesn't sleep because the money doesn't sleep. Even after World War Two, Tin Pan Alley continued to operate at full power.

During the 1950s, it seemed for a moment that Southern rock 'n' roll and BMI might change the balance of power in the music industry dramatically, but Tin Pan Alley and the major records companies were able to recover. They returned to their natural place in the "moment" between Elvis Presley's enlistment in the army in 1958 and The Beatles' landing in America in early 1964. Rock historians described this era as the "Middle Ages," supposedly connecting two pop music explosions.

Despite the stereotype of this era as "the Middle Ages," it was and still is important and crucial when it comes to songwriting and musical production, even if it lacks the cultural explosion associated with Presley and The Beatles. The latter two have influenced music sales patterns and passing fashions, releasing hidden energies that surfaced. They cut through class and race lines, dividing society by age. They altered the way of walking, talking, dressing, symbolizing cultural heroes, and probably the generation's dreams. These pop promoters accelerated changes in sexual, sometimes political, and cultural patterns of thinking.[328]

Compared to this volcano in pop culture, the late '50s and early '60s seemed like a return to a safer routine: the House of Representatives began an investiga-

---

[328] Greil Marcus, "The Beatles", in *The Rolling Stone's Illustrated History of Rock and Roll*, edited by De Curtis Anthony and Henke James (New York: Rolling Stone Press, 1992), 214.

https://doi.org/10.1515/9783110723168-010

tion into the Payola scandal (the bribe payments by rock 'n' roll independent labels to radio stations), which crushed the power of broadcasters like Alan Freed. Southern rock 'n' roll artists who broke out in the mid-1950s remained jobless: Presley went into the army, Jerry Lee Lewis was out of the music business for a few years (due to his marriage to his minor cousin once removed), Little Richard was reborn as an evangelist, Chuck Berry was in legal trouble and later sent to prison, and Buddy Holly died in a plane crash.[329]

The major record companies recruited handsome guys (many of Italian-American origin) to fill the void left by Elvis, and an entire industry once again needed songs. They all turned to the Brill Building, which was near Broadway, but symbolized a whole area of publishers' houses. The major record companies regained their strength, and the music industry believed it was back in a "normal" position.

The Jewish network in the Brill Building was formed in the late 1950s and early 1960s between a host of records labels and publishing houses, one of which belonged to two Jews, Al Nevins, and Don Kirshner, who sat across the road on 1650 Broadway.

Kirshner was a Jewish songwriter who went into business. In 1958, together with another songwriter, Nevins, he founded Aldon Music Publishing Agency, whose name was composed of a connection of their first names. Kirshner was a real hustler; Mike Stoller defined him as giving commercial motivation and persuasion a "new meaning."[330] The myth insists that he introduced himself as a publisher even before he had any songs at all. The first pair of songwriters recruited by Kirshner was Neil Sedaka and Howie Greenfield, who were rejected by some other publishers, but found allies in Aldon. Sedaka recalled bringing 12 songs with him only to see the publisher busy washing the floor.[331]

Kirshner based his 'song factory' on the Jewish social environment of Carole King and her husband Gerry Goffin, who had studied with Sedaka. Other neighbors were Barry Mann and his wife Cynthia Weil, and in the Brill Building, Jeff Barry and Ellie Greenwich were making their first steps. Paul Simon attended Queens College with them, made new efforts as a writer in Tin Pan Alley, though he set himself on a different musical career. Neil Diamond was in the area but was able to launch his career with an Atlantic Records' subsidiary. Those who

---

[329] Ari Katorza, *Come Together: Rock 'n' Roll, Liberalism, Mass Bohemianism and the Sixties* (Tel Aviv: K-Academics Publishing, 2019), 46–65.
[330] Jerry Leiber and Mike Stoller with David Ritz, *Hound Dog: The Leiber and Stoller Autobiography* (New York: Simon & Schuster, 2009), chap. 17, Kindle.
[331] Tom Nolan, "Neil Sedaka: Second Stairway to Heaven," *Rolling Stone* (4 December, 1975).

completed the picture were Burt Bacharach and his older Jewish partner Hal David, who worked on the other side of the street in another publishing house.

Bacharach studied classical composition while Sedaka was at the Juilliard School of Music, but many in this Jewish milieu enjoyed a semi-formal music education (at least classical piano studies). Many of them also went through their artistic experiences in the Catskill Mountains, a vast and famous vacation resort in eastern New York.[332] In contrast to the Southern rock 'n' roll artists, who came from working-class backgrounds, the attraction of young Jews to the popular music field was a combination of the music education they received in conjunction with their desire to escape middle-class expectations and norms.[333]

The songwriters were more eloquent in their work than they used to think. Many of the songs were directed explicitly at the lives of teenagers. They dealt with shared passions, desires, and imagery from the era. Still, each of the writers also touched on other topics: Goffin and King wrote songs about urban alienation in "Up On the Roof" and gender violence in "He Hit Me (And It Felt Like A Kiss)"; Barry Mann and Cynthia Weil introduced "Uptown," which dealt with class disparities; however, most of the time they were committed to creating hits. Familiar to all the writers was the professionalism, the rich musical background and fusion between rhythm and blues, Latin rhythms, and classical European harmonies. Although there were different writing groups with different approaches, the music industry branded their sound as "The Brill Building Pop Sound."

Many of the performers of those songs were black. This social and professional connection was not intrinsically new, but the Jewish-black relationship during the "Brill Building" era was completely alive.[334] This musical alliance was bolstered by the multiracial energy that bubbled from Martin Luther King's vision and the Civil Rights Movement, which encouraged the tremendous liberal dream.

Goffin and King wrote hits for various black girl groups, including The Shirelles; Cynthia Weil and Barry Mann, Ellie Greenwich and Jeff Barry, led by producer Phil Spector, wrote for African-American girl group The Crystals and The Ronettes; Burt Bacharach and Hal David split wings with singer Dionne Warwick. Unlike the wild 1950s rock 'n' roll artists from the South, which had fright-

---

[332] Greg Shaw, "Barry Mann: Rock & Roll Survivor," *Phonograph Record* (July 1975)
[333] Ibid.; Tom Nolan, "Neil Sedaka: Second Stairway to Heaven," *Rolling Stone* (4 December, 1975).
[334] Greg Shaw, "The Brill Building Pop," in *The Rolling Stone's Illustrated History of Rock and Roll*, edited by De Curtis Anthony and Henke James (New York: Rolling Stone Press, 1992), 143–152; Marcus, Greil, "The Girl Groups," in Ibid., 189–191.

ened America, the Brill Building's music was based on a compromise and combination of the old Tin Pan Alley music and the new rock 'n' roll sound. At this point, the writers preferred to concentrate on writing. Still, some were almost able to establish a career as performers.

Sedaka was the first, and he certainly didn't look like Elvis Presley. He looked innocent and unathletic and had a loud, beeping voice, but he became a model after gaining the attention of the industry. The boy whose mother made him play the piano was a school celebrity. Friends like Paul Simon, Neil Diamond, and Carole King could sense the possibilities outside the door, and the influences and motivations seemed mutually inspiring: Sedaka, inspired by Carole King, wrote, "Oh! Carol" (1958) that infiltrated the Top 10 in the *Billboard* chart (1959), and King answered it with a song, " Oh! Neil "that didn't get very far.[335]

The Brill Building writers were not the only ones influenced by Leiber and Stoller, whose work was very evident in American music of the early 1960s. The combination of stories of mass attraction and depth, caricatures of the adolescent world in American daily life, and a rich European orchestration combining blues and gospel elements, was also popular on the West Coast. In Los Angeles, Jewish writers and producers Lou Adler and Herb Alpert started a series of The Drifters-style productions for the African-American singer, Sam Cook. They would both be set to play a crucial part in the rise of the rock wave in California.

In New York, the producers focused on a new wave of music: the girl groups. They were young and mostly African-American. They looked like Amy Winehouse looked in the 2000s when she brought the world to its knees, but instead of self-destruction and the image of the martyr-and victim that suffers-for-everyone's-sins, the girl groups sang about the perfect guy to bring home to mom and dad; the boy with whom they will go to church and in the end bring home the longed for ring. However, these songs seemed to be more than that. "What makes the songs matter, beyond this rather timeless theme, is their beautiful construction, their unbelievable desire, their lust, their staggering demand for life," wrote Greil Marcus, "all riding on the voice of a single girl pushed by her sisters in the chorus."[336]

Something was misleading about the girl groups. They were devoid of autonomous authority, and the themes of their songs were incredibly conservative, but for the most part, the racial fabric of the girl groups showed a desire for a priv-

---

[335] Tom Nolan, "Neil Sedaka: Second Stairway to Heaven," *Rolling Stone* (4 December, 1975).
[336] Greil Marcus, "How the other half lives: The Best of Girl Group Rock," *Let It Rock* (May 1974).

ileged place in society and utopian life that was echoing from "below." The excellent products (in part) associated with them brought to light the old conflict between art and capitalism.[337]

Psychologically, the world of black/white identities might have confronted a mass audience with their private and public Jungian shadow archetype, but black femininity may have combined the shadow with primeval images of male-female duality: the anima. In moments of creative brilliance, Carl Gustav Jung explained that the anima is like a collective unconscious cast as spiritually sublime, imbued with images of danger, magic, communicating with our souls like the serpent in Eden.[338]

Some of the girl groups looked like "neighbor's girls," domesticated and conservative, but producers also brought African-American nymphs and Lolitas to the pop world in the early 1960s, in multicultural images, often full of magic and seduction. This time, for a change, women also gave them their voices.

Broadway and rock 'n' roll exotics

Carole King was one of the prominent writers of the Brill Building. She was born in 1942 in Brooklyn to a middle-class Klein family. Both her parents, second-generation immigrants from Eastern Europe, attended college, and her mother was responsible for her artistic-musical education. At the age of four, she was already practicing piano. Later she went on to study at the School of the Arts. She remembers that Broadway musicals and rock 'n' roll exotics from Alan Freed's radio show at WINS had impacted her musical maturity.[339] In 1955, she even watched Freed's rock 'n' roll shows in a Brooklyn theater, facing white and black groups dancing in segregation.

Two years later, she stood in amazement at Little Richard's stage performance roaring with his captivating gibberish, while during her upbringing at home she delved into the opera Carmen, Mozart, and the best of European classical music. Many parents believed that the rock 'n' roll that Freed broadcast was dangerous, but she remembers her sexual maturation and rock 'n' roll went hand in hand. She naturally accepted Elvis Presley's landing on American television in 1956, but it seems that it didn't have the same dramatic effect that Lennon and

---

[337] Greil Marcus, "The Girl Groups," in *The Rolling Stone's Illustrated History of Rock and Roll*, edited by De Curtis Anthony and Henke James (New York: Rolling Stone Press, 1992), 189–191.
[338] Jung, Carl Gustav, "The Archetypes and The Collective Unconscious," *Collected Works of C. G. Jung*, Vol. 9, Part 1, 54.
[339] Carole King, *A Natural Woman: A Memoir* (New York: Grand Central Publishing, 2012), 38.

McCartney experienced across the ocean ("before Elvis there was nothing," Lennon's myth claims).

She had dreams of acting on Broadway, but as time went on, the music seemed like the real destination. At the age of 15, she encountered the world of the Beat poets and their culture in Greenwich Village, but it was particularly her vocal group and local talents (Neil Sedaka) that made her start writing. She even played songs for Wexler and Ertegun at Atlantic, who thought she had a talent and asked her to come back with a few more. ABC-Paramount also got excited, offered a contract, and she even recorded some songs for them. In the meantime, these were just preliminary attempts.

Carole changed her last name from Klein to King to avoid an ethnic label and began attending Queens College. She made friends there with student Paul Simon, and the two began recording demos together. The future, however, blended into the life of another student, Gerry Goffin. In her memories, she says she felt she knew him from a painting she had drawn as if she was born with his character in her mind. He was an elitist, loved jazz and Broadway songs; he came from a rich literary background but eventually agreed to write to rock 'n' roll as an intellectual exercise. Faster than they expected, artists began recording their songs.

In 1959, they got married. Jerry worked as a chemist, but not for long. Sedaka had connected them with Kirshner. Because Goffin was busy with his day job, Carole went alone to a meeting at Aldon Music. She remembered an office whose design, she said, recalled a brothel. During the audition, Kirshner winked at her after every song, and Nevins enthusiastically praised her. She said Aldon Music had invested $6,000 in three-year advances, which probably made millions through Goffin and King especially after Kirshner launched a marketing venture with his typical enthusiasm, which would bring fast results with the band The Shirelles.

King and Goffin offered "Will You Love Me Tomorrow" (1960) to a group on the label Scepter Records, owned by a Jewish woman named Florence Greenberg. Hal David and Burt Bacharach also worked with her. Bacharach testifies in his memoirs that Greenberg had a great talent for choosing the least successful songs, but not this time.[340]

King remembers that she ran with a handwritten of a Goffin lyrics page to play the song to Greenberg and music producer Luther Dixon, and they loved it. She recorded a demo, played the piano in the studio, and arranged the string

---

[340] Burt Bacharach, *Anyone Who Had a Heart: My Life and Music* (New York: Atlantic Books, 2014), 127.

instruments into a huge hit. King captured the spirit of the era. She also won the essence of the girl groups, even though a man wrote the lyrics.

"Will You Love Me Tomorrow" dealt with pre-marital sexual intercourse and documented a typical pre-feminist pattern that wondered, "will the man respect the girl in the morning after." This hit, now considered one of the masterpieces of proto-feminist rock music, is about sex in a more sophisticated and respectful way for the mainstream than the so-called semi-pornographic post-war rhythm and blues.

The historical importance of the song also lies in the fact that an African-American girl group performed it. With lyrical depth and carrying a popular idea, "Will You Love Me Tomorrow" situates race and ethnicity respectfully in the public discourse. In contrast to the hits that Leiber and Stoller wrote for The Coasters, "Will You Love Me Tomorrow" was free of black lingo, but legitimized both a black and a feminine presence. Critic Charlie Gillett appreciated the unique way in which "Will You Love Me Tomorrow" conveyed sincerity, sexual attraction, and emotional realism in an authentic way.[341] Other critics praised the song and vocalization, which expresses sexual attraction without vulgarity, claiming that it was more than a perfect record and that after eight hours continuous listening only sounds better.[342]

King remembers that they sought inspiration from Rodgers and Hammerstein and even Aaron Copland, but they channeled the black female world mainly through the vision of Leiber and Stoller:

> They had a tremendous influence on me, especially on the first songs [...] The idea of connecting the R&B of the street with classical influences [...] It was amazing because my background and Jerry's was classical music, It was pretty strong here, but we also liked rock 'n' roll and street music, so we put them together.[343]

In her memoirs, she writes that The Drifters' "There Goes My Baby" recording was the model.[344] New York's ethic of professionalism influenced the whole conduct, which was different from the rougher recordings of rhythm and blues by the independent labels. After recording the rhythm section, the string instrument's turn came, and Carole was euphoric, especially as the musicians record-

---

341 Charlie Gillett, *Sound of The City: The Rise of Rock and Roll* (London: Da Capo Press, 1984), 195.
342 Greil Marcus, "How the other half lives: The Best of Girl Group Rock," *Let It Rock* (May 1974).
343 Paul Zollo, "Carole King," *Songwriters on Songwriting* (Cincinnati: Da Capo Press, 2003), 146.
344 Carole King, *A Natural Woman: A Memoir* (New York: Grand Central Publishing, 2012), 96.

ed what she wrote for them. She was only eighteen. After selling more than a million copies, Goffin allowed himself to leave his job as a chemist.

Songs and hits came one by one. In 1962 Goffin and King wrote a new song, "The Loco-Motion," and recorded his demo with the African-American babysitter of their children, Eva Boyd. After a brief and unsuccessful attempt to connect it to a performer, Kirshner decided that instead of persuading records labels to record his songs, he would instead open one himself. So he launched Dimension Records, where his producers and writers recorded songs for the record label. Kirshner branded Eva Boyd as Little Eva, and in the summer of 1962 "The Loco-Motion" reached the top of the charts for weeks, with a dance invented by Little Eva that became a fashionable frenzy. "Not a song. A sound," wrote the critic Dave Marsh in perspective, "created from an overly enthusiastic girl, applause, baritone sax," while the other details, he emphasized, including the lyrics, and the fact that Eva was the babysitter, "really don't matter."[345]

Goffin, who became the artistic director of the new label, made it, along with King, an incubator for African-American stars: not only Little Eva, but The Cookies, and a particularly successful girl group, The Chiffons. Goffin and King wrote "One Fine Day" (1963) for the group, which has production qualities, rich harmony, and a vision of writing. "One Fine Day," it was stated, "lay in the witty, accurate and attractive illustration of the female fantasy of a stable and exciting relationship."[346]

However, it is not just girl groups that recorded their songs. King and Goffin wrote the acclaimed "Up on the Roof" (1962) for The Drifters, which was a song about urbanity, passion, and horror. Jimmy Webb, the renowned American songwriter of the 1970s, argued that the quality of the song lies in the idea, its mystery, ambiguity, and sexuality. He presents Goffin and King's song as a masterpiece and a model for songwriting.[347]

The work required, King said, "a good ear" and attention to social sensibilities, perspective, and balance between quality and mass taste. "When I say good I mean something that's right, marketable, that has something to say," Goffin added in a newspaper interview. "It has to go through a lot of different ears; different people have to decide if it's something that people want to hear."[348]

In her memoirs, King felt regret at not receiving credit as a co-producer for her work on Label, claiming that a feminist consciousness had not yet been solid

---

[345] Dave Marsh, *The Heart of Rock & Soul: The 1001 Greatest Singles Ever Made* (New York: Da Capo Press, 1989), 41.
[346] Ibid., 34.
[347] Jimmy Webb, *Tunesmith* (New York: Hachette Books, 2013), 38.
[348] Bruce Pollock, *In Their Own Words* (New York: Collier, 1975), 11.

enough to demand it, and they did not have the time for too many gender issue thoughts, as all of them were busy creating hits. Kirshner, who felt safe in his nascent New York empire, began operating in Los Angeles through a pair of Jewish producers Lou Adler and Herb Alpert, who oversaw his West Coast branch. In between, he connected King and Howie Greenfield's "Crying in the Rain" (1962) to The Everly Brothers, who were King's youth heroes.

Feel the earth move under their feet

Everything was progressing wonderfully, but it stopped on one bright day. The British invasion, which began on February 7, 1964 with The Beatles landing in New York, amounted to a formative event in pop culture and a trauma for many American artists. It undoubtedly shifted the industry's center of gravity to new voices. African-American artists such as Ben E. King, The Drifters, and many of the bands were pushed aside by the British invasion, and there was a particular paradox that the admiration of The Beatles, The Rolling Stones, and other groups for African-American rock 'n' roll and rhythm and blues forced the American mainstream to acknowledge it so completely.

Leiber and Stoller claimed they weren't interested in the invasion, and Leiber, unlike his partner, believed The Beatles' singles weren't "funky" enough. Yet, the fact that British white lads admired black music changed the game. At last, a white performance in a black dream seemed to be the real thing, adding a new notion of authenticity, which did not come from the "provincial" and "schizophrenic" South, but from "stylish" England. The British revealed to the Americans the cultural and musical wealth that lay there in their own backyard. America returned to minstrelsy, but this time of English taste and in sync with the Constitutional amendments regarding Equal Rights led by President Linden B. Johnson, culminating in the summer of 1964. These together changed the path of American music and history.

The British invasion brought with it not only music, but style, fashions, European exotics, and Anglophilic fantasies originating in the artistic world that also shaped itself from the plethora of British art schools. These were set up in the United Kingdom after World War Two and many British rock artists studied there. London in the era of The Beatles' success became overnight the undisputed pop center of the universe: art pop galleries, absurd theater, an attractive cinema center for the best European directors, and a fashion center with young designers and modern boutiques. *The Times* magazine called the British capital in 1966 "Swinging London." Among these were the Mods and Rockers, tribes, subcultures of young people, who were trying to define for themselves an alternative identity that tried to bridge the gap between their class and the possibilities of British social mobility. For the first time, Britain had its own "American Dream."³⁴⁹ Yet, the Brits based an essential part of their early repertoire on music written by Jews and performed by blacks in America. Even after the invasion, British producers used to travel to New York to queue for songs.

The Beatles performed songs from Leiber and Stoller, such as "Some Other Guy," "Young Blood," and "Searchin'," and later recorded "Kansas City." Early recordings, bootlegs, and their own lives and radio appearances reveal that they loved performing "To Know Him Is To Love Him" (Phil Spector), as well as "Keep Your Hands Off My Baby" (Goffin and King). In their debut album, Please Please Me (1963), they included hits from girl groups such as "Baby It's You" (Bacharach, Dixon, Davis), "Chains" (Goffin and King), and of course "Twist and Shout" (Berns, Medley), which was performed by The Isley Brothers, and became one of their flagship songs. John Lennon confessed on a television show that he and his partner Paul McCartney aspired to be "the Goffin and King" of London." King and Goffin admitted years later that they considered Lennon's words "a very big compliment."³⁵⁰

The Rolling Stones based their first two albums on the Chicago blues sound, and their first major American hit, "Time Is on My Side," was the product of Jewish producer and composer Jerry Ragovoy. The Hollies recorded "Honey and Wine" (Goffin and King); and after The Animals invaded with "We Gotta Get Out of This Place" (Mann and Weil), Manfred Mann reached number one on the US and British charts with "Do Wah Diddy Diddy" (Barry and Greenwich).

The song's composition had undergone a transition from rhythm and blues to the pop hits of Goffin, King, and their friends. The Brill Building composers combined rock 'n' roll with the Broadway-musical style, which includes a mix of familiar structures (e.g., ABAB, AABA), while the verses had a refrain, conveying the basic idea of the song. Sometimes as in "Be My Baby" and "Baby, I Love You" by The Ronettes (written by Barry, Greenwich, Spector) the songs had sophisticated verses or resembled the structure of verse-pre-chorus-chorus, which became more popular in rock music from the 1970s onwards (from the Swedish band ABBA to Oasis).

The songwriters cultivated the second part of the songs, the middle eight (or bridge), in AABA, while deepening its harmonious, melodic, and lyrical dimensions. The middle eight might sometimes move between tonal centers and lean

---

349 Ari Katorza, *Come Together: Rock 'n' Roll, Liberalism, Mass Bohemianism and the Sixties* (Tel Aviv: K-Academics Publishing, 2019), 94.
350 Paul Zollo, "Carole King," *Songwriters on Songwriting* (Cincinnati: Da Capo Press, 2003), 146.

on harmonic substitutions as the composers returned "home" at the end of the part to the basic tonality of the song.

Harmonically, the songs were based on the tonality of Western music but characterized new combinations that became the musical elements of 1960s rock. Leiber and Stoller wrote many of their songs on the 12-bar blues structure and its harmonic degree (I7, IV7, V7), though The Drifters' best work relied on harmonic degrees associated with doo-wop hits (I, vi, IV, V7), which today is associated with the harmonies of the 1950s.

The Brill Building writers expanded their rock n 'roll compilations. They rejected the swing style a la Duke Ellington, that sounded anachronistic to their era, and reverted to triad chords at the tonic, even if there were elements of jazz harmony that were gently present in the songs (e.g. the cadence ii7-V7 in a multitude of hits). Many of the songs had a series of suspense and resolution (secondary and extended dominant chords progression). These were typical of the writing from Tin Pan Alley and Broadway: starting with "Will You Love Me Tomorrow," through "Crying in the Rain," and ending In "Breaking Up Is Hard to Do" (Sedaka and Greenfield, 1962) and "Be My Baby" (Barry, Greenwich, Spector), which is an shining example of a harmonic tension series, which goes from the song scale and takes the song for a "walk" from the tonic to the euphoric chorus.

The Brill Building writers did not hesitate to use modulations between different parts of the song (e.g. "One Fine Day," Goffin and King, 1963). Sometimes they combined modal interchange, meaning "borrowings" of chords from parallel major and minor scales, such as "Uptown," highlighted in a virtuoso flamenco guitar under Phil Spector's production, which dealt with an uncharacteristic theme for girl groups: class difference.

The Beatles, as well as other British bands, relied on all these elements designed by the Brill Building writers; however, although they did not have a musical education, but intuitively refreshed these structures, harmoniously and melodically. Except that The Beatles were, King says, "everything men want to be, and everything women would like to love, their music was impressive:" Their songs had catchy melodies, smart words, imaginative harmonies, and energetic arrangements," she admitted.[351]

The Beatles based their songs on more blatant combinations of blues and rock 'n' roll energy with Western harmony. The blue notes sparkled like diamonds in their songs that were not necessarily bluesy in their orientation (e.g., "From Me to You"). Melodically, The Beatles were bolder, like their empha-

---

[351] Ibid., 146.

sis on octave jumps in tune (e.g., "I Want To Hold Your Hand"), and with expressive and powerful combinations of horizontal melodies (limited range of notes) to vertical (wide range of notes). Lennon, McCartney and Harrison established modal interchange compositions that were based on borrowing chords from parallel major and minor scales and subsequently deepening the use of the church modes. All of these created the prominent harmonic sound of rock music in the 1960s. Musicologists who studied The Beatles' hits at the time of the invasion pointed out the modal dimensions in their songs. A famous commentary ("What Songs the Beatles Sang …") was offered by the classical music critic William Mann in *The Times* in December 1963 on their use of "Aeolian cadence," and Lennon answered cynically and jokingly that the term "Aeolian cadence" sounds like exotic birds to him. Mann was among the first to recognize their musical quality and crowned them as outstanding English songwriters, while the media was busy with Beatlemania.

After the British Invasion, and probably in light of the blues sounds of bands such as The Rolling Stones, The Kinks (in the beginning) and The Yardbirds, some of the Brill Building's song writers tried to fight back with a more bluesy sound with songs like "We Gotta Get Out Of This Place" (Mann, Weil) and "River Deep – Mountain High" (Spector, Barry and Greenwich), and turned more to modal interchanges with rock borrowings based on parallel scales such as in "You've Lost That Lovin 'Feelin'" (Barry, Greenwich and Spector, 1964). However, it was Burt Bacharach, who combined his best ammunition, especially asymmetrical bars, modulations, and, at times, a real Latin aroma and jazz harmony that managed to stay in the game against Motown Records' pop-gospel hits and British blues-rock.

Soul in 'lost and found'

Carole King confesses that she and Goffin believed that President Johnson's Equal Rights Act was "progress." Their support for the struggle for social justice was also due to their ties with African-American artists, but certainly because they shared a sense of outrage over injustice.[352] The famous murder of the three civil rights activists between Mississippi and Alabama in 1964 hit them hard, especially since they knew the mother of one of the victims, Andrew Goodman, personally. The radical youth movements that focused their hostility on the establishment after Kennedy's assassination mainly influenced Goffin, who

---

[352] Carole King, *A Natural Woman: A Memoir* (New York: Grand Central Publishing, 2012), 119.

sought to expand his consciousness with hallucinogens and writing songs with a more poignant social message. Yet, many folk singers had already grasped the nettle and communicated with the audience on this issue. The salvation came through the collaboration of three Jews with an excellent African-American female singer, Aretha Franklin. This recording brought the musical Jewish-black alliance to one of its highlights, probably its feminist peak.

Franklin had been recording at Columbia Records since the early 1960s, but after years of failures, she was invited by Jerry Wexler in 1966 to join Atlantic Records. Although the company was slightly skeptical of her ability to reach mass audiences, Wexler believed in her greatness. He decided to return it to the most authentic place associated with her songs: to the church. He chose rough and honest blues and gospel songs for her, and he did so with a band of southern white musicians from Muscle Scholes, Alabama.

Wexler recalls in his autobiography that his role as a music producer was "to pick the best songs, pick the best musicians or most appropriate ones, sit Aretha at the piano and let her roar." Franklin, he said, was a singer who didn't need guidance, but only "a suitable workspace."[353] Franklin was 25 years old at the time of their work, and she was a singer with a unique voice expressing the emotion and experience of someone much older than her age. In his own words, "I urged Aretha to be Aretha."[354]

By the time Wexler got out of his black limo to ask Goffin and King to write Franklin a good rhythm and blues song, she already had some huge hits, which crowned her senior position in American music. Wexler asked them for a song titled "A Natural Woman," and Goffin and King knew it was a great title.[355]

The work process was simple: in her memory, King writes that after dinner with radio stations in the background, and after putting her children to sleep, she went to the piano, and her hands just fell on the right chords. Goffin claims that the 6/8-time signature helped him write quickly. His imagery worked great, like the soul in "Lost and found," which formulated the uplift from depression and existential meaning with the help of true love. It was a song about being uplifted, that allows a woman to feel all the beauty that exists in her naturalness.

King describes first hearing Franklin's performance as "a rare moment with no ability to speak."[356] Franklin's excellence exceeded every reasonable expect-

---

[353] Jerry Wexler and David Ritz, *Rhythm and the Blues: A Life in American Music* (New York: Alfred Knopf, 1993), 208.
[354] Ibid.
[355] Carole King, *A Natural Woman: A Memoir* (New York: Grand Central Publishing, 2012), 119.
[356] Dave Marsh, *The Heart of Rock & Soul: The 1001 Greatest Singles Ever Made* (New York: Da Capo Press, 1989), 20.

ation, and the performance touched King more than any other production of a song she was involved with. She defined Franklin as "the most expressive vocal instrument of the twentieth century." Goffin and King's gospel received the excellent strings arrangement by Arif Mardin and authentic sonics by sound engineer Tom Dowd, and especially good production by Wexler, the visionary who, throughout the second half of the 1960s, tried to preserve Atlantic's liberal black vision in all its operations. In every sense, the song culminated in what Leiber and Stoller started in the late 1950s. The rendering of the elegant European orchestration alongside the gospel voice of an African-American singer echoed The Drifters and turned into one of the top moments of American music in the 1960s.

The performance revealed a female character who intensified the process of self-discovery into a complete personality. The single "(You Make Me Feel Like) A Natural Woman" became an artistic and commercial sensation and crossed generations of listeners. Critic Dave Marsh dubbed it "the greatest song ever written about female sexuality."[357]

California dreaming

Even before the British Invasion, Kirshner sold Aldon Music to Screen Gems, a Columbia subsidiary. His goal was to expand his influence on the film industry. The songwriters were frustrated with the sale, but he assured them it would be to their advantage. Kirshner produced a TV series, *The Monkees*. It imitated the mood of The Beatles' films as well as the sound of their hits from that era. Goffin and King were involved in the project with "Pleasant Valley Sunday" (1967) and "Porpoise Song (Theme from Head)" (1968), two songs that resembled The Beatles' psychedelic sound and even included similar elements of composition (modal interchange and modality together), which were not really typical of the duo.

The rise of counterculture and protest singers like Bob Dylan also unexpectedly affected the couple. According to King, Goffin's jealousy of Dylan's artistic freedom, his attraction to bohemianism, and hallucinogenic drugs led to his mental decline, and their separation and divorce. They moved, individually, to California.

Fortunately for King, the California music industry was no less Jewish than New York. Kirshner appointed Lester Sill, the friend of Leiber and Stoller and

---

[357] Ibid.

Phil Spector's former partner, as the director of his new venture. A longtime acquaintance, Lou Adler, who started with Dunhill Records, among others, opened Ode Records in 1967 and was involved in Kirshner's ventures. Adler became one of the most successful music men in Los Angeles and the manager behind King.

Adler was synchronized wonderfully with California's folk-rock wave in the middle of the decade: The Mamas & the Papas were a huge success, as was Barry McGuire, a folk-rock singer who triumphed commercially with "Eve of Destruction" (1965). A young Jewish songwriter, P.F. Sloan (born Philip Gary Schlein), managed by Adler, wrote the song and popularized folk-rock, while turning folk protest into a new capitalist fashion.

In the late 1960s, the changes were even more blatant. With the onset of the psychedelic wave, a host of bohemian and post-hippie artists established a successful new musical movement in Los Angeles. After years of ideological drifting, artists forged an imaginary alliance with the South as they stepped back into Southern mythology and pantheism. The Band, Creedence Clearwater Revival, The Flying Burrito Brothers and The Eagles created a new Southern dream and a new version of rock 'n' roll: country rock, one of the most influential musical waves during the 1970s, replacing the fashion for psychedelic hallucination with American heritage and history.

James Taylor, Crosby Stills and Nash, Neil Young and Joni Mitchell, established another musical wave of singer-songwriters. Two Jews, David Geffen and Elliot Roberts, managed many of them. These singers went on to form something similar to Dylan's folk-rock that redefined the sound of California, which they updated for the Me Decade. King arrived at this creative paradise with fantastic timing.

After years of writing hits and some unsanctioned solo career attempts, she had been on a quest to find her unique voice. Her relationships with James Taylor and other musicians who encouraged her filled her with renewed energy. Her performances at Sunset Boulevard Club were full of college girls (and their mothers). King wrote some great songs. She fused a non-fake romanticism version of the Tin Pan Alley style that combined ingredients of New York's jazz music and Latin traditions with California's sense of rock and freedom. These came together at the end of the journey with the bestseller *Tapestry* (1971).

King's songs stood out with the aroma of jazz harmony (seventh, 9, 11 and 13 chords) and musicals, but with the addition of up-to-date approaches from the rock age (modality and pentatonic melodies), even though in many ways it was close to the traditions of Berlin, Rodgers, Gershwin, and Goffin and King's own songs. She wrote most of the songs about relationships. Still, the audience might interpret them in light of the political atmosphere of those years. King's turned hymns about the breakup of love relationships into an expression regarding the disappointments of 1960s counterculture. Other songs were about empowerment and friendship and positive thinking, and King's writing was brilliant as ever (and included what perhaps sounded like very Jewish sentences: "Doesn't anybody stay in one place anymore"). Above all, her stage persona seemed to have undergone a process of individuation, completion, maturation, and balance. What began in the early 1960s as a display of African-American world charisma with the girl groups, and continued through the self-discovery process written for Aretha Franklin, came to maturity in King's process of artistic individuation and completeness, at least for this album.

Tapestry has sold around 25 million copies to date, and King captured the Grammy Grand Slam in March 1972. It won the Record of the Year, Album of the Year, Best Female Vocal Performance of the Year, and Song of the Year. "You've Got a Friend" performed by James Taylor, won that year's Male Vocal of the Year performance. For a moment, she felt that the earth moved under her feet.

Chapter 10: River Deep – Mountain High: Phil Spector, Burt Bacharach and the Ghost on the Second Floor of the Bus

One cold day, the teenager Burt Bacharach was on his way to his piano class with teacher Rose Raymond on 86th Street in Manhattan. Once a week, he would travel to Queens to work on the discouraging finger exercises. Although, at that point, he felt he lacked talent and hated to practice, he was still meticulous about switching transportation and getting to classes while traveling and thinking on the second floor of a bus.

One man who seemed strange to him sat down next to him. When the boy Burt whistled a tune, the man asked, "Is that 'Two O'Clock Jump'?" "Yes, how do you know that? Are you a musician?" Burt asked. The man answered yes, and Burt wondered if he was playing at the local bars. "No actually I am a conductor," the man replied, "the New York Philharmonic." "Come on, I know who conducts the New York Philharmonic. Bruno Walter," the boy replied. "Well, I am assistant conductor," the stranger corrected. The two continued to talk. Just before getting off the bus, Burt said goodbye to him, "Well, I'll see you up someday, Lenny."[358]

Bacharach had hoped to meet the musician sometime on the second floor of the bus, not knowing that the next day the *New York Times* would publish a profile article about the new young conductor, Leonard Bernstein.

Years after the torch was passed between the Jewish conductors (Walter and Bernstein), Bacharach and the famous conductor met again in 1980 at Bernstein's sister's house, after going through dizzying careers. They both participated in Ted Kennedy's election campaign for the Democratic Party, but Bernstein asked him to stop telling everyone they met on the second floor of the bus: "That never happened. You just dreamed it up," the maestro hissed. It sounded even more wonderful, Bacharach thought to himself.

Bernstein was perhaps the most prominent figure in the world of classical music, trying to communicate with popular music. Not just the best-selling *West Side Story*, but as a dictator of public opinion. On Valentine's Day of 1967, he presented a television show, Inside Pop: The Rock Revolution (CBS) in which he introduced new rock music, said what he liked about it and admitted it was five percent of what was happening. But when he talked about The Beatles

---

[358] Burt Bacharach, *Anyone Who Had a Heart: My Life and Music* (New York: Atlantic Books, 2014), 17.

or Brian Wilson and Janis Ian, it was evident that he had great appreciation and interest in the world of young people.

This chapter, however, is about two characters who were pioneering in the opposite direction – in the connection between the pop world and high art: Burt Bacharach and Phil Spector. In many ways they were completely different from each other. Bacharach belonged to the jazz generation, Spector to the rock generation. Bacharach was a composer with a formal education, while Spector was a talented musician with great intuitions. Bacharach was a man of the existing order, while Spector broke every law of the entertainment world. Bacharach looked like an accountant, while Spector was notorious for being one of the crazies of show business. However, they both continued the trend of combining popular and high-end art into works that had overwhelming influences on American pop music as a whole. Both took off in the early 1960s through the Brill Building in New York. They both came out of hit the production factory characterized by Jewish dominance and business acumen. They both achieved this through the use of African-American femininity.

'It's pure gold coming out of these speakers' (Phil Spector to Sonny Bono)

Sometime in the late 1960s, British-Jewish journalist and writer Nik Cohn waited for days at a Spanish-style hotel for a car to take him to Phil Spector's estate.[359] His idea was to write a book about someone he perceived as one of the most influential figures in the decade's popular music: The producer behind the Wall of Sound recording technique, the first real rebel in rock, the Wagner of the pop world and the first tycoon of teens.

Cohn's meeting with Spector, however, resembled meeting a ghost. Cohn described Spector as short and not a nice-looking man with a painful childhood, against all the odds of reinventing himself, while briefly winning an unprecedented artistic prominence in the pop world. To him, Spector, for all the paranoia that hounded him, was the embodiment of America in this American century.

Cohn described the mansion as in a manner reminiscent of a combination of Hitchcock and David Lynch films. The voice of singer Ronnie Spector (Bennett originally) in a hallway that suddenly appears and disappears, a fun and momentary pool game, *Rolling Stone* magazine pages scattered and marked with ar-

---

[359] Nik Cohn, "Phil Spector," in *The Rolling Stone's Illustrated History of Rock and Roll*, edited by De Curtis Anthony and Henke James (New York: Rolling Stone Press, 1992), 180–183.

ticles about Spector himself, a Rolls Royce with blacked out windows for invisibility, and above all a character who spoke of his glorious past in an impossible present. Spector wasn't even 30 years old, but he seemed to have been living in the industry for decades. He was gone, over, finished. Kaput. After a few days, Cohn abandoned the idea of the book.

Spector, for his part, later traveled to England to save The Beatles' *Get Back* project in what for a moment seemed like a lightning comeback (and ended controversially).[360]

He was working on John Lennon and George Harrison's first solo albums, but months later, things turned out badly. His mental illness left him no rest. He walked around with guns, wretched people, ran away with tapes, and then, according to the myths, threatened the Ramones that he would add classical strings instruments to the recording of their punk songs. Since the early 1980s, except for some bleak attempts, nobody wanted to hire him anymore. He barricaded himself on his estate, devoid of purpose, music, and love, longing for a time when he had the urge and initiative reserved for true pioneers until the bitter end.

In the early 1960s, the Brill Building worked full force, but it seemed that the influence of the hit factories reached a new peak with Spector's work. Spector, who was paranoid, schizophrenic, charismatic and cruel, created his economic mini empire in his early twenties with the help of the Jewish network in the music industry in general, and Brill Building in particular.

Spector was born in late 1940 in New York to a family with a history of mental illness. His father, a second-generation immigrant from Russia, committed suicide when Spector was a child. His mother moved with him to the largest Jewish neighborhood in Los Angeles, Fairfax. He attended the same high school that Jerry Leiber had studied at, which bore the neighborhood's name. Hollywood's glamor, on the one hand, and pop culture and physical sports on the other, shaped the world of the poor, short Jewish boy. He, who was described as having terrible hair and skin – had to grow up in the Californian world of golden sunny, athletic, and good-looking surfers.

Spector played some jazz guitar and was good at it, but soon realized he was attracted to the backstage work. During his high school studies, when he was

---

[360] Some critics didn't like Spector's bombastic production of "Let It Be" and "The Long and Winding Road" specially the choirs and string orchestra's arrangements he ordered to add. The Beatles' producer George Martin, too, confessed in The Beatles anthology that Spector missed the band's uniqueness in his production. Paul McCartney demanded in a special letter to remove Spector's extras. The lack of an answer to his letter precipitated the official declaration of the dissolution of The Beatles.

only 17, he formed a band with four other Jews, including singer Annette Kleinbard and Marshall Leib, who remained with him to form The Teddy Bears. The Los Angeles musical environment outlined the career path: Young Spector recorded at Gold Star Studios, which was in contact with a local label, Era/Dore Records.[361] The label was scanty but full of Jewish presence; Spector started his career there, as did repertoire directors Lou Adler and Herb Alpert, who began their journeys as successful labels owners and managers in the music industry.

Shortly after that, he wrote his first hit, "To Know Him Is to Love Him" (1958), which he based on a sentence engraved on his father's tombstone. Spector played, arranged, and produced it, submitting a master more reminiscent of Broadway than rock 'n' roll. Although the single was relatively primitive in terms of production, it contained features that would appear down the road: layers of double-tracking vocal harmonies, beautifully composed lead vocals by Kleinbard, a middle eight rich in the keys of the moment, tonal centers, tensions and a resolution of secondary dominant chord progressions. After a while, a DJ discovered it on California radio and streamed it across the state. It sold more than one million copies and reached the top of the *Billboard* chart.

Unfortunately, mismanagement of the band led Spector back to the starting point. He was involved in several mediocre singles, continued to roam among various labels, and finally discovered a new channel with Lester Sill, one of the best contacts in the Los Angeles music scene.[362]

On the advice of the new mentor, Spector was preparing to move to the most coveted place for him: the New York-based musical complex of Leiber and Stoller. Los Angeles may have been the movie capital, but as far as Spector was con-

---

361 The Label Era was owned by Lew Bedell, a former broadcaster on a local radio station, and his cousin, Herb Newman. Despite being a small label, Era managed to put out hits at the national level ("The Wayward Wind"). In 1958 Bedell and Newman launched another label, Dore, dedicated to rock 'n' roll. They appointed Lou Adler and Herb Alpert, two young musicians of Jewish origin, to the artists' directors and repertoire, in order to discover new talents. Adler also later ran the Kirshner label's California branch, Dimension Records.

In the mid-1960s Alpert launched a very successful career as a musician and one of the two partners of successful Californian label A&M. He also released bestselling albums under his band, Herb Alpert & the Tijuana Brass. Lou Adler was equally successful as a music producer, the owner of the label Dunhill Records, and as one who discovered, among other things, The Mamas & the Papas. As a music producer and executive producer, he was also responsible for Carol King's bestseller Tapestry (1971).

362 Dave Thompson, *Wall of Pain: The Biography of Phil Spector* (New York: Sanctuary Publishing, Ltd., 2003), 34.

cerned, the rock 'n' roll center was in New York.[363] There, the important record companies and publishing houses operated. Jerry Leiber recalls Sill asking him to hire Spector as an apprentice. "He was living in Los Angeles at the time and Los Angeles wasn't that exciting," he reiterated.[364] Jerry Wexler, who would develop a friendship and professional relationship with Spector, remembers that Sill introduced him as a "prodigy," as one who plays musical instruments, composes, produces and does everything, and as someone who "learned in the same school as Jerry and Mike" (even if it was only partially true).[365] Spector convinced his mother that he would travel to New York as an apprentice in translation work, which wasn't easy for someone who was suffering from a fear of abandonment. "He was scared to death of being left alone," recalled Leiber, who thought he was terribly ambitious and smart, but admitted he never liked him.[366]

In the meantime, Kirshner and Nevins established their own songwriting enterprise with a series of writers who came every morning to work, and were responsible for dozens of American hits of the era.[367] Spector couldn't help but be impressed by the way Kirshner and Nevins, the ethnic "outsiders," built themselves up in the entertainment industry with a very successful initiative.[368] Now he has beginning his own network spinning. He began collaborating with Doc Pomus, who wrote songs, among others, for Ray Charles and Elvis Presley. Pomus remembered that Spector used to rent a car and drive to visit his home, during which he would enjoy his wife's Jewish cooking; "Then the big songs started coming," he said.[369] They co-wrote "First Taste of Love" for Ben E. King, which did not get the commercial credit it deserved.

But Spector had no time to hesitate: Through Stan Shulman, the Jewish manager of singer Ray Peterson ("Tell Laura I Love Her"), he produced the single "Corrine, Corrina," which reached the Top 10. Now, after weeks of pleading, he got a chance to play with the big guys and write with Leiber and Stoller.

---

363 Ibid., 40.
364 Ibid., 41.
365 Jerry Wexler and David Ritz, *Rhythm and the Blues: A Life in American Music* (New York: Alfred Knopf, 1993), 141.
366 Jerry Leiber and Mike Stoller with David Ritz, *Hound Dog: The Leiber and Stoller Autobiography* (New York: Simon & Schuster, 2009), chap. 17, Kindle.
367 Dave Thompson, *Wall of Pain: The Biography of Phil Spector* (New York: Sanctuary Publishing, Ltd., 2003), 43.
368 Ibid.
369 Ibid., 41.

Spector was listening to Debussy's "Ibéria" and Ravel's "Rapsodie espagnole," and offered something Spanish. Various reasons prevented Stoller from arriving, so Spector and Jerry Leiber wrote and produced Ben E. King's "Spanish Harlem," a delicate and lyrical work with gospel vocals, saturated with marimba, strings arrangement and Brazilian art and a delicate Latin flavor.

His New York success led Spector back to Los Angeles, this time as a sought-after producer. Influenced by the success of Wexler and Ertegun at Atlantic and Kirshner and Nevins for Aldon, he sought to establish himself as a record tycoon. At the end of 1962, he launched their record label, Philles Records with Lester Sill, which consisted of merging their first names (it would not be long before his partner left). He embarked on a mode of artistic and business warfare, eventually crowning him one of the most influential music producers of his generation. In no time, he combined Oscar Wilde-style rebellion, a saturated battle of self-persecution in the industry and a pioneering artistic world, wearing dark ethereal shades, a three-piece suit, and using his recording technique, the wall of sound.

Apocalypse and teenage dreams

The art of recording underwent a revolution in the late 1950s. If in the Swing era, orchestras were supposed to commemorate their best performance, the studio in the age of rock gradually became a musical instrument itself. The multi-track tape recorder, the famous echo chambers, and capacity to control the reduction of the dynamic range of the recorded signals with a limiter and compressor enabled the creation of original 3D musical sound. Technological development enhanced the possibilities of directing in the studio.

Producers began to work on various highlights that were essential to the success of songs: starting with the movement, speed, and flow of the song; through volume and size achieved through double-tracking of musical instruments and multicolored layers; and finally to the use of 'colors' in the tradition of classical impressionism. But gradually through the 1960s, they did it with the use of various technologies: reverberation, varispeed, an alternative method of recording tapes (backward play, for example), and subsequent developments of multiple effects such as flange and phasing, distortion, and more.

The evolution of the music producer also evolved rapidly: from label owners who recorded artists, to artist and repertoire men who oversaw diverse recordings, to the producer becoming an artist in his own right. In this case, the producer carried with him a musical, visual, and technological vision and used the artist to convey that vision. The producers came from a variety of backgrounds:

music, technology, and artistic mentoring, but some, like Spector, were prominent in all three of them.

In much the same way that Jewish lyricists and composers were nurturing the American art of songwriting, the producers were responsible for expanding its musical and technological spectrum. They connected the foundations of African-American music to the aesthetics of high European orchestration with the use of technology. Sometimes, romanticized by notions of musical authenticity, they acted in the opposite direction and made sure to bring their clients, the black artists, back to their "authentic" environment.

The musical production also had to include a psychological aspect that was communicated with control and manipulation. George Goldner, one of the first Jewish musical producers, designed some of the hits of the 1950s and strengthened the Jewish-black alliance in the music industry. Writer Greil Marcus wrote about his work with The Chantels:

> There were five of them, young black girls from New York City; lead singer Arlene Smith was all of fourteen. Their producer was George Goldner [...] He was the archetypal cigar-smoking Jewish businessman who took black singers off the street, hustled, bought, stole, pleaded and hyped to put their records across and then left them behind [...] He was also a magnificent record producer. The sound he and arranger Richard Barret worked out for the "Chantels" was simple: one very steady drum beat; rolling piano triplets climbing up and falling away, over and over again; a little guitar; a virtually inaudible bass. In the nave, a pleading choir from four "Chantels"; at the pulpit, with everything surrounding her, Arlene. And somehow, the sound was huge, overpowering, like Judgment Day.[370]

Spector went on precisely from where Goldner, Leiber and Stoller left off; but he then went a few steps ahead, at least with his ambition. He redefined the role of the music producer as an artist in his own right. In Spector's world, the artists played a secondary role, if any. The wall of sound he produced was a multicultural force throughout.

Spector used the assistance of the arranger Jack Nitzsche, sound engineer Larry Levine, and the best Los Angeles studio players known by the name The Wrecking Crew. He also collaborated with the Brill Building songwriters: Carole King and Gerry Goffin, Barry Mann and Cynthia Weil, Jeff Barry and Ellie Greenwich. However, the songs needed a vision of sounds. He came to the wall of sound straightforwardly: under the influence of Leiber and Stoller, he used a large number of musicians sitting in one recording room but increased the size to an army of musicians. Its purpose was to create as great a sound as pos-

---

[370] Greil Marcus, "How the other half lives: The Best of Girl Group Rock," *Let It Rock* (May 1974).

sible. The musicians were divided into groups by musical instruments, and these musicians played in the same musical ranges. With the leak from every player's microphone, and with the use of the echo chamber, he achieved an enormous volume of sound compared to the rest of his work during his time. Although he produced a diverse line of artists, he became more well-known than any other producer who shaped the sound of the girl groups The Crystals and The Ronettes.

The Brill Building writers knew they were capturing the traditions of the Tin Pan Alley, Broadway, and rock 'n' roll, but Spector was most fascinated by the concept of high art and to sell it to a mass audience. "It's gold, pure gold coming out of these speakers," his assistant Sonny Bono remembered Spector's words.[371]

On the other hand, the mythologists liked to tell that he adored the works of German composer Richard Wagner, but he stole and borrowed from everyone and whatever he could: from Schubert to Walt Disney. He called his works "little symphonies for teens." Praise was bestowed on the relation between the high and mighty sound and human sensibilities. Writer and music critic Nik Cohn believed the huge apocalyptic sound was Spector's revenge on the psychological traumas that accompanied his life, as well as a mental compensation for his small physical stature.[372]

Either way, Spector moved the Hollywood tycoon myth into the music industry. He drove a Rolls-Royce car with dark windows and a bodyguard driver, seeing and not being seen; he combined innocent teenage stories with a brutal and dramatic sound, teenage dreams with the apocalypse. Rock writers loved to embrace the mythology around him, such as being a mad producer, a disturbed, genius scientist of sounds, and he probably believed what they were writing as he read the fairy tales about him at his California estate. Greil Marcus wrote about Spector's achievement in "He's Sure the Boy I Love":

> This was Phil Spector's first breakthrough into ecstasy. A dramatic fanfare – just on long note on a horn' and then a completely confident female voice announcing over the impatient rumble of too many drums: 'I always dreamed the boy I loved would come along, and he's be tall and handsome, rich and strong. Well, now that boy has come to me – but he sure ain't the way I thought he'd be!" And so, the Spector saga begins. In one swoop, pianos, more drums, sax, the full assault, and – I think – Darlene Love, holding on to the explosion, so proud of herself and her boy she can't hold back anything at all. No excuses, no regrets, all he's got are unemployment checks, but she loves him, and you'd better believe

---

[371] See the inside booklet of the record box of Spector's hits Back to Mono (1958–1969).
[372] Nik Cohn, "Phil Spector," in *The Rolling Stone's Illustrated History of Rock and Roll*, edited by De Curtis Anthony and Henke James (New York: Rolling Stone Press, 1992).

it. The Crystals are tossing out lines and Darlene throws them back with a smile that stretched all over America the year this record became a hit.[373]

The writing on Spector focused on the special balance he made between mass culture and high art. On the one hand, Nik Cohn writes, Spector created his own creative and imaginary universe, which he saw as the "test of every true artist."[374] In other words, he was very serious about his artistic ambitions. And yet, at the same time, he maintained the "nonsense" spirit of rock 'n' roll and was driven by commercial intuitions per se. "He stole from any source he could," Cohn writes, "Wagner, Leonard Bernstein, Broadway shows, a thousand or a million other singles, past and present – and was still completely original." In this paradox, "he managed to combine the two great rock 'n' roll romances – rebellion and teen dream – into one."[375]

The hit that introduced the wall of sound to the world was "He's a Rebel" (1962). Spector gave it a Latin-flavored production and the song hit the top of the chart. Another significant hit was "Da Doo Ron Ron" (1963) which represented a tour de force of the wall of sound style with tympany drums, saxophone, layers of vocal harmonies, piano introduction in triplets, and a literal "hook" that was open to sexual interpretation of the perfect guy's infatuation.

However, the perfect prototype for girl group hits was the "Be My Baby" by The Ronettes (1963), a rock 'n' roll adaptation of a Brazilian baion rhythm to a profoundly resonant intro weaved into a multicultural saga. With an image of Lolita, singer Ronnie Bennett, with her African-American, Native American, and Irish mix of origins, redefined music and exoticism (Spector fell in love with her, but tormented her during their horrible marriage). A basic verse structure, the tension resulting from extended dominant chords progression in the pre-chorus and vocal counterpoint in the chorus were crafted on layers of strings of electric and acoustic guitars, Spanish castanets, and gradually wind instruments and strings. The drums "hook" pattern in the introduction came back a moment before the final chorus, all of which saw the song to second place on the *Billboard* chart as it became one of the most influential songs in American pop culture.

---

[373] Greil Marcus, "How the other half lives: The Best of Girl Group Rock," *Let It Rock* (May 1974).
[374] Nik Cohn, "Phil Spector," in *The Rolling Stone's Illustrated History of Rock and Roll*, edited by De Curtis Anthony and Henke James (New York: Rolling Stone Press, 1992), 183.
[375] Ibid.

Tomorrow's sound, today!

In 1964, the swing of the girl groups was halted. The media was concentrated on The Beatles' landing on February 7 in New York, after breaking through in America with the late 1963 single "I Want to Hold Your Hand" as if it signaled a changing of the center of musical gravity. New York radio stations declared "Beatles Time," and the British invasion resembled alien landings. "It was not something in the air, but the air itself," Marcus wrote.[376] America responded to The Beatles' music as if they listened to music for the first time.

The Beatles portrayed the image of Shakespeare's buffoons with excellent timing. And they made great music. Like Gershwin before them, Lennon and McCartney intuitively combined the best of European traditions with the blues (blue notes, pentatonic scales, roaring vocals), modal elements, and various forms of modal interchange (borrowing from parallel major and minor scales), to make a fresh new rock sound.[377] They loved rock 'n' roll, doo-wop, and American musical comedy songs (as well as old British music), but gradually, they moved out of the musical world as designed by Leiber and Stoller and the Brill Building songwriters, and redefined it. In general, with some rare exceptional cases, they rejected the swing harmony a la Duke Ellington and moved on from where Gershwin had stopped songwriting during the 1930s, but with a heavier emphasis on blues to rock language that would impact the decades to come.

Spector answered the British invasion with a new song that was a collaboration with the duo Weil and Mann, "You've Lost That Lovin' 'Feelin'." This time he tried his hand with a duo of white rhythm and blues singers: The Righteous Brothers. When the song came out, it became known as a masterpiece of musical production and the best expression of the wall of sound, with the emphasis on counterpoint voices by female ensembles, classical strings arrangements, heavy reverberation, an advanced and rocky structure of verse-pre chorus-chorus, and dramatic low male vocals. Musically, it contained a bluesy-rocky bVII harmonic degree (and a modal interchange of major and minor scales), and Spector added a third part based on the three "Guantanamera" chords in a winning white-black-Latin multicultural mix.

"You've Lost That Lovin' 'Feelin'" is also endowed with simple, high-praise lyrics. The subject is about a love crisis and the breakup of a relationship, but

---

376 Greil Marcus, "The Beatles," in *The Rolling Stone's Illustrated History of Rock and Roll*, edited by De Curtis Anthony and Henke James (New York: Rolling Stone Press, 1992), 214.
377 Dominic Pedler, *The Songwriting Secrets of the Beatles* (London: Omnibus, 2003).

the simple lyrics convey a deep and authentic emotion of heartbreak. The song has a circular sequence as the first and last sentences complete a course of ideas. This bestseller was praised by songwriter Jimmy Webb, who explains that the song's virtues lie in the small details. The way the song begins with the speaker's diagnosis that the object of his passion "never close[s]" her eyes anymore when he kisses her puts the listener in an intimate relationship on a voyeuristic level while listening to only one side of a song that makes the narrative more exciting and mysterious.[378]

Spector had to change the key in order to fit the low, dramatic voice of Bill Medley that stands out in most of the song. Legend has it that when the other singer in the duo, Bobby Hatfield, asked about his involvement regarding the song, Spector replied that he could "go to the bank".[379]

"You've Lost That Lovin 'Feelin'" not only reached the top of the charts but was probably one of the most played songs on American radio and defined Spector's status. Spector's British promo-man Andrew Loog Oldham released the song while describing it as Spector's greatest production and "tomorrow's sound, today!", in the United Kingdom, a promise that was only partially true.[380]

Through the Jewish-Black Alliance, Spector spread the sound of African-American girl groups, and the black charisma and glorification of African-American beauty to the world and into the mainstream of American entertainment. He did so with more than a dozen songs, in part performed by black Lolitas, reaching the Top 10. Writer Tom Wolfe dubbed him "The First Tycoon of Teens."[381]

Despite the successful Jewish-black artistic collaboration, the rumors of exploitation regarding non-royalty payments and abuse grew louder in the context of the producer and the artists. Spector's madness took over his talent (until the court convicted him of murder in 2009), and he – even at a time when he produced The Beatles in their late days as a band and Lennon and Harrison on their first solo albums – failed to recapture the days when a small, pale Jew was reborn in self-belief that he was the last Emperor of American music.

---

[378] Jimmy Webb, *Tunesmith* (New York: Hachette Books, 2013), 41–42.
[379] Back to Mono (1958–1969).
[380] Michael Billig, *Rock 'n' Roll Jews* (London: Five Leaves Publications, 2001), 108.
[381] Tom Wolfe, *The Electric Kool-Aid Acid Test* (New York: Farrar, Straus and Giroux, 2008 [1965]).

Burt Bacharach: What the world needs now is love

In the mid-1960s, the Brill Building songwriters seemed to gone off track: Leiber and Stoller navigated their way to a calmer lifestyle; Spector had become increasingly confined to his California estate; and the writers of Aldon Music and others, even if they made excellent hits for the British bands, had trouble continuing the momentum of the beginning of the decade. The American audience, magnetized by dramatic changes in pop culture, listened to Bob Dylan's prophetic tone; the new groove of Motown's gospel whipped cream, and the British bands, that after their dizzying initial invasion, began the occupation phase.

Of the writers of the Brill Building, the duo Burt Bacharach and Hal David managed to fight back. On paper, they belonged to another era. Bacharach and David were born in the jazz era of the 1920s and grew up during the Great Depression and World War Two. Hal David admired Irving Berlin, and Bacharach idolized Gershwin and Bernstein. Considering their character and image, they had nothing in common with protest marches, flower power, and free love, Vietnam, long hair, loud fuzz guitars, and hallucinogens. However, during the turbulent days of the British invasion, the duo wrote, composed, and produced a series of hits that became classics – both American and British – that bridged across generations. They made links between Irving Berlin and Gershwin, through rich jazz harmony and a Latin rhythm world, to the energetic spirit of Kennedy and Johnson liberalism, all remembered with the gentle, educated and controlled African-American voice of Dionne Warwick.

Bacharach was born in 1928 in Kansas City to a Jewish family with German roots and grew up in Queens in New York. Physically he was small in stature during his youth but experienced a perfectly normal adolescence in a middle-class family. Bacharach remembered his mother as having great taste in music and art, and their home as being beautifully decorated. He admired his father, who was an editor and a journalist. Except for the Pesach ritual with relatives, they hardly kept in touch with the Jewish community. Bacharach recalled that the Catholic environment in which he grew up influenced his ethnic identity, so he was never thrilled to say that he was Jewish.

He remembered his parents going to the recreation centers regularly because his father used to write about the places he spent time in. In their car, by the way, the Bacharach family would listen to the New York Philharmonic. His mother forced him to study piano not because she hoped he would be a musician, but because she believed it was important to him in life. He says that for years, he was a reasonably mediocre piano student and even more terrible at school. He continued to study piano, he said, only because of the "Jewish guilt" feelings he had.[382]

He had never been able to understand school, but luckily at the age of 15 he was blown away by the magic of music. He used a fake ID to enter Manhattan jazz clubs and watch at first-hand the African-American jazz bebop artists. During World War Two, they revolutionized New York clubs as they reshaped and expanded the art of modern jazz improvisation and harmony. At this point, however, the appeal was not their harmonic insights, but their approach to life, the self-confident look of these hipsters, the rebel image, and the complete charisma that accompanied these jazz wizards. Bacharach recalls:

> Dizzy Gillespie was the guy I loved the most and he became my hero. I worshipped him because everything he did was so cool and I loved the way he looked onstage playing that funny-looking trumpet of his. One night I saw him standing out on the street with a monkey on his shoulder, so I went right home and asked my mother and father if I could get a monkey, too [...].[383]

Bacharach experienced a revelation. For a while, he changed his stage name to Happy Baxter so he wouldn't sound too Jewish; and he still had braces on his teeth. He discovered Debussy and Ravel's concerted impressionism and navigated himself to music with full force after only winning second place in a piano competition. The prize had been a tutorial with the best teachers, but Bacharach found his path.

His terrible grades at school left no doubt about higher education possibilities. He attended music classes, including composition with French-Jewish refugee Darius Milhaud. He experimented with writing in 12 tones but was also interested in the atonality of Schoenberg and his students. During one exercise, he felt he wrote too melodically, but his teacher explained that "you should never be ashamed to write a melody that can be hummed." He gave him a lesson he would not forget, and he also taught him to eat Mexican tacos.[384]

But Bachrach believed that the classic composer's life could be arduous. He didn't want to teach at university and thought about the possibilities in the field of popular music.[385] He never completed his music studies and joined the US army during the Korean War. After showing wretched incompetence as a soldier

---

[382] Burt Bacharach, *Anyone Who Had a Heart: My Life and Music* (New York: Atlantic Books, 2014), 22.
[383] Ibid., 23–24.
[384] Ibid., 36.
[385] Paul Zollo, "Burt Bacharach and Hal David," *Songwriters on Songwriting* (Cincinnati: Da Capo Press, 2003), 207.

during recruitment, he was sent to play piano at the Officers' Club and passed the time until the army appointed him as a music arranger to one of the US army's entertainment centers in Germany. After his release, he went on to study composition, among others, with the avant-garde figure, Henry Cowell. He even visited a concert by the then well-known John Cage during which 24 musicians held 12 radios while Cage conducted them. In everyday reality, he accompanied Broadway singers, Las Vegas crooners, earned additional income at Catskill, and began writing songs. The rock 'n' roll of Bill Haley or Elvis Presley, Bacharach said, never "did it" for him. He always found that a major seventh chord with a jazzy aroma was more interesting to him than a triad chord.

In the mid-1950s, he began working at the Brill Building in the Famous Music Publishing Company, which was owned by Paramount Studios. There, he first met Hal David, a son of Jewish immigrants from Austria who was seven years older. After World War Two, David followed his brother Mack, who himself was a lyricist. As Bacharach, David was an "ordinary" person, with no eccentricities. He didn't even dress like people in show business.

Bacharach and David saw themselves as the successors to the Tin Pan Alley tradition and were proud of it. In a press interview, David confessed his great appreciation for Berlin. "Irving Berlin was an absolute genius," David explained. "He could say the most honest, beautiful, and thoughtful things in just a few lines, which is the key to songwriting."[386]

They used to write together and continued in separation each at his home. Sometimes it started from an idea, a title, sometimes from a melody, and sometimes they wrote the whole song right together. Bacharach remembers that David was a non-stop smoker. They wrote for Johnny Mathis and Perry Como, and the money that came in helped further down the road, but what fueled his career was Bacharach's encounter with Marlene Dietrich.

In her mid-50s, the German singer and actress who fought a conscious struggle at the time with Nazi Germany was still quite active, becoming Bacharach's mentor. Dietrich gave him confidence and faith in himself and appointed him the musical director of her show. She took him on tour, including one particularly moving experience in Israel. She tried to connect him to Frank Sinatra (still unsuccessfully), and on the night of her performance, introduced him like a real star. When he abandoned her in the 1960s, she was devastated.

Meanwhile, Bacharach wrote songs with several lyricists, and through his acquaintance with African-American music producer Luther Dixon came to Scepter Records, owned by a Jewish woman named Florence Greenberg. As the mu-

---

[386] Terry Staunton, "We're In Love with This Guy: Hal David," *Music365.com* (27 May, 2000).

sical scene of the girl groups of the late 1950s made a noise, Bacharach and David had to adjust. He "calmed down" his intuition to include jazz harmonies and settled on more straightforward approaches that fit the world of rhythm and blues and Leiber and Stoller's proto-soul. "Baby It's You," which was a collaboration with Mack David, received triple credit after Dixon added "Cheat, Cheat" to give it a darker tone. It reached the Top 10 with The Shirelles, even though it was supposed to be a B-Side. Later on, the song received a beautiful version by The Beatles that they included in their debut album (1963).

Bacharach continued to weave the network after writing a song for The Drifters. In collaboration with David, Leiber and Stoller, they decided to form a joint publishing company, a decision he would later regret. But now Bacharach began to learn their way of musical production. Although he was several years older, they preceded him by several steps in each field. Everyone was in sync with their love for the Brazilian baion rhythm, which he discovered on tour with Dietrich in Brazil. The rhythm would contribute an essential part to their success.[387]

During a vocal rehearsal "Mexican Divorce" (1962) written for The Drifters, he met one of the backing singers, Dionne Warwick. "I thought she had a very special kind of grace and elegance that made her stand out," recalls Bacharach, "had really high cheekbones and long legs, and she was wearing sneakers and her hair was in pigtails. There was just something in the way she carried herself that caught my eye. To me, Dionne looked like she could be a star."[388] About six weeks later, Warwick, Bacharach and David began working together.

However, not everything progressed as expected. One of the songs, "Make It Easy On Yourself," found its way to Vee-Jay, an African-American label who suggested to Bacharach to produce the song for their singer, Jerry Butler, instead of Warwick, and he had to agree. It was the first time he had gained full control of the studio, and with all the weight of his career on his shoulders, he arranged, conducted and produced what sounded very much like The Drifters, and sent the single to the Top 20 in the pop charts. It could have been a more profound breakthrough in the business relationship between Jews and blacks, but Bacharach didn't continue with the label. Controversy over the single's print quality ended the short connection.

Warwick was disappointed with the sequence of events, but now the three began releasing a series of hits, with Bacharach pushing for more time signature changes, more modulations, an excellent range of notes, and more luxurious

---

[387] Burt Bacharach, *Anyone Who Had a Heart: My Life and Music* (New York: Atlantic Books, 2014), 76.
[388] Ibid., 108.

productions, which at their best had Latin rhythm. He liked the fact that Warwick was musically educated and read notes, and she remembers that he asked her to give "more of herself." Sometimes dozens of vocal takes were needed to get the right result, especially given that he liked to record everything, including strings orchestra, together.

Bacharach and David deepened the human expression of the characters in their songs in what they tried to present as songs that would sound "like a movie." David's stories were diverse in different genres: rhythmic waltz ("Wives and Lovers"), country-flavored pop hits ("Twenty-Four Hours from Tulsa"), but the real meat was the collaboration with Warwick. Her magic lies in her conservatism. In a performance that combines drama, suspense, gentleness, and the image of a nymph and a heartbroken diva, she moved away from the blatant sexuality of their original black rhythm and blues and became part of the sound of conventional multicultural America.

In spite of having the outer costume of a composer of rhythm and blues, inside, he was a jazz and musical composer. He built many of his big hits on seventh chords, jazz harmony, and movement between keys of the moment. Unlike The Beatles, his tunes have relatively little use for blue notes, pentatonic scales, modal harmony, and all the elements that characterized rock music in the 1960s. In that, he was similar to Jerome Kern and Richard Rodgers. When it came to rhythm, however, he was closer to Gershwin. Bacharach was famous for irregular bars; Warwick once said, "you had to have a music degree to sing Bacharach."[389]

Bacharach loaded the single "Anyone Who Had a Heart" (1963) with its asymmetry bars. The song's structure consists of sequential bars of 5/4 and 4/4 to a tension that only intensified the sound of Warwick's heartbreak. Bachrach used a great deal of ammunition that includes the circle of fifths, modulations, modal interchange, and a sense of elusiveness and ambiguity in the tonal center, or in fact, a multidimensionality harmony. Warwick's band players complained that it made life difficult for them with a 7/8 bar, but Bacharach didn't notice it while he wrote the music.[390] "Anyone Who Had a Heart" gained a lot of cover versions, among others, from British female singers Dusty Springfield and Cilla Black, who led the song to first place in the UK chart in 1964, positioning Bacharach and David as a vital part of the British industry.

Bacharach remembers recording "Walk On By" (released in 1964) in the same session as "Anyone Who Had a Heart." "While I was writing 'Walk on

---

[389] Barney Hoskyns, "Back to the Brilliance of Bacharach," *The Times* (22 August, 1990).
[390] Paul Zollo, "Burt Bacharach and Hal David," *Songwriters on Songwriting* (Cincinnati: Da Capo Press, 2003), 209.

By,' I was hearing the whole arrangement," he recalls. "I love flugelhorns and they're on there and I heard the piano figure being played by two different pianos. Because they were never exactly in synch with one another, that gave the song a very different, jagged kind of feeling."[391]

Musically, the Latin rhythm section blends in with the tonal ambiguity, or multidimensional "elusiveness" that Leonard Bernstein liked, say, in Chopin's music, Wagner and Mahler. At first, it seems like Bacharach starts with a modal flavor, but then it moves to another minor key of the moment, and finally the major basic tonality is slowly exposed, but as it remains somewhat vague when the lyrics deal with the theme of heartbreak this ambiguity is very powerful.

Bacharach liked to write jazz harmonies in the pop world. The single "A House Is Not a Home" (1964) performed by Warwick reminded in-depth, multi-dimensionality and with the ambiguity of its predecessors, mainly due to the quick jump to what sounds like a chorus after just one sentence. Another single, "Alfie" (1966), a theme song for the movie with the same name and beloved by Hal David, continued this approach while radiating jazz harmony and using harmonious costumes one by one as it passed through momentary centers. The transition to the middle eight (bridge) of the song, endowed with one of Bacharach's memorable melodies and sophisticated harmony, passes through a familiar tension note to the chord ending the verse and the one beginning the bridge. Although initially recorded by British Cilla Black with Bacharach himself and produced by George Martin, he was very successful with Warwick's version.

As British artists took up more and more space in America, David and Bacharach's songs were blended beautifully into British radio. The single "There's Always Something There to Remind Me" was also recorded by singer Sandie Shaw and paved the way to the top of the British chart (1964). In contrast to the jazzy Broadway-esque sensibility of "A House Is Not a Home," Bacharach composed the beautiful lyrics of "(There's) Always Something There to Remind Me" in a more rock 'n' roll harmonious feel with modal interchange and a sense of wholeness between the words and the music, with Shaw keeping the delicacy and heartbreak without falling into kitsch.

From 1965, the year President Johnson ended the passing of civil rights amendments that were the result of the struggle for social justice, the Brill Building network lost its grip, albeit gradually, in the music field. The writers still gave songs and hits to various pop artists, even to British bands. But bit by bit, the scene

---

[391] Ibid., 212.

began to change. With the escalation of the war in Vietnam, the radicalization of the New Left, the rise of the separatist Black Power movement, and the emergence of hippies, the music had undergone a more experimental, surrealistic, sometimes political and psychedelic direction. West Coast and UK underground bands were dominant in the years to come. The Beatles documented the new mood with greater success than anyone else.

Spector tested his strength in a single with Ike and Tina Turner, "River Deep – Mountain High" (1966), defined by many as his best work. Songwriters Barry and Greenwich have argued that Spector's megalomania took over this humble blues and presented an unprecedented attack in popular music. "It was total brainstorm – Spector was louder, wilder, more murderous than he'd ever been, and Tina Turner matched him, big earth woman, one scream of infinite force," Nik Cohn wrote.[392] The single was successful in Europe but failed in America, which seemed to lose interest in the wall of sound. Without his hallmark, Spector retired for three years, and when he returned he was no longer the same person.[393]

Bacharach, who was one of Brill Building's most successful men, continued to flourish. He wrote music for James Bond and other films, won an Oscar, was invited to compose classical music and participated in television specials that saluted him. He continued to challenge his performers with time signature changes and irregular bars (listen to "Promises, Promises") that even prompted modern composer Frank Zappa to praise the duo's achievements.[394] Later Bacharach, David and Warwick got into unnecessary legal disputes and wasted valuable time. Not many people noticed this in real-time, but he, too, found it challenging to keep up the momentum. Voices in the industry began to call him "the new Gershwin," but without the multicultural and multiethnic feel of the first

---

392 Ibid, 121. Barney Hoskyns, "Phil Spector's Ghosts: The Spooky World of the Greatest Producer in Pop Music," *Slate* (February 2003).
393 In 1969, Spector was invited to work on a remake of the Beatles' Get Back project, which came out at the end as Let It Be in 1970. He then worked with John Lennon and George Harrison on their first solo albums. From the mid-1970s he had a career saturated with ethical problems, characterized by paranoid behavior and, he said, even schizophrenic. The ending was particularly miserable: Phil Spector was charged with murdering actress Lara Clarkson in 2003. He was convicted in 2009. He died in January 2021 in a California jail from Covid-19. See Nick Brown, *Tearing Down the Wall of Sound: The Rise and Fall of Phil Spector* (London: Vintage, 2007). Spector's official statement that he was suffering from mental illness appeared for the first time in an interview with journalist Nick Brown, which was first published in 2003 and printed in his biography on the producer.
394 Paul Zollo, "Burt Bacharach and Hal David," *Songwriters on Songwriting* (Cincinnati: Da Capo Press, 2003), 198.

half of the 1960s, his songs lost their edge despite their impressive complexity. In Nietzschean terms, his art suffered from an overdose of Apollonian order and lacked a balance with Dionysian sensibilities. Either way, the 1970s was, in the end, a pale shadow of the previous decade.

Spector, Bacharach, and the Brill Building writers brought their liberal voices and images into American life through exceptional, multicultural radio hits, forms of equality, and enlightenment that were in sync with the political struggle. However, from the middle of the decade onwards, the political spirit required more bohemian and experimental cultural images – a new kind of far-reaching liberalism. Folk musicians adopted electric instruments, black soul music gradually became more rugged, and the remaining relevant British bands were the most artistic. The direction was more radical. As The Beatles began navigating the places where flower power music would go, Bacharach and David answered the world with one of their most beautiful songs, "What the World Needs Now Is Love" (1965), and they were right.

Chapter 11: The Sounds of Silence – Folk, the Blues and the Spirit of Capitalism Between Grossman, Bloomfield and Zimmerman

They disliked the comfort of the Eisenhower era, the suburban circuits, the routine, and what they perceived as a culture drained of content. They preferred to go to Greenwich Village in New York, sleep on friends' couches, read Sartre and Camus, praise Ginsberg, starve for the next dose, and believe that America was sick. They performed their songs with an acoustic guitar in coffee houses, and they became known as folk singers. Pioneering Jewish entrepreneurs recorded them, while sometimes managing them from a marginal dark corner before becoming an integral part of the ongoing historical story of American music.

Inside Llewyn Davis (2013), the Coen brothers' film, redefined this phase in the history of American music. The film tells the (fictional) story of a folk singer with a sputtering career in New York of the early 1960s. The Coen brothers-based Llewyn Davis' character on singer Dave Van Ronk, who was a major activist in the renewed movement in Greenwich Village – in the same folk revival that began in the second half of the 1950s, and declined when Bob Dylan moved to rock a decade later.

The Coen brothers' film discusses the contrast regarding the purity of folk music and commercial cynicism. One of the hilarious personages featured in the movie is Mel Novikoff – the head of a small record independent label with which the Coen brothers' anti-hero is signed. The Coen brothers probably based him on a real character, Moses Asch, the Jewish owner of Folkways Records – one of the most important labels in the folk genre. Asch was a passionate entrepreneur, with a stingy approach and vital bargaining power. For decades he conducted a recording operation that became a significant part of American folk music heritage.

Another character in the film is Bud Grossman, who the Coen Brothers based on Albert Grossman, the Jewish manager of Bob Dylan, and many successful folk and rock bands. In one scene, Grossman sends Llewyn Davis back from Chicago to New York, claiming he "doesn't see big money here," a statement about the great paradox of the folk story in America.

People and songs in an imagined community

Throughout the Europe of the modern era, new nations have used folk music to build their own nation's myths and unite imagined communities. But the concept of folk takes has different meanings in different parts of the globe. In America alone, the nickname is given throughout history to almost every music style: from Indian tribal ballads, singing cowboys, country music, bluegrass bands, religious anthems, gospel quartets, minstrelsy, blues, Hawaiian music, and whatnot.

Over time, however, it was precisely in capitalist America that folk music turned into an unique style with ethics that were allegedly anti-commercial. American folk was a response to a threatening modernity, which was disruptive when reaching many rural areas, some of which gained something from it only with Roosevelt's New Deal. Folk became a style during the Great Depression of the 1930s and embraced Marxist agendas, dealing with injustice and exploitation, while folk artists were perceived not as pop stars, but as part of the community.

World War Two, followed by the McCarthy witch hunt, along with the rise in living standards and the liberal consensus of the 1950s, pushed aside folk music for more than a decade. It returned to relevance only in the second half of the 1950s and reached its commercial peak in the first half of the 1960s against the backdrop of Kennedy's pragmatic liberalism and growing awareness of America's dark side. The resurrection of folk rested on Woody Guthrie's legacy but updated itself in the struggle for social justice led by Martin Luther King Jr., pacifism, Cold War protests, and the capitalist threat to the human psyche and personality.

The roots of the folk revival began to grow in New York in the late 1940s with the activity of The Weavers, of which Pete Seeger was a member. This group was part of *People's Songs*, an organization of musicians who published and distributed songs (also through a quarterly magazine) of the American labor movement, and supported the Progressive Party campaign led by Henry Wallace for the United States presidency. Not long after, the folk community concentrated on the Bohemian scene of Greenwich Village, though there were other centers as well.

Contrary to the prevailing stereotype, folk artists such as Woody Guthrie and Pete Seeger were prominent, but so were African-Americans such as Lead Belly and Josh White. The instruments were acoustic: accordion, banjo, dulcimer, harmonica, violin, mandolin, and more. The dynamics were supposed to be anti-commercial and anti-capitalist, rural, communal, leftist, and protest-based, and in short, it was a platform for social change. But beneath the surface, folk roots were immersed in a kind of sublime and universal consolation, imprisoned in religiosity-filled images.

In the late '50s and early '60s, a new generation of artists, young and political, provided the content of New York's Greenwich Village cafés, alongside veteran Pete Seeger, Joan Baez, Tom Paxton, Ramblin' Jack Elliott, Bob Gibson, Dave Van Ronk, and others. Romantic and altruistic, radicals full of hopes, they fueled a lively movement. Folk was about to accelerate rock 'n' roll's artistic development, enabling, among other things, the connection between folk traditions and high poetry.

This land is your land

Although it was anti-capitalist in its message, folk needed a commercial mechanism to distribute the music, and some Jewish entrepreneurs penetrated this space and established independent records labels in this field. One of them was Moses Asch.

He was born in Poland to an educated Jewish family. His father was the author and Yiddish intellectual Sholem Asch, who left antisemitic Poland for France even before the First World War. During the war, the family emigrated from there to New York. Unlike his father, Moses was attracted to technology and also studied electronics in Germany. Asch prompted his interest in recordings by *The Jewish Daily Forward* where his father worked to install a radio transmitter for them to broadcast in Yiddish. The meeting with the world of technology and the airwaves led him to the recording world.

In the beginning, he documented secular and religious Yiddish music in America. Asch recorded, lost money, went bankrupt, but resurrected his business in the late 1940s and devoted his life to recording folk artists, even if his activity was broader and included jazz, poetry, and ethnic music.

Woody Guthrie recorded with Asch, including the monumental "This Land Is Your Land," which Bruce Springsteen crowned in a 1985 performance as one of the most influential songs ever written about the American Promise.[395] "Woody was a true hippie," Asch recalls. "illustrative of Walt Whitman. He had a frame and he used the music of American folk song as a base for his words."[396] In ad-

---

[395] See <www.youtube.com/watch?v=1yuc4BI5NWU> (last accessed 11.03.2021). Guthrie wrote the song as a critical response to Irving Berlin's "God Bless America," an ironic fact in the story of this book.
[396] Kip Lornell, *Exploring American Folk Music: Ethnic, Grassroots, and Regional Traditions in the United States* (Jackson: University Press of Mississippi, 3rd edition, 2012), 293.

dition, Asch documented the work of African-American Lead Belly with "Goodnight, Irene" and many more. His recordings today sound noisy, partly due to the constraints of the period, but some indicate that the print quality was primitive even in those years.[397]

Either way, he made history. In the early 1950s, filmmaker and folklorist Harry Smith incorporated many of these recordings into the *Anthology of American Folk Music* (1952) collection, which contained Anglo-American ballads and social music, which Smith categorized into subtypes. This collection, after years, even received congressional recognition.

Before Asch became established in the folk anthology, the brothers Maynard and Seymour Solomon, of Jewish descent, founded their own company, Vanguard Records, in the early 1950s. They began their label recording classical music, ranging from spiritual to swing, but positioned themselves as leading members of the folk world. Politically, they went a step further and recorded musicians from Senator Joe McCarthy's black boycott lists. They signed The Weavers with Pete Seeger, the African-American musician Paul Robeson, and later Joan Baez and a host of other artists.

Another essential company was Elektra Records, founded by Jac Holzman. Holzman grew up in a democratic and liberal Jewish home with a father who was a successful but oppressive medical doctor. His maternal grandmother was associated with Franklin Delano Roosevelt, and his grandfather was a rabbi who was expelled from the community, he says, because he married Jews and gentiles, as well as Jews and blacks.[398] Holzman defined himself as an unmotivated student, and his father hoped he would at least be a pharmacist. The best moments for him in college were during Friday's philosophy evenings, as well as in the state-of-the-art electronics lab. Holzman fell in love with the radio when he used to accompany his grandmother to broadcast at various stations and realized during his studies that he was an audiophile. In the dorm, he became familiar with the folk of Susan Reed, Lead Belly, and Josh White. In October 1950, while a student, Holzman turned the idea of a record label into a reality. The college management recommended that he withdraw for a year to understand what he wanted to be. In the decade and a half to come, he became a very successful man in the music industry.

Holzman recorded folk music quickly and cheaply, with an emphasis on designer covers and photographs and high-quality printing. Although Folk was the

---

397 Jac Holzman and Gavan Daws, *Follow the Music: The Life and High Times of Elektra Records in the Great Years of American Pop Culture* (Santa Monica, CA: FirstMedia Books, 2000), 46.
398 Ibid.

catalyst for the company, he recorded a variety of styles, including gypsy and Jewish music. For a long time, Jewish singer Theodore Bikel commercially held the small company together with a series of recordings in various languages, including Israeli folk songs in Hebrew.

While Elektra was able to survive, a Chicago entrepreneur by the name of Albert Grossman broke into the New York arena and shuffled the cards. His influence played an essential role in the connection between folk and capitalism.

Grossman was born in Chicago to Jewish-Russians immigrants and studied economics in college. In 1957, he and a classmate launched a club called Gate of Horn in Chicago. Peter Yarrow (of the folk trio Peter, Paul and Mary) testifies that he was very intuitive, brave, familiar with the street and brilliant, adding that he was an effective manipulator.[399] Journalist Fred Goodman described Grossman as a "builder": "He built houses, restaurants, theaters, recording studios, power stations; he even built his own town in Upstate New York."[400]

Grossman soon recognized the artistic yearning around folk and made himself the "protector" of art in the face of business, even though he was more "the business" than anyone else. He surrounded himself with folk talents, Bob Gibson and Odetta, and found he would rather spend time with artists than with the club. He positioned himself as the "king of the center of the room." He teamed up with two jazz festival outlets for PAMA management company, and they all discovered that behind the business creativity stood a tough man to negotiate with.

However, Grossman created a precedent by demanding that the industry treat his clients as artists.[401] Against the backdrop of his rising power, Joan Baez became interested in his organization, even if she eventually chose another manager. Idealists such as Peter Yarrow put their trust in Grossman, since he genuinely believed in his taste, judgement and ability to determine what was authentic and what was not.[402]

Grossman used to take at least 25 percent of his clients' profits, and another quarter of every deal they earned against a third party, so he actually earned a lot from every artist. He would excuse this by saying that "every time you talk to me

---

399 Fred Goodman, *The Mansion on the Hill: Dylan, Young, Geffen, Springsteen, and the Head-On Collision of Rock and Commerce* (New York: Vintage, 1997), 87.
400 Ibid., 83.
401 Ibid., 87.
402 In the Coen brothers' movie, the fictional character Grossman offers Davis to join the trio he is setting up, just as Albert Grossman suggested to Peter Yarrow, as well as Dave Van Ronk, to join a trio he set up with a blonde singer who he was banned from tanning. Van Ronk gave up the trio and the fame from the stage that would feature Peter, Paul and Mary

you're ten times smarter than before."[403] At the same time, he allowed his artists complete autonomy over the creative process, which sounded like science fiction in the early 1960s. He created a commercial environment that allowed his artists to make money and maintain artistic integrity, even staying political, if they wanted to. Bob Dylan penetrated this environment.

The ballad of thin man

Bob Dylan was born in 1941 as Robert Allen Zimmerman, a son of Jewish shopkeeper parents from Duluth, Minnesota. He probably grew up quite normally in a patriotic family. His hometown was a source of memories of blue-gray skies, mysterious fogs, wild storms, and howling and merciless winds that rise from the big, black river with treacherous waves several feet high. He remembered that from a political point of view, the region supported agricultural and social-democratic political parties. He remembered parochialism.

At school, he was exposed to the ongoing warning campaign about the danger of Communism. In the absence well-developed media to help learn about the world, he spent time in the area's natural and water districts, and later on drive-in movies, car racing and baseball, and even watched blackface minstrelsy shows. He played a bit of guitar and sang and read the Beat poets. He knew African-American folklore about gunman Stagger Lee and black working-class hero John Henry. He wasn't a fan of American bandstand TV shows, but he loved Buddy Holly, and said he was looking for what Allen Ginsberg called the "hydrogen jukebox."

At university, he discovered folk, which was a reality of a brighter dimension. For him it transcended all human understanding. [404] Dylan's attraction to the folk was, he says, like a mythological world full of sharply and metaphysically drawn archetypes. He went to a musical instrument store, replaced the acoustic guitar for an electric guitar, and opened the door to a whole musical world of folk and old blues records.

An English professor introduced him to the world of mythical ballads, and he began appearing in nearby coffee houses. At that time, he had first heard of Woody Guthrie, and he felt as if "my life had never been the same since."

---

403 Fred Goodman, *The Mansion on the Hill: Dylan, Young, Geffen, Springsteen, and the Head-On Collision of Rock and Commerce* (New York: Vintage, 1997), 89.
404 Ibid, 229.

With Guthrie's songs, he recalls, "[w]hen I first heard him it was like a million megaton bomb had dropped."[405]

He listened to Ramblin' Jack Elliott and Joan Baez and decided to move to New York. He disguised himself as a copy of Woody Guthrie and introduced himself as a nomad, devoting time to building a new identity. He started with the name: His first intention was to change it to Robert Allen, but Dylan sounded better than Allen; until he finally decided that Bob sounded better than Robert.

Like Al Jolson before him, Zimmerman was a trickster. Instead of a black mask replacing identities, he was reborn as another character. He had a particularly high level of intelligence. Zimmerman was a bourgeois Jew, and technically a very limited singer, but disguise allowed him to present himself as a joker who held "secret knowledge," such as having information on the world's problems, and the ability to point them out precisely, if not solve them. Like Leiber and Stoller, he played with identities and turned them on their heads. Dylan was a guy with a well-developed conscience but realized that show business was the image business. Like mythological tricksters, he refused to subordinate himself to existing laws.

Dylan managed to fit in well in New York. He learned a lot from the members of the scene, hosted in their homes, read their books, listened to their records, and created a whole cultural world for himself. But by the age of 20, he hadn't written many good songs. That didn't stop Columbia producer John Hammond, who was drawn by his charisma and mystery, from signing him to the record label. His unflattering voice was an exception in pop music, so the people at Columbia saw his signing as Hammond's folly; but since his recordings were very cheap (guitar, harmonica, and vocals only), they let the American aristocrat "have fun."

Dylan combined the folk influences of Woody Guthrie, Dada, Allen Ginsberg, Jack Kerouac and Arthur Rimbaud, and his background as a Jew, as an outsider, gave him a different view of America.

The common theme about Dylan and his Judaism is that he used to deny his origins, adopting a WASPish appearance as a "ticket from the Midwest"; but that is far from accurate, because Dylan actually converted the WASP American into another, more universal American.[406] The effect was to offer an alternative to the Yankee myth of the "three-dimensional man" who built the nation radiating the gospel that all immigrants should be like him. He introduced some minor Marxist influences and criticism of employee exploitation and was in favor of pacifism. He tried to create in his songs a kind of alternative republic.

---

405 Ibid.
406 Michael Billig, *Rock 'n' Roll Jews* (London: Five Leaves Publications, 2001), 120–121.

In *Chronicles*, Dylan claimed that his songs were "my preceptor and guide into some altered conscious of reality, some different republic, some liberated republic"; he writes, "it wasn't that I was anti-popular culture or anything and I had no ambitions to stir things up. I just thought of mainstream culture as lame as hell and a big trick [...] It was like the unbroken sea of frost that lay outside the window and you had to have awkward footgear to walk on it."[407]

Musically, folk had similar harmonies to religious and gospel anthems rather than the blues, and Dylan's start was no exception. Over the decade, with his conversion as a folk rock artist, his songs absorbed heavier elements of blues.[408] He used to listen to blues' records at the student dorm, but the day he signed a contract with Columbia he received from John Hammond a collection record by black Mississippi blues artist Robert Johnson. He describes in *Chronicles* the enormous influence that this blues had on his work:

> When Johnson started singing, he seemed like a guy who could have sprung from the head of Zeus in full armor. I immediately differentiated between him and anyone else I had ever heard. The songs weren't customary blues songs. They were perfected pieces [...] Johnson's voice was in the room and I was mixed up in it [...] over the next few weeks I listened to it repeatedly, cut after cut, one song after another, sitting staring at the record player. Whenever I did, I felt like a ghost had come into the room, a fearsome apparition [...] I copied Johnson's words on scraps of paper so I could more closely examine the lyrics and patterns, the construction of his old-style lines and the free association that he used, the sparkling allegories, big-ass truths wrapped in the hard shell of nonsensical abstraction – themes that flew through the air with the greatest of ease.[409]

Johnson himself was a trickster. The mythology around him says that he met the devil at the crossroads and converted his soul for a unique talent. Of course, that wasn't true, but he sounded like it. Scholars such as Craig Werner have tried to explain the origin of the blues songs from African Yoruba mythologies about the Esu-Elegba, a spirit who creates chaos in human life.[410] On the other hand, writer Greil Marcus saw the blues as a desperate reaction to the idea of the Puritans' notion of pre-destination that (without being aware of it) had an impact on

---

[407] Bob Dylan, *Chronicles, Volume 1* (New York: Simon & Schuster 2004), 34–35.
[408] The minor pentatonic scale has five notes from the minor scale: the tonic, the third, fourth, fifth and seventh. The blues scale is very similar to it, but includes another note, the fifth step down to a semi-tone.
[409] Bob Dylan, *Chronicles, Volume 1* (New York: Simon & Schuster 2004), 282–285.
[410] Craig Werner, *A Change is Gonna Come: Music, Race and the Soul of America* (New York: Plume, 1998), 66–67.

the blues artists and their belief about their place in this life.[411] Whatever the origins, Dylan used mythology and mystery to redefine American popular music.

After signing the recording contract, John Hammond sent Dylan to Lou Levy, the Jewish owner of Leeds Music Corporation, a publishing company at Tin Pan Alley. Levy asked Dylan questions about his resume, and Dylan answered that he came from Illinois, his father was an electrician and he came to New York by cargo train. He also said he didn't see anyone like himself in the music scene today. Except for the last confession, none of these details were completely accurate. "Everyone" knew that the imaginary biography suffered from a lack of credibility, but "everyone" was inexplicably drawn to this identity changer.

Blowin' in the wind

His first album, *Bob Dylan* (1962), included mostly cover versions of a number of protest folk songs and African-American spirituals. Dylan confessed that it was an unsuccessful effort and told director Martin Scorsese that he wanted to delete it as soon as he listened to it.[412] However, he was so ambitious compared to the humble spirit of the folk, that Albert Grossman entered the picture.

Grossman's initial strategy was to terrorize the people of Columbia Records while threatening to demand the cancellation of the contract, claiming Dylan had signed it when he was a minor. Hammond, the closest thing to an American nobleman, despised what he perceived as Grossman's bullying and pettiness. But Grossman believed that the liberal WASP didn't see far enough. Clive Davis, Columbia's Jewish lawyer, reached out to reconcile the parties. Within a few years he was given the keys to the CBS Empire, and Grossman had free access to it whenever he wanted.

Grossman moved lightly within the Jewish business maze; except for depositing Dylan's performances with Harold Leventhal, he moved Dylan from the Leeds of Lou Levy to Witmark publishing house, under the management of Artie Mogull. The publishing company began to plug his songs for artists. The first big success came with Peter, Paul and Mary performing "Blowin' in the Wind" (1963) and "Don't Think Twice, It's All Right" (1963).

The single "Blowin 'in the Wind," as performed by Peter Paul and Mary, almost reached the top of the pop charts. It cemented the revival of the folk as a

---

411 Greil Marcus, *Mystery Train: Images of America in Rock 'n' Roll Music*, 5th ed. (New York: Plume, 2008).
412 Martin Scorsese, *No Direction Home* (2005).

mass movement, but that was just a taste of what happened in the next act. "Blowin' in the Wind," also included in his second album, *The Freewheelin' Bob Dylan* (1963), targeted the indifference of Americans in the face of racial discrimination in the South, and Dylan was for a moment part of the political movement. He participated and sang with Joan Baez in the Civil Rights Movement's march led by Martin Luther King Jr. in Washington in 1963. Peter, Paul and Mary also attended and performed that hit at that crucial moment, one of the most critical events in the history of the civil rights struggle in the United States.

The editors of *Rolling Stone* magazine chose it years later as one of the most important songs of all time because of its poetic qualities and specific form of protest, and how public apathy was seen as "a crime almost equal to racism itself."[413] It was as if at that moment Dylan was a knight in the war for justice. In an interview from that time, he claimed: "I hate injustice, that's why I sing about racial discrimination and freedom. I'm not spreading disillusionment by singing the truth."[414]

Within months, Dylan established himself as an imaginative and visionary songwriter, turning folk from association with bohemian circles and college students into a mass fashion. His songs between the years 1962 to 1964 dealt with everything that engaged the Civil Rights Movement: "Oxford Town," "The Death of Emmett Till" and "Only a Pawn in Their Game" discussed the impact of racism on the decline of Southern conscience, the justice system, to the stranglehold of the Ku Klux Klan and the helplessness of the individual to escape this morbid and formidable "matrix" of the segregation policy in the South.

Dylan also dealt with the threat of nuclear apocalypse in a prophetic biblical expression of people's law and sins ("A Hard Rain's A-Gonna Fall"), pacifism ("Masters of War"), generation gaps ("The Times They Are a-Changin'"); but his most important protest song was "With God on Our Side." Michael Billig wrote about Dylan's self-identity and the song:

> [...] Dylan presents himself as a typical American (non-Jewish) Mid-Westerner. "We remain the Americans" – even though "We" are criticizing ourselves with force. The Jew is singing as a Christian American, while criticizing Christian America.[415]

Nevertheless, Dylan was more likely to ironically insist on rejecting the Puritan myth of "God-save America." The vision of an alternative republic had only begun to develop. Dylan's poetic writing has had a profound and tangible impact

---

413 "The 500 Greatest Songs of All Time," *Rolling Stone* (February 2004).
414 Andria Lisle, "Bob Dylan in Mississippi," *The Oxford American* (Summer 1999).
415 Michael Billig, *Rock 'n' Roll Jews* (London: Five Leaves Publications, 2001), 127.

on the world of popular music and even critics who remain cynical about Dylan's ambition to compose high art into a mass medium such as a rock 'n' roll agreed that Dylan was a historical revolutionary, mainly because he influenced many of the artists to engage in politics, social injustice and life philosophies.[416]

However, in 1964 Dylan began to move away from the politics of the Civil Rights Movement. Feeling that he had become a propaganda voice for a political organization he withdrew and turned his writing to testing the boundaries of intuitive writing derived from the unconscious and into a new kind of radical liberalism. His enlistment in the struggle for social justice made him feel like he was a politician, and politics, as a concept and way of life, he said, lowered them (activists for social justice) to the rank of racists themselves.[417] Dylan further stated that the connection between music and politics had reduced the power of the message and justice itself, and that the movement had neglected other sectors that needed help.

His first albums were a mix of public protest hymns and personal experiences, but from 1964 he began with more personal and surreal writing. His album *Another Side of Bob Dylan* (1964) featured a collection of personal songs about his private world as an artist, and in 1965 he caused a great uproar at the Newport Folk Festival in New York when he chose to perform with an electric band and switched from his folk ethics. He also began a trilogy of his important rock albums: *Bringing It All Back Home* (1965), *Highway 61 Revisited* (1965), and *Blonde on Blonde* (1966), which were rife with absurdity and cynicism, paranoia and mystery, allegory and surrealism.

Chicago's black and electric flag

Dylan's folk-rock trilogy introduced a bohemian imagery subverting the Yankee-WASP tradition. The rock press didn't really emphasize that, but in the process of Dylan's move into rock came a crucial number of Jewish musicians from the New York blues scene, such as the keyboardist Al Kooper (originally Kuperschmidt), bassist Harvey (Goldstein) Brooks, and drummer Bobby Gregg; one of the crucial figures in Dylan's move to rock, who accompanied him even more from the riot of the folk festival, came from the Chicago blues scene. His name was Michael Bloomfield, and he was an excellent guitarist if a complicated personality.

---

[416] Nik Cohn, *WopBopaLooBop LopBamBoom: Pop from the Beginning* (London: Paladin, 1969), 170–171.
[417] Andria Lisle, "Bob Dylan in Mississippi," *The Oxford American* (Summer 1999).

Decades after his move into rock, Dylan declared he still missed that fine guitarist. He believed that Bloomfield was the best guitarist with whom he played. Either way, his guitar licks on the *Highway 61 Revisited* album still resonate with inspiration. "He had so much soul," Dylan recalls, "[a]nd he knew all the styles."[418]

Bloomfield was born in 1943 in Chicago. His mother had acting aspirations and was a daughter of a financially unstable businessman who at one point ran a pawn shop. His father was a Jewish industrialist, and he made his fortune selling kitchen utensils and other products. The father was tough and athletic, while Michael was slightly chubby and not athletic at all. Bloomfield's friends recalled that the father was ashamed of him in the Jewish sports and country club he was accepted to (given that his entry into the WASP clubs was still banned), thus undermining the stability of young Michael for his entire life.

The Bloomfield family was affluent but lived in an atmosphere of potential crisis that was the legacy of the economic slump and previous disasters that plagued the family in the process of assimilation to America. In a house where shaky parent relationships prevailed, Michael found solace in the African-American maid. He would run away to her, enjoy her cooking and the music around her. Black music, including blues, spirituals, and gospel became a constitutive force, while the mainstream white world was something fake and disconnected. Like Leiber and Stoller, Michael grew up to be a White Negro.

His parents ripped him from the bustling streets of North Chicago to Glencoe, a suburban-rich community village with a significant presence of city Jews. Michael grew up there with a complete lack of a sense of belonging. In an athletic, snobby, and closed world, Michael was attracted to open streets and to homeless people, art and music, and the "other" people's world on the southern side of the city. His immediate surroundings consisted of Jews growing up with black maids and sharing the same sense of suburban boredom. At around his Bar Mitzvah, he received a transistor, a guitar, some lessons, and the rest learned was on his own to become one of the guitarists of the decade.

Michael' and his friends loved going to town, walking around their grandfather's pawnshop or Maxwell Street, where black musicians sang blues and gospel, and street dealers communicated with each other. The blacks called Maxwell Street, "the Jewish city," and according to musician Barry Goldberg's memories, they believed the music was good for business. This concept was unusual even in

---

[418] Douglas Brinkley, "Bob Dylan's Late-Era, Old-Style American Individualism," *Rolling Stone* (14 May, 2009).

the United States after World War Two. The Maxwell Street blues had a dramatic impact on Michael's life.⁴¹⁹

At about the age of 15, he formed a band with his suburban friends, and as non-conformist as he was, he had to go through several prestigious schools until he barely graduated. He progressed wonderfully and quickly on the guitar as a blues and folk player. He loved Scotty Moore, Elvis's guitarist, and rock 'n' roll artists like Eddie Cochran, but at one point, he became a true blues missionary. He was the American equivalent of Eric Clapton. They both allegedly gave up wider success to devote themselves to the blues and turn the "sanctity of the blues" into a mythology in itself. Bloomfield recalls:

> Muddy Waters, he was like a god to me. Well, if he was a god, B.B. King was a deity where I couldn't even imagine ever knowing someone of his magnitude and greatness. But Muddy was in Chicago. I would go down the street, and from two blocks away I'd hear that harmonica come out of the club. I'd hear that harp, and I'd hear Muddy's slide. I'd be tremblin'. I'd be like a dog in heat. [...] I would strive to sing like Ray Charles if I could, and play exactly like B.B. King. If I could play exactly like B.B., be B.B. Junior.⁴²⁰

Bloomfield made harmless exaggerations that were part of his charisma. His memories were of sexual experiences in clubs. "All the women who would lift their dresses over their heads," and he recalls his attraction to African-American sexuality, apparently exaggeratingly, "[...] and shake it right in your face. Oh, man, it's so embarrassing."⁴²¹ Chicago was blown away by music. He took lessons for folk and blues guitar, but around them played jazz, gospel, Latin, and Greek music, and Michael remembers real Jewish music, Chassidic hymns in old synagogues. "The music sounded like blues, the wailing of it," he said about Jewish music.⁴²² But most notably, after World War Two, Chicago again became a serious blues center, as it had been during the 1920s. Many blues artists migrated from the South and helped it thrive with the independent label Chess Records.

Beyond the real and imaginative musical influences around Bloomfield, Chicago was a relatively liberal environment. The University of Chicago became a philosophical and scientific incubator for some of the important voices of the time. Writer Saul Bellow, Hannah Arendt, and art critic Harold Rosenberg lectured there. The music communicated with the spirit of the city. At the university

---

419 Barry Goldberg, *Two Jews Blues* (np: St. Paul Books, 2012), chap. 2, Kindle.
420 Jan Mark Wolkin and Bill Keenom, *Michael Bloomfield – If You Love These Blues: An Oral History* (np: Backbeat Books, 2015), chap. 3, Kindle.
421 Ibid.
422 Ibid.

he studied Elvin Bishop, who was to become the guitarist for a tough Irish-American harmonica player and vocalist, Paul Butterfield. Another immigrant son, Nick "The Greek" Gravenites, was one of the most prominent figures in the Chicago blues scene (and in its connection to California) and who would collaborate with Bloomfield and Grossman in the composition of the group The Electric Flag.

Butterfield and Gravenites, both white and self-indulgent, were tough "street" men, moving north to south of the city freely and becoming an accepted part of the black blues community. Gravenites argues that the anti-black justice system helped them move in the black ghetto because they could feel a sense of superiority in their daily conduct. While African-Americans believed Gravenites was "dangerous," he was confident enough to introduce the black clubs to Butterfield.

Bloomfield recognized Butterfield's talent. He was fascinated by him, but also scared of him at the same time. He was impressed with his independence. He realized that to receive something from the black musical 'authorities," you had to step in the blues field of fire and prove yourself. Butterfield had to receive recognition from Muddy Waters and the harmonica wizard Little Walter; Bloomfield needed Freddie King's "stamp" and Buddy Guy's "license." "You should have been a man there," Bloomfield recalls, "and if you didn't go through it properly, you would be lost."[423] At his grandfather's pawn shop, he met Susan, who would be his wife even before he was 20, and piously accompanied him on a journey to the heart of the blues' darkness.

Paul Rothchild, a senior music producer for Elektra Records, had already met Butterfield and Gravenites in Berkeley, California (and even published Gravenites' "Born In Chicago" in Electra's successful collection), but he had not forgotten him when he came in after a warm recommendation to a Chicago club to listen to Paul Butterfield's new band. "I walked into Big John's and heard the most amazing thing I'd ever heard in my life. It was the same rush I'd had the first time I heard bluegrass," Rothchild recalls, thinking to himself, "[h]ere is the beginning of another era. This is another turning point in American music."[424] After the show, they went to watch the competing band in which Bloomfield played. Rothchild believed that two guitarists would be good for the group. Rothchild used his Jewish intellectual jargon to convince the guitarist to join Butterfield, Bloomfield made his first steps in a new blues band that was momentarily important in America's culture during the struggle of L.B. Johnson for its liberality and equality.

---

[423] Ibid.
[424] Ibid., Ch. 9.

Rothchild loved Butterfield and Bloomfield's sense of urbanity and their ultimate identification with the black world. The debut album, *Paul Butterfield Blues Band* (1965), came out after the original studio recording was to be archived. A live performance recording that conveyed the stage power took its place. Under the influence of the British invasion, they purchased suits, and Rothchild arranged gigs for them at clubs he knew, but they needed a stronger figure to drive their career. Albert Grossman was invited to listen to them and stated that he'd see them at the Newport Festival, even before he met them.[425]

Now it was time for Dylan and Bloomfield to meet at the crossroads. The first time the guitarist listened to the king of folk, he believed he was terrible. Columbia's attempts to compare Dylan's harmonica to Little Walter offended Bloomfield. "He couldn't really sing," Bloomfield recalled after watching him perform at The Bear Club, "[b]ut to my surprise he was enchanting."[426] Bloomfield succumbed to Dylan's charm, but also impressed him with his abilities in their restaurant and jam session. Dylan called a while later and invited him to record a new album. The guitarist arrived in New York carrying an uncovered Fender Telecaster guitar and met Grossman, who looked like Benjamin Franklin. He remembered that except for the slogan "We're going to make a folk-rock album," no one had any idea what it was going to be, and producer Tom Wilson didn't really control the studio. According to his recollections, it was improvised and half-baked, and Bloomfield remembers that Dylan was fascinated by the rock versions other artists made of his songs. Barry Goldberg, his friend from Chicago and a blues musician himself, claims that it was him who showed Bloomfield the ascending chords progression that Bloomfield would then show Dylan in their work on "Like a Rolling Stone."[427] Dylan even asked him to play like Roger McGuinn of The Byrds and not the "B.B. King clichés." But the Jewish guitarist came to New York to play like the king.

Bloomfield said he didn't like the lack of rigor in working with Dylan, but in the end, it was his most significant career achievement, an artistic triumph that he probably never could realized alone. On the verge of international fame, he preferred to return to the real and imagined a magical world in Chicago. Bloomfield assured Al Kooper that he would play with him on the next recordings. He insisted that even though Dylan asked him to stay by his side, he would never leave Paul Butterfield and his band. Paradoxically, he did abandon Dylan, and it took him no more than a few months to quit Butterfield. Fortunately, playing

---

425 Ibid.
426 Ibid.
427 Barry Goldberg, Two Jews Blues (np: St. Paul Books, 2012), Ch. 11, Kindle edition.

with Dylan connected the scene from Chicago with New York musicians to a host of ensembles and projects composed of Jewish blues dreamers.

Meanwhile, Paul Butterfield and Bloomfield's band performed at the Newport Festival. They got into a riot after one of the organizers, Alan Lomax, disparaged them as white boys trying to sing blues. Grossman immediately went on the attack to defend their honor, while the band introduced the Chicago blues sound to the white folk audience. The next day Bloomfield performed with Dylan at the festival, and his guitar wails took part in a dramatic turning point in rock history.

The Sodom and Gomorrah of bourgeois tranquility

If Dylan based his first albums on the rewriting of English, Scottish, and Irish ballads, and spirituals hymns with protest messages, Zimmerman now penetrated deeper into the blues. He custom-built the trickster archetype dimension, with a more paranoid tone, and wrote songs that resembled Robert Johnson's world, whose picture appeared on the first of the three albums. He revived the vision of the Beat poets regarding the roads. "What's wrong goes much deeper than the bomb," he told his friend, Jewish-American folk singer Phil Ochs in 1965, "what's wrong is how few people are free."[428]

Dylan presented a version of radical liberalism and wrote about existential insignificance and anti-capitalist messages, most notably through absurdity and highlighting moral deterioration in a trilogy that sounded like a mythical account of one of the bible's prophets. America was seen as an impossible monster to control, a kind of Sodom and Gomorrah of bourgeois tranquility. Salvation would not come through politics, but in psychology, wider consciousness, in the "freedom" of the person, in the ways in which the imposition of the influence of the surrounding social system would lead to finding a more developed and real personality.

His greatest achievement was his journey of absurdity in *Highway 61Revisited (1965)*. For him, this highway dates back to Duluth Minnesota and the South End, and became associated with the wanderlust of legendary blues artists. Influenced by Kooper and Bloomfield, Dylan not only donned the costume of the Beat poets and blues artists but did so in a way that was reminiscent of Leiber and Stoller as he intensified the impact of the imagery and especially the African

---

[428] David Pichaske, *A Generation in Motion: Popular Music and Culture in the Sixties* (Granite Falls, MN: Ellis Press, 1979), 63–64.

American sound as ammunition to inspire the journey of self-discovery of young people around the globe.

The accolades were excellent, both in real-time and even more retrospectively. Critics used biblical and religious references. They described him as the Isaiah of Minnesota who examined America's traps and limitations.[429] The trilogy was seen as "an introduction to the hippie scene that will emerge in the second half of the decade," and in which the horror-prophetic imagery, as revealed by the unconscious, predicted the rise of psychedelia.[430] The year 1965, it was written, was when the perception of the new generation occurred, when, like the taste of "forbidden fruit," it was accepted.[431]

The most important song in this trilogy, as mentioned, was "Like a Rolling Stone" which came out as a single and was a major radio hit despite its length (more than six minutes); it reached second place on the *Billboard* chart. The song introduced a new language for songwriting, which was a combination of everyday slang and Ginsberg's and Kerouac's poetry. Dylan had cynically and comfortably exposed "the roads" as a dangerous but essential place for finding one's complete self. The roads, in his view, were an alternative to American bourgeois values due to their perilousness and way of contributing to one's self-identity. Bloomfield's guitar and Al Kooper's organ were smeared all over the track.

Rolling Stone magazine editors chose "Like a Rolling Stone" in 2004 as "The Most Important Song of All Time" due to its lyrical language and impressionism and the way Dylan expresses this language, alongside the way Dylan's band played a blues-gospel song that evoked an apocalyptic feel.[432] Critic Dave Marsh also chose this as one of the greatest single of all time as he described the way Dylan reinvented English expression.[433] Greil Marcus dedicated a book to this song and explained that it was like a cave – that as you enter to it, you discover new dimensions.[434] Dylan seemed to be showing the way to convey emotional multidimensionality in popular music using epic lyrics. He had an

---

[429] Greil Marcus, *Stranded: Rock 'n' roll for a Desert Island* (New York: Random House Inc., 1978), 267.

[430] Mick Farren, "Remember Those Fabulous Sixties? An NME Consumer's Guide to Bob Dylan," *NME* (9 February, 1974).

[431] Jon Savage, "Dylan is 60," *Mojo* (June 2001).

[432] "The 500 Greatest Songs of All Time," *Rolling Stone* (February 2004).

[433] Dave Marsh, *The Heart of Rock & Soul: The 1001 Greatest Singles Ever Made* (New York: Da Capo Press, 1989), 20–21.

[434] Greil Marcus, *Like a Rolling Stone: Bob Dylan at the Crossroads* (New York: PublicAffairs, 2005).

overwhelming impact on the world of popular music, and Grossman's prophecy came true as his client became a great artist.

Lancelot and Dracula

As Dylan gained an unprecedented status as an American songwriter and his new signings from Chicago become musical meteors, Grossman established his management company (ABGM) in New York. It was a small corporation that included a booking company, several publishing companies, public relations, show managers, and even musical producers. Grossman dominated the dynamics with Clive Davis in Columbia and Mo Ostin in Warner, making personal connections worth millions. No record company dared refuse Grossman artists; the question was what the deal included. If Dylan had expanded the boundaries of songwriting, Grossman expanded the boundaries of business. Artists and executives left in a rage, lawsuits were part of the day-to-day, and Grossman would not hesitate to negotiate new contracts during current negotiations. Jerry Wexler of Atlantic thought that Grossman was a bothersome person, but the lucrative folk and blues artists – Dylan, Peter, Paul and Mary, The Band, Mike Bloomfield, and Paul Butterfield, and Janis Joplin of the San Francisco psychedelic scene – were under his control.

Grossman could make people come to him. His body movements, the way he would answer the phone call, the way a cigarette could almost be burned between his fingers, this combination of Lancelot and Dracula paved the way for the mini-empire he built. He even convinced artists to move to Woodstock, including Dylan, The Band, Tim Hardin, and others, and turned the bohemian scene around him into an essential source of profit. Andy Warhol may have assembled quirky artists and freaks around the Factory, but Grossman brought the images of the hippies and the freaky Diggers theater from San Francisco to the forefront of popular culture.

However, he did not have enough time to focus on the troubles of each of his artists. He couldn't control his young Chicago blues artists. Mike Bloomfield didn't stay long in Paul Butterfield's band. Tensions with the second guitarist, Elvin Bishop, and Butterfield himself, caused him to leave. He set up a multi-racial group, The Electric Flag. The band, which purported to bring together different extremes of American music, survived for only nine months but managed to perform at the Monterey Festival in the summer of 1967. At the Festival, Jerry Wexler offered Bloomfield and his band a contract with Atlantic, but Grossman vetoed it with the accusation that the record label was "exploiting blacks." Wexler remained stunned. Bloomfield was sent to Columbia records and would regret it all his life.

He continued with Al Kooper for the album *Super Session* (1968), even if he didn't finish the recordings. He became addicted to heroin, suffered from chronic insomnia, failed to fulfill his obligations with appearances, and also failed to concentrate on one convincing path except for his eternal love for the blues. Grossman couldn't save him, but no one could save him anymore. He continued to play the blues until his early, sad and unsurprising death in the early 1980s.

Dylan did not appear in Woodstock in the summer of 1969, but the subject of Grossman's contract renewal came up in tandem with the festival. A year or so before, he recorded the song "All Along the Watchtower," stating that "business men drink my wine," and probably echoed his skepticism about his relationship with his manager. Dylan became the most influential artist of his generation, doubting that Grossman had anything else to offer.

There were more disputes, and it was over. Grossman, some say, lost momentum. His artists were in trouble: Mike Bloomfield was a junkie, singer Paul Butterfield was alcoholic, Janis Joplin was both an alcoholic and a drug addict. Grossman, by himself, survived another decade and a half. His acquaintances claimed he distanced himself from the world he once ruled, but we may remember him as having created a business dynamic that allowed him and Dylan and the rest of his artists to take folk with a blues tone to the forefront of American music.

The folk Talmud

While President L.B. Johnson succeeded in passing the Voting Rights Act of 1965 that successfully ended the constitutional struggle for social justice, traditional folk music remained only a musical setting and poetic tradition. Political ideology faded as a passing fashion. In California, entrepreneur and music producer Lou Adler drove his small empire with massive hits in the folk-rock wave: The Mamas & the Papas, as well as Barry McGuire, who sang young Jewish songwriter, P.F. Sloan's protest anthem "Eve of Destruction "(1965). The single was a huge success and sounded like a parody of the original folk intention, even if not as poking fun at the scandalous pseudo-political folk-rock of Sonny & Cher.

The anthem, which was in line with President Johnson's victory, belonged to another Jewish songwriter. Paul Simon, influenced by gospel quartets, Doo-wop groups, Latin poetry, and Dylan, Simon wrote "The Sound of Silence" months earlier. Simon, as he continued Dylan's "Blowin' in the Wind," approached the darkness of the unconscious, of fears and hopes, to awaken people from their indifference to the same racial shadow that Berlin, Gershwin, Leiber and Stoller had faced in their works. The original folk-acoustic version of the song didn't make much noise, but a remix with a rock production sent Simon & Garfunkel to the top of the charts in 1965. Like Dylan, the successful duo would also communicate with the masses through a large corporation, Columbia Records. It was probably the last political folk anthem of that altruistic folk revival that had begun a decade ago.

The folk record labels survived years after that historic "revival." The most successful was Elektra Records. After Dylan's transition to rock, Holzman simply "followed the music" and recorded the best of The Paul Butterfield Blues Band, as well as Love, led by African-American Arthur Lee, and of course The Doors with the combination of French poetry, the Beat poets' rebellion, blues, and Frank Sinatra, cabaret and other eclectic influences to great success. In 1967 Elektra became a major asset and merged alongside Atlantic with the Warner Communications Corporation. Later, David Geffen took over Elektra and got rid of most of the old folk artists who had made it what it was in the first place.

In contrast, while continuing to run the company every day with his secretary in their small office, Moses Asch from Folkways continued to record folk music until his death. People say that he never deleted recordings or artists from his repertoire, nor let his momentary popularity affect him. Many saw the incredible and historical collection that he created as the *Talmud* of folk music.

Chapter 12: Walk On the Wild Side – Jews, Gangsters, and Rock 'n' Roll

> "[...] I have an arrangement with Muddy Waters"; Leonard (Chess) says that night. "Muddy," I tell him, "when your stuff [...] stops selling, you can come over to my house and do the gardening." "Funny, but I got a different kind of deal with (Big Joe) Turner," Ahmet says... "if his records don't sell, I can be his chauffeur." Leonard thinks we're crazy to pay our artists as high as 5 percent, as high as the majors... but Leonard counters there are virtually no defections from Chess. "They're (The Negroes) just happy to be making records... The records get them club work." (Jerry Wexler, *Rhythm and the Blues*, 1993)[435]

> We have the talent. They have the expertise [...] they are the managers, the agents, and they are the accountants. And that's why our black artists [...] got fame [...] but died poor; because somebody else got their money. They sent their children to the finest schools, and are able to continue to rule, while you pass on nothing to your children but the legacy of your fame [...] but today they developed a new strategy. Let's make our Negroes rich. (Louis Farrakhan)[436]

One of the most mysterious characters in the American television series *The Sopranos*, written by David Chase, is Herman "Hesh" Rabkin. The figure in the series is a Jew who made his fortune in the music industry. He is also close to the mafia. Chase probably based him on the image of two Jews from the record industry: Morris Levy and Hy Weiss.

Tony Soprano is aware that Rabkin made his fortune from exploiting the talent of black musicians because this myth has become part of the partly anti-Semitic stereotype that has become commonplace. After all, the mafia, lust for power, and poor morals lead to exploitation. Indeed, in the music world, the boundaries between crime, social legitimacy, and ethnic relations have always been a gray area. These relationships were not exclusive to Jews and blacks, but since it was probably impossible to understand the history of the American music industry in the twentieth century without understanding this relationship, it contributed a particular dimension to this story.[437]

In the ethnic discourse, there are different perspectives regarding this relationship: while the central Jewish view of Jewish-black relations is evident in

---

[435] Jerry Wexler and David Ritz, *Rhythm and the Blues: A Life in American Music* (New York: Alfred Knopf, 1993), 100–101.
[436] See <www.youtube.com/watch?v=OiQG23S2cZ4> (last accessed 11.03.2021).
[437] Jeffrey Melnick, *A Right to Sing the Blues: African Americans, Jews and American Popular Song* (Cambridge: Harvard University Press, 1999), 32.

its altruistic dimension, a lateral and decisive view of the more radical African-American interpretation argues for the exploitation of blacks by Jews.

The problem lies in the fact that the Jews (artists, writers and entrepreneurs) – from minstrelsy, through ragtime and jazz to rock 'n' roll – made use of African American musical materials. However, these two minority groups moved on different levels in the music field and gained different power. Jews were the ones who gained control of African-American cultural products, both as performers and creators of these materials and as owners of the means of production: publishers, owners, and managers of independent and major record labels, publishing agencies, and more. The success of Jews in entertainment led to their control of the sources of music and the careers of artists.

Back in the 1960s, the African-American intellectual Harold Cruse thought that the cultural system was cynically exploiting black artists and writers, leaving them in the degree of arrested development.[438] In 1991, African-American lecturer Leonard Jeffries introduced the theme that Hollywood was a Jewish white supremacist production house the role of which was the destruction of the black man in America. In 1990, African-American film director Spike Lee documented a stereotype of two Jewish club owners trying to take advantage of the black jazz player performing at their club. This image, he argued, was based on "many, many, many" Jewish club owners who exploited black artists who pleaded for pennies.[439] Singer Michael Jackson, who had a close relationship with Jewish executives, stated in the middle of the first decade of the 2000s that he had been exploited for years by a battery of agents, record labels and film companies, and lawyers of Jewish origin. This issue is still a matter of dispute. The film *Straight Outta Compton* (2015), directed by African-American Gary Gray, which recreates the story of the NWA hip-hop band in the late 1980s, is also about their financial exploitation by their Jewish manager Jerry Heller. Although most of these voices were never backed up with compelling evidence and data, black-Jewish relations were associated with the "discourse on exploitation." This discourse has its roots in the initial meeting of Jews and blacks, in minstrelsy and the Tin Pan Alley. Power relations that created a constant fear of arrogance and exploitation, against the backdrop of a racist America, as in the following case:

Publisher Isidore Witmark says he met two African-American writers, one of them was James Weldon Johnson, who came from Florida to New York. He met

---

[438] Harold Cruse, *The Crisis of the Negro Intellectual* (New York: NYRB Classics; Main edition, 2005 [1967]).
[439] Murray Freedman, *What Went Wrong?: The Creation and The Collapse of the Black-Jewish Alliance* (New York: Free Press, 1994), 109–110.

with them for a few hours and was enthusiastic about the songs; after presenting it to visitors and guests at the publishing house, he did not hesitate to say, perhaps with humor, that they might be able to steal something from the opera that both gentlemen wrote. The guests laughed, while James Weldon Johnson himself states that he and his friend "didn't quite understand the joke."[440]

In another case, Isidore Witmark told of a dispute he had with two other African-American writers, Will Marion Cook and Paul Laurence Dunbar. In 1898, they wrote the operetta *Clorindy, or The Origin of the Cake Walk*, which was published by the Witmark publishing house. The power relationship affected the relationship between employers and employees. Witmark called Dunbar "an outstanding poet of the Negro race," but he did not forgive his colleague, Cook, who demanded additional royalties through his lawyer. The Witmark House unequivocally assured Cook that they would no longer publish any of his songs if only to illustrate that the one who controls the money controls everything.[441]

Some cultural scholars believe that Jews exploited African-American music and artists as part of a general white supremacist ideology. On the other hand, others insist that even if black exploitation did occur, it was within the broader framework of "employee exploitation." After all, Jewish writers and composers also suffered from the exploitation of their publishers.[442]

For a long time, from the beginning of the twentieth century until after World War Two, blacks had difficulty in establishing themselves as entrepreneurs in the music business. While there were some African-American publishing companies in Tin Pan Alley and later blacks managed some labels (that Motown Records was owned by African-Americans was exceptional). Still, in most cases, until the 1970s and 1980s, they did not dramatically affect the music industry's activities. It seems that the copyright law enacted in 1909 and the establishment of the ASCAP mechanism, designed to collect royalties for the writers and composers, did little to protect African-American songwriters.[443] If that is not enough, the connection between the underworld of crime and the big money in the music industry exposed black (and white) artists to various avenues of exploitation.

One of the interesting phenomena that link Jews' movements through the margins of American society is the activity of Jewish gangsters in the music

---

[440] Isidore Witmark and Issac Goldberg, *From Ragtime to Swingtime* (New York: Lee Furman, 1939), 198.
[441] Ibid., 197.
[442] Jack Gottlieb, *Funny, It Doesn't Sound Jewish: How Yiddish Songs and Synagogue Melodies Influenced Tin Pan Alley* (New York: University of New York Press, 2004), 194.
[443] Jeffrey Melnick, *A Right to Sing the Blues: African Americans, Jews and American Popular Song* (Cambridge: Harvard University Press, 1999), 34.

world. Arnold Rothstein (one of the compelling characters in the HBO series, *Boardwalk Empire*), was one of the most famous of them. Rothstein was a supporter of successful jazz pianist Fats Waller and financed various shows. Legend, which might be true, has it that Jewish gangster Dutch Schultz, who financed the musical Hot Chocolates (1929), by the African-American Andy Razaf, even demanded at gunpoint that another song dealing with the difficulties of "colored people" be added. However, the mix of mafia business and music was not all fairy tales.

Joe Glaser, who was the manager of Louis Armstrong from 1935, was a close associate of Al Capone's criminal organization and his supervisor at Cafe Sunset and the prostitution business. The MCA empire, the most powerful artists and actors' agency in the United States throughout most of the twentieth century, was characterized by special relations between its senior executives and the mob. Its original Jewish owner Jules C. Stein, had a close relationship with various groups in the Italian mafia, including Capone; this is even though Stein was not a gangster or a bohemian musician but a professional businessman capable of moving smoothly between these social worlds.[444] However, even though MCA preferred to please the audience with white orchestras, Stein was the one who began marketing King Oliver and Louis Armstrong, and the New Orleans Jazz wizards. This relationship between the mafia and executives and agents and their African-American artists was more than usual and affected what went on, as was the case with Joe Glaser, who began managing Louis Armstrong as he returned to America after being forced to flee to Europe due to a conflict with the mafia.[445]

Jews promoted performances by black artists, but the connection to the world of crime led to the emergence of those taking control of black cultural capital. In the history of the Harlem Renaissance in the 1920s, Jews' control of theaters in the city was evident in the conversion of many cultural venues into entertainment sources for white audiences.[446] The Apollo Theater, which became a vital arena for African-American music after World War Two, involved Jewish figures: Sydney Cohen owned the place, and Morris Sussman managed it until they transferred it to other American Jews, Frank Schiffman and Leo Brecher, who owned other clubs in Harlem. Jay Faggen and Moe Gale founded the Savoy Ballroom. Bernard Levy was one of the founders of the Cotton Club, but had to sell it to Irish gangster Owney Madden. Lou Walters (the father of broadcaster Barbara

---

[444] Dennis McDougal, *The Last Mogul: Lew Wasserman, MCA, and the Hidden History of Hollywood* (New York: Da Capo Press, 1998), 141.
[445] Ibid., 19.
[446] Ralph Cooper and Steve Dougherty, *Amateur Night at the Apollo: Ralph Cooper Presents Five Decades of Great Entertainment* (New York: Harpercollins, 1990), 196.

Walters) owned the Latin Quarter, and Monte Kay of the Birdland Club, one of the centers of bebop music) in collaboration with Morris Levy, a food and underworld businessman who entered the publishing business and later owned several independent record companies.

Jewish gangsters owned many entertainment and music venues. In New York, Dutch Schultz retained the Ambassador Club, and Charles "King" Solomon controlled the Boston Coconut Grove. In Newark, Abner "Longie" Zwillman owned the Excise Mirror and Casablanca Club. Jewish singers and entertainers such as Al Jolson, Eddie Cantor, Fanny Brice, and Sophie Tucker frequently appeared in mafia-controlled clubs.[447]

Rock historians tend to romanticize pioneers of the independent labels. While major record companies, alongside the publishers of Tin Pan Alley, were indeed slow in understanding rock's economic potential, there were small entrepreneurs – many of them Jewish in origin – who rushed to record black music.[448] At least some of the pioneers are certainly entitled to praise for the vision and "foresight," but many did so while economically exploiting poor African American performers who lacked the means to gain legal advice and protection. Journalist, Fredric Dannen wrote about "The Pioneers":

> Many of them were crooks. Their victims were usually poor blacks, the inventors of rock & roll, though whites did not fare much better. It was a common trick to pay off a black artist with a Cadillac worth a fraction of what he was owed. Special mention is due Herman Lubinsky, owner of Savoy Records in Newark, who recorded a lineup of jazz, gospel, and rhythm and blues artists and paid scarcely a dime in royalties.[449]

Lubinsky's influence may not have been broad, but – as his daughter testifies – this behavior was demonstrated to everyone, whites, Europeans and blacks alike.[450] Lubinsky was one of many Jewish entrepreneurs operating on the fringes of the music industry. Among them were Hy Siegel and Bess Berman (Apollo Records), the Bihari brothers (Modern Records), Eddie, Leo, and Ira Messner (Aladdin Records), Al Silver (Herald and Ember Records), Sol Rabinowitz (Baton Records) Sam and Hy Weiss (Old Town Records), Florence Greenberg (Scepter Records). These were just some of the Jewish names associated with the

---

[447] Robert A. Rockaway, *But He Was Good to His Mother: The Lives and Crimes of Jewish Gangsters* (New York: Gefen Publishing House, 1993), 205–206.
[448] Fredric Dannen, *Hit Men: Power Brokers and Fast Money Inside the Music Business* (New York: Anchor, 1991), 31.
[449] Ibid.
[450] Mark Lisheron, "Rhythm and Jews," *Common Quest: The Magazine of Black Jewish Relations* 2 (Summer 1997): 20–33.

record business, which often recorded African-American artists. All these are in addition to the characters I have already mentioned: the Jewish brothers Leonard and Phil Chess recorded Chuck Berry, and Syd Nathan at King Records in Cincinnati who introduced James Brown to the audience. Art Rupe, the owner of Specialty Records, recorded Little Richard. Lew Chudd, the owner of Imperial Records, recorded Fats Domino; and there are many other examples. Some of these ventures were on the brink of legal business and business related to the American crime world, and others did not hesitate to promote their companies and their artists in illegal ways.

The prototype of the Jewish gangster in the music industry was Morris Levy, owner of Roulette Records. Levy was a Jew of Spanish origin from the Bronx, and he went further and more aggressively compared to the other entrepreneurs. While the others had fallen over the years, he remained a strong institution. He was in contact with the mafia – he was never a real member of the organization, but he did business with several crime families.[451]

Levy obtained his fortune (about $75 million before his death in 1990), by dominating the various sides of the music industry. Levy, who started in the food business, opened the New York bebop Club, Birdland, in the late 1940s; in the mid-1950s, he launched the label Roulette Records, but also made his fortune from taking over copyright in the Tin Pan Alley area through his publishing company, Patricia Music. Except for the underworld business, he focused on purchasing bankrupt labels (including their catalogs), forging record prints, editing song collections, and establishing a network of record stores.

Through marketing his jazz shows, he discovered promotion through payola, namely providing bribes to broadcasters and radio show editors. Therefore it was no wonder he knew Cleveland Jewish broadcaster Alan Freed, who was the one who gave rock 'n' roll its name. Freed was one of America's most influential broadcasters during the 1950s and established rock 'n' roll as a successful and legitimate musical genre. He also based his power on payola that independent labels would pass on.

Throughout the 1950s, Levy moved forward in the Jewish network through his relationships with producer and Jewish talent discoverer George Goldner, and with Alan Freed, who conducted rock 'n' roll all shows over America and was a partner in his record label's profits. In the early 1960s, under pressure from the big record companies, the House of Representatives began investigating labels and broadcasters in what became known as the Payola Affair. While most

---

[451] Fredric Dannen, *Hit Men: Power Brokers and Fast Money Inside the Music Business* (New York: Anchor, 1991), 32–33.

broadcasters and corporate owners came out unharmed, Freed lost his world after being convicted and died in 1965 suffering from alcoholism.

Levy, however, survived. In 1973, the Jewish community even held an evening in his honor, attended by music industry leaders. Until his conviction (and his death shortly after that) in 1990, he continued his relationships with the Jewish network, including affiliations with CBS Records lawyer, Walter Yetnikoff.[452]

The relationship between Levy and Yetnikoff knew its ups and downs, but was intimate, or more precisely included a kind of "Jewish intimacy," each addressing each other by their Yiddish names: Yetnikoff called Levy Moishe, and Levy called Columbia's lawyer Velvel. Yetnikoff admitted he admired "strong people like Morris Levy."

The following conversation between Yetnikoff, then a promising lawyer for Columbia, and Levy – taken from Yetnikoff's memoirs – reveals the Jewish underworld's worldview about bribery and the "American way":

> "Mr. Levy, I'm here to discuss the matter of your debt to Columbia Records in the amount..."
> "Don't you think I know how much I owe?"
> "I'm here because..."
> "You're here because you're a fucking lackey. What's your name again?"
> "Yetnikoff"
> "'A nice Jewish boy" [...] "Call me Moishe, I like your Chuzpah, Yetnikoff, but I still don't see how the fuck you're going to collect this debt."
> "The contract is explicit"
> "I use contracts to wipe my ass [...] You got to learn, successful transactions don't have shit to do with contracts."
> "Then what do they have to do with?"
> "Moxie. Raw fucking moxie"...

When Clive Davis was fired from CBS-Records in 1973 for using the company's money to fund his son's Bar Mitzvah celebration, Yetnikoff spoke to Levy about the issue:

> "So Moishe, What about this Clive business?"
> "CBS has their head up their ass. Clive is a Cub Scout. If he took, he took peanuts. Do they think they're running a record company or a fucking nunnery?"
> "It's a clean-cut corporation."

---

[452] Walter Yetnikoff and David Ritz, *Howling at the Moon: The Odyssey of a Monstrous Music Mogul in an Age of Excess* (New York: Abacus, 2003), 61–71, 81.

"Ain't no such animal. How do you think Paley signed Bing Crosby? You don't think someone got greased. In this business, someone's always got greased. It's the American way."[453]

Hy Weiss, the Jewish owner of Old Town Records, was a friend of Morris Levy and began his career as a distributor and promoter for Atlantic Records. Weiss emigrated with his family from Romania and settled in the Bronx, in the neighborhood where Levy grew up. Dannen quotes him as justifying Levy's gangster behavior: "Given where we came from," Weiss argued, "we were capable of many things." They did not hesitate to use violence. An example of this is the story that he and Morris Levy traveled with baseball bats to "stop" a factory forging their records, according to various sources, and Weiss said they didn't hesitated to push men from windows to settle business, and that he was not afraid to use illegal violence to settle differences in financial matters.[454]

Weiss established his distribution network by sharing his rewards with record store owners and sellers in exchange for placing his records in the top ranks and prominent places for the consumer. However, Weiss promoted his label by payola. "Also he made sure to write himself as co-writer": "I may be the writer of the thing but it was just a few lines," he said. He was known to have "invented" the concept of the Fifty-Dollar-Hand-Shake with the DJs, as a nickname for the way he used to bribe DJs and radio editors for song promotion.

However, not only entrepreneurs with connections in the underworld like Weiss and Levy promoted themselves through payola, but also other label owners, some of them highly respected, such as Atlantic Records. It happened – not only, but also – because the law for radio stations was not clear enough and decisive concerning radio promotions (only after the inquiry by the House of Representatives was the law clarified again). Dickie Klein, Atlantic's sales and public relations promoter in the South and Midwest, confessed that the standard of those days was to "send money to editors and broadcasters in exchange for broadcasting the record."[455]

Jerry Wexler remembered that he used to bribe Alan Freed regularly. During one of Atlantic's tough times, Wexler says, when there wasn't even money to pay salaries to employees, he asked Freed to freeze the payments and at the same time, continue to broadcast records from Atlantic. Freed refused. However, he

---

[453] Ibid.
[454] Dorothy Wade and Justine Picardie, *Music Man: Ahmet Arthgun, Atlantic Records, and the Triumph of Rock 'n' Roll* (New York: W. W. Norton & Co. Inc., 1990), 68.
[455] Ibid., 66.

adds that despite taking payola, Freed promoted black music not only due to profits but also because he "felt" that it was part of his life. Wexler wrote:

> He'd be good to the Chess brothers in Chicago – they couldn't have conquered the Midwest without him [...] He viewed the Erteguns and me as Marks, paying customers. I was happy to be in the ball game at all [...] remember that Allan and I had the same affinity for the music. He adamantly played original black versions, not white covers."[456]

The brothers Leonard and Phil Chess, Jewish immigrants from Poland, started their career in the food and beverage business in Chicago and later moved on to the music business. They recorded blues music performed by black artists such as Muddy Waters, Howlin' Wolf, John Lee Hooker, and Bo Diddley, but gained even greater success with African-American rock n 'roll artist Chuck Berry.

In his autobiography, Berry describes his relationship with his employers, the Jewish Chess brothers. He emphasized how he signed the contract. He received a standard contract, with no company logo at the top or bottom of the printed page, and he did not understand most of the legal concepts. Nevertheless, he made himself look like a well-versed reader on the legal issues as he noticed Leonard Chess was surprised by Berry's "scope of legal knowledge."[457]

The Chess brothers rewarded broadcasters not only in the form of cash, drugs, and women but also by payment through copyrights. They were not the first. Hy Weiss used to register himself as one of the songwriters regularly, and although he said he did not write them, he only added "a few lines here and there [...,]" the Chess brothers included this by paying payola as a partnership in royalties.[458] They encouraged broadcaster Alan Freed to promote "Maybellene" (1955), Chuck Berry's song, to national hit status, after listing him as one of the songwriters; this is even though Berry wrote the song alone. Fredric Dannen testified that Freed admitted to taking $2,500, but explained that it was gratitude and that the payment had no effect on the song's broadcast. Freed, wrote Dannen, forgot to clarify that the Chess brothers added his name to the copyright as one of the songwriters and in that way he was legally paid for each play as any songwriter is entitled.[459]

---

[456] Jerry Wexler and David Ritz, *Rhythm and the Blues: A Life in American Music* (New York: Alfred Knopf, 1993), 130.
[457] Chuck Berry, *The Autobiography* (New York & London: Harmony Books, 1987), 104.
[458] Dorothy Wade and Justine Picardie, *Music Man: Ahmet Arthgun, Atlantic Records, and the Triumph of Rock 'n' Roll* (New York: W. W. Norton & Co. Inc., 1990), 69.
[459] Fredric Dannen, *Hit Men: Power Brokers and Fast Money Inside the Music Business* (New York: Anchor, 1991), 43.

It is unclear whether Berry shared in this conspiracy, or that the Chess brothers unknowingly sold some of his rights for broadcast, but Berry suggests that a review of Chess's royalty books revealed that they had not paid him the full royalties. Berry recalls in his memoirs:

> I was surprised to learn that I had been paid the same songwriter royalties for an LP as I was receiving for a single record. Chess claimed to be unaware of this "mistake," as if they had never noticed that an LP had between eight and ten songs on them.[460]

African-American singer Little Richard (Richard Penniman) also felt he was a victim of exploitation.[461] Penniman, a young bisexual man from Georgia and a member of a disadvantaged family, broke out in 1955 with the hit "Tutti Frutti," which reached the top 20 of the pop charts and almost went to the top of the rhythm and blues hit parade. He confessed selling the rights to some of his songs for pennies to Art Rupe, the Jewish owner of Specialty Records. Penniman explains, "I didn't know anything about the record business," adding, "I was very dumb. I was just like a sheep among a bunch of wolves that would devour me in the moment." Penniman explained that he was "exploited," in part because he was "uneducated." He believes the record label treated him inhumanly and that they made millions and left him nothing.[462]

In fact, Art Rupe owned not only the master recordings but also the publishing rights to his songs. Rupe, like other label owners operating in the 1950s, created a situation in which the publishing company he owned was supposedly also the owner of his record label, and the songs recorded for the record label were "pre-sold" to the publishing company.

For example, the song "Tutti Frutti" was sold from the record label to the publishing company – both owned by Rupe – for only $50. Therefore, Rupe profited from record sales as well as from copyright royalties and would bite into the profits that songwriters should have received. In Penniman's case, instead of getting two cents on each record sale or radio broadcasting, he earned one single cent, while the difference remained with the company owner. Rupe made it happen because he defined this form of royalty payment at BMI, which was the publisher's songwriting organization, and was responsible for collecting royalty payments from the airwaves and other commercial areas that broadcasted the songs. Penniman and other rock 'n' roll stars said they didn't understand any-

---

[460] Chuck Berry, *The Autobiography* (New York & London: Harmony Books, 1987), 246–247.
[461] Charles White, *The Life and Times of Little Richard* (New York: Omnibus Press, 1984), 58–59.
[462] Ibid.

thing about the royalty payment system and could not follow this relationship between various copyright payments. In 1957 Penniman, as his stage persona, Little Richard, was reborn as an evangelist. He sold the rights to some of his songs (apparently) for pennies. Years later, he filed a lawsuit against Art Rupe, but the court acquitted the label owner.

Jewish producers who were also very successful businessmen, such as producer Phil Spector, were controversial in their relationship with the artists they produced in general, and African Americans in particular. In 1997, a US court ordered Spector to pay $263,000 to Darlene Love, his lead performer in The Crystals' songs (though not officially a member of the band). The court accused Spector of failing to pay her all the royalties she deserved over the years. In 2000, a US court forced Spector to pay about $2.6 million to The Ronettes for their royalty fees. The girl group members also sought to claim some of the rights to the master recordings, but the court rejected their request under the erroneous explanation that Spector's contribution to their success was crucial. However, the court unequivocally ruled that Spector did not pay them full royalties. Nevertheless, two years later, the Supreme Court accepted Spector's appeal and overturned the decision. The Supreme Court upheld the validity of the 1963 contract signed.[463]

Hints of exploitation also arose in the face of the fate of African-American performers, such as in the relationship between Gerry Goffin and Carole King and black singer Eva Boyd, known as Little Eva. King and Goffin discovered Boyd when she served as a nanny for their children. The Jewish duo wrote and produced several great hits in the early 1960s, including "The Loco-motion." The records came out under the name Little Eva in Label Dimension Records, founded by publisher Don Kirshner. Nevertheless, given the popularity of the British bands after The Beatles' success, King and Goffin had trouble reconstructing the first successes with the African-American singer. During the 1960s, Goffin and King's marriage broke up and they split and artistically as well. Goffin, who suffered a mental crisis, became a songwriter for several Hollywood films and

---

[463] Dave Thompson, *Wall of Pain: The Biography of Phil Spector* (New York: Sanctuary Publishing, Ltd., 2003), 207–208. Despite Spector's victory, the Supreme Court did not overturn a decision to transfer to the band additional royalties from hit collections and other uses of material not included in the old contract. The Supreme Court returned the issue to a lower court to determine the level of royalties to be paid to the band, but the band felt it had lost its central demand.

According to the Allmusicguide.com Encyclopedia, the African American girl group The Shirelles, which recorded for Florence Greenberg's label Scepter, has filed lawsuits against Greenberg for failure to pay royalties.

occasionally went on to write for significant stars. King, who released the phenomenal bestseller *Tapestry* in 1971, became a major singer-songwriter star during the 1970s. Little Eva, on the other hand, performed the hits that earned her relatively little while she was a star, disappeared, retired on and off from the music industry, and found herself working for various periods in occasional jobs in North Carolina.[464]

Atlantic Records became a small and successful independent company in the 1960s since it was also able to adapt to new fashions. It expanded its catalog of recordings of Southern soul music, and from the middle of the decade had increased its interest in white, American, and British rock bands. Atlantic also expanded its hold on African-American music by producing, marketing, and distributing an agreement with two Southern labels: the first was Stax, located in Memphis, and the other – Fame, located in Alabama. These two labels were established and run by Southern whites. Atlantic had been proud of its decent treatment of black artists for years, but accusations of exploitation have increased concerning their relationship with Southern white labels.

Stax, owned Jim Stewart and his sister Estelle Axton, was established as a country music label and converted itself to rhythm and blues. The label's house band, Booker T. & the MG's, consisted of two blacks and two Southern whites (keyboardist Booker T. and drummer Al Jackson were African American; guitarist Steve Cropper and bassist Donald Duck Dunn were white), and built a unique sound repertoire. They presented a standard that affected the pop world on both sides of the Atlantic.[465] The multi-racial composition of the house band gave a liberal image to the record label. Practically, they fulfilled Martin Luther King Jr.'s dream. The African-American vice-president, Al Bell, was one of Dr. King's associates. Stax's artists included Otis Redding, Sam & Dave, Rufus Thomas, and others.

In the light of Stax's success, Atlantic began bringing its artist Wilson Pickett to Stax's studio in Memphis. While Memphis musicians, they say, brought with them the funk, that is, the rhythmic authenticity of black music, Wexler brought the taste of the mass audience, the fresh fashions in New York City, alongside a

---

[464] Ralph Cooper and Steve Dougherty, *Amateur Night at the Apollo: Ralph Cooper Presents Five Decades of Great Entertainment* (New York: Harpercollins, 1990), 196.
[465] Russell Reising, ed., *Every Sound There Is: The Beatles' Revolver and the Transformation of Rock and Roll* (London: Routledge, 2002).
  The Beatles, for example, were heavily influenced by the sound of Motown, the most successful black company in the United States, and the sound of Stax. These effects were evident even in the early records, but especially in the albums Rubber Soul (1965) and Revolver (1966).

broader artistic and economic worldview. However, the economic cooperation ended in harsh realities due to legal and financial controversies, and a feeling of the Southern label owners that they were being culturally and economically exploited.

In 1968, Stax's biggest star, Otis Redding, was killed when his plane crashed en route to the show. According to Peter Guralnick, music critic and historian of Southern soul music, said Stax's "Heart and Soul" died with him.[466] But Jim Stewart, the owner of the label, was to make another startling discovery: Atlantic heads informed him that the label's master recordings, recorded in collaboration between the two companies, were owned exclusively by Atlantic Records. Stax was embarrassed by its ridiculous naivety. Wexler claimed that he wanted to return the masters, but the attorneys did not allow it.[467]

During the breakup of the relationship with Stax, Wexler found another creative outlet to which he sought to connect Atlantic artists – the label Fame studio, owned by Southern white engineer Rick Hall, located in Muscle Shoals, Alabama. This studio brought to the world one of the greatest hits of 1966, "When a Man Loves a Woman" performed by the African-American Percy Sledge, which was successfully marketed by Atlantic.[468] Encouraged by the surprising success, Wexler decided to copy the focus of Muscle Shoals and produce some of the new African-American songs by Wilson Pickett. Pickett's success encouraged him to record the album of his new sensation, singer Aretha Franklin.

Franklin's recording process reveals the tensions between blacks and southern white during musical collaboration. This story shows just how much Wexler was a mediator within this impossible relationship. It is surprising to find that this recording, which was loaded with racial slurs, became a milestone in the connection between music and King's struggle. Franklin's voice became the one most associated with the struggle for social justice. While Stax introduced a mixed house band (whites and blacks), the studio at Muscle Shoals included a group of Southern white players. Tensions between the races began when Ted White, Franklin's husband, and then manager, complained to Wexler that "all the musicians are white." Wexler, who tried to fix this "mistake," was late.

---

[466] Peter Guralnick, *Sweet Soul Music: Rhythm and Blues and the Southern Dream of Freedom* (New York & Boston: Back Bay Books, 1986), 357.
[467] Ibid.
[468] The song "When a Man Loves a Woman" performed by Percy Sledge had a huge impact on pop music around the world. The most tangible example was the rendering and production by British producer Denny Cordale to the song "A Whiter Shade of Pale" by Procol Harum, which contained the same musical elements, most notably the sound of the Hammond organ.

The atmosphere was heated when one of the trumpeters made some "offensive comments" toward Franklin.[469]

Later that evening, at the hotel where the singer and her husband were staying, label and studio owner Rick Hall tried to straighten things with the singer and her husband, but the conversation descended into shrill tones that included blasphemy, until Franklin and her husband decided to leave the city. Wexler, furious at Hall for ruining something that had gone so well, had to return to New York with complete recordings for the song "I Never Loved a Man (The Way I Love You)," and the beginning of another song, "Do Right Woman, Do Right Man." Rick Hall recounted years later how Wexler took advantage of rural Southerners:

> Jerry never came back. We never cut anymore sessions together. We are good friends now [...] but that ended our relationship, and of course Wexler went after my musicians [...] they would put me out of business [...] He broke with Stax, he broke with me [...] Wex was a strong-willed and a tremendous businessman. He could use you, pit you against me, me against this guy, and he did that, especially to us Southern boys [...] he wasn't a musician [...] but he was the best businessman I ever met."[470]

Syd Nathan, the Jewish owner of Label King Records of Cincinnati, had a tumultuous relationship with his biggest star, James Brown. During the 1960s, Brown became the most influential black artist standing for Black Power's separatism and pride, both in verbal slogans ("Say It Loud – I'm Black and I'm Proud"), and in "re-enacting" the African rhythmic foundations of funk music.[471] His story reveals the complexity of an employee-employer relationship, in this case, between a Jew and a black.

While journalists had a feeling that whites "were irrelevant to him,"[472] Brown had a heated relationship with Nathan. King Record's Jewish artist and repertoire Ralph Bass was the one who "discovered" Brown in Atlanta and obtained him after competing with other small labels, such as Chess Records (Bass paid Brown $200 to not sign Chess' contract). James Brown and the Famous Flames were signed at the end of January 1956 and came to record in Cin-

---

[469] Peter Guralnick, *Sweet Soul Music: Rhythm and Blues and the Southern Dream of Freedom* (New York & Boston: Back Bay Books, 1986), 342.
[470] Ibid, 344.
[471] Robert Palmer, "James Brown," in *The Rolling Stone's Illustrated History of Rock and Roll*, edited by De Curtis Anthony and Henke James (New York: Rolling Stone Press, 1992), 170–193. James Brown was introduced in an entire band playing melodic instruments as percussion, with an emphasis on the first beat – the "One."
[472] Nik Cohn, *WopBopaLooBop LopBamBoom: Pop from the Beginning* (London: Paladin, 1969), 110–111.

cinnati in early February. Nathan, who listened to the first single "Please, Please, Please," written under the heavy influence of gospel, called what he heard "[a] piece of shit." He was sure it was a certain loss of his money, and at the end of the recordings, he fired Bass. Guralnick described Nathan as "cruel" and an aggressive man who has never generous or sensitive.[473]

Jewish-American Seymour Stein, who successfully managed the record label Sire Records in the 1970s and 1980s, began as a sales promoter for Nathan's company. He said Nathan's "roughness" and "toughness" were not directed exclusively at his African-American artists, but also toward white workers and even his own family members. Nathan, emphasizes Stein, did not hesitate to use physical and verbal violence towards them.[474]

Despite Nathan's fears, Brown's debut single has reached – albeit slowly – a gold record status. The success was a result of the attractive stage show, which established Brown's status as "The Hardest Working Man in Show Business." While Nathan believed that the way to sell records was through "cultivating" them and adapting them to the mainstream, Brown proved that it was precisely the extroverted ghetto image, or the stereotype he cultivated, that incorporated "the beauty of the ugliness," that worked for him. At the end of the 1950s, after several singles, Brown sought to record another song, "(Do the) Mashed Potatoes," but Nathan refused. With no choice, Brown had to put it out a few months later under another name on another label. To Nathan's surprise, the song reached the Top 10 in the rhythm and blues chart.

Brown, who in the meantime became a sensation and attraction for an African-American audience, included the show as a very theatrical African ceremony. Brown sought to record the special ecstasy of live performances by recording a live show album at New York's Apollo Theater. However, Nathan believed that the rhythm and blues industry was based on singles, and refused to fund these recordings. Brown, again, decided to get the money himself, and the result: *Live at the Apollo* (1963) was a huge commercial and artistic success. Brown leveraged himself as the African-American artist most loyal to African traditions while incorporating the idea of black capitalism.[475] The album, according to many critics,

---

[473] Peter Guralnick, *Sweet Soul Music: Rhythm and Blues and the Southern Dream of Freedom* (New York & Boston: Back Bay Books, 1986), 226.
[474] Dorothy Wade and Justine Picardie, *Music Man: Ahmet Arthgun, Atlantic Records, and the Triumph of Rock 'n' Roll* (New York: W. W. Norton & Co. Inc., 1990), 63.
[475] Brown became famous as a Richard Nixon voter, and in the 1980s as a supporter of Ronald Reagan and the Republican Party and their economic policies. This was not an obvious choice for an African American. Brown also used to fine musicians who made a mistake during performances, to demonstrate the extent of the "hard work" ethic.

created a new musical language. Guralnick likened the album's release to the design of neo-realistic Italian cinema, and Brown, in every sense, became the hero of African-American culture.[476]

Although under contract, Brown abandoned King Records in 1963 in favor of Smash Records. Legal disputes accompanied the departure and the filing of counterclaims between Brown and Nathan. However, two years later, Brown asked to return. Although he could join any record corporation he wanted, he chose in 1965 to renew the King contract. Nathan gave in to all his demands and gave him full ownership of the song rights, higher royalties, and additional benefits. Nathan also declared after a while that "it is impossible not to admire James Brown for his determination and the way he did it." After Nathan's death in 1968, Brown put on his desk a gilded placard: "I Remember the Man Syd Nathan."

Love and theft, distance and closeness

The discourse regarding exploitation in the popular music field includes not only references to Jewish business people who exploited African American cultural capital, but to the artists (writers and producers) themselves.[477] Cultural scholars have tried to claim that the Jewish writers of the early twentieth century created a particular way of introducing an approximation of black materials and at the same time, expressed a distance from them.

In this concept, Irving Berlin, who began his career as a singer-waiter, "learned" the work of unsighted African-American songwriter Blind Sol. While Berlin was crowned the "King of Ragtime," he admitted that he never understood "what exactly was ragtime." Over the years, there have been accusations that Berlin stole the motif of his hit "Alexander's Ragtime Band" from Scott Joplin's *Treemonisha* opera. Berlin was exposed to Joplin's work, allegedly, through Henry Waterson, his close friend and publishing partner at Tin Pan Alley.

Africans-Americans and other critics directed these charges against Gershwin. Gershwin's career was nourished by European classical music and black musical traditions, but African-American musicians argued that *Porgy and Bess* was more an opera about blacks than black opera.[478] African-American

---

[476] Peter Guralnick, *Sweet Soul Music: Rhythm and Blues and the Southern Dream of Freedom* (New York & Boston: Back Bay Books, 1986), 240.
[477] Jeffrey Melnick, *A Right to Sing the Blues: African Americans, Jews and American Popular Song* (Cambridge: Harvard University Press, 1999), 43.
[478] Ibid., 48.

jazz composer Duke Ellington accused Gershwin of stealing materials from everyone. The acquisitions weren't exclusive to blacks: critic Virgil Thomson believed Gershwin shouldn't even have tried to write it.

African-American musician Eubie Blake believed that Gershwin was greatly influenced and perhaps even copied his first ragtime songs from composer and black pianist Luckey Roberts.[479] Other accusations were that Gershwin used motifs from Eubie Blake's "Shuffle Along" from 1921 for his song "I Got Rhythm," and there were even those who questioned Gershwin's use of the Charleston rhythm developed by his friend, James P. Johnson, for a dominant element in his work "Concerto in F."[480] And there are many more examples.

Yet, Gershwin acknowledged the importance of imitation in the development of a composer and shared his notions regarding studying the popular:

> I learned to write music by studying the most successful songs published. At nineteen I could write a song that sounded like Jerome Kern [...] But imitation can go only so far [...] The younger songwriter may start by imitating a successful composer he admires, but he must break away soon as he has learned the maestro's [...].[481]

Louis Armstrong, a son of an African-American prostitute, was related to the New Orleans Jewish Karnofsky family, who rescued him from his stay in an orphanage and took him under their wing. Yet, the story is bigger than this altruistic anecdote. The influences were mutual and acted on both sides. Cultural scholars and musicologists have claimed that African-Americans Fats Waller and Andy Razaf used Gershwin motifs in their musical *Hot Chocolates*. Louis Armstrong, who played in the musical, enriched the introduction with influences from Gershwin's "Rhapsody in Blue." Will Wodrey, who was Duke Ellington's teacher, was also an African-American composer who worked on some of the best works by Jewish composers. He helped orchestrate Gershwin's "Blue Monday." The African-American orchestrator Will Marion Cook assisted Harold Arlen with his arrangements. Jewish-American singers, such as Fanny Brice and Sophie Tucker, leaned on the musical skills of African-American composers and arrangers. And there were (possibly) influences from Jewish music: musicologist Jack Gottlieb claimed that Scott Joplin, for example, who

---

479 Terry Waldo, *This is Ragtime* (New York: E. P. Dutton, 1976), 113.
480 Murray Freedman, *What Went Wrong?: The Creation and The Collapse of the Black-Jewish Alliance* (New York: Free Press, 1994), 117.
481 George Gershwin, "Making Music," in *The George Gershwin Reader (Readers on American Musicians)*, edited by Robert Wyatt and John Andrew Johnson, 1st ed. (Oxford University Press, 2007), 136.

blamed Berlin for "musical borrowings," "stole" for his piece "Magnetic Rag," a theme of Jewish music from "Avreml Der Marvikher."[482]

A sober look at the music industry reveals that black-owned publishing companies became known for not paying their writers. Duke Ellington recounted that African-American writers would sell their songs several times to several different companies and became known for "borrowing and stealing" ideas from his bandmates; African-American composer Willie "The Lion" Smith explains that early jazz musicians didn't understand the economic significance of copyright.

Despite stories of business tensions, let's look at the facts: it is not difficult to determine that the Jews helped open up the cultural dead end imposed on blacks. Jews, who owned clubs, were among the first to open their doors to black artists. Jewish jazz artists broke the barriers between the jazz orchestras. Benny Goodman not only employed black arrangers like Fletcher Henderson – but paid tribute to African-American soloists such as Teddy Wilson and Lionel Hampton and guitarist Charlie Christian. Jewish jazz artist Artie Shaw went out of his way to bring singer Billie Holiday on tour.[483]

In the rock age, there is no trace of this discourse about the theft of African-American cultural products by Jews, but by white artists (the discussion about Led Zeppelin's "musical thefts" is perhaps the most obvious example). The critical elite – almost unaware of the ethnic origin of the creators – have crowned Jewish songwriters and producers as very successful interpreters of what they have termed black music. African Americans also praise the works of Jewish "rockers" as authentic works and even enjoy their cultivation by the Jews. The debate, if any, still stands on financial disputes.

Pragmatism and survival

At least in the music field, I certainly believe that Jews lacked strong and oppressive social and political institutions (compared to the role the Catholic Church had on Irish and Italians immigrants), which encouraged the need for pragmatism. In the new American world, it seemed, if you did not know how to "get along," the Jews had no possibility of religious and social escapism. "I have nothing to hide and I've always been pragmatic," Wexler admits, "at Christmas

---

[482] Jack Gottlieb, *Funny, It Doesn't Sound Jewish: How Yiddish Songs and Synagogue Melodies Influenced Tin Pan Alley* (New York: University of New York Press, 2004).
[483] Murray Freedman, *What Went Wrong?: The Creation and The Collapse of the Black-Jewish Alliance* (New York: Free Press, 1994), 118.

you give a tip to the guard not to celebrate the birth of Jesus [...] but against the evil eye of next year; if you didn't know the power of the broadcasters and program editors, you were out of business."[484]

Indeed, blacks were not the only victims of exploitation. Financial disputes have also emerged among powerful Jews. Leiber and Stoller, in fact, left Atlantic in the early 1960s due to a dispute over royalty payments. In an accounting review conducted by Leiber and Stoller of Atlantic, their accountants found that the company owed them another $18,000. Wexler was adamant when he argued against them to "forget about it" (and keep working with them, or take the money and not work with us anymore), and this is when the three of them had a "friendship relationship."[485] Bob Dylan, too, departed from his Jewish manager Albert Grossman due to a dispute over the distribution of royalties. Relationships among Jews in the music industry were often extremely difficult.[486]

We should take quotes about love and hatred of blacks and Jews skeptically. Still, the fact is that despite the political alliance, the march to Washington, Jewish philanthropy in black education, and especially the unique creative collaboration in the popular music field, blacks and Jews didn't cooperate in the economic sphere. It is not easy to find a record label, artist agency, or publishing house that shared a serious Jewish-black commercial initiative. This fact reinforced the African-American voices that believed the relationship was accompanied by "ongoing exploitation." Jerry Wexler could have argued that he shouldn't have identified with the lower classes since he was of inferior status, but historically this was not true, and the relationship between Jews as owners of the means of production and the African-American artists was undoubtedly not simple.

The year 1968, with the assassination of Martin Luther King Jr., marked the end of the dream of artistic integration in this format. Blacks – influenced by the phenomenal success of African-American label Motown among white audiences –stepped up economic entrepreneurship in the music field toward the end of the decade with the fantastic success of Philadelphia International Records.

Jewish-black entrepreneurship came to fruition years later. It was Rick Rubin and Russell Simmons, a Jew and a black, who, during the 1980s, created the label Def Jam Recordings, which recorded and distributed successful hip-hop music, and in the first place had everything it needed to be in the American music revolution of the twentieth century.

---

[484] Jerry Wexler and David Ritz, *Rhythm and the Blues: A Life in American Music* (New York: Alfred Knopf, 1993), 130–131.
[485] Ibid.
[486] Fred Goodman, *The Mansion on the Hill: Dylan, Young, Geffen, Springsteen, and the Head-On Collision of Rock and Commerce* (New York: Vintage, 1997), 105.

Chapter 13: Hard Rain Is Gonna Fall – Popular Music, Hegemonic Rifts, and New American Culture

In 2012, President Barack Obama presented the Gershwin Award – the highest honor regarding popular music – to Hal David and Burt Bacharach. A year later, he awarded it to Carole King, who was also the first woman to win the award. Paul Simon and Billy Joel also had the honor of winning it. The reverberations of the history of Jews in the American music industry and Jewish-black musical alliance as part of this story reminded us that American Jews had completed their journey in American music.

However, understanding the influence of this political and musical cooperation and fragile alliance on American culture has made it possible for me to become acquainted with my understanding of the world of British cultural studies. These were developed after World War Two at The Center for Contemporary Cultural Studies in Birmingham, England. I'd like to present their essence in this chapter.

Culturalism and structuralism

Members of the Center for Cultural Studies were associated with the British Left. Some of them left the Communist Party after their disappointment with the Soviet model. Thus, they established the British New Left and tried to reformulate Marxist theory and criticism. Two primary schools of thought influenced their research methods: culturalism and structuralism.[487]

Culturalism based its research on the study of literature and history using a Marxist approach. This paradigm continued in the works of Richard Hoggart, Raymond Williams and E.P. Thompson.[488] It engaged with the process of democratizing culture, understanding that high culture is a product of social negotiation, held a humanistic belief in the ability of the masses to create a progressive society, and promoted the perception that man "makes history."

---

[487] Stuart Hall, "Two Paradigms," in *A Cultural Studies Reader*, edited by J. Munns and G. Rajan (New York: Longman, 1995), 194–200.

[488] Raymond Williams, *Culture and Society, 1750–1880* (London: Columbia University Press, 1983 [1958]); E.-P. Thompson, *The Making of the English Working Class* (London: Penguin, 1963); Richard Hoggart, *The Uses of Literacy* (London: Penguin, 1957).

There were differences in their works, but they changed the study of popular culture by applying a new definition of culture. Their idea was to understand "culture" not in the sense of "the best artistic works" or "the best of what humanity has written, said and done." Instead, they wanted to examine culture as a complex of interactions between the various texts and mediums, and that people needed and used in everyday life.

These scholars democratized the concept of culture since they believed that culture in the sense of the "best" was a form of negotiation within society. Therefore, they tried to perceive culture as a "way of life." Culture under the new terms was related to anthropology: a lifestyle that expresses particular meanings and the values of institutions and everyday behavior. The definition of culture has gone from the realm of art and literature to a whole world of clarifying the implicit meanings and values expressed in a particular way of life. In these terms, Coca Cola, football, pub life, Eurovision, pulp fiction, and soap operas embody social and political meanings. They made sure to apply criticism applied to high literature in parallel fields of mass communication and popular arts.

The second school, structuralism, was fundamentally French and relied on the philosophy of Claude Levi-Strauss, Ferdinand de Saussure, Roland Barthes, and later in combination with Louis Althusser, who fused the psychological theory of Jacques Lacan with Marxism to a revisionist reading of Marxism.

Structuralism sees human activity as a product of social "structures," depth mechanisms of a social system that eliminate the individual's role in the development of humanity. Human history, therefore, was seen as the product of those "structures" and their power. According to this concept, man does not create his own history. Instead, he is "in" the "prison" of those structures.

Linguistics and, at times, Annales school of history influenced structuralism, but its essential philosophers reinterpreted Marx's writings, including the early works, which dealt with what we might perceive as liberating man from his ignorance and an alienating consciousness that matched the mood of the New Left. Throughout the 1960s many radical Leftists converted the deep disappointment with Soviet Marxism after the invasion of Prague in 1968, with the adoption of Maoism and the Cultural Revolution in China. They thought this Cultural Revolution would bring the "path to utopia" but without knowing much about it.[489]

Roland Barthes was one of them. He stirred up British cultural studies scholars with his insights on the semiotics of myths and signs. Barthes sought to dis-

---

[489] Richard Wolin, *The Wind from the East: French Intellectuals, the Cultural Revolution, and the Legacy of the 1960s* (New Jersey: Princeton University Press, 2010).

cover the meanings of everyday cultural behavior that seemed to society to be completely natural; he tried to show how natural and spontaneous rituals of contemporary bourgeois society are a way of distorting their meaning while drowning in their artificial "naturalness." Barth believed that ideology surrounded Western civilization, hidden in everyday life. For his concept, the press, the movies, theater, literature (especially popular forms), ceremonies, concepts of justice, diplomacy, clothing, "comments about the rain" – everything in everyday life depends on the representative relationship that exists in the bourgeois world.[490]

He examined the same naturally hidden laws, codes, and insights, through which the dominant groups and classes in society declared their authority and status. Barthes found signs of this ideology in the most neglected cultural products (tourist guides, for example), which acted as if they were "natural" and based on common sense. They functioned like myths. In doing so, Barth provided a new world of possibilities for examining culture as a "way of life."

Leaning on the assumption of the base\superstructure, Karl Marx had explained that the dominant ideology is the ideology of the ruling class. He believed that ideology, by definition, permeated beneath consciousness, as a "natural" element in everyday life. Under this influence, Stuart Hall, the head of the Birmingham Institute, explained that it was precisely its "spontaneous" nature, its transparency, its "natural" environment, its refusal to examine the underlying premises, and the closed circle in which it moved. All these made our common sense at the same time "spontaneous," ideological and unconscious.[491]

Hall was greatly influenced by Louis Althusser, who believed he had found a way to combine the early Marx of "German ideology" with the later Marx of "Capital," as well as to read Marx through Lacanian psychoanalysis. Althusser believed that "ideology" is not separate from everyday life, and is not a set of political agendas or an abstract worldview that operates behind "false consciousness"; it is present, he argued, as a "structure" acting on the unconscious.

The structure, in this sense, is an infrastructure of oppressive mechanisms such as political, military, police, and ideological devices that also include the basic structure of society, such as the family and education system. All aspects of culture are inherent in semiotic value, and even phenomena taken for granted function as constituting elements of communication systems governed by mean-

---

[490] Roland Barthes, *Mythologies* (London: Farrar, Straus and Giroux, 1972).
[491] Louis Althusser, "Ideology and Ideological State Apparatuses," *Lenin and Philosophy and Other Essays* (New York: Monthly Review Press, 1971), 85–126.

ingful laws and codes. These signs, therefore, affect social relations in a society that has an ideological dimension to each symbol.

Althusser writes:

> Not only does the State apparatus contribute generously to its own reproduction (the capitalist State contains political dynasties, military dynasties, etc.), but also and above all, the State apparatus secures by repression (from the most brutal physical force, via mere administrative commands and interdictions, to open and tacit censorship) the political conditions for the action of the Ideological State Apparatuses.[492]

Nevertheless, since signs and images have semiotic significance, many diverse ideologies – representing the interests of different social groups – may emerge from the surface. A power determines these ideologies. A privilege that allows the dominant classes to control the quantity, way, and manner of representation. Not every social group has the same power to impose their ideologies on the others. Inevitably, there are more dominant ideologies.

Marx believed that the dominant position in material and economical means also controlled intellectual power. But Althusser ruled out the concept of a "subordinate" class as a single-entity entity. Instead he developed the notion of interpellation and the Subjective Individual.[493] Ideology builds the individual's imaginative participation in a complex of social processes that fulfill his consciousness, but each of the entities that make up the society develops differently. The negotiations take place in several spheres: political, economic, and ideological. In the political and economic spheres, subordination to the dominant class is palpable, but on the ideological level, there is the possibility of cultural resistance. A system of representation of images and myth demonstrates this subversion. These same elements were identified by Birmingham scholars as "Resistance through Rituals" through speech, clothing, and style, even if the dominant classes eventually succeeded in neutralizing resistance expressed through the image by embedding it in the economic system.

After the failure of the student revolution in May 1968, Althusser was momentarily the fashionable voice in the academic world. Still, the academy soon found an even more effective intellectual treasure in Antonio Gramsci's writings, translated towards the end of the decade.[494] Gramsci adopted the concept of hegemony to explain the complexity with which the ruling class tries to

---

[492] Ibid. retrieved from https://www.marxists.org/reference/archive/althusser/1970/ideology.htm.
[493] Ibid.
[494] Antonio Gramsci, *Selections from the Prison Notebooks* (London: International Publishers Co, [1971], 1989).

control society. Although society is built up of conflicting interests of various classes, the ruling class manages to make its tastes and interests dominant.

Hegemony, in its "normal" practice is characterized by the combination of government and the consensus, balancing each other in varied ways, without the aforementioned governing authority over-enforcing the consensus; On the contrary: it will try to make the government appear to be supported by the majority. Gramsci wrote:

> The 'normal' exercise of hegemony on the now classical terrain of the parliamentary regime is characterized by the combination of force and consent, which balance each other reciprocally, without force predominating excessively over consent. Indeed, the attempt is always made to ensure that force will appear to be based on the consent of the majority, expressed by the so-called organs of public opinion – newspapers and associations – which, therefore, in certain situations, are artificially multiplied.[495]

Stuart Hall explained the term "hegemony" as a situation in which transitional alliances of certain social groups can exert "total social authority" on subordinate groups by agreeing on the naturalness and legitimacy of these groups' dominance. So the subordinate groups, if not controlled, are at least surrounded by an ideological space produced in the name of the dominant classes – perceived as "natural."[496]

At the same time, cultural scholars found another source of influence for the positive possibilities for exploring cultural meanings in the field of mass communication: Walter Benjamin. This German-Jewish intellectual continued in the 1930s to set his theism against Theodor Adorno's contempt concerning the artistic possibilities inherent in popular arts. Benjamin optimistically examined the democratization of art through modern mechanical reproduction, arguing for a change in the nature of art under the culture of consumption. He believed that mass culture dulled the hallowed "aura" of the original work. Art in the mass culture era offered another practice: the politics of defiance that shocks one in everyday existence.[497]

---

[495] Ibid, 248.
[496] Stuart Hall, "Culture, the Media and the 'Ideological Effect,'" in *Mass Communication and Society*, edited by J. Curran, M. Gurevitch and J. Wollacott (London: Edward Arnold, 1977), 315–348.
[497] Walter Benjamin, "The Work of Art in the age of mechanical reproduction," in *A Cultural Studies Reader*, edited by J. Munns and G. Rajan (New York: Longman, 1995), 88–96.

From ideology to the politics of culture apparatuses

British cultural scholars channeled this theory to engage with various aspects of young British working-class culture and popular music, such as their research on subcultures (Teddy Boys, Mods, Punk, etc.). They put particular emphasis on the adoption of a unique style as a ritual of cultural resistance. Cultural scholars have assumed that the historical conditions of the post-war era, which characterized the generation gap, created a new belief in social mobility, which created a sharp contrast with the real state of young people. The subculture responded to its class and experiential subordination in creating a unique style, connecting fragments of different and diverse styles and forms of the dominant culture into the space of youth culture. On the one hand, style expressed an experience; on the other, it allowed members of the subculture to live with the contrast by constructing an identity that was sometimes "forbidden" and "imaginary." This was opposed to the prevailing and parental culture and class, but offered nothing more than a "magical" solution in its contrast.[498]

Towards the end of the 1970s, the study of popular music presented a new path by using post-structuralist and postmodern theories of power, text and representation. They were heavily influenced, among others, by the French philosophy of Michel Foucault.[499] Foucault sought to study culture in terms of "power relations." Unlike Marxists, he refused to perceive power as a repressive or oppressive concept, that is, a conspiratorial tool of one institution versus another. Power, in his view, is expressed as a whole complex of forces. Even a tyrant and aristocrat not only "hold" power, but are empowered by a "discourse" – acceptable ways of thinking, writing, talking, and activities. The power in this sense, is also productive and allows for new growths and new forms of subjectivity. The study of culture, in this view, is intensified by the history of memory learned from everyday life (diaries, architecture, court decisions, medical forms), which reveal the moments of transformation in the discourse. This alternative presented a research-de-

---

[498] Stuart Hall and Tony Jefferson, eds., *Resistance Through Rituals: Youth Subcultures in Postwar Britain* (Birmingham: Hutchinson, 1976); Dick Hebdige, *Subculture: The Meaning of Style* (London: Routledge, 1979). Some of the institute's students criticized the subculture theory with an emphasis on its naivety, its non-compliance with the role of media, and disagreement about the "passivity" concept of the rest of the population. See, S. Clark, "Response to Dick Hebdige," in *On Record* (New York: Routledge, 1990), 120–130; Lawrence Grossberg, "The Political Status of Youth and Youth Culture," in *Adolescents and Their Music: If It's Too Loud, You're Too Old*, edited by S. Jonathon (Boston: Epstein, 1994), 25–46; Bill Osgerby, *Youth in Britain since 1945* (London: Wiley, 1995).
[499] Lynn Hunt, ed., *The New Cultural History: Essays* (Berkeley: University of California Press, 1989).

pendent cultural research method and a more complex view of the relationship between social forces and the production of culture. American music and cultural scholar, Lawrence Grossberg, has settled into this context.

Grossberg dealt with popular culture, political power relations in the United States, and the relationship and power between popular music and politics. Grossberg combined the work of Stuart Hall with a host of intellectuals from continental French theory, believing that popular culture is a necessary and positive psychological force in everyday life. He skipped over Althusser's anti-humanist sensebilities and radicalized the combination of cultural discussion and interpretation under historical conditions.[500] Grossberg explained "articulation" as

> [...] a continuous struggle to reposition practices within a shifting field of forces, to redefine the possibilities of life by redefining the field of relations – the context – within which a practice is located.[501]

Articulation, re-articulation, and disarticulation, therefore, are part of an intellectual and historical activity that forms a unique force of power, and stereotypes that define society and culture.

Popular culture is more than a field of ideological representation but lends itself to calmness, privacy, pleasure, passion, and emotion.[502] He refuses to see people as passive consumers on the one hand, and not utterly active on the other. People do not make history just by themselves; on the other hand, they are not merely the product of structure. Grossberg argues that people are not always "rebellious" (and not always in the way that the academic scholar wants them to rebel), but this does not indicate that they are "passive cultural consumers." People, he argues, "make history" under uncontrollable conditions. They struggle and fight for territories and spaces where they will have "control," and he believes that in this "struggle" popular culture has an important place, as it accompanies the person in his daily life and personal biography. It may serve as an emotional grip on the "pessimism" that accompanies the realities of everyday life in the neo-capitalist world.

Grossberg explains that apparatuses of culture influence everyday life. These are ensembles of diverse activities related to discourse, institutions, forms of architecture, regulations, law, certain types of administration, scientific statements, philosophy, morals, and underlying assumptions of philanthropy (an example of this is, for example, the cultural apparatus of rock music). They bring

---

500 Hayden White, *The Content of the Form* (Baltimore: John Hopkins University Press, 1973).
501 Lawrence Grossberg, *We Gotta Get Out of This Place* (New York: Routledge, 1992), 397.
502 Ibid., 79.

together activity regimes, technologies, and behavior programming. These systems – which are alliances between institutional and other apparatuses and between audiences and cultural products – create structures of power. This power functions through various forms of its mechanisms (censorship, legislation, differentiation, oppression, consensus, activation of an existential alternative). There are also social structures that guarantee the production and distribution of power to specific sections of the population.

Grossberg distinguishes two forms of apparatuses: "differentiating" and "territorializing," which are responsible for producing different social identity systems that are different from other identities, and identify areas and spaces related to stability and mobility, that is, the organization of everyday life in places and spaces. These apparatuses work to reinforce the binary differences associated with social identities, which are defined differently (male / female; white / black; young / adult).

The interpretation of culture is in constant struggle and under the influence of agency, forces that enable broad structures of articulation (capitalism, nationalism, liberalism, etc.), and pressure groups (which he calls agents), which influence the emergence of cultural texts and their interpretation. These groups try to change the production and distribution of a cultural text, but they are not always responsible for creating the text, and there is not always one identity between the pressure groups and the text.[503]

Grossberg's study explained the "politicization" of rock music as a process that happened "behind his back," through attacks by local governments, the education system, and the church. However, I would like to argue that the politicization of popular music was influenced by the activities of another agent: the Jewish-black Alliance.

Grossberg's definition of "agent" is as follows:

> [T]he actors, institutions and groups which act to change or direct history consistent with the interests of particular agencies, although this may not be intentional.[504]

Thus, the Jewish-black Alliance, as a type of pressure group, was an agent that functioned at various and varied levels of politics, society, and culture, between which there was no conscious connection. Politically, it was an alliance of political bodies that sought to influence public and ethnic discourse, to be a liberating body from discriminatory and restrictive laws. Culturally, as the music field demonstrated, they were responsible for cultural products (sounds, slogans, and

---

503 Ibid., 397.
504 Ibid.

images), which unintentionally altered cultural capital, the array of images, and normative concepts. Liberalism is itself an agency:

> [T]he actual forces producing the larger structures of articulation; the long-term forces which struggle to determine the direction and shape of history. For example: nationalism, capitalism.[505]

In this context, these forces that produced large structures of articulation that influenced the course of history drained what I called in this book post-war liberalism.

Music, identity, aesthetics, and liberation

While Grossberg deals with the everyday politics of popular music's apparatus and how this creates a consumer desire and investment mechanism, his discussion is less about the music itself. Simon Frith use cultural studies to understand the aesthetic value of popular music.[506]

Liberation as an aesthetic experience may illuminate how the music itself, based on African-American elements, not only brought with it anti-WASP elements but contained within it the same meanings and dialectics that relate to search for authenticity and a sense-of-difference identity sought by the music fan.

Critics and scholars have previously linked the relationship between the influence of "Africa" and liberation as the product of the id, the source of man's creative and sexual instincts. However, the argument about the sexual qualities of African-American music (and their influence on ragtime, jazz, and rock) is sociological and not just musicological. The connection between rhythm and "Africa" is a Western idea (African music is incredibly diverse). But the meaning of rhythm lies not in simplicity or directness, but in flexibility and sophistication, not in its physical expressiveness, but its communicative traits: its ability to make all body movements coherent. Thus, the "dance" resulting from listening to the rhythm is not only physical but mental. The sexuality of music stems from the tension and contrast between the flexibility of the voice (as a musical instrument) and the disciplined and dependent rhythmic body movements. In the end, popular music may have sexual connotations – not because it makes us "move," but rather because the way the movement makes us feel present.

---

[505] Ibid.
[506] Simon Frith, *Performing Rites: On the Value of Popular Music* (New York: Oxford University Press, 1996).

Frith adds to this insight the idea of "time": music is by nature irrational or analytical, but also offers an experience that conveys the sense of "ideal time." Frith displays the notions of individual and society, the body and the mind, stability, and change, the different and the similar, the past and future to come, passion, and fulfillment. Music in this sense resembles a sexual act. The rhythm is necessary as it does not release physical impulses but extends the time when listeners can feel that they are truly living in the present tense.

Lyrics in songs are important. Songs' lyrics are not "poetry" because we, as listeners, can't separate the lyrics from the context of the performance (and interpretation). The pleasure and enthusiasm for the best songs stem from a singer's "failure" to connect the musical and semantic meanings. The best pop songs sound like a struggle between rhetoric and revelry, between the singer and the song. The singers, in this context, are "character imitators."

In this sense, the written content is secondary because the same "love song," for example, may express different emotions according to different performers. The voice becomes not just someone's identity but a tool for changing identities. We use voice to pretend that we are someone who we aren't. With the voice, the performers "lie" to show someone "the truth," namely it is a tool of disguise that aims to confirm authenticity.

Music constructs our sense of identity through experiences it offers to our body, time, and sociality, experiences that allow us to place ourselves in imaginary cultural narratives. This fusion of imaginative fantasy and physical activity integrates aesthetics and ethics. The transcendence stemming from the music we love, he argues, means it takes us out of ourselves and puts us elsewhere. What makes music special – even for identity – is the construction of boundless space. Popular music is a cultural form that allows you to cross boundaries because sounds pass over fences, through walls, oceans, classes, races, and nationalities. Frith believes that music has been (at least for a few moments during the twentieth century) an essential way in which we learned to understand ourselves in relation to historical, ethnic, class, and gender issues; sometimes under conservative and sometimes liberal values. The music may turn into a game of "sense of identity" that fits (or does not) into where we positioned ourselves in society, and even declares our dissatisfaction and incompleteness.

Liberalism, radical liberalism, multiculturalism and hegemony

Popular music of the 1960s, liberalism and mass bohemianism participated in changes of the fabric of American hegemonic images: The White Negro, the hippies, the beautiful Italian, the black ghetto, long hair, gurus of Zen and Buddhism, Cuban guerrillas, Catholic radicals, Jewish anarchists, and civil rights fighters who all made the 1960s' noise. Popular music presented a black dialect, an African-American visual and more blatant sexuality, which stood aside from the territories and the daily order of the WASP's cultural hegemony.

These images confronted America's shadow, but the next process was that of canonization. Liberal critics from the 1920s to the 1960s allowed for a broad articulation process that legitimized multiculturalism. The liberation from Victorian codes was developed throughout the twentieth century, but the 1960s were a period of significant shifts in hegemony, the 'natural' status of which was questioned.[507]

The fluctuations of power influenced this new and liberal fabric of images in American society: two progressive presidents, who operated under various pressure groups, ranging from student politics to other minority alliances, considered liberalism and multiculturalism as solutions to society's ills. Post-war liberalism was a force that produced large structures of academic, political, cultural, and historical activities that disrupted previous power relations and created new stereotypes that redefined society and its culture.

The liberalism of 1960s' rock music (some even turned it into radical liberalism and mass bohemianism as in the case of Dylan), despite its various and contradictory voices, took part in this process and intensified the social discourse about a more pluralistic American society. Even if Anglo-American popular music only occasionally explicitly dealt with racism and sexism or class hierarchies and patriarchy, listeners placed themselves in a parallel imaginary place of pleasure, freedom, independence, utopia, criticism, and the possibilities that these fantasies created for the fans. Radical liberalism and rock music influenced fans in various dimensions of the chance of escaping from the everyday 'prison,' confirming alternative identities and experiencing authenticity through an alternative culture.

The 1960s were not a sudden breaking point in which American culture became more multicultural, but instead a significant and turbulent period that continued previous liberal trends. Long hair, sexual liberation, ethnic pride, reflections on postmodern culture, a revision of official history – all these things,

---

[507] Regarding multiculturalism's minorities and the "war" concerning American music between the WASP elite versus modernist composers and liberal writers from liberal background, see MacDonald Smith Moore, *Yankee Blues: Musical Culture and American Identity* (Bloomington: Indiana University Press, 1985).

which attested to a crisis in the authority of the WASP hegemony, were only parts of the liberal wave that shaped the century.[508]

The Kinsey Reports revealed that American sexuality was liberated even before the 1960s' revolution, although the decade prompted a more radical change concerning informality. American courts legitimized obscenity, which freed Hollywood and allowed the emergence of the pornographic industry. In 1969, English language dictionaries included for the first time the words "Fuck" and "Cunt." In August 1971, *Penthouse* magazine revealed female genitalia in an unprecedented manner, and *Playboy* had no choice but to catch up five months later. In 1967 *Newsweek* exploited the explosion of the mini-skirt fashion to report that the old normative codes were "dying," and that a more permissive society had taken its place. Violence became more common in popular culture with a wave of horror films. On Wall Street, employees began to call managers by their first name, and labor policy became looser than they were in the past. Doctors and stockbrokers grew their hair wildly. Magazines began to give advice on using language, liberating women, and how to get professional help with housework. Newspaper columns provided recommendations and guidelines for breast-feeding in public, free dress, and drug use. Columnists often went against the old ethics of male/female relations and wrote about the need to change simple codes relating to equality between the sexes.

Various courts refused to accept defiant clothing as a violation of the law or censorship and abolished restrictions on offensive words spoken publicly. The court had to redraw the lines between behavior and violence, leaving a more extensive space for rude words and liberation from puritanical codes, although, in workplaces and educational institutions, the law left rigid dividing lines and tolerated the changing of the meaning of the term good taste.[509]

The "noise" that characterized student politics and their image as anarchists that accompanied it only reinforced the need among many sectors of the population for "law and order," the slogan that Nixon favored in the 1968 presidential election. In the 1972 election, which gave Nixon a more impressive victory, it was evident that the American public rejected Kennedy and Linden Johnson's liberal vision, and in particular, the idea of the Great Society and welfare policies supporting the weaker among the population. All this happened while Japan began to take the place of the United States as the country with the most impressive economic development.

---

508 Kenneth Cmiel, "The Politics of Civility," in *The Sixties: From Memory to History*, edited by David Farber (Chapel Hill: The University of North Carolina Press, 1994), 292.
509 Ibid.

The election of Ronald Reagan in 1980 seemed to shut down the 'sixties.[510] Reagan, who argued that government is not the solution to the problems of the state, but the source of its [economic] problems, finally buried the idea of the Great Society and cut government involvement in the economy.[511] Reagan's choice enabled a blatant right-wing attack (old and new) on the post-World War Two liberal consensus. The state abandoned its role as an intermediary between capital and labor. It supported policies regarding trade union attacks, minimum wage freeze, and reliance on third-world labor utilization, consumer saturation markets, and national debt growth. Economic turmoil in the 1980s detached itself from the puritanical ethics of hard labor. It offered images regarding luck as a way of life (lottery and stock exchange), while the sheer volume of the popular mass culture in public life turned – blatantly and self-consciously – the control over the images into political, economic and ideological capital. The 1980s replaced the legitimacy of hedonism and leisure, with various images linking transcendence through discipline, which included the supervision of nicotine, cholesterol, and alcohol. American popular culture may have expressed a clear sense of sexual and narcotic permissiveness, but the polls showed that slightly less than one-third of Americans had this moral orientation.[512]

Conservative thinkers such as Alan Bloom expressed the New Right's agenda. They accused the extreme liberalism of the 1960s (and even rock music) of reducing the role of the humanities and of causing the absence of a spiritual structure for American youth.[513] More conservative imagery characterized the 1980s. Popular culture portrayed 1980s' youth culture as more conformist than the baby boomers. American TV broadcast role reversals between adults and their children, with a flush of soap operas dealing with youth traditionalism, and a popular media of censorship organizations such as the PMRC.

Even if President Bill Clinton held a far more liberal policy later than Republicans, he could not return to Johnson's legacy. And still, I'm convinced that post-'sixties American culture is more permissive, more pluralistic and multicultural, and that the WASP's hegemony is less dominant.

---

510 Lisa McGirr, *Suburban Warriors: The Origins of the New American Right* (New Jersey: Princeton University Press, 2002).
511 Bruce J. Schulman, *Lyndon B. Johnson and American Liberalism* (Boston: Bedford/St. Martin's, 2007), 155–165.
512 Paul W. Kingston, *The Classless Society* (Stanford: Stanford University Press, 2000), 146.
513 Alan Bloom, *The Closing of the American Mind* (New York: Simon & Schuster, 1989).

Epilogue

> When I started in this business, rock 'n' roll was defined like this: Two Jews and a guinea recording four *schvartzes* on a single track. Now it's changed so much, it's not even recognizable as the thing people used to be so afraid of.
> (Richie Finestra, *Vinyl*, HBO, 2016)

In my city, the local theater screens a movie about singer Amy Winehouse. She's been dead for some years, but I still remember the first time I listened to her. In her early twenties, she sounded like an old-fashioned jazz singer. On the album cover, she looked like a Lolita from one of Phil Spector's girl groups, even if she was far more impressive than any of them. The musical production of her record has placed this contemporary Jewish-British Billie Holiday against a remarkably up-to-date wall of sound reminiscent of Spector's, the girl groups and Motown's, yet sounding ever more relevant. The music producer was Mark Ronson, a British Jew who, in many ways, resembles the fantasized passion of artists we discussed regarding the White Negro ethos. While writing this book, he finished a very successful year in his collaboration on "Uptown Funk" (2014) with Bruno Mars, who conquered the charts all over the world. The Hawaiian pop star (with Latin-Jewish roots), managed to stir up a whole world of black language and movement, that sounded like updated Michael Jackson meets The Coasters.

Even if we deal with slightly different stories in different historical periods, these sounds would not have been possible without the dramatic change that had taken place in American popular music during the twentieth century, as I have described in this book. The flame continues to burn in a stylish, elitist, and humanistic encounter. Ronson's and Mars' single was a flashback of social and musical harmony in a world that deals with entirely different topics: terrorism, Islamic nuclear threat, overcrowding, and scarcity of resources. Even if it occasionally also experiences painful reminders of racist remnants that still resonate in the American experience.

In recent years, the counterculture victory seemed more palpable with a (half) black president in the White House, but in the late 1960s, the feeling reminded many of social dissolution. The murder of Martin Luther King Jr. in April 1968 marked various things for diverse people, including the disintegration of the Jewish-black political alliance. It seemed that after the political victory with the amendments to the constitution in 1964 to 1965, which dealt with equality of rights and the abolition of Southern segregation, no joint issues remained for the two minorities to fight for. However, after King's death, all that remained was to be cut off.

The African-American alternative to Martin Luther King Jr.'s liberal policy, in the form of black power and African-American separatism, has kept Jewish (and non-liberal) activists away from black issues. Disputes between Jewish and black leaders regarding affirmative action have reflected the gap in social and political perceptions.

The economic gaps and differences in the intensity of the motions between the two minorities were evident throughout the twentieth century, but from the 1970s, the controversies increased significantly. Jews reached their real golden age in the United States as anti-Semitism rates dropped drastically, and their economic position in the American middle class was firm and stable, almost without traditional discrimination across all economic niches. African Americans, on the other hand, even as they began to improve their situation following the achievements of the Civil Rights Movement, were still left behind.

In the entertainment industry in general and music in particular, it was evident that the 1970s entailed a different form of activity. These were the years when the power of the big corporations increased. The era when small labels could compete with the major record companies was a long distant memory. Most independent records labels have disappeared or been acquired and merged with the majors. Jews no longer stood out as small entrepreneurs they used to be on the fringes of the record industry, even if there were some who continued to act independently. In the major corporations, however, they sustained their active role, but the era of cooperation between minorities was gone since these definitions lost their original meaning.

During the 1980s, Jewish entrepreneur and music producer Rick Rubin, alongside the African-American Russell Simmons, succeeded in collaborating with black hip-hop artists and had great success with their label, Def Jam. They also had great success with the hip-hop band, the Beastie Boys, all three of whom are of New York Jewish origin. Later on, Lyor Cohen led the label and went on to a successful career in the music industry. The successful hip-hop singer Drake is a son of a black father and a Jewish mother; the veteran rock star of the late 1980s, Lenny Kravitz, is a son of a Jewish father and a black mother. Nevertheless, black-Jewish collaborations in popular music since the 1970s are part of another story.

The black-Jewish Alliance in politics and music was historic. The intersection where Jewish entrepreneurship and Jewish-black creativity met, and the long-standing struggle for social justice, enabled the American music revolution from 1890 to 1965, which was different from the original vision of the WASP elite. These Jewish entrepreneurs and artists waved the flag of another minority because popular culture and the mass industry required pragmatic survival. The musical revolution took place because it thumped against the racial tension at the heart of American music and pulse. It made America recognize its unflattering shadow. Through racial charisma, Jews could define their social identity and interference by embracing a culture with an image of a more urban, rooted, cosmopolitan, and universal America.

What remains of this revolution are timeless images: the trickster's mimicry and the replacement of Al Jolson; the Jewish ghetto soul and the black world in Gershwin's folk opera; the pride of Irving Mills in the African-American jazz duke he crowned as a king; The White Negro identity of Jerry Wexler, Doc Pomus, Jerry Leiber and Mike Stoller; the female empowerment led by Goffin and King through a host of African-American singers; Spector's wall of sound and the multidimensional harmonies of Burt Bacharach that penetrated to a mass audience through the use of black femininity; and the identity games of Dylan and Mike Bloomfield on Robert Johnson's blues highway.

Against the complex racial and ethnic realities of everyday life, the sounds – in the words of Pomus and Shuman written for The Drifters – provided magic moments. They showed how popular art in general, and songs in particular, might radiate the world's hidden beauty.

Bibliography

"The 500 Greatest Songs of All Time," *Rolling Stone* (February, 2004).
Alexander, Michael. *Jazz Age Jews* (New Jersey: Princeton University, 2001).
Althusser, Louis. *Lenin and Philosophy and Other Essays* (London: Monthly Review Press, 1971).
Altschuler, Glenn G. *All Shook Up: How Rock 'n' Roll Changed America* (Oxford: Oxford University Press, 2003).
Anderson, Benedict. *Imagined Communities* (New York: Verso, 1983).
Bacharach, Burt. *Anyone Who Had a Heart: My Life and Music* (New York: Atlantic Books, 2014).
Bailey, Beth. "Sexual Revolution," in *The Sixties: From Memory to History*, edited by David Farber, 235–262 (Chapel Hill: The University of North Carolina Press, 1994).
Banfield, Stephen. *Jerome Kern*, 1st ed. (New Haven: Yale University Press, 2006). Kindle.
Baron, Salo W. *Steeled by Adversity: Essays and Addresses on American Jewish Life* (New York: Jewish Publication Society, 1971).
Barthes, Roland. *Mythologies* (London: Farrar, Straus and Giroux, 1972).
Bayor, Ronald. *Neighbors in Conflict: The Irish, Germans, Jews, and Italians of New York City, 1929–1941* (Urbana: University of Illinois Press, 1988).
Bell, Daniel. *The End of Ideology* (Illinois: Free Press, 1959).
Benjamin, Walter. "The Work of Art in the age of mechanical reproduction," in *A Cultural Studies Reader*, edited by J. Munns, and G. Rajan, 88–96 (New York: Longman, 1995).
Berdyaev, Nicolas. *The Russian Revolution* (Michigan: Ann Arbor Paperbacks, 1961).
Bergreen, Laurence. *As Thousands Cheer: The Life of Irving Berlin* (New York: Da Capo Press, 1996). Kindle.
Bernstein, Leonard. *The Unanswered Question: Six Talks at Harvard* (Cambridge: Harvard University Press, 1976).
Berry, Chuck. *The Autobiography* (New York & London: Harmony Books, 1987).
Berry, David Carson. "Gambling with Chromaticism? Extra-Diatonic Melodic Expression in the Songs of Irving Berlin," *Theory and Practice* 26 (2001): 21–85.
Billig, Michael. *Rock 'n' Roll Jews* (London: Five Leaves Publications, 2001).
Birmingham, Stephen. *"The Rest of Us": The Rise of America's Eastern European Jews* (New York: Syracuse University Press, 1999).
Bloom, Alan. *The Closing of the American Mind* (New York: Simon & Schuster, 1989).
Branch, Taylor. "The Uncivil War," in *Bridges and Boundaries*, edited by Jack Salzman, Adina Back and Gretchen Sullivan Sorin, 50–69 (New York: George Braziller, 1993).
Brinkley, Douglas. "Bob Dylan's Late-Era, Old-Style American Individualism," *Rolling Stone* (14 May 2009).
Brodkin, Karen. *How Jews Became White Folks and What That Says About Race in America* (New Brunswick: Rutgers University Press, 1998).
Brown, Norman O. *Life Against Death: The Psychoanalytical Meaning of History* (New York: Vintage, 1959).
Bruck, Connie. *Master of the Game: Steve Ross and the Creation of Time Warner* (New York: Penguin Books, 1995).
Buhle, Paul. *From the Lower East Side to Hollywood: Jews in American Popular Culture* (New York: Verso, 2004).

Christgau, Robert. *Experience Music Project, Seattle, Washington* (16 April 2005).
Christopher, Robert C. *Crashing the Gates: The DE-WASPing of America's Power Elite* (London & New York: Simon & Schuster 1986).
Clark, S. "Response to Dick Hebdige," in *On Record*, 120–130 (New York: Routledge, 1990).
Cmiel, Kenneth. "The Politics of Civility," in *The Sixties: From Memory to History*, edited by David Farber, 263–290 (Chapel Hill: The University of North Carolina Press, 1994).
Cohn, Nik. *WopBopaLooBop LopBamBoom: Pop from the Beginning* (London: Paladin, 1969).
Cohn, Nik. "Phil Spector," in *The Rolling Stone's Illustrated History of Rock and Roll*, edited by De Curtis Anthony, and Henke James, 180–183 (New York: Rolling Stone Press, 1992).
Colburn, David R., and George E. Pozzetta. "Race, Ethnicity, and the Evolution of Political Legitimacy," in *The Sixties*, edited by David Farber, 119–148 (Chapel Hill: University of North Carolina Press, 1995).
Cooper, Ralph, and Steve Dougherty. *Amateur Night at the Apollo: Ralph Cooper Presents Five Decades of Great Entertainment* (New York: Harpercollins, 1990).
Cruse, Harold. *The Crisis of the Negro Intellectual* (New York: NYRB Classics; Main edition, 2005 [1967]).
Dannen, Fredric. *Hit Men: Power Brokers and Fast Money Inside the Music Business* (New York: Anchor, 1991).
Dawidowicz, Lucy. "From Past to Past: Jewish East Europe to Jewish East Side" *Conservative Judaism* 22, no. 2 (1968): 19–27.
Dehing, Jef. "Jung's Shadow," (2002), <www.cgjung-vereniging.nl/home/files/jef_dehing.pdf> (last accessed 23.10.2017).
Dickstein, Morris. *Gates of Eden: American Culture in the Sixties* (New York: Basic Books, 1977).
DiMaggio, Paul. "Cultural Entrepreneurship in Nineteenth-Century Boston. Part 2: The Classification and Framing of American Art," *Media Culture and Society* 4 (1982): 303–322.
Diner, Hasia. *In the Almost Promised Land: American Jews and Blacks, 1915–1935* (Westport, Conn.: Greenwood Press, 1977).
Dinnerstein, Leonard. *Antisemitism in America* (New York: Oxford University Press, 1994).
Dollinger, Marc. *Quest for Inclusion: Jews and Liberalism in Modern America* (New Jersey: Princeton University Press, 2000).
Douglas, Ann. *Terrible Honesty: Mongrel Manhattan in the 1920s* (New York: Farrar, Straus & Giroux, 1996).
Douglas, George. *Postwar America: 1948 and the Incubation of Our Times* (New York: Krieger Publishing Company, 1995).
Dylan, Bob. *Chronicles, Volume 1* (New York: Simon & Schuster 2004).
Ellington, Duke. *Music is My Mistress* (New York: Da Capo Press, 1976).
Erenberg, Lewis A. *Steppin' Out: New York Nightlife and the Transition of American Culture, 1890–1930* (Chicago: The University of Chicago Press, 1984).
Erikson, Erik H. *Identity: Youth and Crisis* (New York: W. W. Norton, 1968).
Farber, David. *The Age of Great Dreams: America in the 1960s* (New York: Hill and Wang, 1994).
Farren, Mick. "Remember Those Fabulous Sixties? An NME Consumer's Guide to Bob Dylan," *NME* (9 February 1974).
Feingold, Henry L. *A Time for Searching: Entering the Mainstream 1920–1945* (Baltimore: Johns Hopkins University Press, 1992).

Freedman, Murray. *What Went Wrong?: The Creation and The Collapse of the Black-Jewish Alliance* (New York: Free Press, 1994).
Frith, Simon. *The Sociology of Rock* (London: Constable, 1978).
Frith, Simon. *Sound Effects: Youth, Leisure and the Politics of Rock'n'Roll* (New York: Pantheon Books, 1981).
Frith, Simon. *Music for Pleasure: Essays in the Sociology of Pop* (London: Routledge, 1988).
Frith, Simon. *Performing Rites: On the Value of Popular Music* (New York: Oxford University Press, 1996).
Fromm, Erich. *Escape from Freedom* (New York: Open Road Media, 2013 [1941]).
Fromm, Erich. *Man for Himself: An Inquiry into the Psychology of Ethics* (New York: Open Road Media, 2013 [1947]).
Fuchs, Lawrence H. "Sources of Jewish Internationalism and Liberalism," in *The Jews: Social Patterns of an American Group*, edited by Marshall Sklare, 595–613 (New York: Free Press, 1958).
Furia, Philip. *The Poets of Tin Pan Alley: A History of America's Great Lyricists* (New York: Oxford University Press, 1992).
Gabler, Neal. *An Empire of Their Own: How the Jews Invented Hollywood* (New York: Crown Publishers, Inc., 1997).
Galbraith, J. K. *American Capitalism: The Concept of Countervailing Power* (New York: Martino Fine Books, 1952).
Galbraith, J. K. *The Affluent Society* (New York: Library of America, 1958).
Garofalo, Reebee. *Rockin' Out: Popular Music in the USA* (Boston: Prentice Hall, 1997).
Gershwin, George. "Making Music," in *The George Gershwin Reader (Readers on American Musicians)*, edited by Robert Wyatt and John Andrew Johnson, 1st ed. (Oxford: Oxford University Press, 2007).
Gershwin, George, "Rhapsody in a Catfish Row: Mr. Gershwin Tells the Origin and Scheme for His Music in That New Folk Opera Called Porgy and Bess," in *The George Gershwin Reader (Readers on American Musicians)*, edited by Robert Wyatt and John Andrew Johnson, 1st ed. (Oxford: Oxford University Press, 2007).
Giddins, Gary. *Riding on the Blue Note* (New York: Da Capo Press, 1980).
Gillett, Charlie. *Sound of The City: The Rise of Rock and Roll* (London: Da Capo Press, 1984).
Gitlin, Todd. *The Sixties: Years of Hope, Days of Rage* (New York: Bantam, 2013).
Glazer, Nathan. "The American Jew and the Attainment of Middle-Class Rank: Some trends and Explanations," in *The Jews: Social Patterns of an American Group*, edited by Marshall Sklare, 138–146 (Free Press, New York, 1958).
Glazer, Nathan, and Patrick Daniel Moynihan. *Beyond the Melting Pot: The Negroes, Puerto Ricans, Jews, Italians, and Irish of New York City* (New York: The MIT Press, 1970).
Glazer, Nathan. "Negroes and Jews: The New Challenge to Pluralism," in *Bridges and Boundaries*, edited by Jack Salzman, Adina Back and Gretchen Sullivan Sorin, 99–107 (New York: George Braziller, 1993).
Goldberg, Barry. *Two Jews Blues* (np: St. Paul Books; 2012). Kindle.
Goldberg, Isaac. *George Gershwin: A Study in American Music* (New York: Ungar, 1958).
Goodman, Fred. *The Mansion on the Hill: Dylan, Young, Geffen, Springsteen, and the Head-On Collision of Rock and Commerce* (New York: Vintage, 1997).
Goren, Arthur Aryeh. "Freedom and its Limitations: The Jewish Immigrant Experience," *Forum* 42/43 (1981): 83–99.

Gottlieb, Jack. *Funny, It Doesn't Sound Jewish: How Yiddish Songs and Synagogue Melodies Influenced Tin Pan Alley* (New York: University of New York Press, 2004).
Gramsci, Antonio. *Selections from the Prison Notebooks* (London: International Publishers Co, [1971], 1989).
Grossberg, Lawrence. "Another Boring Day in Paradise: Rock and Roll and the Empowerment of everyday life" *Popular Music* 4 (1984): 225–258.
Grossberg, Lawrence. *We Gotta Get Out of This Place* (New York: Routledge, 1992).
Grossberg, Lawrence. "The Political Status of Youth and Youth Culture," in *Adolescents and Their Music: If It's Too Loud, You're Too Old*, edited by S. Jonathon, 25–46 (Boston: Epstein, 1994).
Grundy, Stuart, and John Tobler. *The Record Producers* (London: St. Martins Pr., 1982).
Guralnick, Peter. *Sweet Soul Music: Rhythm and Blues and the Southern Dream of Freedom* (New York & Boston: Back Bay Books, 1986).
Gurock, Jeffrey. *When Harlem was Jewish, 1870–1930* (New York: Columbia University Press, 1979).
Hall, Stuart, and Tony Jefferson, eds. *Resistance Through Rituals: Youth Subcultures in Postwar Britain* (Birmingham: Hutchinson, 1976).
Hall, Stuart. "Culture, the Media and the 'Ideological Effect,'" in *Mass Communication and Society*, edited by J. Curran, M. Gurevitch and J. Wollacott, 315–348 (London: Edward Arnold, 1977).
Hall, Stuart. "Two Paradigms," in *A Cultural Studies Reader*, edited by J. Munns, and G. Rajan, 194–200 (New York: Longman, 1995).
Hardcastle, Cleothus. "The Unearthing of Howard Tate," *Rock's Backpages* (April 2001).
Harrington, Michael. *The Other America: Poverty in the United State* (New York: Penguin Books, 1962).
Hebdige, Dick. *Subculture: The Meaning of Style* (London: Routledge, 1979).
Heinze, Andrew. *Adapting to Abundance* (New York: Columbia University Press, 1992).
Hobsbawm, Eric J. *Nations and Nationalism since 1780: Programme, Myth, Reality* (Cambridge: Cambridge University Press, 1992).
Hobsbawm, Eric J., and Terence Ranger. *The Invention of Tradition* (Cambridge: Cambridge University Press, 1992).
Hofstadter, Richard. *The Paranoid style in American Politics and other Essays* (Cambridge: Harvard University Press, 1962).
Hoggart, Richard. *The Uses of Literacy* (London: Penguin, 1957).
Hollinger, David A. *Science, Jews, and Secular Culture* (New Jersey: Princeton University Press, 1996).
Holzman, Jac, and Gavan Daws. *Follow the Music: The Life and High Times of Elektra Records in the Great Years of American Pop Culture* (Santa Monica, CA: FirstMedia Books, 2000).
Hoskyns, Barney. "Back to the Brilliance of Bacharach," *The Times* (22 August 1990).
Hoskyns, Barney. "Bert Berns," *Mojo* (March 1998).
Hoskyns, Barney. "Phil Spector's Ghosts: The Spooky World of the Greatest Producer in Pop Music," *Slate* (February 2003).
Howe, Irving. *World of Our Fathers* (New York: Simon & Schuster, 1976).
Hunt, Lynn, ed. *The New Cultural History: Essays* (Berkeley: University of California Press, 1989).

Johnpoll, Bernard K. *Pacifist's Progress: Norman Thomas and the Decline of Socialism* (Chicago: Quadrangle Books 1970).

Jung, Carl Gustav, Gerhard Adler and R. F.C. Hull, eds. *The Archetypes and The Collective Unconscious (Collected Works of C.G. Jung)*, Vol. 9, Part 1, 2nd ed. (New Jersey: Princeton University Press, 1968).

Kaiser, Charles. *1968 in America: Music, Politics, Chaos, Counterculture, and the Shaping of a Generation* (New York: Grove Press, 2018).

Kaplan, Mordecai M. *Judaism as a Civilization: Toward the Reconstruction of America – Jewish Life* (New York: Reconstructionist Press, 1956).

Katorza, Ari. "Walls of Sound: Leiber and Stoller, Phil Spector, the Black-Jewish Alliance, and the 'Enlarging' of America," in *Mazal Tov, Amigos: Jews and Popular Music in the Americas*, edited by Amalia Ran and Moshe Morad, 78–95 (Leiden: Brill Academic Press, 2016).

Katorza, Ari. *Come Together: Rock 'n' Roll, Liberalism, Mass Bohemianism and the Sixties* (Tel Aviv: K-Academics Publishing, 2019).

Katznelson, Ira. "Between Separation and Disappearance: Jews on the Margins of American Liberalism," in *Paths of Emancipation*, edited by Pierre Birenbaum and Ira Katznelson, 157–205 (New Jersey: Princeton University Press 1995).

Kaufmann, Eric P. *The Rise and Fall of White-Anglo America* (Cambridge: Harvard University Press, 2002).

Kazin, Alfred. "The Jew as Modern Writer," in *The Ghetto and Beyond; Essays on Jewish Life in America*, edited by Peter Rose (New York: Random House, 1969).

Kellner, David. *Television and the Crisis of Democracy* (Oxford: Westview Press, 1990).

Keniston, Kenneth. *Young Radicals: Notes on Committed Youth* (New York: Harvest, 1968).

Kennedy, Rick, and Randy McNutt. *Little Labels – Big Sound: Small Record Companies and the Rise of American Music* (Indiana: Indiana University Press, 1999).

King, Carole. *A Natural Woman: A Memoir* (New York: Grand Central Publishing, 2012).

King, Tom. *The Operator: David Geffen Builds, Buys, and Sells the New Hollywood* (New York: Broadway Books, 2000).

Kingston, Paul W. *The Classless Society* (Stanford: Stanford University Press, 2000).

Konvitz, Milton R. "Judaism and the Pursuit of Happiness," *The Menorah Journal* 49 (1962): 127–128

Kun, Josh. "'If I Embarrass You, Tell Your Friends': The Musical Comedy of Bell Barth and Pearl Williams," in *The Song is Not the Same: Jews and American Popular Music*, edited by Bruce Zuckerman, Josh Kun and Lisa Ansell (Indiana: Purdue University Press, 2010).

Kuznets, Simon. "Economic Structure and Life of the Jews," in *The Jews: Their History, Culture, and Religion*, edited by Louis Finkelstein, 2nd ed. (Philadelphia: Jewish Publication Society of America, 1966).

LaChapelle, Peter. "Dances Partake of the Racial Characteristics of the People Who Dance Them: Nordicism, Anti-semitism and Henry Ford's Old-Time Music and Dance Revival," in *The Song is Not the Same: Jews and American Popular Music*, edited by Bruce Zuckerman, Josh Kun and Lisa Ansell, 29–70 (Indiana: Purdue University Press, 2010).

Lasch, Christopher. *Culture of Narcissism* (New York: W. W. Norton & Company, 1979).

Leary, Timothy. *The Psychedelic Experience: A Manual Based on the Tibetan Book of the Dead* (Boston: Progressive Press, 1964).

Lederhendler, Eli. "American Jews, American Capitalism, and the Politics of History," in *Text and Context: Essays in Modern Jewish History and Historiography in Honor of Ismor Schorsch*, edited by Eli Lederhendler and Jack Wertheimer, 504–546 (New York: Jewish Theological Press, 2005).

Lederhendler, Eli. *Jewish Immigrants and American Capitalism, 1880–1920: From Caste to Class* (Cambridge: Cambridge University Press, 2009).

Leiber, Jerry, and Mike Stoller with David Ritz. *Hound Dog: The Leiber and Stoller Autobiography* (New York: Simon & Schuster, 2009). Kindle.

Levine, Lawrence M. *Highbrow/Lowbrow* (Cambridge: Harvard University Press, 1988).

Lhamon Jr., W.T. *Raising Cain: Blackface Performance from Jim Crow to Hip-Hop* (London: Harvard University Press, 1998).

Liebman, Arthur. *Jews and the Left* (New York: Wiley, 1979).

Lisheron, Mark. "Rhythm and Jews," *Common Quest: The Magazine of Black Jewish Relations* 2 (Summer 1997): 20–33.

Lisle, Andria. "Bob Dylan in Mississippi," *The Oxford American* (Summer 1999).

Lornell, Kip. *Exploring American Folk Music: Ethnic, Grassroots, and Regional Traditions in the United States*, 3rd ed. (Jackson: University Press of Mississippi, 2012).

Lott, Eric. *Love & Theft: Blackface Minstrelsy and the American Working Class* (New York & Oxford: Oxford University Press, 1993).

Magee, Jeffrey. *Irving Berlin's American Musical Theater* (New York, Oxford University Press, 2012).

Mahar, William J. *Behind the Burnt Cork Mask: Early Blackface Minstrelsy and Antebellum American Popular Culture* (Illinois: University of Illinois Press, 1999).

Mailer, Norman. *The White Negro: Superficial Reflections on the Hipster* (San Francisco: City Lights Books, 1970 [1957]).

Marcus, Greil. "How the other half lives: The Best of Girl Group Rock," *Let It Rock* (May 1974).

Marcus, Greil. "The Girl Groups," in *The Rolling Stone's Illustrated History of Rock and Roll*, edited by De Curtis Anthony, and Henke James, 189–191 (New York: Rolling Stone Press, 1992).

Marcus, Greil. "The Beatles", in *The Rolling Stone's Illustrated History of Rock and Roll*, edited by De Curtis Anthony, and Henke James, 214 (New York: Rolling Stone Press, 1992).

Marcus, Greil. *Mystery Train: Images of America in Rock 'n' Roll Music*, 5th ed. (New York: Plume, 2008).

Marsh, Dave. *The Heart of Rock & Soul: The 1001 Greatest Singles Ever Made* (New York: Da Capo Press, 1989).

Matuso, J. A. *The Unraveling of America* (New York: Harper and Row, 1984).

May, Lary. *Screening Out the Past: The Birth of Mass Culture and The Motion Picture Industry* (Chicago and New York: The University Of Chicago Press, 1980).

McDougal, Dennis. *The Last Mogul: Lew Wasserman, MCA, and the Hidden History of Hollywood* (New York: Da Capo Press, 1998).

McGirr, Lisa. *Suburban Warriors: The Origins of the New American Right* (New Jersey: Princeton University Press, 2002).

Melnick, Jeffrey. *A Right to Sing the Blues: African Americans, Jews and American Popular Song* (Cambridge, Massachusetts: Harvard University Press, 1999).

Millard, Andre. *America on Record: A History of Recorded Sound*, 2nd ed. (Cambridge: Cambridge University Press, 2005).
Miller, Douglas T., and Marion Nowak. *The Fifties: The Way We Really Were* (Garden City, N.Y.: Doubleday & Co., Inc., 1977).
Moore, MacDonald Smith. *Yankee Blues: Musical Culture and American Identity* (Bloomington: Indiana University Press, 1985).
Morgan, Edward. *The Sixties Experience: Hard Lessons about Modern America* (Philadelphia: Temple University Press, 1991).
Nolan, Tom. "Neil Sedaka: Second Stairway to Heaven," *Rolling Stone* (4 December 1975).
Osgerby, Bill. *Youth in Britain since 1945* (London: Wiley, 1995).
Palmer, Robert. "James Brown," in *The Rolling Stone's Illustrated History of Rock and Roll*, edited by De Curtis Anthony and Henke James, 170–193 (New York: Rolling Stone Press, 1992).
Palmer, Robert. *Deep Blues: A Musical and Cultural History, From the Mississippi Delta to Chicago South Side to The World* (New York: Penguin Books, 1982).
Palty, Arnon. *Connecting Points in Jazz Dialects: The Metamorphic Process* (Kiryat Ono Academic College, 2017).
Park, Robert A. *Race and Culture* (Glencoe: The Free Press, 1950).
Pedler, Dominic. *The Songwriting Secrets of the Beatles* (London: Omnibus, 2003).
Peiss, Kathy. *Cheap Amusements: Working Women and Leisure in Turn-of-the-Century New York* (Philadelphia: Temple University Press, 1986).
Peterson, Richard. "Why 1955? Explaining the advent of Rock Music," *Popular Music* 9 (1990): 97–116.
Pichaske, David. *A Generation in Motion: Popular Music and Culture in the Sixties* (Granite Falls, MN: Ellis Press, 1979).
Podhoretz, Norman. "My Negro Problem – And Ours," in *Black and Jews: Alliances and Arguments*, edited by Paul Berman, 77–96 (New York, Delacorte Press, 1993; Reprinted from *Commentary*, 1963).
Pollack, Howard. *George Gershwin: His Life and Work* (Los Angeles: University of California Press, 2007).
Pollock, Bruce. *In Their Own Words* (New York: Collier, 1975).
Raab, Earl. *What Do We Really Know About Antisemitism and What We Want to Know?* (New York: American Jewish Committee, 1989).
Reising, Russell, ed. *Every Sound There Is: The Beatles' Revolver and the Transformation of Rock and Roll* (London: Routledge, 2002).
Rischin, Moses. *The Promised City: New York Jews, 1870–1914* (Cambridge: Harvard University Press, 1970).
Rockaway, Robert A. *But He Was Good to His Mother: The Lives and Crimes of Jewish Gangsters* (New York: Gefen Publishing House, 1993).
Roediger, David R. *The Wages of Whiteness: Race and the Making of the American Working Class* (New York: Verso, 1991).
Roediger, David R. *Working Towards Whiteness: How America's Immigrants Became White* (New York: Basic Books, 2005).
Rogin, Michael. *Blackface, White Noise: Jewish Immigrants in the Hollywood Melting Pot* (Berkeley: University of California Press, 1998).

Rothman, Stanley, and Simon Lichter. *Roots of Radicalism: Jews, Christians, and the Left* (New York: Transaction Publishers, 1985).
Rotundo, E. Anthony. "Jews and Rock and Roll: A Study in Cultural Contrast," *American Jewish History* 72.1 (1982): 82–107.
Savage, Jon. "Dylan is 60," *Mojo* (June 2001).
Saxton, Alexander. *The Rise and Fall of the White Republic: Class Politics and Mass Culture in Nineteenth Century America* (New York: Verso, 1990).
Schiff, David. *Gershwin: Rhapsody in Blue* (Cambridge: Cambridge University Press, 1997).
Schlesinger, Arthur M. *The Vital Center: The Politics of Freedom* (New York: Transaction Publishers, 1947).
Schrag, Peter. *The Decline of the WASP* (New York: Simon and Schuster, Inc., 1973).
Schuller, Gunther. *Early Jazz: Its Roots and Musical Development* (New York: Oxford University Press, 1986)
Schulman, Bruce J. *Lyndon B. Johnson and American Liberalism* (Boston: Bedford/St. Martin's, 2007).
Schulman, H. B. *The Seventies: The Great Shift in American Culture, Society and Politics* (New York: Da Capo Press, 2001).
Scorsese, Martin. *No Direction Home* (2005).
Shaw, Greg. "Barry Mann: Rock & Roll Survivor," *Phonograph Record* (July 1975).
Shaw, Greg. "The Brill Building Pop," in *The Rolling Stone's Illustrated History of Rock and Roll*, edited by De Curtis Anthony, and Henke James, 143–152 (New York: Rolling Stone Press, 1992).
Sklare, Marshall. *Conservative Judaism: An American Religious Movement* (New York: Schocken Books Inc., 1955).
Sklare, Marshall, ed. *The Jews: Social Patterns of an American Group* (Free Press, New York, 1958).
Sklare, Marshall. *Jewish Identity on the Suburban Frontier: A Study of Group Survival in the Open Society* (Chicago: University of Chicago Press, 1979).
Sowell, Thomas. *Ethnic America: A History* (New York, Basic Books, 1981).
Staub, Michael. *Torn at the Roots: The Crisis of Jewish Liberalism in Postwar America* (New York: Columbia University Press, 2004).
Staunton, Terry. "We're In Love with This Guy: Hal David," *Music365.com* (27 May 2000).
Stearns, Marshall. *The Story of Jazz* (London: Oxford University Press, 1970).
Steigerwald, David. *The Sixties and the End of Modern America* (New York: St. Martin's Press, 1995).
Steinberg, Stephen. *The Ethnic Myth: Race, Ethnicity, and Class in America* (New York: Beacon Press, 2001).
Storm, Yale. *The Book of Klezmer: The History, the Music, the Folklore* (Chicago: Chicago Review Press, 2002).
Stratton, Jon. *Jews, Race and Popular Music* (Surrey: Ashgate, 2009).
Suisman, David. *Selling Sounds: The Commercial Revolution in American Music* (Cambridge, MA: Harvard University Press, 2012). Kindle.
Svonkin, Stuart. *Jews against Prejudice* (New York: Columbia University Press, 1999).
Teachout, Terry. *Duke: A Life of Duke Ellington* (New York: Gotham Books, 2013). Kindle.

The Charleston News and Courier. "George Gershwin Arrives to Plan Opera on Porgy," in *The George Gershwin Reader (Readers on American Musicians)*, edited by Robert Wyatt and John Andrew Johnson, 1st ed. (Oxford: Oxford University Press, 2007).

Thompson, Dave. *Wall of Pain: The Biography of Phil Spector* (New York: Sanctuary Publishing, Ltd., 2003).

Thompson, E. P. *The Making of the English Working Class* (London: Penguin, 1963).

Wade, Dorothy, and Justine Picardie. *Music Man: Ahmet Arthgun, Atlantic Records, and the Triumph of Rock 'n' Roll* (New York: W. W. Norton & Co. Inc., 1990).

Waldo, Terry. *This is Ragtime* (New York: E. P. Dutton, 1976).

Webb, Jimmy. *Tunesmith* (New York: Hachette Books, 2013).

Weber, William. *Music and the Middle Class: The Social Structure of Concert Life in London, Paris and Vienna* (London: Routledge, 1975).

Wenger, Beth S. *New York Jews and the Great Depression: Uncertain Promise* (New Haven: Yale University Press, 1999).

Werner, Craig. *A Change is Gonna Come: Music, Race and the Soul of America* (New York: Plume, 1998).

Wexler, Jerry, and David Ritz. *Rhythm and the Blues: A Life in American Music* (New York: Alfred Knopf, 1993).

Whitcomb, Ian T. *After the Ball – Pop Music from Rag to Rock* (New York, Allen Lane/Penguin, 1972).

White, Charles. *The Life and Times of Little Richard* (New York: Omnibus Press, 1984).

White, Hayden. *The Content of the Form* (Baltimore: John Hopkins University Press, 1973).

Whitfield, Stephen J. *In Search of An American Jewish Culture* (London: Brandeis, 2001).

Whyte, William H. *The Organization Man* (New York: Simon & Schuster, 1956).

Williams, Raymond. *Culture and Society, 1750–1880* (London: Columbia University Press, 1983 [1958]).

Witmark, Isidore, and Issac Goldberg. *From Ragtime to Swingtime* (New York: Lee Furman, 1939).

Wolfe, Tom. *The Electric Kool-Aid Acid Test* (New York: Farrar, Straus and Giroux, 2008 [1965]).

Wolin, Richard. *The Wind from the East: French Intellectuals, the Cultural Revolution, and the Legacy of the 1960s* (New Jersey: Princeton University Press, 2010).

Wolkin, Jan Mark, and Bill Keenom. *Michael Bloomfield – If You Love These Blues: An Oral History* (np: Backbeat Books, 2015). Kindle.

Wood, Ean. *George Gershwin: His Life and Music* (New York: Sanctuary Publishing, 1999). Kindle.

Wyatt, Robert, and John Andrew Johnson, eds. *The George Gershwin Reader (Readers on American Musicians)*, 1st ed. (Oxford: Oxford University Press, 2007).

Yetnikoff, Walter, and David Ritz. *Howling at the Moon: The Odyssey of a Monstrous Music Mogul in an Age of Excess* (New York: Abacus, 2003).

Zollo, Paul. "Burt Bacharach and Hal David," *Songwriters on Songwriting* (Cincinnati: Da Capo Press, 2003).

Zollo, Paul. "Carole King," *Songwriters on Songwriting* (Cincinnati: Da Capo Press, 2003).

Zuckerman, Bruce, Josh Kun and Lisa Ansell, eds. *The Song Is Not the Same: Jews and American Popular* (Indiana: Purdue University Press, 2010).

Index

A Hard Rain's A-Gonna Fall 210
A House Is Not a Home 198
Aaron Copland 44, 76, 89, 173
Abbie Hoffman 142
Aberbach brothers 157
Abraham Goldfaden 85
Abraham Lincoln 29
Afro-Americans 1, 11, 46 f., 49, 53 f., 56, 66, 71, 86, 89
Ahmet Ertegun 10, 119 f., 151, 160
Al Bell 232
Al Jolson 1, 12, 16, 21, 23, 26–28, 31 f., 39, 48, 70, 73, 86 f., 94, 207, 225, 255
Al Kooper 211, 215, 217, 219
Al Nevins 10, 167
Allen Ginsberg 206 f.
Albert Grossman 10, 12, 19, 120, 123–125, 201, 205, 209, 215, 239
Aldon Music 10, 167, 171, 179, 193
Alexander's Ragtime Band 31, 70, 236
Alfie 198
All Along the Watchtower 219
All the Things You Are 82
Altruistic approach 14
American culture 4, 6, 8 f., 13–15, 20, 22, 24 f., 33 f., 37 f., 40 f., 43, 45, 55 f., 58, 61, 71, 75, 78, 92, 141, 146, 153, 155, 236, 240, 250, 252
An American in Paris 87, 90
Andrew Jackson 23
Andrew Loog Oldham 192
Annales school 241
Anne Caldwell 79
anti-Semitism 12, 14, 17, 33, 41, 55, 58, 130, 254
Anton Rubinstein. 84
Antonio Gramsci 243
Anyone Who Had a Heart 156, 160, 171, 182, 194, 196 f.
Aretha Franklin 82, 156, 178, 181, 233
Art Rupe 10, 119, 226, 230 f.
Arthur Rimbaud 207
Arthur Taylor 125

Artie Mogul 124
Artie Shaw 97, 123, 238
ASCAP 78, 116, 149, 223
Atlantic Records 8, 10, 104, 119 f., 151, 163, 165, 167, 178, 228 f., 232 f., 235

B.B. King 213, 215
Baby, I Love You 67, 151, 165, 175
Baby It's You 175, 196
BANG 163, 165
Barbara Streisand 126
Barney Biggard 108
Barry Mann 167 f., 188
Be My Baby 175 f., 190
Beat poets 134, 141, 143, 148, 171, 206, 216, 220
Ben Bloom 85
Ben E. King 128, 161, 163, 174, 186 f.
Benny Goodman 2, 91, 97, 111, 123, 238
Bert Berns 152, 163–165
Big Bands 10, 100, 147, 150
"Big Joe" Turner 151
Big Mama Thornton 155
Bill Clinton 82, 252
Bill Haley & His Comets 118, 149
Billboard 116, 119, 123, 150 f., 157, 169, 185, 190, 217
Billy Joel 126, 240
Bing Crosby 111, 115, 228
Birdland 225 f.
Birth of a Nation 28
Black-Jewish alliance 6, 13–16, 18, 20, 48, 128, 135 f., 138, 140, 153, 222, 237 f.
blackface minstrelsy 2, 12, 16, 19, 21, 23–26, 29, 33, 56, 60, 94, 147, 206
blacks 3, 12 f., 15 f., 18, 22–24, 28 f., 32, 34 f., 40, 45–47, 51, 58, 65 f., 93, 97, 100, 104, 108, 113, 123, 128–130, 132, 134 f., 137, 139 f., 149, 151, 155, 165, 175, 196, 204, 212, 218, 221–223, 225, 232 f., 236–239, 266
Blowin' in the Wind 209 f., 219

Index

blues 1, 4, 10, 13f., 19, 22, 41, 43, 47–51, 53, 58f., 69f., 72f., 79, 81f., 89f., 95, 98–100, 103–105, 108–111, 116–119, 121f., 124, 147–152, 154–161, 163, 165, 168f., 172, 174–178, 186, 191, 196f., 199, 201f., 206, 208f., 211–221, 223, 225, 229f., 232–236, 239, 250, 255
BMG 119
BMI 116, 123f., 149, 166, 230
Bob Dylan 2, 8, 10–12, 19, 120, 123f., 163, 179, 193, 201, 206, 208–211, 217, 239
Bob Gibson 203, 205
Bobby Gregg 211
Booker T. & the MG's 232
Breaking Up Is Hard to Do 176
Brian Wilson 183
Brill Building publishing industry 18f.
British cultural studies. 20, 240
Broadway musicals 1, 12, 16f., 57, 74, 120, 170
Bruce Springsteen 126f., 203
Bruno Mars 158, 253
Bubber Miley 105
Bud Powell 92
Buddy Guy 214
burlesque 21, 27, 64, 67, 75, 79–81
Burt Bacharach 12, 18, 59, 72, 90, 97, 156, 160, 168, 171, 177, 182f., 193f., 196f., 199, 240, 255
Butterfield 214–216, 218f.

Can't Help Lovin' Dat Man 81
Cantorial music 49
Caravan 109
Carole King 12, 18, 149, 160, 166f., 169f., 172, 175, 177f., 188, 231, 240
Casablanca Records 125
CBS Records 8, 113, 120f., 227
Center for Contemporary Cultural Studies 20
Charles Hambitzer 84
Charles Ives 44, 88
Charles K. Harris 65f.
Charleston 57, 73, 86, 93f., 237
Charlie Parker 13, 92, 155
Chick Webb 91
Chess Records 119, 159, 213, 234
Chopin 88, 198

Chuck Berry 156f., 159, 167, 226, 229f.
civil rights amendments 12, 142, 159, 198
Civil Rights Movement 2f., 130, 141, 168, 210f., 254
Clive Davis 11, 120f., 124, 209, 218, 227
Clorindy, or The Origin of the Cake Walk 102, 223
Clyde McPhatter 151
Cole Porter 9, 50, 66, 72f., 76f.
Colonel Tom Parker 157
Columbia 15, 35–37, 44, 47, 55, 87, 115–121, 124, 143, 179, 207–209, 215, 218f., 227, 240
Columbia Records 114, 178, 209, 220, 227
Communist Left 7
Communist Party 130, 138, 240
Concerto in F 87, 90, 237
corporations 1, 8, 11, 36, 114f., 120, 131, 138, 254
cosmopolitan 1, 5, 16, 41, 54, 59, 71, 75, 145, 153f., 255
Cotton Club 106–108, 110f., 224
Count Basie 155
country music 10, 116, 147, 149, 202, 232
Creedence Clearwater Revival 180
Creole Rhapsody 110
Crosby Stills and Nash 126, 180
Crying in the Rain 174, 176
Cultural Revolution 241
culturalism 240
Cynthia Weil 167f., 188

Da Doo Ron Ron 190
Daniel Bell 133, 138
Dave Van Ronk 201, 203, 205
David Geffen 12, 119, 120, 121, 122, 123f, 124f, 125, 126, 127
David Sarnoff 115
Debussy 87–89, 95, 187, 194
Decca 115, 118f.
Democratic Party 24f., 31, 46, 182
Dimension Records 173, 185, 231
Dionne Warwick 59, 168, 193, 196
Do Wah Diddy Diddy 175
Doc Pomus 158, 160, 161, 164, 186, 255
Don Kirshner 10, 167, 231
doo-wop 10, 160f., 176, 191, 219

Dorothy Fields   106
Dr. Martin Luther King Jr   18
DuBose Heyward   93
Duke Ellington   12f., 17, 32, 44, 73, 90f., 95f., 98–101, 105–107, 109–111, 176, 191, 237f.
Dvořák   44, 70, 81f., 102
D.W. Griffith   28, 42

E.P. Thompson   240
Earl Warren   136
East St. Louis Toodle-Oo   105
Eddie Cantor   8, 31, 225
Edison Records   114
Edna Ferber   79, 81
Edward Elgar   81
Elektra Records   8, 11, 123f., 204, 214, 220
Eli Lederhendler   34f., 37f., 40, 137
Ellie Greenwich   167f., 188
Elliot Roberts   124f, 180
Elvis Presley   2, 11, 100, 118, 147, 152, 156f., 159, 161, 166, 169f., 186, 195
Era/Dore Records   185
Erich Fromm   135f.
Erik Erikson   135, 142
Ethel Merman   91
Eubie Blake   85, 101, 237
European   1, 6–9, 17, 22, 25, 30f., 33f., 36f., 39, 42–44, 46, 48f., 53, 56, 59f., 62, 70, 76, 78, 85–87, 90, 97, 99, 114, 118, 122, 125, 128, 130, 134f., 137, 144, 147, 152f., 159–161, 164, 168–170, 174, 179, 188, 191, 225, 236
Existentialism   142

Fanny Brice   8, 225, 237
film industry   1, 28, 34, 42f., 47, 134, 179
Fletcher Henderson   90f., 102–104, 109, 111, 238
Florenz Ziegfeld   28, 107
folk   7, 10–12, 14, 19, 41, 44, 48, 53, 57, 59, 76, 92f., 95f., 108, 120, 123–125, 129, 148, 154, 163, 180, 200–211, 213, 215f., 218–220, 255
folk-jazz opera   2
folk singers   178, 201
Folkways Records   11, 201

Fordism   131
Frank Saddler   79
Frank Sinatra   115, 147, 164, 195, 220
Franz Liszt   89
Freddie Beinstock   157
Freddie Keppard   117

Gennet   117
George Gershwin   1f., 12, 17, 31f., 44, 49, 62, 66, 74–77, 82f., 85, 87, 89, 92, 94–96, 152, 237
George Goldner   162, 165, 188, 226
George Harrison   184, 199
George Jessel   21, 31
George Martin   184, 198
Gerry Goffin   160, 167, 171, 188, 231
Get Back   184, 199
Giacomo Puccini.   81
Gilbert and Sullivan   76f., 154, 157
Girl Crazy   91
Girl Groups   18, 168, 170
Goddard Lieberson   120
gospel   4, 10, 48, 82, 102, 116, 128, 149, 151, 158, 161f., 164, 169, 177–179, 187, 193, 202, 207f., 212f., 217, 219, 225, 235
Gotham-Attucks Music   66
Gravenites   214
Great Society   251f.
Guantanamera   163, 191
Guns N' Roses   126
Gunther Schuller   99, 105, 109f.
Gus Kahn   75
Gustav Mahler   88

Hal David   59, 160, 168, 171, 193–195, 197–199, 240
Hannah Arendt   135, 213
Harlem   40, 46f., 73, 84, 93, 101, 103, 106f., 110f., 117f., 122, 148, 159, 187, 224
Harlem Hit Parade   154
Harold Arlen   1, 32, 48, 50, 75, 97, 152, 237
Harold Cruse   96, 222
Harold Leventhal   124, 209
Harry Gennett   117
Harry Von Tilzer   26, 64f.
Harvey (Goldstein) Brooks   124, 211

He Hit Me (And It Felt Like A Kiss) 168
hegemonic 4–6, 13, 20, 145, 240, 249
hegemony 3, 5f., 14, 20, 43, 46, 54, 145, 243f., 249–252
Henry Ford 15, 55, 131
Herb Alpert 169, 174, 185
Herbert Marcuse 141
He's Sure the Boy I Love 189
Highway 61 Revisited 211f.
hippies 3, 144, 199, 218, 249
Hoagy Carmichael 50, 103
Hollywood 1, 9, 14f., 21, 29, 31f., 38, 42, 45, 48, 52–57, 64, 67, 73, 77, 79, 82f., 97, 102, 107f., 114f., 119, 121f., 134, 149, 154f., 157, 184, 189, 222, 224, 231, 251
Hound Dog 58, 147, 152, 154–158, 167, 186
Howie Greenfield 167, 174
Hy Weiss 221, 225, 228f.

I Got Rhythm 87, 91, 237
I Want to Hold Your Hand 177, 191
Igor Stravinsky 88
I'll Build a Stairway to Paradise 87
independent record labels 1, 7, 203, 254
Inside Llewyn Davis 201
Ira Gershwin 8, 73, 75, 84, 91, 94, 147
Irving Berlin 1, 8, 12, 17, 31f., 39, 48, 50, 52, 61–64, 66–69, 72, 74f., 84, 87, 152, 154, 193, 195, 236
Irving Caesar 86
Irving Mills 12, 17, 73, 98, 100, 103, 107, 255
Isidore Witmark 9, 34, 67, 222f.

Jac Holzman 11, 120, 123–125, 204
Jack Gottlieb 7, 49, 76, 223, 237f.
Jack Kerouac 207
Jackie Robin 36, 39
Jacksonian era 23
Jailhouse Rock 100, 157
James Brown 10, 226, 234, 236
James P. Johnson 86, 101, 103, 154, 237
James Reese Europe 86
James Taylor 126, 180, 181
James Weldon Johnson 222f.
Janis Joplin 123, 164f., 218f.

jazz 2, 4, 10, 12–14, 17–19, 21f., 28, 31f., 44f., 48, 51f., 57, 62, 70, 73, 75–77, 79, 81f., 84, 86–95, 97–103, 105–110, 114, 117f., 147, 150–152, 155f., 171, 176f., 180, 183f., 193f., 196–198, 203, 205, 213, 222, 224–226, 237f., 248, 253, 255
jazz operas 1
Jeff Barry 167f., 188
Jeffry Katz 125
Jelly Roll Morton 109, 117
Jerome H. Remick and Company 66
Jerome Kern 2, 8, 12, 17, 28, 32, 50, 66, 74–77, 82, 93, 108, 152, 197, 237
Jerry Kasenetz 125
Jerry Leiber and Mike Stoller 2, 8, 18, 58, 100, 128, 147, 152, 154, 158, 165, 167, 186, 255
Jerry Ragovoy 152, 164, 175
Jerry Wexler 2, 10, 12, 59, 104, 119–126, 150–152, 156, 158, 160, 163, 165, 178, 186, 218, 221, 228f., 239, 255
Jewish activists 7, 130, 136
Jewish immigration 12, 17, 33f., 37–39, 54
Jewish modes 49, 86
Jewish music 7, 17, 49, 76, 85f., 119, 124f., 205, 213, 237f.
Jimmy McHugh 106
Jimmy Page 164
Jimmy Webb 173, 192
Joan Baez 203–205, 207, 210
Joey Levine 125
John Coltrane 2
John Hammond 44, 104, 111, 124, 207–209
John Howard 92
John Lennon 90, 175, 184, 199
Johnson 3, 87, 89, 92, 94–96, 174, 177, 193, 198, 208, 219, 237, 251f.
Joni Mitchell 126, 180
Joseph Rumshinsky 85
Joseph Stern 9, 67f.
Josh White 202, 204
Juan Tizol 107, 109
Jules Stein 45, 119
Julius Witmark 26, 67
justice 1f., 7, 37, 55, 57, 75, 93, 136, 139, 210f., 214, 242

K.C. Lovin'   155
Kansas City   155, 175, 193
Karl Marx   242
Keep Your Hands Off My Baby   175
Kennedy   2f., 117, 128, 130, 140f., 177, 182, 193, 202, 251
Kenneth Keniston   142
Keynesianism   131
King Oliver   102, 117, 224
King Records   10, 119, 151, 226, 234, 236
Kirshner   167, 171, 173f., 179f., 185–187
KKK   32
Kurt Lewin   135

L.B. Johnson   12, 214, 219
La La-Lucille!   86
Latin   22, 128, 152, 155, 159–163, 168, 177, 180, 187, 190f., 193, 197f., 213, 219, 225, 253
Lawrence Brown   109
Lawrence Grossberg   13, 29, 131, 150, 245f.
Lead Belly   202, 204
Led Zeppelin   126, 164, 238
Leiber and Stoller   12, 18, 58, 147, 152–159, 161–163, 165, 167, 169, 172, 174–176, 179, 185f., 188, 191, 193, 196, 207, 212, 216, 220, 239
Lennon and McCartney   72, 97, 171, 191
Leo Feist   9, 32, 66, 73
Leo Frank   129
Leonard Bernstein   2, 75f., 88–90, 96, 182, 190, 198
Leonard Cohen   8
Lew Dockstader   21, 27
Liberalism   3–6, 8, 14f., 18, 36–38, 44, 52, 55f., 59, 112, 129, 132, 138, 140f., 145–147, 159, 167, 175, 193, 200, 202, 211, 216, 247–250, 252, 266
Like a Rolling Stone   215, 217
Little Richard   10, 148, 156, 167, 170, 226, 230f.
Lorenz Hart   8, 33, 73, 75, 78
Lou Adler   169, 174, 180, 185, 219
Lou Levy   209
Lou Reed   8
Lew Wasserman   45, 119
Louis Althusser   13, 241f.

Louis Armstrong   32, 89f., 97, 102, 107f., 117, 151, 224, 237
Louis Bernstein   9, 66
Luckey Roberts   86, 101, 237

management companies   1
Mark Ronson   158, 253
Marshall Sterns   120
Marxism   144, 241
Masters of War   218
Maurice Shapiro   9, 66
Max Dreyfus   32, 66, 73, 78
Max Horkheimer   135
Max Roach   92
Maybellene   229
Maynard and Seymour Solomon   11, 204
MC5   11
MCA   45, 119, 126, 224
Mezz Mezzrow   156
Michael Bloomfield   211, 213
Michael Jackson   113, 126f., 222, 253
Michel Foucault   245
middle-class values   24, 37
Mike Bloomfield   12, 19, 124, 218f., 255
Miles Davis   13, 92, 97
minority alliance   3, 250
Miriam Beinstock   152
modernism   4, 44, 145
Molly Picon   8, 31
Mood Indigo   108
Morris Levy   221, 225–228
Mort Shuman   160
Moses Asch   11, 201, 203, 220
Motown Records   8, 177, 223
multicultural   1, 12, 32, 59, 75, 157–160, 170, 188, 190f., 197, 199f., 250, 252
musical comedy   17, 21, 27f., 33, 54, 74–79, 82, 85–87, 91, 93, 97, 154, 157f., 191
musicals   4, 13, 21, 75, 79, 85, 93, 97, 158, 180

Nathan Glazer   34, 36, 41, 45–47, 56
Neil Bogart   120, 125
Neil Gabler   42
Neil Sedaka   167–169, 171
Neil Young   126, 180

Nesuhi Ertegun 156
New Left 3f, 7, 130, 140, 141, 142, 143, 144, 199, 240f.
New York 1, 4–7, 9–11, 14–17, 19, 22–24, 26, 29, 31–43, 45–49, 51f., 55, 57–60, 62–64, 66, 68–70, 72, 74, 76–78, 83, 89, 94–96, 99, 101f., 104–110, 113f., 116, 118f., 121–125, 127–131, 133, 135–145, 147, 149–154, 156, 158, 160–162, 164, 166–175, 177–180, 182–194, 196, 201–203, 205–209, 211, 215–218, 221–240, 242, 244–246, 248, 252, 254
Nick The Greek Gravenites 222
Niger Mike 67
Nik Cohn 22, 59, 148, 150, 158, 163, 183, 189f., 199, 211, 234
Nirvana 126
Nixon 235, 251
Norman Mailer 148, 153, 156

Oh, Kay! 78, 87, 93, 169, 213
Ol' Man River 81f., 108
One Fine Day 173, 176
Only a Pawn in Their Game 210
Original Dixieland Jass Band 86, 114
Oscar Hammerstein 2, 8, 32, 50, 73, 75, 79, 93
Oscar Levant 87, 96
Otis Redding 232f.
Otto Hardwick 109
Oxford Town 210

P.G. Wodehouse 78
Patricia Music 226
Paul Butterfield Blues Band 124, 215, 220
Paul Goodman 141
Paul Laurence Dunbar 102, 223
Paul McCartney 90, 126, 175, 184
Paul Robeson 81f., 154, 204
Paul Rothchild 11, 124, 214, 215
Paul Simon 2, 8, 167, 169, 171, 219, 240
Paul Whiteman 88, 102, 110
pentatonic scales 69, 72, 99, 191, 197
Perry Como 115, 195
Pete Seeger 202–204
Peter Paul and Mary 123, 209

Peter Yarrow 123, 205
Phil and Leonard Chess 10, 119
Phil Spector 2, 8, 12, 18, 59, 152f., 160, 168, 175f., 180, 182f., 185f., 189f., 199, 231, 253
Piece of My Heart 164
Pleasant Valley Sunday 179
Poison Ivy 158
PolyGram 125
pop culture 2, 67, 69, 123f., 127, 166, 174, 184, 190, 193, 204
popular music 4, 6, 8, 10, 13–15, 20, 22, 40, 45, 54f., 60, 64, 66, 82, 84, 92, 97, 101f., 116, 118, 127, 149, 151, 153, 162, 168, 182f., 194, 199, 209, 211, 216–218, 236, 239f., 245–250, 253f., 266
popular song 6, 14, 41, 47f., 53, 58, 64f., 70, 73, 82f., 106, 108, 153, 221, 223, 236
populist 4
Porgy and Bess 2, 57, 81, 87, 92, 95f., 109, 236
Porpoise Song (Theme from Head) 179
Port Huron statement 142
post-war 18, 20, 58, 100, 118, 130, 133, 137, 140, 147, 162, 172, 245, 248, 250
postmodern 4, 20, 52, 142, 245, 250
pre-modern 24
protest movement 3, 140
publishing houses 1, 9, 26, 47, 65–67, 74, 79, 85, 103, 115, 167, 186
publishing industry 4, 12, 17, 26, 32, 34, 62, 64f., 74, 78, 84, 114
Puritan 5f., 23, 44, 50f., 132, 134, 145, 208, 210
Puritan ethics 24
Puttin' On the Ritz 73

radio 6, 10, 32, 34, 73, 107f., 114–118, 120f., 123, 131, 149, 154, 160, 167, 170, 175, 178, 185, 191f., 195, 198, 200, 203f., 217, 226, 228, 230
ragtime 1, 12f., 17, 19, 22, 28, 31, 34, 44, 51f., 61f., 69f., 74, 84–86, 99, 101, 118, 147, 150, 222f., 236f., 248
Ramblin' Jack Elliott 203, 207
Ramones 184

Randy Newman   2
Ravel   84, 87, 90, 105, 187, 194
Ray Charles   151, 163, 186, 213
Raymond Williams   240
R&B   10f., 15, 18, 59, 151, 172
RCA-Victor   115, 118f., 121
record labels   6, 8, 11, 124, 167, 173, 220, 222
Red Bird label   163
Red Seal   114
Remick 66, 73, 85, 86,
Rhapsody in Blue   84, 86–89, 237
Rhythm Changes   91f.
Richard Hoggart   240
Richard Rodgers   2, 8, 32f., 50, 66, 74f., 77f., 97, 197
Richard Wagner   1, 189
River DeepMountain High   177, 182
Robert Allen Zimmerman   206
Robert Russell Bennett   82
Robert Johnson   50, 117, 208, 216, 255
rock and roll   9, 11, 13, 19, 117, 119, 153, 166, 168, 170, 172, 183, 189–191, 232, 234
Rock Around the Clock   71, 118, 149
rock music   4, 10, 82, 97, 116, 125, 145, 147–149, 162, 172, 175, 177, 182, 197, 246f., 250, 252
Roland Barthes   13, 241f.
Rolling Stone magazine   10, 148, 156, 183, 210, 217
Ronald Reagan   235, 252
Roosevelt   27, 115, 123, 202, 204
Roulette Records   226
78 rpm records   116
Ruth Brown   151

Saint Louis Blues.   86, 104
Save the Last Dance for Me   161
Savoy Records   10, 119, 225
Schoenberg   88, 90, 94, 194
Shubert brothers   21, 28, 45, 78,
Scott Joplin 17, 69, 70, 85, 236, 237
Scotty Moore   213
SDS   140, 143
Searchin'   158, 175
second Viennese school   88

Sholom Secunda   85
Show Boat   2, 79f., 82, 93, 108
Simon Frith   60, 66, 115, 147f., 248
Simon & Garfunkel   220
slavery   14, 23f., 29, 31, 33, 46, 53, 59, 110f.
Sloan, P.F.   180, 219
socialism   52, 136f., 142, 145
Someone to Watch Over Me   75, 87
Sonny Rollins   92
Sony   126
Sophie Tucker   8, 31, 86, 225, 237
Sophisticated Lady   109
Specialty Records   10, 119, 226, 230
Spike Lee   222
stairway to Paradise   1, 16, 266
Stand by Me   128, 161,
Stax   164, 232–234
Stephan Foster   25, 31, 65, 69, 71, 85, 87,
Stephen Weiss   135
Steve Ross   11, 119
Stride   86, 101, 152, 154,
structuralism   20, 52, 240f.
struggle for social justice   3f., 7, 12f., 16, 130, 136, 139, 177, 198, 202, 211, 219, 233, 254
Stuart Hall   13, 240, 242, 244–246
student politics   3, 140, 250f.
subcultures   13, 174, 245
Sun Records   11, 118, 159
Swanee   32, 86f.
Swanee River   31, 71, 87
swing   2, 17, 66f., 70, 73, 89–91, 98–100, 105, 111, 115, 118, 123, 147, 150, 176, 191, 204
Swing era   10, 187
Syd Nathan   10, 119, 151, 226, 234, 236
Syncopation i   62

Tapestry   180f., 185, 232
Ted Snyder   66, 68
The Band   123, 180, 218
The Brill Building Pop Sound   168
The Center for Contemporary Cultural Studies   240
The Coasters   153, 157, 158, 160, 172, 254

The Coen brothers 202
The Cookies 173
The Crystals 168, 189f., 231
The Death of Emmett Till 210
The Doors 11, 220
The Drifters 151, 157, 159–163, 169, 172–174, 176, 179, 196, 255
The Eagles 126, 180
The Ed Sullivan Show 122
The Electric Flag 214, 218
The Flying Burrito Brothers 180
The Freewheelin' Bob Dylan 210
The Jazz Singer 2, 27–29, 32, 56, 73, 115
The Loco-Motion 173
The Mamas & the Papas 180, 219
The Mamas & the Papas 185
The Monkees 179
The Rolling Stones 126, 174f., 177
The Ronettes 168, 175, 189f., 231
The Shirelles 168, 171, 196, 231
The Times They Are a-Changin' 210
The Witmark brothers 66, 73, 124
Thelonious Monk 92
Theodor W. Adorno 135
Theodore Bikel 205
There Goes My Baby 160f., 172
There's Always Something There to Remind Me 198
Time Is on My Side 175
Tin Pan Alley 7, 9–12, 15, 17, 26, 32, 34, 45, 47, 49, 52, 57, 61f., 64–66, 72–76, 79, 84f., 89, 103f., 108, 114–116, 118, 120f., 149–151, 166f., 169, 176, 180, 189, 195, 209, 222f., 225f., 236, 238
To Know Him Is To Love Him 175
Tom Hayden 142
Tom Paxton 203
totalitarianism 138
Treemonisha 69, 236
Truman 131, 138
Twist and Shout 163, 175

Up On the Roof 168

Vanguard Records 11, 204

vaudeville 1, 21, 27, 34, 41, 43, 45, 47, 49, 64f., 67f., 75, 83, 86, 115, 117, 158
Victor 107, 114f., 117, 119, 121
Victor Herbert 76f.
Victor Talking Machine Company 114
Victorian 1, 6, 15, 41–44, 54, 62, 65, 68, 75f., 78, 85, 103, 134, 250
Vincent Youmans 66, 75
Virgil Thomson 89, 237

W.C. Handy 86, 95, 106,
Wagner 2, 88, 96, 183, 190, 198
Walk On By 197
Walter Benjamin 244
Walter Yetnikoff 12, 113, 120–125, 127, 227
war in Vietnam 3, 199
Warner Communications 8, 11, 119, 122, 220
WASPs 3, 5f., 15, 17f., 22, 33f., 42–44, 48, 60, 113, 121, 124
Watch Your Step 86
Waterson, Berlin & Snyder 66, 68f., 72, 104, 236
We Gotta Get Out Of This Place 29, 131, 150, 175, 177, 246
West Side Story 120, 182
White Negro 18, 58, 147f., 156, 161, 212, 249, 253, 255
white supremacy 23
Whiteness 14f., 22, 24, 58
Will Marion Cook 102, 223, 237
Will Wodery 86, 88
Will You Love Me Tomorrow 18, 166, 171f., 176
William Paley 11, 115, 119, 121
Willie "The Lyon" Smith 86, 101, 238
With God on Our Side 210
Woody Guthrie 11, 202f., 206f.
Wright Mills 141

Yakety Yak 158, 160
Yankee composers 15, 44
Yip Harburg 1, 8, 75
Young Blood 158, 175
You've Got a Friend 181
You've Lost That Lovin' 'Feelin' 177, 191f.

Author information

Dr. Ari Katorza is a historian, a cultural studies scholar, and a musician. His research concentrates on popular music, society, and history. He lectures in various Israeli academic colleges and universities as Rimon – School of Music, the Academic Center at Kiryat Ono, and the Inter-Disciplinary Center at Herzlia. Amongst his previous publications: *Come Together: Rock 'n' Roll Liberalism, Mass Bohemianism and the Sixties* (2020), *Pink Floyd: Tear Down the Wall (2014)*, *Unknown Noises: Punk, Post-punk, and New-wave* (2019), *Tomorrow Never Knows: Rock in the Twentieth Century* (2012). *Stairway to Paradise: Jews, Blacks and the American Music Revolution, 1890–1965*, is his fifth book.

www.ingramcontent.com/pod-product-compliance
Lightning Source LLC
Chambersburg PA
CBHW020224170426
43201CB00007B/314